Crisis and Control

T0345894

MAX-PLANCK-INSTITUT FÜR GESELLSCHAFTSFORSCHUNG
MAX PLANCK INSTITUTE FOR THE STUDY OF SOCIETIES

Renate Mayntz is Director emeritus at the Max Planck Institute for the Study of Societies, Cologne, Germany.

Renate Mayntz (ed.)

Crisis and Control

Institutional Change in Financial Market Regulation

Campus Verlag
Frankfurt/New York

Publication Series of the Max Planck Institute for the Study of Societies, Cologne, Germany, Volume 75

Schriften aus dem Max-Planck-Institut für Gesellschaftsforschung Köln, Band 75

Bibliographic Information published by the Deutsche Nationalbibliothek.
The Deutsche Nationalbibliothek lists this publication in the Deutsche Nationalbibliografie.
Detailed bibliographic data are available in the Internet at http://dnb.d-nb.de.
ISBN 978-3-593-39671-2

Printed on acid free paper.
Printed in the United States of America

This book is also available as an E-Book.
www.campus.de

Contents

1
Institutional Change in the Regulation of Financial Markets: Questions and Answers

Renate Mayntz

The formation of a research network

The near-collapse of the international financial system in 2008, with its dire consequences for the real economy and state budgets, has generally been perceived as a major global crisis. Crises command the attention of politicians, experts, and the general public and are expected to trigger responsive action. The financial crisis focused political attention first on measures to contain it—in other words, on crisis management—while economists and social scientists started to analyze its causes. Soon there was wide agreement that one prominent cause had been the failure to regulate the internationally expanded financial markets in such a way that their crisis potential—the "market failure" to which they were prone – would be contained. The existing formal rules had significant gaps and created incentives for circumvention and deviation. Banks had not been required to retain on their books part of certain securities they issued; hedge funds and private equity firms were not required to comply with the capital standards of Basel II; and the over-the-counter (OTC) trade of derivatives did not have to be registered, to name just a few of the regulatory gaps that permitted the financial markets to become bloated with "toxic" assets. In unregulated spaces, new practices developed which contributed to the crisis. This holds for the construction of "innovative" financial instruments, such as structured asset backed securities and credit default swaps. At times the effort to avoid compliance with existing rules led to the invention of innovative forms of circumvention; a prominent example is the creation of special purpose vehicles by banks. The new practices that had developed within the given regulatory framework helped to spread the financial crisis to other sectors and other countries when the bubble based on US subprime mortgages burst. "Market discipline" and efforts at self-regulation had obviously been insufficient to prevent the financial crisis; changing the regulation of financial markets therefore appeared the appropriate response.

The observation and analysis of regulatory responses to the crisis was an obvious challenge to sociologists, political scientists, and political economists interested in institutional change. Relevant research started in many places, but clearly no single research institution was able to set up immediately an empirical project covering all aspects of institutional change triggered by the crisis. This also held for the Max Planck Institute for the Study of Societies (Max-Planck-Institut für Gesellschaftsforschung or MPIfG), whose research program focuses on markets and on institutional change. The MPIfG therefore decided to provide instead a platform for the formation of a collaborative network of researchers dealing with specific aspects of the process of institutional change triggered by the financial crisis.

The study of institutional change requires specification of its empirical referent. The term "institution" is applied to specific normative regimes, to normatively structured social sub-systems, and even to single organizations such as constitutional courts. Financial markets can also be regarded as institutions. They are based on general norms such as property rights, and are peopled by market actors shaped by and subject to legal norms and collectively agreed standards. However, for the network project we decided not to focus on possible future change in financial markets, but on change in the institutions designed to regulate them. Research into institutional change in respect of financial market regulation addresses the structure and practice of supervision, as well as the formulation of new rules, the amendment of existing laws, and the modification of existing standards taking place at different political levels, from the national to the European and the international.

The first steps of network formation were taken in the fall of 2009. In December 2009, Renate Mayntz invited a number of social scientists known to be engaged in relevant work to join the project. In the same month, Till Kaesbach joined the MPIfG to assist with network coordination, and to collect material to keep abreast of the unfolding reform process. The purpose of the network was to gain insight into features of the many-faceted change process that cannot be obtained in a project covering only one component of the financial and regulatory system: features such as the phase structure of the overall process, the relative dominance of activities at different political levels, or the role played by different types of agents, both supporters and opponents of regulatory change. It is this emphasis on the dynamic and characteristics of the macro-process of institutional change then under way that distinguished the MPIfG enterprise from the multitude of studies devoted to a particular agency, financial instrument, or country. In February 2010, seventeen scholars met for a workshop to discuss the aim, design, and guiding questions of the network enterprise, and to suggest additions to the group. Future network members were to contribute, based on their ongoing research, an account of regulatory reform taking place either in a specific country, at the European level, or with respect to an international agency, regulatory standard or financial instrument. Institutional change was to be studied not simply as an outcome, but as a process unfolding over time (see Hall 2006).

When network formation started in 2009, the financial crisis had already led to a wide-ranging reform discourse. It did not seem unreasonable at the time to assume that by 2011 the process of institutional change would have reached a stage warranting assessment and analysis. At the workshop in February 2010 network members therefore planned to reassemble in a year to present the results of their studies. By the summer of 2010, the network counted 22 members from six different countries. As planned, the concluding workshops of the network took place at the MPIfG in February and March 2011, respectively.

This volume contains a selection of the workshop contributions, nearly all of them in a substantially revised form; revision lasted until September 2011. Not all network members are found among the authors of this book. The aim has been to produce a volume of manageable length, concentrating on events at the three political levels involved in the change process—the national, the European, and the international—and paying more attention to changes in agencies and in rules applied to market actors than in financial instruments. Special emphasis has been put on studies dealing with regulatory change in given countries, for one thing because it turned out that the national level—and in particular the United States and the big European countries—has played and continues to play a dominant role in the regulatory reforms under way globally. This neglects, but does not intend to disavow the importance of the emerging economies to the development of the global financial system—a topic treated in other publications (for example, Underhill/Blom/Mügge 2010). An attempt has been made to have the country chapters answer a common set of questions, but as the network project had not been set up as a comparative study of national responses to be analyzed, for instance, within the framework of the varieties of capitalism approach (VoC), there are considerable differences in the approach, style and implicit normative flavor of these chapters.

The process of change in financial market governance triggered by the financial crisis of 2007/2008 had not fully run its course when, towards the end of 2011, this book went into print. Meanwhile, a second shock wave—the sovereign debt crisis—has overlaid the shock wave of the financial crisis, and the attention of politicians and social scientists alike has shifted to the new crisis. This gives some post-hoc justification to the initial decision to follow institutional change in financial market regulation only until 2011, when it could still be connected to the financial crisis of 2007/2008. As analysts of institutional change are well aware, change processes have no objective beginning or end, but are entities defined by those who decide to investigate a given stretch of sociopolitical development; whatever happens during that period will take on a new meaning if looked at from some later point in time. The open-endedness of the process analyzed in this book inevitably makes its assessment provisional.

Questions

The questions the network project set out to answer refer to the macro-process of institutional change, but to answer them the individual contributions had to supply factual accounts and focused explanations of what happened in a given country, a given agency, or with respect to a given financial standard. Having graciously accepted this discipline, all authors set out to collect data specifically for this publication. As a result, the chapters in this volume provide valuable case analyses; taken together they give at least tentative answers to the more general questions that were formulated at the beginning of the collective enterprise.

The guiding empirical questions were directed at the process of change, its outcome, and the factors at work in generating that outcome. Macro-processes of planned institutional change move through several phases. Gaps can develop between initial reform intentions and subsequent action, and reform targets can change. Since national, European, and international decision-makers were involved, the question of the relative dominance of a given political level in the reform process was raised. As for the outcome of the change process, we were interested in changes of regulatory structure, and changes in rules. Would there be a pronounced shift away from self-regulation, would agencies disappear or be newly created at the different political levels? Would existing rules become stricter, would there be new rules (legal norms, standards) to guide the behavior of financial market actors and market transactions? With respect to change factors, both the role of potential change agents (drivers as well as opponents) and the role of perceptions and ideas were to be looked at. Since these empirical questions referred to features of governance rather than markets, answers to them were to be interpreted mainly within the framework of theories of institutional change, and of governance. However, all authors were free to develop their own theoretical perspective.

When the results of research undertaken in 2010 were presented and discussed at the workshops in 2011, attention had shifted from the question of *what* was changing, to the question of why so *little* change had taken place. This became a paramount topic in most of the chapters in this book. The results of the collective enterprise thus contribute, more than initially expected, to a theory interested not generally in the trajectory of change processes, but specifically in the conditions making for either radical or incremental institutional change.

The financial crisis did appear to be a "big bang" event that could well have led to radical change. Why did this not happen? When do shocks fail to engender radical change? The case-specific answers to this question may be the major theoretical contribution of this volume.

Answers

In the following sections of this introduction I attempt to formulate answers to the questions that have guided the network enterprise. These answers are based nearly exclusively on the material presented in the eleven following chapters, making good on the promise that the individual contributions of the network members will make it possible to answer more general questions about the institutional change in financial market regulation after the crisis of 2007/2008. What I am presenting is my own summary of this material, not the consensual view of all authors. To make reading easier, I have tried to limit the number of explicit references to chapters in the book by adopting the following rule: whenever one of the countries that are the subject of chapters 2–6 is mentioned by name (for example, the United Kingdom/British) and no other reference is cited, reference is to the corresponding chapter in this book.[1]

The macro-process of change

To identify change presupposes knowledge of the status quo. By necessity, the chapters in this volume therefore devote space—some more, some less—to the institutional arrangements of financial market regulation in a given country or agency or at a given political level as they had developed up to the outbreak of the crisis. The changes in financial market regulation motivated by the financial crisis of 2007/2008 are part of a long historical process. Since World War II, the globalization of financial markets, and financial crises in different parts of the world, have repeatedly led to institutional change in financial market regulation. Starting in the late 1970s, two parallel developments took place. As shown in several of the country chapters, there has been, on the one hand, increasing regulation: supervision was strengthened and tended to become integrated, and standards claiming compliance internationally were developed. On the other hand, however, in the financial markets, both market actors and transactions

---

1 US = chapter 2; Britain/UK = chapter 3; France = chapter 4; Germany = chapter 5; Switzerland = chapter 6.

were increasingly deregulated. Rather than being contradictory, these developments were two sides of the same coin. As the liberalized financial markets continued to change without commensurate changes in the regulatory framework, a regulatory gap developed which became manifest in the crisis of 2007/2008.

The changes in financial market regulation that occurred in response to the crisis can hardly be described as a single change process. A multitude of heterogeneous actors operating in a multitude of different sites were involved in the generation of the crisis, and in the response it triggered. In contrast to a natural event such as an earthquake or tsunami, "the financial crisis of 2007/2008" is an aggregate of many events; as a single event it is a cognitive construction. The process of institutional change we set out to study is again composed of many separate, but interdependent change processes. And yet it is possible to discern something like a macro-pattern.

The immediate reaction to the crisis was crisis management: at the national, European, and international levels. As crisis management succeeded in preventing the "meltdown" of the financial system and a sudden and major disruption of the real economy, it opened the way for reforms—in other words, for a process of planned change in the governance of financial markets. Public discussion focused first on guilt attribution, while financial experts in central banks and other institutions, as well as academics tried to understand how the unexpected crisis developed. Guilt was attributed to "greedy bankers," before the focus shifted to the behavior of rating agencies, the unregulated use of recently invented derivatives, and the structure of modern banks. Guilt attribution and causal analysis led to the formulation of demands for change. More quickly than public opinion, policymakers realized that in a culture in which the pursuit of individual interest is legitimate, moral suasion will not suffice to change the behavior of the financial institutions accused of having caused the crisis. In unusually wide agreement, politicians, heads of supervisory agencies, and academic experts reasoned that since financial markets had evidently failed to regulate themselves through what is euphemistically called "market discipline," radical regulatory reform was needed. Reform demands summarized in a flurry of official reports prepared, among others, by the Stiglitz commission (United Nations 2009) and the OECD (2009) were comprehensive, and directed at the financial system as a whole. This was expressed clearly by the heads of government at the G20 Summit in London: "We have agreed that all systemically important institutions, markets, and instruments should be subject to an appropriate degree of regulation and oversight" (G20 2009).

As time went on, reform demands became more concrete—and more selective. Although the chapters in this book show that there were differences between levels and countries, reform plans by and large tended to be directed first at uncontested causes of the crisis, where the necessary change was at the same time relatively easy to define. From the compensation schemes for bankers, the capital reserves that banks were obliged to hold, and the behavior of rating agencies, the reform agenda moved to more difficult topics, such as ways to reduce the moral hazard posed by systemically important banks that were "too big to fail." As reform demands were translated step by step into concrete legislative initiatives and international standards, reform plans at all political levels and in all the countries we analyzed met with opposition. This resulted in compromises and in significantly delayed implementation requirements. Even before the sovereign debt crisis made regulatory reform of the financial markets appear less urgent, the slowing reform impetus was publicly noted and criticized by experts, as well as by heads of government.

This summary description of the change process as it emerges from the chapters of this book glosses over the interesting differences between political levels, countries, and agencies in the way the reform process played out. It is nevertheless evident that this particular change process differs from the familiar model of a policy cycle. A "policy cycle" starts with the identification and articulation of a problem, followed by political agenda-setting, the formulation of alternative solutions, choice of an alternative, and finally implementation (see, for instance, Windhoff-Héritier 1987). Different from most policy processes, the financial crisis was not a problem that needed identification and definition before it made its way onto the political agenda. It imposed itself suddenly and forcefully as a problem of systemic importance on politics, market actors, and the general public alike. There was no doubt that immediate action was needed. In other words, the financial crisis was generally perceived as a "big bang" event that shattered an arrangement believed to be fundamentally stable, notwithstanding periodic ups and downs.

The dynamic of policy processes provoked by a crisis obviously differs from that of policy processes preceded by a period of relative stability, with a slowly shifting change in the balance of power between critics and supporters of the status quo that leads finally to the articulation of a policy problem. As is generally recognized in institutional theory, particular institutional arrangements have distributional consequences that motivate supporting or opposing, defending or trying to change the status quo (Streeck/Thelen 2005; Hall/Thelen 2008; Mahoney/Thelen 2010). In the contest between social groups supporting or wanting to change the status quo, political actors may take sides or serve as mediators (Amable/Palombarini 2008). In our case, however, the pre-crisis mixture of regulation and deregulation that appeared to support economic growth had prevented the development of two opposed social blocs, one challenging and one defending the status quo. As noted in some of the chapters here, there were experts and regulators who would have preferred stricter regulation, but they remained voices crying in the wilderness. It was the crisis that led to a wave of criticism and the demand for radical reforms, but the critics scarcely formed a single social bloc. As the reform plans impinged upon (previously unchallenged) vested interests, they stimulated the formation of opposition. But again this opposition, created by the incipient policy process, was not a coherent social bloc. As the chapters in this volume show, those who supported and those who opposed regulatory reform varied from issue to issue, between political levels, and between countries. Even in the phase of deciding on concrete reforms we cannot speak of two circumscribed social blocs pitted against each other.

Nevertheless, the outcome of the interaction between supporters and opponents of change was a loss of momentum: the change process slowed down over time. While a movement from broad to narrow and from ambitious to modest is not exceptional for planned institutional change in a non-revolutionary situation, it is unusual that this is encountered already in the early stages of the process by publicly voiced disappointment and criticism. The widespread public denunciation of the gap between initial reform demands and the forthcoming changes attests to the strength of the initial conviction that substantial change was needed.

Changes in financial market governance

Turning to the changes in the overall structure of financial market governance that took place in direct response to the crisis of 2007/2008, the most obvious effect has been a shift away from private self-regulation towards public regulation. Existing regulatory and supervisory agencies at all political levels of course reacted to the crisis. Most immediately and visibly, however, political actors became involved. On all political levels, the process switched suddenly from the previous "low politics" to "high politics." Symptomatic of politicization at the international level was the mutation of the G20, formerly a low-key body of central bank governors and finance ministers—who rarely attended in person— to the "premier forum for our international economic cooperation" at which heads of government meet for highly publicized summits (Leader's Statement, Pittsburgh Summit 2009, Preamble point 19[2]). In Germany, the crisis reinforced existing demands for regulation. But also in, for example, the United Kingdom and the United States, where self-regulation and light-touch public regulation had been the order of the day, politicians and even heads of government now

---

2 Available at: http://ec.europa.eu/commission_2010-2014/president/pdf/statement_20090826_en_2.pdf.

called publicly for stricter regulation. Given that reform was felt to be urgent, it was the executive rather than political parties and parliaments that first became involved. In the United States, it was the Treasury that drafted the plan for comprehensive reform that became the basis of the Dodd-Frank Act; in Germany, the Finance Ministry together with the Ministry of Justice drafted the restructuring law later passed by parliament. What formerly appeared to be technical issues to be dealt with by experts was transformed into a publicly observed process of high-level policymaking. According to Helleiner and Pagliari (2010), the financial crisis, reinforcing a trend towards banking regulation already under way, may lead to a further shift from private and decentralized to public and centralized governance. The shift to public regulation is evident also in our study, but whether there is also a shift towards centralized regulation is doubtful, as will become evident when we turn to changes in the governance structure.

Contrary to early demands, regulatory change has been neither comprehensive nor internationally coordinated. Given the horizontal and vertical differentiation of the pre-crisis governance structure, an integrated reform process guided by a master plan covering all aspects of the internationalized financial system that had proven so problematic was not to be expected. Demands for a coordinated, international response, voiced in public statements of political representatives as well as in the reports and memoranda issued by the G20 and by national bodies (for example, Financial Services Authority 2009; Wissenschaftlicher Beirat 2010) met with the reality of a geographically (horizontally) and politically (vertically) differentiated governance structure. Regulatory competences were concentrated at the national level. The EU had largely refrained from using its legislative powers for the purpose of market shaping rather than market making (Scharpf 2010). The international standardization bodies—the Basel Committee BCBS, the International Organization of Securities Commissions IOSCO, and the International Accounting Standards Board IASB—depended on voluntary compliance with the rules they developed. As the chapter on France suggests, demands for reform at the international level sometimes went together with a weak domestic reform impetus. But by and large, there was an early flurry of disparate national initiatives, including the one-time British tax on bankers' bonuses and the German ban on short selling. At the same time, national authorities were also the dominant actors in negotiating higher level agreements: heads of state at G20 summits and the European Council, and representatives of finance ministries, central banks and supervisory agencies in the Financial Stability Board FSB, and the BCBS (chapters 11 and 10). National actors were thus the key change agents in the reform of financial market regulation (Mayntz 2010).

As is evident from the chapters in this volume, governance structures have changed most at the national and least at the international level. At the international level there were changes in the mandate, composition, and weight of some agencies in the overall process of regulation. Examples are the change of the former Financial Stability Forum into the FSB (chapter 11), the additional resources given to the IMF (chapter 12), and the focal role assumed by the BCBS in the reform process (chapter 10). But no new agencies were established at the international level, nor were existing bodies given the competence to make binding decisions for lower level jurisdictions and market actors. International bodies are still restricted to monitoring, recommending, and trying to coordinate.

More substantial change took place, at least formally, at the level of the EU, where a new agency, the European Systemic Risk Board, was created and where the three previously existing committees that were supposed to coordinate national supervisors were transformed into European supervisory agencies. These agencies have some decision-making power, and the competence to intervene, under certain conditions, in areas hitherto under exclusive national jurisdiction (see chapter 7).

Agency change has been most pronounced at the national level. In several countries, new bodies to administer fiscal rescue programs have been created and, especially in the United Kingdom and the United States, new regulatory agencies have been established. The most innovative change has been the new emphasis on macro-prudential supervision; in the United States and the United Kingdom new bodies were even created for this purpose, while in other cases existing bodies were explicitly given this task. Other changes in the supervisory structure appear less significant. While in the United Kingdom the integrated supervisory agency FSA is being dissolved and the central bank is becoming appreciably more powerful, in most countries there has only been some redistribution of regulatory competences between central banks and supervisory agencies. Whether supervision over banks, securities, and insurance should be integrated or not, and whether central banks should also perform supervisory functions has been an issue for decades. The financial crisis brought old domain conflicts to the surface again and provided a window of opportunity for reform initiatives that previously did not receive political attention and support.

In the course of organizational change at the different political levels, public agencies were given, by and large, more powers. At the same time, there has been an—albeit limited—upward shift of de facto power, and an even more limited upward shift of formal competences, the latter especially in the EU. But since legislative competence is still concentrated at the national level, this upward shift has meant that the downward connection between levels has become more important. Supported by the FSB, the G20 has strongly voiced the need for specific reforms and has "tasked" international organizations—notably the IMF, BCBS and IASB—as well as national and regional jurisdictions to become active (chapters 11, 12, and Bradford/Lim 2010). The standards formulated by international bodies, notably the BCBS, have been integrated into EU directives and have thus become legally binding for market actors and supervisory agencies in member countries (see chapter 7). Expecting a new or amended EU directive, member countries have in fact put off introducing new rules by themselves; this also holds for directives the EU developed independently.

The policy recommendations and standards formulated by international bodies have also shaped regulatory decisions taken by states that are not EU members. Legislative powers to effect institutional change are still concentrated at the national level, but national decisions are affected by higher level demands and rulings. In the formulation of these demands and rulings, national actors have again been active, but there is a difference between the domestic and international decision-making contexts, not least with regard to the interests pursued by the actors involved and the resulting conflicts of interest. The connected upward and downward movements in this multi-level policymaking process are reminiscent of the dialogue model found to characterize the relationship between the political leadership and the bureaucracy in German federal ministries (Mayntz/Scharpf 1975). The post-crisis policymaking process has still been fragmented, but by virtue of the cross-level connections it has clearly become, if not more centralized, more international.

Publicly voiced initial reform demands focused on legal provisions and standards, more than on regulatory agencies. Rules were to be tightened, to cover all critical components of the financial system, and to be coordinated at the international level in order to be applied uniformly down to the level of market actors and their transactions. Although rule change and agency change are two closely related aspects of institutional change, the evidence amassed in this volume suggests that rule changes may have been more deep-cutting than agency changes. Existing rules that mainly targeted banks have been tightened and extended, as in the case of the Basel Accord (see chapter 10). Regulation has also been extended to new targets, such as hedge funds, rating agencies, and OTC derivatives. Most of the changes in standards developed by the BCBS, IOSCO, and the IASB and already agreed on are micro-prudential, and bank-centric. There is, however, also increasing emphasis on the need for macro-prudential regulation, manifested in the introduction of countercyclical buffers (in Basel III) and national resolution regimes for failing financial institutions (as in Germany). In support of macro-prudential regulation, monitoring financial market stability has been re-emphasized at the international, European, and national levels.

In practically all the chapters in this volume, the regulatory changes realized when pending legislative decisions have been taken, new agencies are up and running, and new and amended rules are finally implemented are judged to be incremental rather than radical. Doubts are voiced particularly with regard to the ability of regulation to discipline risk taking by banks, to deal with the problem of a moral hazard presented by financial institutions too big to fail, and to counter the threat of domino effects resulting from the high degree of interconnectedness among market actors and transactions. There is, however, some ambivalence in most chapters concerning their assessment of the observed reforms, and naturally the authors' views sometimes differ on this. Thus while Jabko (in chapter 4, pp. 97–118) judges institutional change at the EU to be a "major transformation of its financial supervisory architecture," Quaglia (in chapter 7, pp. 171–195) is more skeptical, emphasizing that "the new agencies have limited competences and it remains to be seen whether they will be able to regulate the financial sector effectively." It is true that the radical changes in regulation demanded by some politicians and scientific experts when the crisis became manifest have not been achieved: required bank equity is still below 10 percent, the new, highly structured securities and credit default swaps have not been prohibited, tax havens have not been completely closed, and financial institutions have not returned to concentrating on their classical functions instead of seeking profit by proprietary trading. But there have been changes, and sometimes a set of related small changes may add up to a transformative change. The question is whether the given change is sufficient or insufficient to solve the problem. At the time, the problem was defined as the in-built proclivity of the financial system to undergo major disruptive crises. Regulatory reform was supposed to solve this problem, but the pervasive view now is that it has fallen short of this goal. By the end of 2011, the perception of what is amiss has of course changed, pushing the critique of failed regulatory reform into the background.

Factors shaping the process and its outcome

The changes in financial market regulation emerging from the chapters in this book and summarized in the previous section pose two closely related questions: why has change taken place with respect to some aspects of the pre-crisis status quo and not others, and why has it not been more radical? Both properties of the process outcome—its selectivity and its intensity—have been affected by a set of change factors that operated not only in one country, one agency, or at one political level.

One generally important factor determining the political response to the financial crisis of 2007/2008 has been the kind and severity of the threat it posed.

The impact of the crisis was felt most directly at the national level, but it was not a disruptive shock to all the countries dealt with in this volume. The severity of the impact and the extent to which it was banks, the real economy, or households that were affected, depended on particular features of the given financial industry. In the United States, households unable to pay their mortgages were severely affected. In Germany, the failure of the HRE, which had to be taken over by the state, shaped the problem: the goal of regulatory change was to avoid future costly public bailouts that delegitimize the political system. Where the impact was limited and coping quick and effective—as was the case in France—the general public and the media were enraged by bonuses and scandals involving individual traders, but perceived no vital threat and did not demand radical institutional change. As put succinctly by Johal, Moran and Williams (in chapter 3, pp. 67–95), "crisis management both opened up and closed off possible paths to the post-crisis institutional order."

Although this study does not provide data with which to measure comparatively the impact of the crisis, it seems that the two liberal market economies, the United States and the United Kingdom, suffered a severer shock than the three other countries dealt with in this volume. This certainly applies to the ideological impact of the crisis, which varied with the ideological undergirding of the regulatory status quo. The empirical falsification of the belief in the efficiency of unregulated markets hit hard in the United Kingdom and the United States, but the impact was milder in coordinated market economies such as Germany and France. In Switzerland, the crisis challenged a belief in self-regulation based on the historical legacy of self-reliance and individualism rather than the efficient market theory of liberalism. Behind the discredited British "narrative" of successful liberal opposition to the threat of an interventionist democratic state, convincingly described in the chapter on the United Kingdom, there lies the old issue of the balance between state and economy. The crisis of 2007/2008 appeared to have shifted this balance back towards the state.

The institutional changes following the financial crisis are the outcome of the preferences of and interactions between advocates and defenders of the status quo. The most visibly active reform agents were political actors. Their orientation and actions were influenced by several contextual factors, although it is difficult to generalize about them. It is an open question, for instance, whether elected members of parliament, party leaders, and politicians in high executive positions differed in characteristic ways in their reform orientation. Members of the European Parliament appear to have been more reform-oriented than, for instance, the European Commission; in countries where the government was forced by the crisis to take a stand immediately, parliamentarians became involved only at a later stage. It is plausible that the party composition of governments played a role. In Switzerland, the persistent dominance of conservative parties has shaped the response to the crisis. But there is no uniform relationship between the left/right orientation of a government and the strength of its reform orientation. In the United States, the Democrat Barack Obama at least initially did not stand up as strongly for regulatory reform as the Conservative David Cameron did in the United Kingdom. The country chapters suggest that institutional arrangements are another factor that shaped the policy response to the crisis, but again it is hardly possible to generalize about the kind of impact made by different institutional arrangements. In the United States, for instance, relations between the executive and the legislature played an important role in the gradual development of the Dodd-Frank Act. In the EU, the Commission acted as agenda-setter, the European Parliament pushed for reform, and the Council had to agree on compromise solutions. Political constellations, such as power relations between the governing party or coalition and the opposition, the imminence of a general election, and congressional power politics clearly influenced the course of national reform initiatives. Elections especially are situations that can be used to demand or reject change, and have been used in this way particularly in the United Kingdom. In the United States, the campaign promises of the incoming Obama government on health care reform tended to push financial market reform into the background for a time.

Since change in political power constellations follows its own dynamic, political factors are a source of contingency in shaping the details of regulatory change. Another source of contingency are institutional entrepreneurs, individual political actors with power and backing who make a specific reform issue their own project, as Elisabeth Warren and Paul Volcker did in the United States. In fluid situations with many actors pursuing different and often contradictory goals, a determined political actor can make a difference. To sum up, political actors were the most visibly important actor category in the process of planned regulatory change, but substantively their influence was highly contingent once crisis management had been provisionally successful.

Less visible than the influence of political actors has been that of central banks and supervisory agencies on the direction of the reform process. Agency reform in particular was affected by the distribution of regulatory competence between central banks and supervisory agencies. Most importantly, however, up until the crisis national central banks and supervisory agencies had close and cooperative relations with the financial industry and its organizations. It may not be surprising that in the United States and the United Kingdom, regulators, policymakers and the financial elite shared the regulatory ideology of efficient market theory. In the French case, this consensual outlook reflected a career pattern that started in the same institutions for the members of both elite groups.

However, elite consensus was not only based on a shared ideological outlook or career pattern, but also firmly rooted in national interests. In all countries represented in this volume, policymakers and regulators alike aimed to create, support, and safeguard a competitive domestic financial industry. Where the pre-crisis elite consensus had supported deregulation and light-touch regulation, it now motivated efforts to save that industry. In this process, a strong element of path dependency is involved. National central banks and supervisory agencies were not destined to become particularly active change agents; they may even have restrained radical change. The action orientation of national regulators and supervisors was also predominantly micro-prudential before the crisis, with bank solvency and investor protection the major goals. In the aftermath of the crisis, more emphasis was put on macro-prudential supervision and financial stability. Where central banks and supervisory agencies old and new become more explicitly responsible for financial stability, the attitude of these regulators vis-à-vis the financial industry may change.

Turning to international regulatory bodies (in the broadest sense), the G20 and the Financial Stability Forum had played the role of guardians of global financial stability already before the crisis. On the basis of this mandate they became, as noted in the preceding section, focal actors in the macro-process of regulatory reform. The international standard-setting bodies channeled the process of rule change towards those aspects of the financial system with which they had already been dealing before the crisis. Thus the Basel Committee started to tighten capital requirements for banks (chapter 10), IOSCO updated its standards for the supervision of securities markets (chapter 12), and the IASB became involved in the debate on whether fair value accounting had contributed to the crisis and needed to be changed (chapter 9). In this way, the pre-crisis structure of these international agencies, with their specific mandates, contributed importantly to the selectivity of the reforms.

The main opposition to institutional change is generally expected to come from those likely to be negatively affected. The ambitious reform plans voiced in direct response to the crisis were generally considered to be too restrictive by the financial industry. But the usual strategies of interest-group pressure on policymakers—the threat of a strike or the mobilization of public opinion against impending legislation—were not available in a situation in which the financial industry itself was seen as the culprit. The chapters in this volume provide only limited evidence on the extent and means of industry lobbying, and the levels at which it preferred to attack and did so most effectively. The industry, being itself negatively affected by the crisis, clearly recognized that something had to change. Since the financial industry is internally differentiated, however, reactions differed between sectors; this lowered the overall intensity of opposition to reform. The intensity of opposition also differed between reforms. In the United States, for instance, the financial industry favored rather than opposed plans to monitor systemic risk, but it tried to ward off interventions that would restrict its freedom of action in the medium and long term. In Germany, savings and mutual banks that had not been involved in the trade with derivatives that proved to be "toxic" were particularly vociferous in protesting against the bank tax which the new restructuring law, which was supposed to address the problem of bank failures, included. Representatives of the finance industry were actively involved in the consultation process involving the regulation of capital requirements for banks, both at the BCBS and in the EU, but lobbying was not always successful. As Woll reports, hedge funds thought themselves exempt from regulation at first and woke up only belatedly to the threat; when regulation seemed inevitable, they cooperated with regulators, trying to make things easier on themselves (chapter 8). In Germany, the joint opposition of the banking association (BdB) and associations of savings and mutual banks failed to prevent the passing of the restructuring law or to change it significantly.

One effective defense for the financial industry was to use the inevitable information asymmetry between financial insiders and outsiders to paint a grim picture of the economic consequences of restrictive regulation: a credit crunch, loss of jobs in the finance industry, and slower growth. Critical views were expressed in official statements by interest organizations, but they were also conveyed through personal contacts in the social networks that existed between the financial elite and the political elite, mentioned especially in the chapters on the United States and the United Kingdom. In the United States, these contacts led to a coalition of financial and policy elites underlying the early preservationist approach to regulatory reform. To interpret such interaction as capture is too simple, however. Even without direct pressure from the financial industry, the national interest in competitiveness counteracted the political impulse to tighten regulation, producing a basic political ambivalence that reform opponents—and particularly the financial industry and its lobbies—could use. If expert industry representatives pointed out that planned regulation would affect economic growth and domestic competitiveness, rulemakers could not but listen to them. The interest of national governments that count on the jobs and tax revenue provided by the financial industry militated against more restrictive interventions.

Cognitive factors thus played a role in downsizing reforms. Planned change generally responds to the perception of the nature and the causes of the problem to be solved. While agreement was soon reached on the proximate causes of this financial crisis, efforts to identify its underlying mechanisms were confronted by the complexity of the financial system whose operation neither bankers nor economists, let alone politicians, had understood. Intervention targeted the obvious causes of the crisis: the risk taking of bankers, the widespread use of certain types of derivatives, and large internationalized banks whose bankruptcy would force governments to bail them out with taxpayers' money. Attention also focused on issues of transparency, true to the teachings of economic theory that it is lack of information that causes market failures. But issues such as global economic imbalances, the financialization of the real economy, and the development of a culture of debt making were touched on only in fleeting asides in the reform discourse immediately following the crisis. It took the sovereign debt and currency crises of 2011 to focus attention on global imbalances, and on public as well as private debt (see, for instance, Bank for International Settlements 2011). The reforms triggered by the financial crisis did not even attempt to get at these causes. Not only were the reforms selective, but even the apparently radical initial reform ambitions were limited.

In democratic states, attention from the media and the general public is important for putting an issue on the political agenda. In the case of the 2007/2008 crisis, media attention was generally immediate and strong, while the reaction of the general public differed between countries. Where crisis management was sufficient to prevent massive immediate repercussions on employment, savings, and the value of money the public did not get angry and did not mobilize. In Germany, France, and Switzerland the effects of the bailout and its dire fiscal consequences, while highly publicized, were not immediately felt by the general public. Successful coping thus served to slow down the reform momentum. The general public was rather enraged by incidents that seemed to support the initial guilt attribution to bankers and financial institutions, as has been the case when the US supervisor, the SEC, filed fraud charges against Goldman Sachs. Only in the United States has public criticism led immediately to the formation of a grassroots organization by consumer groups and labor organizations, called Americans for Financial Reform, which was actively engaged in the regulatory reform process leading to the Dodd-Frank Act. It has taken until 2011 for an organization such as Finance Watch, initiated by a public statement of a group of European Parliament members in July 2010, to be formed at the international level (see www.finance-watch.org).

The most immediate effect of public opinion is on national politics, and it is also at the national level that domestic power politics plays a significant role in determining policy preferences. In international negotiations, national representatives tend to act as economic patriots, and a set of interests different from the one that determines domestic politics comes to the fore. Interests, of course, are subject to definition, and domestic politics, reflecting features of the national financial industry, does influence the definition of national interests. The German central bank, for instance, staunchly defended the interests of German public banks and savings banks in negotiations on capital requirements in the BCBS and the EU. French policy preferences with respect to the EU regulation of hedge funds were similarly affected by the fact that UCITS funds, which had a stake in this regulation, were predominantly located in France (chapter 8). The policy preferences of the United Kingdom were influenced by the fact that, while British banks were not particularly big, the City as an international financial center is of great significance. Where the importance of the financial industry for the national economy is particularly large, there is more fear of the possible negative consequences of stricter regulation. In international negotiations, there is thus a tendency for national representatives to support reforms that would not hurt their own financial industry, but to oppose regulation that would. The result is a pattern of conflicting beggar-thy-neighbor strategies. Given the absence of even a single truly supranational agency with regulatory competence going down to the level of individual market actors, international negotiations tend to end in a so-called joint-decision trap: a situation producing compromises and lowest-common-denominator solutions (Falkner 2011).

A second difference between nations that affects preference formation in international negotiations—a country's position within the global geopolitical order—has been less evident after the financial crisis of 2007/2008. It was felt by big, export-dependent Germany, interested in continuing demand for its products, as well as by small Switzerland that had to ward off international pressure to change its mode of regulation, and particularly the rule of banking secrecy. The US policy process may seem to have been more inward-looking, an effect of the country's historical leading role in international finance and international financial regulation. However, the failure to have the US accounting standard setter FASB converge with the international accounting standard setter IASB (chapter 9) is a sign that this role might now be challenged.

The conditions of radical versus incremental institutional change

What can we conclude from the analyses presented in this volume with regard to the question hovering in the background of the case analyses: namely, under what conditions do big bang events, shocks or crises lead to radical change? What features of the event itself, and what features of the impacted field (or system) can dampen the impulse, and lead to merely incremental change? Even taken together, the network projects cannot answer this question, not only because they deal with a single historical case, but also because the empirical analysis focuses inevitably on proximate causes. But a few observations can be hazarded.

It is common knowledge that reform energies are a limited resource that will soon be exhausted; reform advocates in fact soon warned that the reform momentum would slow down, and urged planners to make use of the crisis while it was still being felt. But what obstacles stood in the way of radical change? The usual answer points to the opposition of vested interests, the banking industry and its wealthy lobby. The explanation that emerges from the chapters in this volume is more complex, however.

One factor clearly dampened the impetus of regulatory reform: the failure of the feared collapse of the real economy to materialize. The suddenness of an event and the severity of its impact define it as a major crisis; the financial crisis came upon us suddenly, but the crisis management undertaken immediately and at all relevant political levels prevented an equally sudden, global economic breakdown. Perversely, the very fear of an economic collapse prevented more radical reforms by spurring attempts to prevent a meltdown of the financial system. Nevertheless, there have been some institutional changes. Media attention and the existence of an ongoing, submerged reform discourse were supportive factors, and so was at least potentially the shift from private to public regulation as a consequence of politicization. But the involvement of political actors in a process of institutional change works to the advantage of radical change only if politicians are firmly set on it. This, however, has not been the case: there was a gap between the early political reform rhetoric and concrete subsequent action. Not only did the outcome of reforms undertaken in direct response to the financial crisis of 2007/2008 lag behind the initial calls for a global and comprehensive change in financial market regulation, but the concrete reform ambitions of the political change agents, formulated domestically and in international negotiations, were modest in comparison with early reform demands.

The fact that reform ambitions were limited is not only the consequence of national interest in a competitive financial industry, elite consensus, and industry pressure. It also expresses a general unwillingness to call into question the institutional underpinning of modern capitalist democracies. A radical change involves getting to the root causes of a problem. The financial crisis was in fact only a symptom of a much larger problem situation, generated by the confluence of several developments impinging on today's wealthy democratic societies with their well-to-do middle classes: liberalization, tertiarization, financialization, and technological developments that substituted computers for human traders and offered new mathematical modeling techniques for risk assessment. A truly radical change of the financial system, and of its operation and importance for the economy, state budgets, and consumers would have required much more than higher capital standards, leverage ratios, and resolution regimes for failing banks. A radical change of the financial system would have involved uprooting the very institutions on which modern, capitalist democracies are built. Among other things it would have required restricting the general dependence on credit, a dependence intricately connected with the inherent future orientation not only of financial markets, but of Western civilization. Whether they realized it or not (most did not), the enormity of the changes that would have been required to get at the root causes of financial crises of the type experienced in 2007/2008 made potential reformers shy away from the task. The strongest impediment to radical institutional change is their close integration with basic features of the societies in which they are embedded. Nothing short of a popular revolution would have sufficed to trigger such radical change, but popular uprisings of the kind we have seen shake the Arabic world in 2011 did not occur in 2009/2010, the period covered by the studies in this volume.

References

Amable, Bruno/Stefano Palombarini, 2008: A Neorealist Approach to Institutional Change and the Diversity of Capitalism. In: *Socio-Economic Review* 7(1), 123–143.

Bank for International Settlements (BIS), 2011: *81st Annual Report*. Basel: BIS.

Bradford, Colin I./Wonhyuk Lim (eds.), 2010: *Toward the Consolidation of the G20: From Crisis Committee to Global Steering Committee*. Seoul: Korea Development Institute, Washington, DC: The Brookings Institution.

Falkner, Gerda (ed.), 2011: *The EU's Decision Traps*. Oxford: Oxford University Press.

Financial Services Authority, 2009: *The Turner Review: A Regulatory Response to the Global Banking Crisis*. London: Financial Services Authority.

G20, 2009: *Declaration on Strengthening the Financial System*. London. < www.g20.org/Documents/Fin_Deps_Fin_Reg_Annex_020409_-_1615_final.pdf>

Hall, Peter, 2006: Systematic Process Analysis: When and How to Use it. In: *European Management Review* 3, 24–31.

Hall, Peter/Kathleen Thelen, 2008: Institutional Change in Varieties of Capitalism. In: *Socio-Economic Review* 7(1), 7–34.

Helleiner, Eric/Stefano Pagliari, 2010: Crisis and the Reform of International Financial Regulation. In: Eric Helleiner/Stefano Pagliari/Hubert Zimmermann (eds.), *Global Finance in Crisis: The Politics of International Regulatory Change*. London: Routledge.

Mahoney, James/Kathleen Thelen, 2010: *Explaining Institutional Change: Ambiguity, Agency, and Power*. New York: Cambridge University Press.

Mayntz, Renate, 2010: Die Handlungsfähigkeit des Nationalstaats bei der Regulierung der Finanzmärkte. In: *Leviathan* 38(2), 175–187.

Mayntz, Renate/Fritz W. Scharpf, 1975: *Policy-Making in the German Federal Bureaucracy.* Amsterdam: Elsevier.

OECD, 2009: Policy Framework for Effective and Efficient Financial Regulation: Regulation: General Guidance and High-level Checklist. In: *OECD Journal: Financial Market Trends* 2009/2. Paris: OECD.

Scharpf, Fritz W., 2010: The Asymmetry of European Integration, or Why the EU Cannot Be a "Social Market Economy." In: *Socio-Economic Review* 8, 211–250.

Streeck, Wolfgang/Kathleen Thelen (eds.), 2005: *Beyond Continuity: Institutional Change in Advanced Political Economies.* Oxford: Oxford University Press.

Underhill, Geoffrey R. D./Jasper Blom/Daniel Mügge (eds.), 2010: *Global Financial Integration Thirty Years On: From Reform to Crisis.* Cambridge: Cambridge University Press.

United Nations, 2009: *Report of the Commission of Experts of the President of the United Nations General Assembly on Reforms of the International Monetary and Financial System* (Stiglitz Commission), September 21. New York: United Nations.

Windhoff-Héritier, Adrienne, 1987: *Policy-Analyse: Eine Einführung.* Frankfurt a.M.: Campus.

Wissenschaftlicher Beirat beim Bundesministerium für Wirtschaft und Technologie, 2010: *Gutachten Nr. 03/10: Reform von Bankenregulierung und Bankenaufsicht nach der Finanzkrise.* Berlin: Bundesministerium für Wirtschaft und Technologie.

2

The Two-Tiered Politics of Financial Reform in the United States

John T. Woolley and J. Nicholas Ziegler

Introduction

The financial crisis of 2007–2008 originated in its key essentials within the United States. Despite the cross-national interdependencies that typify twenty-first century capital markets, American financial institutions were undermined by deep imperfections that originated in US asset markets and then spread to other countries.

The crisis involved tremendous costs and significant disruption to institutions throughout US society. The Lehman Brothers bankruptcy of September 2008 triggered a profound discontinuity in America's financial markets. Three venerable Wall Street institutions—Bear-Stearns, Merrill Lynch, and Lehman Brothers—were absorbed by their competitors or allowed to fail outright.

According to estimates by Deutsche Bank, US financial institutions experienced losses (including asset write-downs) totaling at least $1.1 trillion; funds equal to 30 percent of GDP were committed to supporting the financial sector in the United States (Deutsche Bank 2010). US stock markets fell on average in two consecutive years by more than 14 percent, the first time that had happened since the 1930s. Nationally, housing prices dropped nearly 18 percent from mid 2007 to the end of 2010 but in several important regions, the price decline was upwards of 30 percent (US Federal Housing Finance Agency 2011). The US unemployment rate increased from 4.5 percent in April 2007 to 10.1 percent in October 2009; the number of unemployed increased from 6.8 million to 15.6 million (US Department of Labor 2011). The US Federal budget deficit expanded from about 1.2 percent of GDP in 2007 to nearly 11 percent of GDP in 2011. In 2007, US gross public debt was about 64 percent of GDP. By 2011, that had increased to 103 percent.

The onset of these massive impacts in 2008 was followed closely by a national election in which the financial crisis was a significant issue. The Republicans were swept from office and the victorious Democrats clearly believed they had a mandate for change. In February 2009, Obama told the Business Council that he supported "comprehensive financial reform" to ensure that such a crisis could "never happen again" (Obama 2009a). Previously, US financial experts had a substantial consensus on several reforms to the structure and process of regulation. These ideas were readily available to policymakers in 2009. There was also no shortage of analyses of the causes of the financial crisis.

Given this combination of factors, it is hard to think of periods in post-World-War II America equally ripe for institutional change. One of the central findings in the historical-institutionalist approach is that periods of continuity are punctuated by exogenous shocks that disrupt settled institutions and produce very significant change (Krasner 1984; Steinmo/Thelen/Longstreth 1992; Baumgartner/Jones 2009). Building on this approach, analysts such as Streeck and Thelen have pointed out that cumulatively very significant change can also occur gradually, even without major punctuation points. Thus, when we encounter periods of significant shock, like the financial crisis, it is important to ask how much the response deflects the system from the trajectory that might have been present previously.

The crisis response in the United States seemed to foretell a profound change very unlike anything that might have been otherwise anticipated. A number of large banks were effectively nationalized. The largest insurance company was explicitly nationalized. The two largest government-sponsored enterprises, heavily engaged in mortgage finance, were placed under government conservatorship. Two automobile manufacturers were nationalized. In an effort to keep the financial system afloat, the Federal Reserve abandoned a decade-long practice of avoiding selective credit allocation and instead worked assiduously to support specific market sectors, including the commercial paper market, the secondary mortgage market, investment banks, commercial banks, and money market funds.

But did these events signal a larger shift in the US political economy? Did the shock translate into more enduring institutional change? The Dodd-Frank Act (formally the Dodd-Frank Wall Street Reform and Consumer Protection Act [PL 111-203]), was signed into law on July 21, 2010. It represents the most ambitious overhaul of the country's financial regulations since the 1930s. It establishes a powerful council of regulators to monitor financial markets for signs of systemic risk. This council has extensive new powers to close large firms in financial distress before they collapse. The bill mandates new rules to force most derivatives contracts onto public markets. It redraws a number of bureaucratic boundaries and creates some new funding mechanisms for several of the existing regulatory agencies. It merges one functional regulator, the Office of Thrift Supervision, into an older agency, the Comptroller of the Currency. It includes a number of additional changes in the rules that govern executive compensation, the licensing of credit rating agencies, and the registration of investment vehicles such as hedge funds and private equity groups. Equally important, it creates an entirely new regulatory bureau for consumer financial protection. These changes are very real. They are widely expected by close observers to have far-reaching consequences.

Despite these broad changes, the Dodd-Frank Act falls well short of a new institutional design for financial regulation, and it certainly does not shift the basic contours of the US political economy away from a transaction-based market economy. Rather than a unified or logically consistent plan for reform, the bill comprises an unwieldy set of compromises in several linked domains of regulatory policy. In some domains, industry interests were promoted by a cohesive elite that had dominated financial policymaking for several decades. In other domains, specific policy entrepreneurs, working with the backing of newly mobilized grassroots coalitions, succeeded in opening up the policymaking process to a broader range of actors (Kingdon 2011; Zahariadis 2007). The reforms also failed to pit contending theoretical paradigms against one another as had occurred in some other major instances of economic turmoil and policy change (Hall 1989).

Such an outcome—of significant but less-than-transformational change—requires closer examination. The apparent opening for fundamental redesign of policy and institutions did not lead to any deep-seated change in organizational structures. Only one new agency was created and new regulatory powers were very cautiously drawn. In many more cases, existing powers were reallocated among existing agencies while prior procedures and tools were enhanced. How can we explain the limited scope of reform in comparison to the profound anxiety provoked by the triggering crisis?

Several strands of literature provide plausible hypotheses. One hypothesis from the interest-group literature would hold that concentrated industry interests were able to beat back proposals for unfavorable regulation (Wilson 1980) and to trump more diffuse coalitions (Olson 1965, 1984). Alternatively, it could be that existing regulatory agencies had sufficient autonomy and wielded enough clout to protect their pre-existing jurisdictions (Carpenter 2011). A third possibility, drawn from the institutionalist literature, suggests that incremental adjustments can, over time, allow existing institutions to persist in gradually changing form through exceptionally turbulent environmental changes (Thelen 2004).

Rather than choosing among these alternative explanations, we draw on elements of all in order to emphasize the coalition politics that shaped the Dodd-Frank legislation. More specifically, we argue that this reform required a creative brokering of elites and grassroots interests by Congress and the White House. This complex coalition-building prevented Congress from enacting a consistent overarching design for regulatory reform, but it also allowed for a range of new regulatory powers that may, over time, yield consequences more substantial than apparent from strictly formal changes in the regulatory landscape. The legislation clearly reflected the financial sector's familiar interest-group veto politics, but that politics was altered substantially by a new dynamic of political mobilization. In part, the new mobilization resulted from the Obama Administration's initial legislative proposal, which affected interests far beyond the traditional core financial sector. And, in part, it resulted from the configuration of interests that influenced Congressional action. In particular, this new dynamic hinged on several factors:

– a clear effort by the executive branch to maintain continuity among existing organizations and elites in the finance sector;
– political entrepreneurship by sophisticated, independent policy experts;
– grassroots advocacy organizations new in financial regulation;
– openness to historical contingencies arising from electoral politics and the procedural rules of Congress.

These factors coalesced in a pattern we call two-tiered politics. The pattern of two-tiered politics was anticipated in the executive branch proposals and was further shaped in the Congressional debates that followed. The Obama White House, continuing the approach of the Bush White House, went to great lengths to stabilize financial markets. The Obama Administration continued the same emergency response measures that the Bush Administration put in place in October 2008, and crafted a set of reform proposals that maintained most of the existing regulatory landscape. This "preservationist" approach initially helped the White House maintain strong ties with the financial elite who were seen as necessary for managing the crisis. It was amplified and reinforced by business-friendly blocks in both Congressional parties.

A consequence of the White House preservationist tack was that the most powerful financial firms and associations remained potent. They were able to block many measures they most intensely opposed. They were not, however, able to squelch the proposals of several policy entrepreneurs, most notably Paul Volcker and Elizabeth Warren who, interestingly, were propelled to the forefront largely by the White House. In addition to these policy entrepreneurs, a new coalition of policy advocates injected fresh voices into the policymaking process and limited the sway of the country's financial policy elite. As a result, the second tier emerged, with White House encouragement, and created scope for the most interesting reform efforts.

Accordingly, for both White House and Congressional leaders there were two different logics operating. On the one hand, they worked assiduously to maintain friendly relations with the Wall Street elite whenever possible. Some analysts began to speak of the "gilded network" between Wall Street and Washington (Carpenter 2011), while others claimed the Wall Street elite had become a veritable oligarchy (Johnson/Kwak 2010) more reminiscent of developing countries than advanced democracies. Through its high-powered compensation incentives, the financial elite helped define the upper frontier of an increasingly skewed distribution of wealth and simultaneously consolidated ever stronger ties to the Washington policy community (Bebchuk/Fried 2006; Bartels 2010; Hacker/Pierson 2010). This elite shared a commitment to deep capital markets within the United States, and insisted that any regulatory changes in the domestic market should be carefully geared to corresponding international agreements within the G20 countries.

At the same time that they cultivated this Wall Street elite, Washington leaders wanted to accommodate the popular backlash against precisely the closed elite politics that had previously dominated financial regulation. For this reason, the White House and the Congressional Democrats needed to cultivate coalitions that would confer broader legitimacy on their actions. According to Gunnar Trumbull, such "legitimacy coalitions" had often taken the form of industry alliances with regulators (Trumbull 2011). In the Dodd-Frank discussions, activist-regulator coalitions appeared in the form of grassroots advocacy organizations that mobilized Washington expertise to challenge longstanding industry ties to regulators and key Congressional committees.

The unavoidable tension in this strategy created unusual openness that perturbed a legislative process already vulnerable to quirky developments driven by institutional rules and procedures. Congressional outcomes frequently turned on unpredictable electoral contingencies and rapid shifts in public opinion. The legislative outcome was a mix of significant, if limited, structural change with many provisions for enhanced tools and procedures that would enable existing regulators to supervise a finance industry chastened, but by no means reconstructed, by the crisis. The potential for regulators to adopt important changes was accompanied by the potential for hostile interests to weaken future regulations and the regulatory agencies themselves.

In the following pages, we elaborate this argument in several steps. First, we very briefly review the regulatory landscape before the financial crisis. Second, we provide a compressed chronology of the reform debate, showing how the primary sites of discussion shifted over time. And lastly, we illustrate the distinctive factors that shaped the Dodd-Frank outcome by reviewing debates in the major domains covered by the legislation: systemic risk regulation; consumer protection; the Volcker Rule; and a new regime for derivatives trading.

The existing regulatory landscape on the eve of the crisis

The crisis of 2007–2008 was deeply rooted in the historical development of America's regulatory landscape. For over 175 years, two trends dominated US financial regulation. The first was decentralization. Private banks were initially chartered only by the states. Under the US Constitution, Congress alone has power to "coin money," but States have the power to charter banks. Insurance has always been a state-regulated industry. The Office of the Comptroller of the Controller (OCC) was established in 1863 to provide a unified currency during the Civil War and to anchor more stable conditions for the larger banks that needed a national charter. Not until 1913 was the Federal Reserve System created with 12 regional branches and a central Board of Governors in Washington DC.

The second trend affecting US regulatory structure is competition with industry segmentation. After 1933, the regulatory structure was organized around industry segments which proved, starting in the late 1970s, to be porous. Competition arose between segments, and differentiation between products and firms declined. Nonetheless, groups of firms had well-established links to, and provided important political support for, regulators. This regulatory equilibrium was fundamentally unstable with both industry and regulators typically eager to poach on adjacent turf.

Three further developments in the second half of the twentieth century were especially important. The first of these shifts was the growing preference among finance firms for a holding-company structure that projected their activities into a number of previously prohibited markets. Congress explicitly extended the Glass-Steagall provisions in the 1950s by disallowing deposit banking and securities activities within the same multi-bank holding conglomerate, but many other combinations were permitted. The new holding companies resisted the traditional functional classification and were mostly overseen by the Federal Reserve. Only later did the Securities and Exchange Commission (SEC) and the Home Loan banking agency also gain supervisory authority over those holding companies that chose to designate them as preferred or "lead" regulators. Through this extended shift, the Federal Reserve staff acquired growing knowledge of emerging business models and steadily gained in reputation for sophisticated regulatory policy.

The second significant shift included a compound set of changes in the sophistication of financial instruments, the velocity of transactions, and the geographic scope of financial markets. These changes rapidly gained momentum in the 1990s and early 2000s. They represented a major transformation at the industry level rather than the firm. These changes, often called financialization (for example, Davis 2009; Krippner 2011), meant that vast new markets began to link financial institutions globally, largely outside the purview of existing regulatory agencies.

A final trend involved deregulation, which not only reduced the constraints on firms, but also explicitly eliminated the differentiation between different kinds of financial firms. Thus thrift institutions became largely indistinguishable from commercial banks, and investment banking and commercial banking functions were performed within a single corporate entity. Several turning points are noteworthy:

- Interest rate caps for thrift institutions were removed in 1982.
- A new independent regulator, the Office of Thrift Regulation (OTS), was created in 1989.
- The 1999 Gramm-Leach-Bliley Act (GLBA) effectively repealed restrictions against universal banking activities.
- The Commodities Futures Modernization Act (2000) explicitly barred federal agencies from regulating new markets in derivatives.

In short, consistent with the thesis developed by Streeck/Thelen (2005) and Mahoney/Thelen (2010), the US financial regulatory system gradually and dramatically evolved over a period of 65 years in response to competitive pressures and periodic shocks. These institutional changes, together with a powerful faith in the stabilizing force of market systems, prepared the way for the financial crisis. The deregulatory efforts since 1982 diminished the capacity of existing regulatory agencies. The result was a kind of institutional "displacement" where regulatory institutions were replaced piecemeal by the rules of open market competition. But this result was not a form of dynamic institutional stability. Instead, markets and regulatory institutions became increasingly fragile. The bundling of residential housing loans into so-called mortgage backed securities (MBS) prompted a wild proliferation of newly securitized loans and related financial innovations that created the rapidly growing markets known as the shadow banking system. As early as 2004, government reports noted that the GLBA had made it excessively easy for financial conglomerates to position major activities outside the jurisdictions of the regulatory agencies. With increasing urgency by 2007, official reports were pointing out the jurisdictional gaps between key regulatory agencies such as the SEC and the Federal Deposit Insurance Corporation (FDIC), as well as the OCC and the OTS (GAO 2007). This growing fragility culminated in a dangerous crisis in the economy's key banking and regulatory institutions, which were sustained only through the extraordinary decision making of the Treasury and the Federal Reserve in 2008.

The chronology and political context of reform

Legislative efforts to revamp US regulatory structures followed and had to deal with the consequences of emergency measures adopted to ameliorate the crisis triggered by Lehman's bankruptcy in September 2008. Within weeks, the Bush Administration persuaded a reluctant Congress to enact the Troubled Asset Relief Program (TARP), which authorized the Treasury to spend up to $700 billion for assets tainted by the collapse of mortgage securities (a majority of House Republicans voted against). After Barack Obama won the presidential election in November 2009, his transition team worked closely with Bush Administration officials to refine the TARP program, while planning the new Administration's own legislative agenda. Even before the election, Obama's commitment to preservation was signaled by his reliance on well-connected mainstream economic advisors.

Upon taking office in late January, 2009, the new White House placed top priority on economic stimulus and a plan for health reform; financial reform was a lesser priority in the Administration's very large agenda. In June 2009 the Administration released a White Paper outlining measures for regulatory reform accompanied by a statement by the President (US Treasury 2009; Obama 2009c).

Congressional movement to consider new regulatory laws was quickly apparent in a number of different House and Senate committees. The Treasury proposals of June became the starting point for the broad bills drafted in the House of Representatives by the Committee on Financial Services and in the Senate by the Committee on Banking. Hearings were held by the House Committee, chaired by Representative Barney Frank, through the fall of 2009, followed by passage of the House bill in December.

In October 2009, Goldman Sachs led investment banks in announcing their plan to distribute large bonuses to its executives. In the following weeks, White House polling showed that the public thought Obama was too close to Wall Street (Heilemann 2010). On December 13, Obama appeared on the television news show *60 Minutes* to say pointedly "I did not run for office to be helping out a bunch of, you know, fat-cat bankers on Wall Street." He expressed frustration at the fact that banks that were bailed out "are fighting tooth and nail [...] against financial regulatory reform" (Obama 2009d).

In this context, in January 2010, President Obama again raised the salience of financial reform. He advocated imposing a "Financial Crisis Responsibility Fee," to ensure that the government would be reimbursed for the cost of the bailouts. Shortly thereafter, he appeared with economic advisor and former Federal Reserve Chairman Paul Volcker in support of tough regulations to segregate deposit banking from proprietary trading—the "Volcker Rule." Days

Figure 1   Google Trends graphs of volume of news and of internet searches concerning "health care reform" and "financial reform" in the United States

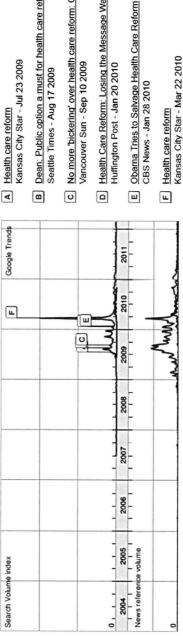

A   Health care reform
     Kansas City Star - Jul 23 2009

B   Dean: Public option a must for health care reform
     Seattle Times - Aug 17 2009

C   No more 'bickering' over health care reform: Obama
     Vancouver Sun - Sep 10 2009

D   Health Care Reform: Losing the Message War
     Huffington Post - Jan 20 2010

E   Obama Tries to Salvage Health Care Reform
     CBS News - Jan 28 2010

F   Health care reform
     Kansas City Star - Mar 22 2010

before, on January 19, Republican Scott Brown had won an upset victory in a special election in Massachusetts to fill the seat of the late Senator Edward Kennedy, a very liberal Democrat. This critically reduced the Democrats' seat share to 59, one less than the 60th pivotal vote required to stop filibusters in the Senate. While Brown was a very moderate Republican on most issues, his election exacerbated an already tense and highly partisan split in Congress.

In March, the Senate Committee on Banking, chaired by Senator Chris Dodd, took up the bill and debated it through April. In April, reforms received a major boost when the SEC filed fraud charges against Goldman-Sachs in connection with the design and marketing of instruments known as credit default swaps (CDS). In subsequent days, Obama gave a forceful speech to the Business Council supporting financial reform. After a number of amendments, the Senate approved its version of the bill on May 20 and requested a conference committee with the House to mesh differences between the two versions. A tough set of conference deliberations occurred from June 10 through June 29, 2010, after which the reconciled bill was passed, easily by the House (June 30) and only by the minimum filibuster-proof majority in the Senate (July 15). The bill became law as the Dodd-Frank Act when President Obama signed it on July 21, 2010.

One of the key factors driving the dynamic of two-tiered coalition-building was the breadth of the interests affected. These involved many groups beyond the traditional core financial interest groups. The Center for Responsive Politics, which tracks lobby registrations and expenditures, identified 697 financial sector lobbying organizations in 2010. Their data also showed that 788 organizations were registered to lobby concerning HR 4173, the Dodd-Frank Bill. Of those Dodd-Frank lobbies, *only 36 percent* were identified as mainstream financial sector groups. Remarkably, nearly two-thirds of the groups mobilized to influence the Dodd-Frank legislation were "non-financial." These proportions reflect the broad reach of the legislation, and helped create opportunities to shake up traditional coalitions.

Even in this heated atmosphere, financial reform engaged the general public far less than health care reform, which passed in March 2010. The agenda-setting media were focused far more intensively on health care reform. In a graphic reviewing major events in 2010, *Time Magazine* prominently mentioned health care reform, but did not mention Dodd-Frank (December 27, 2010, 32–33). The graph in Figure 1 from Google Trends shows, in indexes for the news reference volume as well as Google searches, that the public's attention to financial reform ranked consistently lower. This pattern suggests strongly that even a dramatic crisis did not overcome the political barrier to popular involvement posed by the perception that financial issues are primarily technical in nature.

Systemic risk regulation

The Dodd-Frank Act created (Title I) a new Financial Stability Oversight Council as its central solution to the problem of systemic risk. This new Council groups the main functional regulators together, oversees the financial system as a whole, and exercises the power to establish enhanced levels of regulation for the largest financial services firms.

The idea for such a council appeared as soon as the immediate rescue operations of late 2008 began to take hold, allowing policymakers to focus on longer-term reforms that would prevent similar crises in the future. The Obama Administration followed the prevailing regulatory wisdom by seeking better tools for monitoring so-called "systemic risk" and new powers, in extreme cases, to restructure firms deemed significant enough to endanger the entire financial system. In both respects, the Administration revealed a strong preference for continuity in the regulatory structure and in the major firms that dominated the industry.

While unfamiliar to many members of Congress, the problem of monitoring systemic risk was by no means new to the financial policy elite. Indeed, key members of this elite shared a broad understanding of how the crisis had unfolded and why the recipes of the past failed to work in 2008. In critical respects, the template for responding to systemic risk emerged from the rescue of the famous hedge fund, Long-Term Capital Management (LCTM), in 1998. Since LTCM had been financed by Wall Street's key investment banks, the New York branch of the Federal Reserve convened the heads of a dozen major firms in September 1998 to finance a private-sector bailout. In the space of a weekend, these firms stopped any contagion by taking a 90 percent ownership stake in LTCM (Lowenstein 2001; McKenzie 2008). The senior officials who were to grapple with the impending collapse of Lehman Brothers ten years later were all fully familiar with the LCTM bailout as participants or close observers (see Stewart 2009).

This familiar solution—a solution negotiated with a consortium of market participants convened by the New York Fed—failed in resolving the problems at Lehman Brothers in September 2008. By backstopping J.P. Morgan's acquisition of Bear-Stearns in March 2008, the Fed had signaled its willingness to reverse market outcomes that threatened wider contagion. In mid-September, top policymakers—including Treasury Secretary Hank Paulson, Chairman of the Federal Reserve Ben Bernanke, and Chairman of the New York Fed Tim Geithner—gathered again in lower Manhattan to spearhead a private-sector bailout for Lehman Brothers. When a private-sector solution failed to materialize and policymakers told Lehman to file for bankruptcy, financial centers around the world were gripped by fear. The consequence was a profound crisis of confidence that spread instantaneously, freezing an over-leveraged system of credit markets while dramatically deepening the downturn that soon became known as the Great Recession.

Although Lehman's bankruptcy was not predicted, the gaps in the country's regulatory structure were well understood beforehand. Hank Paulson's earlier experience with LCTM left him acutely aware of the risks posed by highly leveraged and interconnected firms. As Treasury Secretary, he commissioned a major study for redesigning the US regulatory system, entitled *Blueprint for a Modernized Financial Regulatory Structure*, issued in March 2008, six months before the Lehman bankruptcy (US Treasury 2008). The *Blueprint* said the US system of functional regulation by business area made less and less sense as financial firms moved increasingly into multiple parts of the industry—commercial banking, securities brokerage, investment banking, mortgage lending, and their own proprietary trading. The existing framework meant that no single regulatory agency was responsible for monitoring risk across the system as a whole. The Paulson *Blueprint* therefore recommended that a single agency be made responsible for what it called "macro-prudential regulation," while two new agencies should be established, one with consolidated responsibility for day-to-day monitoring and inspection across all financial markets, the other for enforcing overall conduct-of-business regulation.

The main actors

As the Obama Administration took office, the new Treasury Secretary, Timothy Geithner, commanded extensive knowledge of the regulatory problems and prescriptions of the preceding decade. The Administration White Paper of 2009 outlined a new "systemic risk" council. Called the Financial Stability Oversight Council (FSOC), the new council would shift macro-prudential responsibility away from the Federal Reserve (where Paulson's *Blueprint* had proposed putting it). The FSOC would be chaired by the Treasury Secretary. After the Treasury, the Federal Reserve was preeminent, with operational authority for supervising all systemically important companies, but its responsibilities were submerged within a broader set of voting members. These voting members consisted mainly of existing functional agencies. In addition to the Treasury Secretary and the chairman of the Federal Reserve Board, they were to include the Comptroller of the Currency, the Chair of the SEC, the Chair of FDIC, the Chair of the Commodities Futures Trading Commission (CFTC), the Director of the Federal Housing Finance Agency, the Chair of the National Credit Union Administration (NCUA) Board, the Director of the (new) Consumer Financial Protection Bureau, and one independent member with insurance expertise to be appointed by the President with approval by the Senate.

Given the severity of the crisis, the underlying goal of systemic risk regulation was beyond controversy. Neither the firms nor their champions in either party could plausibly claim after 2008 that market discipline alone was sufficient. While the idea of a systemic-risk council quickly gained acceptance, the role of the Federal Reserve remained open to question. The House version of the legislation specified the Fed's role as that of agent of the FSOC (Dodd-Frank 2010: subtitle A., section 1100 of the bill as passed in the House; See also Davis Polk, 2010: 2, 10). The initial Senate Committee drafts in November 2009 proposed, by contrast, to strip all regulatory competencies from the Federal Reserve as part of a thorough regulatory redesign. But by March 2010 the Senate had converged toward the House proposals to group existing agencies into a new macro-prudential council which would include the Chairman of the Federal Reserve (*Washington Post*, 12 December 2009: Brady Dennis. See also DLA Piper, 2010). Within the expert community, some observers felt the duties of day-to-day prudential regulation would burden the Fed with unnecessary tasks that could undermine its independence in monetary policy. Other specialists said the Fed possessed such preponderant expertise that, as former Fed governor Alan Blinder put it, "we would have to tie ourselves in knots" to move the tasks of regulating systemic risk away from the Fed (quoted in *Bloomberg News,* May 9, 2009: Robert Schmidt). Existing regulators, such as Sheila Bair, chairperson of the FDIC, accepted the role of the Fed, but preferred that the super-council of regulators be entrusted with the setting of overall guidelines for macro-prudential regulation (*Bloomberg News,* May 9, 2009). Such proposals echoed earlier efforts to deepen coordination in financial regulation since the late 1970s (FFIEC 2011).

Beyond the precise role of the Fed, Congressional discussion focused on the criteria by which firms would be designated as "systemically important" and therefore subject to heightened regulatory standards. Banks of over $50 billion in assets were automatically designated as "systemically significant." The Senate bill diverged from the House by separating Bank Holding Companies (BHCs) from systemically important Non-Bank Holding Companies (NBHCs). For NBHCs, the Senate proposal called upon the FSOC to develop criteria and decide by a two-thirds majority of voting members that a particular firm would come under the rules of enhanced supervision. The designation of NBHCs seemed like an esoteric issue, but the stakes were high. The details determined whether conglomerates such as General Electric or IBM, as well as hedge funds or private equity groups, would be included under the new requirements for enhanced regulation. At the peak of the crisis, the remaining investment banks became bank holding companies, subjecting themselves to Fed regulation, in order to qualify for help from the Federal Reserve (*New York Times,* September 21, 2008). But nothing prevented them from dropping their bank charters, in which case under the House draft they would escape the new rules for systemic risk monitoring (*New York Times*, 2010).

Outside Congress, the debate over systemically significant firms included more radical remedies. A number of observers saw the Dodd-Frank reforms as too modest. Unless the banks were broken up and capped in size, they would remain "too big to fail." A number of bankruptcy lawyers and respected economists, such as Simon Johnson, recommended this approach, arguing that anything else would either elevate the Treasury Secretary to the position of a restructuring "czar" or simply leave the bank executives in place as virtual "oligarchs" (Skeel 2010; Johnson/Kwak 2010).

Such proposals were never central in Congressional deliberations, although related amendments were soundly rejected. Once the structure of the FSOC was clarified, the main legislative debates revolved around technical matters of definitions, procedures, and degrees of discretion in setting regulatory rules. To bolster the process of macro-prudential oversight, the FSOC was to be supported by a new Office of Financial Research (OFR) with independent subpoena powers and a Director appointed directly by the President. Virtually all versions of the bill directed regulators to align domestic regulations with international agreements, and the Treasury took an active role in preparing to implement the Basel III rules for capital adequacy (Bernanke 2011; see also Goldbach/Kerwer in this volume). The other aspects of macro-prudential regulation were a realm where the specialists' specialists held sway. Congressional Republicans tended to criticize the bill for imposing burdensome compliance costs, while Congressional Democrats had to wrestle with how to define new and more effective instruments of macro-prudential oversight.

Interest-group influence

Given the broad agreement on improving macro-prudential regulation, industry groups were initially restrained in their criticism of the Dodd-Frank proposals. From their viewpoint, a superordinate council that left day-to-day oversight with familiar regulatory agencies had advantages (Ryan 2009). Such a Council would ameliorate the regulatory "gaps" that appeared between the functional regulators as new firms entered the industry. As long as the new information-gathering powers were not used too aggressively, most industry groups affirmed their support for the new FSOC. As the legislation moved from enactment into the implementation phase, however, some divergences among industry groups began to appear.

The Securities Industry and Financial Markets Association (SIFMA) supported a strong macro-prudential regulator. Since its member firms were already highly regulated by the SEC, SIFMA favored a broad ambit for the new risk regulator. The new systemic risk council could then fill important gaps in the regulatory landscape and dampen competition from new and less regulated entrants. The main limit on the council's activities should concern information-gathering, where SIFMA recommended close coordination with existing regulators to avoid duplicative information requirements. The securities traders emphasized repeatedly that US regulators should coordinate closely with the G20 to obtain comparable regulatory standards at the international level (Ryan 2009).

Other industry associations ranged in their comments from supportive to restrained. But few of them saw any mileage in opposing the goal of systemic risk monitoring while the legislation was being formulated. Several months after passage, the American Bankers Association (ABA), highly critical of other elements, clearly favored macro-prudential regulation. The ABA saw systemic-risk regulation as a promising way to subject newer firms to the same kind of rules that its own members—mostly traditional banks—had long lived with. The US Chamber of Commerce expressed far more qualified support. The Chamber's Center for Capital Markets Competitiveness emphasized the negative consequences of defining the concept of "systemically important" too broadly. In contrast to the ABA, the Chamber explicitly opposed "bank-like regulation for large non bank financial institutions," arguing that the process of defining new rules would create unwarranted uncertainties for firms like General Electric or the auto companies' financing subsidiaries (McTighe 2010; Hirschman 2010).

Labor and consumer groups sought a macro-prudential regulator with enough power to bring the entire shadow banking system within its purview. The precise organizational location and structure of a new regulator mattered less than giving it adequate tools to gather comprehensive information that the alternative investment vehicles, hedge funds, and private equity groups had previously been able to keep confidential (Silvers 2009).

By establishing the FSOC as the central executive body for regulatory policy, the Dodd-Frank Act achieves several purposes and sidesteps several irresolvable controversies. By including the Chairman of the Federal Reserve, the FSOC can draw on the Fed's deep expertise without putting macro-prudential monitoring entirely in the Fed's hands. As enacted, the legislation gives the FSOC ten voting members, including the Treasury Secretary as chair. By including the existing functional regulators (except the OTS, now eliminated), the legislation satisfies industry representatives who wanted to avoid the costs of switching from agencies with which most of the country's banks and financial-services firms were already familiar. However, owing to the real power it was given to intervene in cases of systemically important financial distress, the FSOC also responds to those who said that a new and powerful regulatory body was essential.

Consumer protection

A widely-hailed change of the Dodd-Frank bill was the creation, in Title X, of a new, independent Consumer Financial Protection Bureau (CFPB). This bureau has some elements familiar for independent agencies: the Director is appointed by the President for a relatively long term and cannot be dismissed except for cause. However, it differs from many such agencies in that decisions do not need the support from a bipartisan board of voting commissioners. Above all, the CFPB is uniquely located within another independent agency, the Federal Reserve. Funding for the CFPB is defined by law as a percentage of the Federal Reserve's budget and is thus, like the Fed itself, not dependent upon the Congressional appropriations process. Moreover, the Fed explicitly has no role in overseeing the CFPB.

Few observers argue that general consumer lending practices were the central cause of the financial crisis (by contrast to derivatives markets), although they did contribute. The CFPB provides a classic example of the way a well-developed reform proposal, widely discussed prior to the crisis, became politically viable in the subsequent highly charged atmosphere (Kingdon 2011). The adoption of the CFPB was hardly a certainty, and major groups in the financial industry resisted it strongly, winning on some key points. The agency drew powers from many other agencies, including the Fed and the Federal Trade Commission.

Since the biggest and most powerful financial institutions do not earn their profits from lending to ordinary consumers, they were little inclined to fight on these issues. As a result, this issue had the potential to split the industry. Community banks and thrifts, already closely regulated, might be expected to welcome closer regulatory scrutiny for non-bank competitors, including payday lenders, mortgage companies, and consumer credit agencies. Precisely because of its broad reach, however, the proposal could potentially galvanize in opposition the thousands of organizations making consumer loans.

Elizabeth Warren, Policy Entrepreneur

Virtually every account traces the CFPB back to two academic articles by Elizabeth Warren, a professor at Harvard law school (Warren 2007 and Bar-Gill/Warren 2008). The articles powerfully make the case that consumers face a much more risky market for credit products than for physical products because of the relatively lax regulation in the case of credit products. In these articles, Warren called for the creation of a Financial Product Safety Commission. Bar-Gill and Warren (2008: 98) recommended a single new regulatory agency with a broad mandate or "a new consumer credit division within an existing agency (the FRB or FTC)." They did not specify whether it should be an independent agency.

Just as important as those papers, however, was Elizabeth Warren herself. By 2008, she was a seasoned and skilled reformer known as a creative, unflappable and intelligent advocate. Her connections to Obama dated to 2004. She was also close to Hillary Clinton and many other members of Congress. She had achieved prominence in 2005 as an opponent of bankruptcy reform (Sullivan/Warren/Westbook 2001, 2004). Her research was cited repeatedly in 2008 in Congressional hearings and news reports and had been reflected in legislation that long predated Dodd-Frank.

In October 2008, when Congress authorized TARP, it created the Congressional Oversight Panel (COP) to "review the current state of financial markets and the regulatory system" (US Senate, COP). In November, in an important development, Senate Majority Leader Harry Reid named Warren as a COP member and she was subsequently selected as panel chair. The COP was primarily focused on the question of how TARP funds were being used and how banks were accounting for them. Warren became a very visible critic of TARP, frequently interviewed on television.

In late January 2009, the COP issued a "Special Report on Regulatory Reform." This report, prepared by academic consultants, comprehensively surveyed prior investigations and studies concerning financial reform. It was fully up-to-date with the international context, citing the Financial Stability Forum, as well as Basel I and II. The Report included a list of recommendations for policy action, including a call to "Create a New System for Federal and State Regulation of Mortgages and other Consumer Credit Products" (p. 30). This portion of the report closely paralleled Bar-Gill and Warren (2008), and suggested creation of either a new independent agency *or* placing the new regulator within the Federal Reserve Board (p. 35). The report included a lengthy minority analysis which accurately anticipated the arguments leveled at the CFPB in subsequent debates.

In February 2009, Warren blasted the Treasury for failing to spend TARP money as Congress had been promised. The Obama Administration, however, "did not echo the congressional concerns" (*Washington Post*, February 6, 2009: A03). In short, Warren was known to the Obama Administration early on, but was clearly, at that stage, not on the same wavelength as Treasury Secretary Geithner.

On March 25, 2009, the Financial Product Safety Commission Act of 2009, influenced by Warren's ideas, was introduced simultaneously in the House and Senate. It was promoted by House Financial Services Committee Chair Barney Frank (*Newsweek*, April 20, 2009: 34). A group of Senators who had co-sponsored the bill wrote Geithner urging that the consumer finance agency be included in the Administration's plan (*Washington Post*, May 20, 2009: A01). In testimony in late March concerning financial reform plans, Geithner was criticized by consumer advocates for making no mention of consumer issues (*Washington*

Post, March 27, 2010: D01). Reports surfaced in late May 2009 that Secretary Geithner and National Economic Council Chair Larry Summers were discussing including the consumer protection agency in the Administration's reform proposal, but that the Administration was still undecided on the concept (ibid.).

The June 2009 Administration "White Paper" called for creation of a "single regulatory agency," to be called the Consumer Financial Protection Agency, essentially Warren's proposal (US Treasury 2009). Powers over consumer protection in finance would be transferred to the new agency from the several agencies to which they had become dispersed over the years: the Fed, OCC, OTS, FDIC, FTC (Federal Trade Commission), NCUA, and the Department of Housing and Urban Development (HUD). Strikingly, aside from the FTC, there was little bureaucratic resistance to these reforms.

A new coalition

At virtually the same time the Administration unveiled its proposal, a new pro-reform coalition was announced, known as the Americans for Financial Reform (AFR). This coalition, which eventually numbered more than 250 consumer groups and labor organizations, provided for the first time in the history of US financial politics a cohesive non-industry voice. AFR was financially marginal in contrast to the traditional major lobby groups—its annual budget was reported to be around $1.5 million; the Chamber of Commerce reportedly spent over $700 million in lobbying on all issues in 2010.

Comments from representatives of the financial industry earlier in the year suggested that they believed the consumer financial protection proposals were unlikely to be seriously considered. Once they showed up in the Administration's White Paper, the industry began "lobbying furiously" in opposition (Heilemann 2010). The American Financial Services Association stated that they could not accept a solution that involved a new separate agency. A lobbyist for the Financial Services Roundtable said flatly, "our goal is to kill it" (*American Banker,* July 13, 2009: 1). Opposition also came from the American Banker's Association, the American Land Title Association, the Independent Community Bankers of America, the Chamber of Commerce, and many others.

The opponents succeeded in making a number of changes as the legislation progressed. Early on, they eliminated a requirement that lenders be required to offer basic, standardized ("plain vanilla") products to facilitate consumer comparison shopping. They won on strong language requiring coordination and communication between CFPB and other bank regulators. They won requirements for dispute resolution processes when regulators disagreed among themselves. Later in the process they restricted the new agency to *enforcing* (as opposed to writing) regulations only for the largest firms (larger than $10 billion assets), whereas other functional regulators would enforce regulations for smaller firms. Eventually there was an agreement to completely exempt auto dealers (who make consumer loans) from agency oversight.

As 2010 progressed, President Obama repeatedly endorsed the idea of a new independent agency. In April, the SEC brought fraud charges against Goldman Sachs, and in May, opinion polls showed that the public strongly supported stricter bank regulation. In this environment, reform advocates were emboldened. The Senate Bill, passed in late May, placed the CFPB inside the Federal Reserve. Not only had the agency not been killed, it had been granted more robust autonomy. The FSOC may "stay" CFPB regulations (Title X, Section 1023). However, such an action requires a two-thirds vote in the FSOC, and each member voting in favor must represent an agency which has independently determined in a public meeting that the CFPB proposal would put banking system safety and soundness at risk. Contrary to the urging of the financial industry, the CFPB may not preempt state law when state law provides more consumer protection than does Federal law. This was a major change to the status quo.

Implementation

The CFPB received a relatively high number of new rule-making authorities granted under Dodd-Frank (though far fewer than granted to the SEC, FRS, and CFTC). The initial implementation problem confronting CFPB was the creation of an entirely new agency from groups of staff drawn from several existing agencies. Most CFPB authority officially began on July 21, 2011, but as early as March 2011 the agency had a functioning website dispensing advice to consumers, inviting comments, and offering assistance with complaints.

Obama appointed Elizabeth Warren to launch the agency—a decision strongly opposed by Republicans in Congress and most of the financial industry. She went on a "charm offensive" with financial industry executives in order to try to get the agency off to a good start (*Wall Street Journal*, March 15, 2011). She advised bankers that her main targets are non-bank firms making payday and student loans, doing debt collection, and lending for mortgages. She emphasized a "principled approach" to supervision rather than strict enforcement of precise rules.

Of course, the impact of the CFPB remains to be seen. Opponents succeeded in blocking the appointment of Elizabeth Warren as the agency's first director. The fact that the agency exists at all, and has drawn resources from many other existing agencies is a remarkable event. The fact that it is well-financed, headed by a single director, and lodged in, but not controlled by, the Fed, is even more remarkable. At the same time, the agency's enforcement scope is restricted to the very largest financial firms, and it has no mandate to require the creation of the standardized, easily understood instruments initially recommended by Warren. While it is a tremendous accomplishment in some respects, the agency is ultimately of more concern to consumer advocates than to the financial policy elite that cared most about the shadow banking world and its unregulated derivatives products.

The Volcker Rule

The portion of the Act known as "the Volcker Rule" (Title VI sections 619–621) attempts to require banks to separate risky, speculative activity conducted on behalf of the bank, from the basic banking functions serving bank clients. The latter enjoy a variety of explicit public guarantees and supports. The Volcker Rule was also seen as addressing conflicts of interest that might emerge between banks operating in their own interests and those of their clients.

The Congressional debate over the Volcker Rule was highly visible but by some accounts not really very contentious. Contrary to several press accounts, the Volcker Rule did not recreate the bright-line separation of commercial and investment banking of the Glass-Steagall Act of 1933. However, the echo of Glass-Steagall has been widely noted.

The Obama Administration's June 2009 White Paper called for regulatory action to strengthen firewalls between banking affiliates that dealt in OTC derivatives versus the deposit-taking parts of a bank that enjoyed federal guarantees. That proposal was relatively timid compared to what emerged later in the process. Consistent with the initial Administration plan, the version of the legislation passed by the House of Representatives in December 2009 made only a nod toward the kind of separation required by the Volcker Rule—at that time the phrase had not yet been coined.

In response to increasingly negative public opinion about the bank bailouts, the Obama Administration decided in December 2009, as a matter of political strategy, to back stronger legislation and to identify it rhetorically as "the Volcker Rule" in order to draw on the deference accorded the former Fed Chairman. Obama's decision was announced in January 2010, to general surprise because of the widespread belief that this direction was opposed by Larry Summers, Director or the National Economic Council, and Tim Geithner, Treasury Secretary. Obama's announcement followed hard on a White House proposal to place a "Financial Crisis Responsibility Fee" on the liabilities of the largest financial firms in order to repay the loans and subsidies provided by the Government. Both proposals marked a hardening of Obama's approach to financial reform.

In subsequent months, the draft legislation concerning the Volcker Rule became stronger as criticism of Goldman-Sachs became sharper; many observers saw these developments as linked. Shortly after the SEC charged Goldman with civil fraud, a stronger version of the Volcker Rule, known as the Merkley-Levin Amendment (MLA), was introduced in May 2010. Among other differences, Merkley-Levin prohibited proprietary trading as a matter of law, not just prospective regulation, and applied to all "banking entities" rather than only to insured depositary institutions.

Congressional consideration of MLA became linked with another controversial provision, the Brownback Amendment to exempt auto dealers from coverage by the Consumer Financial Protection Agency. Both passed the Senate in late May in an apparent compromise. The MLA was weakened in Conference Committee in order to win the support of newly-elected Massachusetts Republican Senator Scott Brown on a vote necessary to halt debate (Cassidy 2010). In this case, language was inserted that permits banks to invest up to 3 percent of their tier 1 capital (not, as in a prior draft, the more inclusive "common equity") in hedge funds and private equity funds, provided that they do not own more than 3 percent of a fund's capital.

Volcker's entrepreneurship

The idea of restricting banks' involvement with proprietary trading was not among the ideas proposed in prior US regulatory reform documents. Nor had this been an issue for the G20. By 2006, securities regulators, most prominently in Australia, were expressing concerns about proprietary trading as a source of conflicts of interest (Australia, Securities and Investment Commission 2006). However, in late 2008, following the crash, industry observers noted that proprietary trading was "under scrutiny" because of the extensive leverage involved (*Wall Street Journal Market Watch,* October 31, 2008).

The main agenda-setting event was a report issued on January 12, 2009 by the Group of 30 (G30), a private policy-advisory group which was headed by former Fed Chairman Paul Volcker, who had been named by Obama in November 2008 as Chairman of the President's Economic Recovery Board (Group of 30, 2009). The report called for limiting the proprietary activities of "systemically important banking institutions" that "present particularly high risks and serious conflicts of interest." The G30 also called for prohibiting bank sponsorship or management of hedge funds and urged that in the packaging and sale of "collective debt instruments" banks should be required to retain a "meaningful part of the credit risk."

The idea gained no immediate traction. When Volcker outlined the proposal to Congress on February 26 (Volcker 2009), close observers doubted that it would play a significant role in the US reform. There was a widespread impression that, despite his official advisory position, Volcker lacked strong influence with Obama. Consistent with that view, the idea of limiting bank proprietary trading figured modestly in the Administration's June 2009 "White Paper," (p. 31) and it was not mentioned at all in Obama's accompanying public statement (Obama 2009c). The media rarely mentioned the topic. When Obama made a major speech on financial reform in New York City in September 2009, he again omitted any mention of the Volcker Rule or proprietary trading (Obama 2009e). When Volcker continued to advocate prohibition of proprietary trading a few days later, the *Wall Street Journal* (September 17, 2009) speculated that he was likely at odds with the Obama Administration. The *New York Times* (October 20, 2009) observed that Volcker "may not be alone in his proposal, but he is nearly so."

The House bill, passed December 11, 2009 on a strict party-line vote, did not include a *prohibition* on proprietary trading, but it did specify that the Federal Reserve Board could restrict the ability of a financial firm to trade on its own account (Section 1117).

Key events

The progress toward adopting the Volcker Rule was primarily a response to public anger about bailouts and bonuses—anger that came from both the Right and the Left. Obama decided in late December 2009 to reverse course explicitly and prominently support the proposal. In doing this, he had to overcome the objections of Geithner and Summers (Alter 2010; Heilemann 2010). One prominent observer was quoted at the time as saying that the change was a "fundamental shift" (*Washington Post,* January 22, 2010).

The reaction from Wall Street was anger and a sense of betrayal. Congressional reception of the idea was, initially, lukewarm. Within days of Obama's announcement, Volcker testified before the Senate Banking Committee. Chairman Dodd spoke passionately of his commitment to address the problem of too-big-to-fail and his desire to make the idea of future bailouts "absolutely off the charts." He pointed out that the committee had held 52 hearings in the past year that had thoroughly considered the problems of reform. The Volcker Rule issue, he said, came up late and was generally viewed as a political response to the Republican victory in the Massachusetts special election. Dodd warned against trying to do too much, and added, presciently, that "I don't want to go to the floor of the United States Senate begging for a 60th vote." Volcker pointed out that the President's decision long preceded the Massachusetts special election, a point Dodd conceded (US, Senate, Committee on Banking, Housing and Urban Affairs, 2010).

Within a month, there were leaked accounts that the Administration was backing away from the Volcker Rule because they were having trouble selling it to the Treasury and Congress (*New York Post,* February 23, 2010). However, momentum swung back strongly toward the Rule—and all of financial reform—in April, when the SEC filed its civil fraud charges against Goldman. In this environment, many elements of the stronger version of the Volcker Rule, taken from the Merkley-Levin Amendment, prevailed.

Implementation

Ultimately, as passed, the Volcker Rule includes a number of contingencies, exceptions, and limits. Nonetheless, real adaptations have been made already, and the principles articulated in the Volcker Rule permit modes of supervision and monitoring that were previously unknown. The new law directed the FSOC to complete a study within six months including detailed guidance to regulatory agencies required to complete drafts of regulations within another nine months. The law required clarification about the nature of activity related to "marketmaking" that would be permitted. Other terms will be clarified in part through a study to be conducted by the GAO. The FSOC reported receiving over 8,000 public comments about its report, of which 6,550 were substantially the same letter arguing for strong implementation of the Volcker Rule (US, FSOC 2011). This seems to have reflected mobilization by Americans for Financial Reform coalition partner Public Citizen (Krawiec 2011). The remaining comments addressed in detail the ambiguities and problems in implementing the law.

The FSOC report was a statement of intent to strongly enforce the new law. The report innovated in proposing quantitative metrics that can be used to monitor bank investment activities and that may signal an engagement in prohibited proprietary trading. The report notes that its direction will impose additional burdens on regulatory agencies and on banking entities as well.

By the end of January 2011 several major banks had already decided to close down their proprietary trading (*Wall Street Journal,* September 1, 2010; *Business Insider,* September 3, 2010; *Dealbook,* September 29, 2010; *Financial Times,* October 1, 2010). Despite the opportunity for a considerable period in which to implement changes required by regulations yet to be promulgated, the leading investment banks moved quite promptly to reveal plans to eliminate proprietary trading. Skeptics suspected them of essentially reassigning people to permitted areas related to making markets.

The next step is rule making by the SEC; CFTC, FRB, FDIC, and OCC. The proposed regulations were expected in October 2011. Additional joint rule makings "shall" address activities that may threaten US financial stability, additional capital requirements, internal controls, and recordkeeping.

New regime for derivatives trading

Derivatives regulation represented one of the most urgent but difficult reform tasks. This problem was taken up in Dodd-Frank in Title VII, which set new rules for transparent pricing and public documentation in most derivatives markets. Derivatives, as contractual agreements based on underlying assets or commodities or revenue streams, were central to the financial crisis. As a broad class of instruments, they had become a core element in the business strategies of thousands of firms. Since they were private, over-the-counter (OTC) contracts, they could inject inestimable levels of uncertainty into a variety of financial markets. This combination of centrality and uncertainty meant that the prospect of regulating derivatives unleashed a remarkable burst of high-energy politics. Affected constituencies included interest groups from all parts of the business community, labor, professional groups, consumer advocacy groups, and public officials from many federal, state, and municipal jurisdictions.

Reform proponents had two main goals in the derivatives debate: first, to segregate derivatives trading from other banking activities; and, second, to take derivatives out of the unregulated shadow banking system by forcing them into more open venues as fully documented transactions. Both goals provoked bitter resistance from particular segments of the finance industry, but both appeared in the final bill. As enacted, both measures give regulators the tools to limit dramatically excessive risk taking in derivatives, but only if regulators are provided with adequate staffing and expertise.

Despite earlier debates on the subject, derivatives had remained largely unregulated into the early 2000s. They came into existence as hedging instruments, similar to commodities futures, to help market participants insure predictable revenues for agricultural products or anticipated revenues in foreign currencies. As the complexity of the assets underlying derivatives expanded, their notional value began to dwarf all other markets. By the late 1990s, the volume of MBS was growing geometrically and the popularity of the CDS that insured the revenue streams from them appeared to be growing even more quickly. In May 1998, the CFTC, led by chair Brooksley Born, issued a concept paper proposing that derivatives be regulated by the CFTC (CFTC 1998). In an episode famous for its short-sightedness, Treasury Secretary Robert Rubin sided with Fed Chairman Alan Greenspan and other regulators in opposing Born's view. The Commodities Futures Modernization Act, passed in late 2000, legally barred the CFTC (or any federal regulator) from asserting jurisdiction over off-exchange derivatives (Hirsch 2010; McLean/Nocera 2010: 104–106).

Through the early 2000s, the idea of regulating derivatives continued to percolate. Iconic investor Warren Buffett described derivatives as "financial weapons of mass destruction" in 2003 and his remarks were widely quoted (for example, Congressional Record, March 4, 2003: 5309). Between 2005 and early 2008, the Financial Stability Board led discussions of the G20 to ensure that the "operational infrastructure" for OTC derivatives markets was sound. Over the same period, the Federal Reserve Bank of New York held several industry meetings pursuing the same goals (Federal Reserve Bank of New York 2008). By November 2008, the US Treasury had shifted toward an activist position within the G20 by circulating an Action Plan in preparation for the G20 Pittsburgh summit the following September, including efforts to "reduce the systemic risks of CDS," while also bolstering "infrastructure for OTC derivatives" (US Delegation to the G20, 2008). By 2008, all relevant actors acknowledged that financial derivatives had played a key role in the failure of Bear-Stearns in March and in freezing credit markets after Lehman went bankrupt in September.

Key actors

Given the urgency of improving oversight for derivatives, many actors staked out early positions. In early 2009, bills appeared in various Congressional committees to address the danger of speculation in derivatives for energy and agriculture. Seeking to maintain the initiative on financial regulation, Secretary Geithner wrote to House Speaker Nancy Pelosi on May 13, 2009, a month before publication of the Administration White Paper, to outline Administration proposals on derivatives.

The Treasury's plan showed that the financial policy elite was reassessing its earlier views with regard to the derivatives business. The earlier consensus held that sophisticated banks and hedge funds could use derivatives to promote better allocation of risk and resources. But after the crash, regulators had to acknowledge that derivatives could also concentrate risk in "opaque and complex ways." According to the Treasury Department's report, "the build-up of risk in the over-the-counter (OTC) derivatives markets, which were thought to disperse risk to those most able to bear it, became a major source of contagion through the financial sector during the crisis" (US Treasury 2009: 43). Accordingly, Treasury proposed that derivatives be traded through verifiable transactions and guaranteed by registered clearing-house institutions. Instead of the "lax regulatory regime" that had taken shape by 2008, the Treasury report said that adequate regulation required clearing through central counterparties (US Treasury 2009: 47).

This proposal would have effectively reversed the Commodities Futures Modernization Act of 2000. To implement this, the Treasury plan asked the SEC and the CFTC to mesh their rules. The CFTC's duties were to be dramatically expanded to cover most derivatives, while the SEC would cooperate by continuing its oversight of "security-based" derivatives.

Given the stakes involved, a broad range of interests sought to shape the Treasury's proposals as they made their way through Congress. Owing to the unprecedented profits that derivatives had generated, financial services firms mobilized quickly to press for more moderate changes. They wanted to stabilize the market without subjecting the main players to major surgery and, above all, without adding onerous requirements for margin or capital reserves.

Perhaps more surprising, within a few months, the broader grassroots advocacy organizations also met the challenge. They secured the necessary expertise and began to push their own positions on issues of derivatives regulation. By summer 2009, the AFR had begun to articulate alternatives to industry proposals.

The main Congressional bodies involved in derivatives were, again, the House Committee on Financial Services and the Senate Committee on Banking. But the origins of derivatives in agricultural trade meant that these committees shared jurisdiction with the House and Senate agriculture committees. This shared jurisdiction became pivotal at a later point because the two agriculture committees retained oversight for the CFTC, which was now proposed to be the lead agency to oversee the largest financial markets in existence.

The pattern of interest-group activism on derivatives highlighted the two-tiered politics that increasingly confronted elected officials. Initially, the interest-group terrain was characterized by three features. First, while industry groups shied away from opposing the Administration's plans for monitoring systemic risk, they were fully prepared to oppose any measures on derivatives from the outset. Major non-banking firms immediately scrutinized the plans for regulating derivatives. Even before Congressional committees took up the Treasury's proposal, companies including Caterpillar, IBM, and Boeing Aerospace were pushing back against the regulations they anticipated (*Wall Street Journal,* July 10, 2009: Kara Scannell).

Second, derivatives had become so deeply enmeshed in the economy that firms in almost all sectors reacted to the proposals for new regulation. Several industry associations said their members needed customized derivatives to offset specific risks in their everyday business activities—something quite distinct from purely financial speculation that might require special regulatory provisions. One prominent example, the Coalition for Derivatives End-Users, was formed in August 2009 and commented regularly on draft legislation through the fall (Coalition for Derivatives End-Users 2009a). This consortium included many firms that counted as significant players in financial markets, but its component organizations were sufficiently broad in membership that they could plausibly distinguish themselves from the Wall Street banks at the center of the crisis (Coalition for Derivatives End-Users 2009b).

A third feature of lobbying on derivatives was shared across the industry spectrum and the consumer advocacy groups. All of them displayed a tendency to form dedicated, issue-specific coalitions. The Consortium of Derivatives End-Users was one clear example, and the financial services firms adopted a parallel approach. Two associations that represented the main marketmakers and dealers in derivatives were the ISDA (International Swaps and Derivatives Association) and SIFMA (the Securities Industry and Financial Markets Association). They approached the relevant Congressional committees jointly in November and December of 2009. And after the bill was signed into law in July 2010, these two groups began to work also with the Securities Association of the American Bankers Association (ABA) and a number of other industry associations in financial services.

Grassroots advocacy groups from the progressive Left also mobilized surprisingly quickly around the issue of derivatives. Although consumer protection and executive compensation ranked higher among the initial priorities of the AFR, this group advanced informed arguments for serious regulation of derivatives (Tekiela 2011). In August 2009, AFR urged Congress to require that all derivatives be traded on regulated and fully transparent exchanges. The AFR specifically argued against the kind of exemptions proposed by industry groups such as the End-Users Coalition.

The tensions of two-tier politics appeared sharply from the autumn of 2009 onward. The finance industry had reliable entrée to the House of Representatives via the business-friendly members in the New Democrat Coalition. Within days after the Lehman bankruptcy, this group set up a task force on financial reform co-chaired by Melissa Bean (D, NY) and Representative Jim Himes (D, CT), a former banker at Goldman Sachs. The New Democrats prevailed upon the House Financial Services Committee to exempt derivatives end-users from the "discussion draft" of October 2009 (*Propublica,* October 25, 2011: Sebastian Jones/Marcus Stern). When hearings were held on the initial proposals, the CFTC Chairman, Gary Gensler, immediately warned that such "end-users" exemptions would enable banks to shield a major portion of their derivatives business from any new regulatory oversight. The American for Financial Reform supported tough language, testifying that fully public exchanges would provide a safer arena for derivatives trade than would centralized clearinghouses favored by the business-friendly House members (*Washington Post,* October 7, 2009: Brady Dennis; see also Gensler 2009; Johnson 2009).

Key events

As legislative action moved from the House to the Senate, reformers gained resources through unpredicted political events. The Financial Crisis Commission held widely televised hearings in January 2010, and the unrepentant remarks of several Wall Street chieftains shifted the atmospherics in favor of more sweeping measures. Also in January 2010, a popular critic of Wall Street's culture, Michael Lewis, published a bestselling book on the pathologies of the derivatives trade, which became virtually required reading for Congressional staffers. Then, as noted above, came the special election of Scott Brown, altering Senate politics.

As the Senate approached a vote on the financial overhaul in April and May of 2010, the dynamic of two-tier politics became unmistakable. On April 16, President Obama made a point of signaling his intent to veto any bill "that does not bring the derivatives market under control" (Obama 2010). A more surprising source of help for the network of progressive groups came from Senator Blanche Lincoln of Arkansas, the chair of the Agriculture Committee. Lincoln had alienated the left wing of the Democratic party by helping block "the public option" in health care. Then, even more controversially, she opposed President Obama's efforts to strengthen the position of labor unions in plant-level organizing contests. In response, the Arkansas branch of the AFL-CIO labor federation decided to support a far more liberal candidate in the Arkansas primary elections in May 2010. Lincoln reacted by championing tougher language on derivatives regulation than either the House or the Senate committees. Senator Lincoln's amendment strengthened the bill's provisions by requiring all banks to put their derivatives-trading desks into separate subsidiaries that would have to be capitalized independently from all parts of the firm that enjoyed federal guarantees (*Associated Press,* March 1, 2010; *Huffington Post,* June 10, 2010: Sam Stein).

Proponents of stronger derivatives regulation began to coalesce in April and May. As head of the CFTC, Gary Gensler published an essay in the *Wall Street Journal,* arguing that it was time to treat complex derivatives like commodity futures and bring them under the control of clearinghouses with known prices and public record-keeping (Gensler 2010). Those arguments were supported by another business coalition, the Commodity Markets Oversight Coalition (CMOC). Its members included household oil delivery firms, trucking associations, some airlines, farmers, and other retailers. Arguing that they were in fact the genuine users of derivatives in markets that had been flooded by speculators since 2000, this group kept in close touch with the Congressional agriculture panels. They reinforced the views of CFTC Chairman Gensler by arguing against exemptions from the clearing requirements that might allow "hedge funds and other financial players" to shield large portions of their portfolios from scrutiny. For good measure, they explicitly attacked the authenticity of the much larger "Coalition for Derivatives End-Users" by writing that "they are not traditional end-users," and that "it is questionable whether in fact they have the issues of the commercial end-users at heart" (CMOC 2010). Although the AFR did not, as a rule, coordinate with this consortium, its views were so similar on the clearinghouse issue that AFR re-posted the letter on its website within a day.

When the Senate and House conferees met in June to reconcile the bills passed by each chamber, the dynamic of two-tier politics produced unexpected and important consequences. Blanche Lincoln emerged as the exception to a process of legislative dilution that seemed particularly conspicuous in the area of derivatives. While the Volcker Rule spoke generally to preventing speculation by institutions with federal banking guarantees, the Lincoln Amendment required an additional "push-out" of all derivatives transactions, whether client-linked or part of the bank's own proprietary trading portfolio. Now, progressive groups, including the AFR, visibly supported Lincoln's efforts in the conference committee. The finance industry still thought its backers in the New Democrat Coalition would be able to weaken the Volcker Rule and strip the Lincoln Amendment out of the final legislation. The business-friendly group wrote to the conferees on June 16, urging them to restore the House language on limits to the derivatives rules and to remove the Lincoln Amendment (*Huffington Post,* June 14, 2010: Shahien Nasiripour/Ryan Grim; *Propublica,* October 25, 2011: Sebastian Jones/Marcus Stern; *Washington Post,* June 24, 2010: David Cho).

As discussions approached a conclusion, Congressional leaders started to limit their face-to-face contacts with representatives of industry. There was little doubt that the major banks could reach the key contacts by telephone, but many lobbyists began to complain that they were losing face-to-face access (*Wall Street Journal,* June 14, 2010: Aaron Luccetti/Damian Paletta). Since the overhaul was to count as one of the Obama Administration's major legislative achievements, the pressure on key committee members to reach agreement mounted steadily.

At the same time, the role of CFTC chairman Gary Gensler became especially noteworthy. Given the complexity of the derivatives issue, it was not surprising that the heads of the agriculture committees, Senator Lincoln and Representative Collin Peterson, welcomed his availability. Other legislators said it was "a little unusual" to see him conferring with legislators so regularly. According to one account, during a particularly long 20-hour session, Gensler "hovered just behind lawmakers, and could be seen whispering to staff and negotiators as the House and Senate sought to iron out the 2,300-plus page bill" (*Wall Street Journal,* July 15, 2010: Michael Crittenden/Victoria McGrane).

Toward the end of the conference negotiations, Senator Lincoln, resolutely independent, claimed that her language would "make banks get back to being banks and those of us who grew up in small towns in America understand what that means" (*Politico,* June 24, 2010: Carrie Budoff Brown/Meredith Shiner). Ultimately, she compromised but only in part by allowing banks to continue their customary trade in interest-rate swaps and foreign currency swaps, while other derivatives had to go through separate subsidiaries. Whether for electoral reasons or underlying conviction, Blanche Lincoln provided the legislative voice for the same views that the progressive Left had less successfully urged upon Congress in earlier efforts to secure tougher regulation of the derivatives markets.

Conclusion

The financial turmoil of 2008 gave the new Obama Administration no choice but to initiate major financial reforms as it came into office in 2009. At that time, a vague commitment to financial regulatory reform was balanced against economic stimulus, energy policy, education reform, and health care reform as Presidential priorities (Obama 2009). But the reality of financial distress—acute in many cases—gave financial reform even greater urgency among the financial policy elite that dominated the industry.

In passing the Dodd-Frank Act, the Congress produced a broad-gauged piece of legislation. In terms of structural changes affecting key market participants and their corresponding regulators, the changes enacted by the law were significant but cautious. These structural changes included:

- establishing the Financial Stability Oversight Council as a new body composed of existing regulatory agencies;
- eliminating one existing bank regulator, the Office of Thrift Supervision, by merging it into the Office of the Comptroller of the Currency;
- creating a new agency, the Consumer Financial Protection Bureau, with the purpose of setting rules and monitoring compliance of financial products for retail financial products.

As important as these structural changes may turn out to be, the new law mandates important new procedures for governing the key competitors and regulatory agencies in financial markets. Among the central regulatory changes were:

- enhanced prudential regulation for systemically important firms, including the imposition of higher capital and margin requirements at levels to be set by the regulators;
- the spinning off of (most) proprietary-trading activities by banks or other deposit-taking institutions (Volcker Rule);
- the spinning off of (most) derivatives activity, whether as proprietary trader or market-making dealer, by banks or institutions that benefit from federal government guarantees (Lincoln Amendment);
- the shifting of (most) standardized derivatives contracts from private contracts to centralized counterparty transactions.

These changes, both structural and procedural, were important. Their ultimate significance will depend upon implementation decisions and the judicial interpretations that follow. In this period, regulatory agencies will develop the capabilities necessary for their revised missions, propose the new rules that implement the law, receive public comments, and prepare for the legal challenges that make regulatory law a matter of ongoing practice in the United States. While the processes of administrative rule making will remain procedurally normal, they will be contested with heightened vigor in the case of the Dodd-Frank Act. There is no doubt that the parties and interest groups have chosen to fight over financial reform in the legal thickets of post-enactment implementation as much as in the brighter light of public debate. As one Washington newsletter put it in early 2011, a "pitched battle […] has been joined over the regulations that are being written to implement Dodd-Frank" (*Pratt Letter* 2011)

The Dodd-Frank legislation represents an ambitious effort to adapt the underlying structure of core financial and regulatory institutions, but without rebuilding them. In this sense, the Dodd-Frank legislation confounds the simplest predictions from institutionalist theory: that major external shocks are the primary source of institutional transformations. In this case, the external shock was severe but profound institutional transformation did not follow. The Dodd-Frank overhaul therefore provides some support to a more incremental view of institutional change. Despite the magnitude of the external shock, it was not enough to completely delegitimize leading institutions or to shatter old coalitions. Republicans and Democrats alike displayed a consistent preference for maintaining the key institutions in the financial landscape. The deregulatory changes in the decades preceding the crisis can only be characterized as a process of intentional institutional evolution: institutional disassembly via the repeal of key laws and the hollowing out of the regulatory agencies that had previously preserved market stability.

Interestingly, the Dodd-Frank reform included changes that clearly diverged from the other prevalent theories of regulatory policymaking. The creation of the CFPB ran diametrically counter to the goals of some of the most entrenched interest groups in the finance sector, particularly the American Banking Association. And, for similar reasons, the changes in agency jurisdictions do not conform in any simple manner to predictions that bureaucratic agencies can defend their turf successfully.

For these reasons, the Dodd-Frank legislation must be understood as the result of other distinctive factors.

The preservationist approach of the Obama White House put great emphasis on the need to avoid further disruption to the incumbent market participants or the key regulatory bodies. This emphasis on maintaining continuity in the financial policy elite clearly supported the existing interest groups in the financial arena. But the politics of finance were shaken up by a number of unusually knowledgeable and skillful policy entrepreneurs. The efforts of Elizabeth Warren, Paul Volcker, Gary Gensler gave a very different cast to debates that would otherwise have been dominated by familiar dynamics of concentrated interest-group pressure.

At the same time, a form of grassroots mobilization represented by the Americans for Financial Reform reflected popular anger and the efforts of the advocacy groups. The AFR brought together a range of labor unions and consumer groups and, perhaps most important, a reservoir of expertise that pushed the Democratic Party to subordinate the preferences of established industry groups on several occasions. It was partly the organizational skill of the AFR that enabled this result, but also partly the depth of the populist backlash against the financial establishment that forced Congressional leaders to seek broader levels of support than available from the industry groups alone.

The result was a pattern we call two-tier politics, in which both political parties sought to appeal to the established actors and the popular activists at the same time. At the level of elite or top-tier politics, both parties had strong ties to Wall Street, as symbolized by the seamless transition from Hank Paulson to Tim Geithner. Beyond Wall Street, the parties had somewhat different constituencies in the business community, the Republicans with many of the multinational manufacturing and extractive segments, the Democrats with more support from transportation, infrastructure, and domestically-oriented manufacturing segments. At the lower tier of grassroots coalition-building, the party constituencies differed especially clearly. For Democrats, the two-tier strategy meant appealing to labor, consumer advocates, and the broad networks of activists known as the "net roots." For Republicans, the two-tier imperative meant maintaining loyalty from their core business constituencies while also placating the Tea Party and other populist groups that rejected the very elite consensus that had dominated financial policy for several decades.

This two-tier dynamic is likely to appear in other policy areas in the coming years. For financial regulation, the two-tier dynamic distinctly helped policy entrepreneurs such as Elizabeth Warren and Paul Volcker. Without the ongoing scrutiny provided by the Americans for Financial Reform, it is unclear whether the Consumer Financial Protection Bureau or the Volcker Rule would have survived the legislative process.

But another, equally important effect of two-tier politics was the pronounced susceptibility to unpredicted political events. The special election of Republican Scott Brown as Massachusetts Senator in January 2010 led to a significant dilution of the language outlining the Volcker Rule in the Conference negotiations of June 2010. And the electoral challenge that faced Senator Blanche Lincoln within the Arkansas Democratic primary elections in 2010 led her to insist upon much tougher provisions for the regulation of derivatives than would otherwise have found its way into the final legislation.

These final twists in the legislative process directly shaped two of the most important procedural changes to affect US financial markets through the crisis and the regulatory response. The first change, by diluting the Volcker Rule, meant that after Dodd-Frank, the separation of deposit banking from proprietary trading was significantly less clear-cut than it might have been. The second change, by bringing Senator Lincoln's language into the final bill, created a far stronger set of tools than regulators would otherwise have received in their efforts to squeeze excessive levels of risk out of the derivatives markets. Given the centrality of both issues to the workings of contemporary capital markets, it is hard to overstate the importance of political contingency in the Dodd-Frank outcome. Much of the institutional context can be well accounted for by our familiar theoretical perspectives. Key features in the outcome as well as the political process that produced it can only be explained, however, by a new form of two-tier politics in which elected officials have to balance grassroots advocacy organizations with the most powerful elites and interest groups in the political arena.

References

AFR (Americans for Financial Reform), 2009: *Letter on Derivatives Regulation*, August 2. <http://ourfinancialsecurity.org/2009/08/afr-urges-congress-to-regulate-the-derivatives-markets/>

Alter, Jonathan, 2010: *The Promise: President Obama, Year One.* New York: Simon and Schuster.

ASIC (Australia, Securities and Investment Commission), 2006: *Managing Conflicts of Interest in the Financial Services Industry.* Consultation Paper 73, ASIC 06-096. Canberra: ASIC.

Bar-Gill, Oren/Elizabeth Warren, 2008: Making Credit Safer. In: *University of Pennsylvania Law Review* 157, 1–101.

Bartels, Larry, 2010: *Unequal Democracy: The Political Economy of the New Gilded Age.* Princeton: Princeton University Press.

Baumgartner, Frank/Bryan D. Jones, 2009: *Agendas and Instability in American Politics.* Chicago: University of Chicago Press.

Bebchuk, Lucien/Jesse Fried, 2004: *Pay without Performance: The Unfulfilled Promise of Executive Compensation.* Cambridge: Harvard University Press.

Bernanke, Ben S., 2011: *Testimony before the Senate Committee on Banking,* July 21.

Buffett, Warren, 2003: Annual Letter to Shareholders. In: *Fortune,* March 3. <http://latrobefinancialmanagement.com/Research/Individuals/Buffet%20Warren/What%20Worries%20Warren.pdf> (accessed March 9, 2011)

Carpenter, Daniel, 2011: The Contest of Lobbies and Disciplines: Financial Politics and Regulatory Reform. In: Theda Skocpol/Lawrence Jacobs (eds.), *Reaching for a New Deal: Ambitious Governance, Economic Meltdown, and Polarized Politics in Obama's First Two Years.* New York: Russell Sage Foundation, 139–188.

Cassidy, John, 2010: The Volcker Rule: Obama's Economic Adviser and His Battles over the Financial-Reform Bill. In: *New Yorker,* July 26.

Coalition for Derivatives End-Users, 2009a: *Comments on Frank Discussion Draft on OTC Derivatives* (presumably October). <www.nam.org/~/media/5C86F99AECF5436E8ED774A32B649C2D/Coalition_Comments_to_Frankpdf.pdf>

——, 2009b: *Statement to the Senate Agriculture Committee by the Business Roundtable, Financial Executives International, the National Association of Manufacturers (NAM), the National Association of Real Estate Investment Trusts (NAREIT), the Real Estate Roundtable, and the US Chamber of Commerce,* November 18. <www.reit.com/PolicyPolitics/CreditMarketChallengesChanges/~/media/Portals/0/PDF/Coalition%20Statement%20and%20Reid%20Letter.ashx>

CFTC (Commodity Futures Trading Commission), 1998: *Over-the-Counter Derivatives* (Concept release and request for comments), May 6. <www.cftc.gov/opa/press98/opamntn.htm> (accessed September 9, 2011)

CMOC (Commodity Markets Oversight Coalition), 2010: *Letter to Senators Reid and McConnell,* May 4. <www.nefiactioncenter.com/PDF/cmoc_2010may04_final.pdf>, reproduced by the AFR at <http://ourfinancialsecurity.org/2010/05/cmoc-true-derivatives-end-users-don%E2%80%99t-need-any-more-loopholes/>

Davis, Gerald F., 2009: *Managed by the Markets: How Finance Re-Shaped America.* New York: Oxford University Press.

Davis Polk, 2010: *Side-by-Side Comparison Chart—Key Senate and House Bill Issues* (law firm document, June 2).

DLA Piper, 2010: *Senator Dodd Introduces Revised Financial Services Reform Bill,* March 18. <www.dlapiper.com/senator-dodd-introduces-revised-financial-services-reform-bill/> (accessed March 15, 2011)

Dodd-Frank Wall Street Reform and Consumer Protection Act, 2010: Public Law No: 111-203. Washington, DC: Government Printing Office.

Deutsche Bank Research, 2010: *Direct Fiscal Cost of the Financial Crisis,* May 14. <www.dbresearch.com/PROD/DBR_INTERNET_EN-PROD/PROD00000 00000257663.PDF> (accessed September 10, 2011)

FFIEC (Federal Financial Institutions Examination Council), 2011: *Various statements.*

Federal Reserve Bank of New York, 2008: *Meeting Program,* June. <www.newyorkfed.org/newsevents/news/markets/2008/an080327.html> (accessed March 10, 2011)

FSF (Financial Services Forum), 2010: *Joint letter to the SEC and CFTC from the Financial Services Forum, the Financial Services Roundtable, Futures Industry Association, Institute of International Bankers, the International Swaps and Derivatives Association, the Investment Company Institute, Managed Funds Association, and the Securities Industry and Financial Markets Association,* December 6. <www.aba.com/NR/rdonlyres/6322717B-69AC-11D5-AB86-00508B95258D/70015/12 710CommentLetteronRegulatoryProcessandPhaseIn.pdf>

Gensler, Gary, 2009: *Testimony before the House Financial Services Committee,* October 7. <http://www.cftc.gov/PressRoom/SpeechesTestimony/opagensler-13>

——, 2010: Clearinghouses Are the Answer: Complex Derivatives Should Be Regulated like Commodity Futures. In: *Wall Street Journal,* April 21.

GAO (US Government Accountability Office), 2007: *Financial Regulation: Industry Trends Continue to Challenge the Federal Regulatory Structure* (GAO-08-32). October. Washington, DC: GAO.

Group of Thirty, 2009: *Financial Reform: A Framework for Financial Stability.* <www.group30.org/images/PDF/Financial_Reform-A_Framework_for_Financial Stability.pdf> (accessed August 8, 2011)

Hacker, Jacob S./Paul Pierson, 2010: *Winner-Take-All Politics: How Washington Made the Rich Richer and Turned Its Back on the Middle Class.* New York: Simon & Schuster.

Hall, Peter A. (ed.), 1989: *The Political Power of Economic Ideas: Keynesianism across Nations.* Princeton: Princeton University Press.

Heilemann, John, 2010: Obama Is from Mars, Wall Street Is from Venus: Psychoanalyzing One of America's Most Dysfunctional Relationships. In: *New York Magazine,* May 22. <http://nymag.com/news/politics/66188/> (accessed August 8, 2011)

Hirsch, Michael, 2010: *Capital Offense: How Washington's Wise Men Turned America's Future Over to Wall Street.* Hoboken: John Wiley.

Hirschman, David, 2010: *Comment, Center for Capital Markets, US Chamber of Commerce, to FSOC,* November.

Johnson, Robert A., 2009: *Testimony of Robert A. Johnson, Director of Economic Policy, The Roosevelt Institute, representing Americans for Financial Reform, before the House Financial Services Committee,* October 7. <http://financialservices.house.gov/Hearings/hearingDetails. aspx?NewsID= 1124> (accessed March 16, 2011)

Johnson, Simon/James Kwak, 2010: *Thirteen Bankers: The Wall Street Takeover and the Next Financial Meltdown.* New York: Pantheon.

Kingdon, John, 2011: *Agendas, Alternatives, and Public Policies.* Second edition. Boston: Longman.

Krasner, Stephen D., 1984: Approaches to the State: Alternative Conceptions and Historical Dynamics. In: *Comparative Politics* 16(2), 223–246.

Krawiec, Kim, 2011: *Dodd Frank @1: The Volcker Comments.* <www.theconglomerate.org/ 2011/07/dodd-frank-1-the-volcker-public-comments.html> (accessed September 9, 2011)

Krippner, Greta, 2011: *Capitalizing on Crisis: The Political Origins of the Rise of Finance*. Cambridge: Harvard University Press.

Lewis, Michael, 2010: *The Big Short: Inside the Doomsday Machine*. New York: W. W. Norton.

Lowenstein, Roger, 2001: *When Genius Failed: The Rise and Fall of Long-Term Capital Management*. New York: Random House.

MacKenzie, Donald A., 2008: *An Engine, Not a Camera: How Financial Models Shape Markets*. Cambridge: MIT Press.

Mahoney, James/Kathleen Thelen (eds.), 2010: *Explaining Institutional Change: Ambiguity, Agency, and Power*. New York: Cambridge University Press.

McLean, Bethany/Joe Nocera, 2010: *All the Devils Are Here: Hidden History of the Financial Crisis*. New York: Portfolio.

McTighe, Kathleen, 2010: *Testimony on Behalf of the ABA to the FSOC,* November 5, 2010.

New York Times, 2010: *Editorial: "Restarting Financial Reform,"* January 25.

Obama, Barack, 2009a: *Remarks to the Business Council,* February 13.
    <www.presidency.ucsb.edu/ws/?pid=85779> (accessed August 8, 2011)

——, 2009b: *Presidential Address to Congress,* February 24.
    <www.presidency.ucsb.edu/ws/index.php?pid=85753>

——, 2009c: *Remarks on Financial Regulatory Reform,* June 17.
    <www.presidency.ucsb.edu/ws/index.php?pid=86287> (accessed August 8, 2011)

——, 2009d: *Interview with Steve Kroft on CBS's "60 Minutes,"* December 13.
    <www.presidency.ucsb.edu/ws/index.php?pid=88330> (accessed August 8, 2011)

——, 2009e: *Address at Federal Hall in New York City,* September 14.
    <www.presidency.ucsb.edu/ws/index.php?pid=86628> (accessed August 8, 2011)

——, 2010: *Remarks during a Meeting of the President's Economic Recovery Advisory Board and an Exchange with Reporters,* April 16.   <www.presidency.ucsb.edu/ws/index.php? pid= 87771> (accessed September 20, 2011)

Olson, Mancur, [1965]1971: *The Logic of Collective Action: Public Goods and the Theory of Groups*. Second Printing with a New Preface. Cambridge: Harvard University Press.

——, 1984: *The Rise and Decline of Nations: Economic Growth, Stagflation, and Economic Rigidities*. New Haven: Yale University Press.

Pratt Letter, 2011: A. S. Pratt Banking Law Experts, 2011: *The Battle Is Joined Over Dodd-Frank Implementation,* February 16.

Ryan, Timothy, 2009: *Testimony by the Securities Industry and Financial Markets Association before the US House of Representatives Committee on Financial Services,* March 17.

Silvers, Damon A., 2009: *Associate General Counsel of the American Federation of Labor and Congress of Industrial Organizations, Perspectives on Regulation of Systemic Risk in the Financial Services Industry, Testimony before the House Financial Services Committee,* March 17.

Skeel, David A., 2010: *The New Financial Deal: Understanding the Dodd-Frank Act and Its (Unintended) Consequences*. New York: Wiley.

Steinmo, Sven/Kathleen Thelen/Frank Longstreth (eds.), 1992: *Structuring Politics: Historical Institutionalism in Comparative Analysis*. New York: Cambridge University Press.

Stewart, James B., 2009: The Eight Days of the Financial Crisis. In: *The New Yorker,* September 21.

Streeck, Wolfgang/Kathleen Thelen (eds.), 2005: *Beyond Continuity: Institutional Change in Advanced Political Economies*. New York: Oxford University Press.

Sullivan, Teresa A./Elizabeth Warren/Jay Lawrence Westbrook, 2000: *The Fragile Middle Class: Americans in Debt.* New Haven: Yale University Press.

Tekiela, Karolina, 2011: *From Access to Protection: How the Americans for Financial Reform Took on Wall Street.* Unpublished paper. University of California, Berkeley, April 2011.

Thelen, Kathleen, 2004: *How Institutions Evolve: The Political Economy of Skills in Germany, Britain, the United States, and Japan.* Cambridge: Cambridge University Press.

Trumbull, Gunnar, 2011: *Strength in Numbers: The Political Power of Weak Interests.* Harvard University Press, forthcoming.

US Delegation to the G-20, 2008: *Washington Action Plan,* November 15. <www.pittsburgh summit.gov/resources/125137.htm> (accessed March 10, 2011)

US Department of Labor, Bureau of Labor Statistics, 2011: *Labor Force Statistics from the Current Population Survey.* <www.bls.gov/cps/> (accessed August 8, 2011)

US Federal Housing Finance Agency, 2011: *House Price Indexes.* <www.fhfa.gov/Default. aspx?Page=87> (accessed August 8, 2011)

US FSOC (Financial Stability Oversight Council), 2011: *Study and Recommendation on Prohibitions on Proprietary Trading & Certain Relationships with Hedge Funds & Private Equity Funds,* January. <www.treasury.gov/initiatives/Documents/Volcker%20sec%20%20619%20study%20 final%201%2018%2011%20rg.pdf> (accessed August 8, 2011)

US Senate, COP (Congressional Oversight Panel). All materials now archived by Government Printing Office at: <http://cybercemetery.unt.edu/archive/cop/20110401223205/ http:/www.cop.senate.gov/> (accessed August 8, 2011) Special Report on Regulatory Reform is here: <http://cybercemetery.unt.edu/archive/cop/20110401223225/http:// cop.senate.gov/reports/library/report-012909-cop.cfm>

US Senate, Committee on Banking, Housing and Urban Affairs, 2010: *Prohibiting Certain High-Risk Investment Activities by Banks and Bank Holding Companies, Hearing of February 2.* Retrieved from ProQuest Congressional, August 8, 2011.

US Treasury Department, 2008: *Blueprint for a Modernized Financial Regulatory Structure,* March. <www.treasury.gov/press-center/press-releases/Documents/Blueprint.pdf> (accessed on July 21, 2011)

——, 2009: *Financial Regulatory Reform: A New Foundation: Rebuilding Financial Supervision and Regulation.* <www.treasury.gov/initiatives/wsr/Documents/FinalReport_web.pdf>

Volcker, Paul, 2009: *Statement before the Joint Economic Committee,* February 26. <http://jec.senate.gov/public/?a=Files.Serve&File_id=e9b8330c-f68c-49bf-818f-c1af 11794406>

Warren, Elizabeth, 2007: Unsafe at Any Rate. *Democracy Journal* 5/2007, 8–19.

Warren, Elizabeth/Amelia Warren Tyagi, 2003: *The Two-Income Trap: Why Middle-Class Parents Are Going Broke.* New York: Basic Books.

Wilson, James Q., 1980: *The Politics of Regulation.* New York: Basic Books.

——, [1974]1995: *Political Organizations.* Princeton: Princeton University Press.

Zahariadis, Nicolaos, 2007: The Multiple Streams Framework: Structure, Limitations, Prospects. In: Paul A. Sabatier (ed.), *Theories of the Policy Process.* Boulder: Westview, 65–92.

3
Post-Crisis Financial Regulation in Britain

Sukhdev Johal, Michael Moran and Karel Williams

Introduction

The United Kingdom was at the epicenter of the great financial crisis that began, at least as far as the UK was concerned, on September 14, 2007. On that date, depositors queued to withdraw their money from Northern Rock, one of the most aggressively competitive of the new banks created by the financial services revolution in the UK. The event was historically momentous because it was the first public run on a bank in the UK since the Overend Gurney crisis of 1866. But it was momentous also for other reasons. It was one of the precipitating events of the great international financial crisis. Since London was, and remains, a leading global financial centre it was central to the unfolding of the crisis and to its regulatory aftermath—the main concern of this chapter. In short, making sense of the crisis and its aftermath must involve making sense of the British case. That is the justification for this chapter.

The international crisis was the most momentous for at least a generation—perhaps the most momentous for a century. But in the British case it has a further significance. As we shall see, the financial sector was given a special place in official accounts of the character of the British economy in the period of the new long boom that in Britain stretched from 1992 to 2007. The City of London was commonly pictured as the motor of British economic revival. The crisis thus not only called into question the character of the system of financial regulation, but also a whole economic strategy: it terminated a thirty year long experiment in the management of the British economy, an experiment designed to replace one founded on decaying manufacturing industries with a finance-led service sector. Andrew Haldane, the Executive Director for Financial Stability at the central bank (the Bank of England), put the outcome starkly in 2011: "Three years on, the damage from the 2008 crisis remains deep and painful. In

The chapter reports continuing collaborative work conducted at the Centre for Research on Socio-Cultural Change (CRESC) at the University of Manchester, United Kingdom. CRESC is funded by the United Kingdom Economic and Social Research Council.

the UK we are around 10 percent poorer as a nation and 800,000 people have been made unemployed" (Haldane 2011).

There can thus be little doubt of the historical significance of the crisis. From this observation springs the main point of the chapter. A great crisis might be presumed to produce great reform consequences. In the following pages we try to trace where change is occurring, and where it is not occurring. We try to estimate the scale of change, but also to explain where there are blockages to change.

What we have now in the UK has been shaped by the past. Thus, making sense of the present has to start by understanding the historical path along which the UK has arrived at the regulatory practices which were implicated in the great crisis.

The historical legacy

The regulatory legacy of the British system is inseparable from the history of a wider conjuncture, that governing the relationship between financial power and democratic politics in the UK. The City of London is the most deeply historically rooted and the most formidable concentration of power in British society. It was a great centre of economic power and political organization even before the rise of industrial capitalism in Britain. Some of its most important institutions—such as the Bank of England, founded in 1694—date from the beginnings of merchant capitalism in Britain, and were closely tied to the British state and its early ventures in imperial expansion. When industrial capitalism reached its zenith in nineteenth-century Britain the City was already a formidable power. Internationally, it was the centerpiece of the world economy; domestically, it was integrated into ruling aristocratic elites (Kynaston 1994, 1995, 1999; Cannadine 1990: 391–444).

It was also a self-ruling world. Accounting, reporting, business ethics—all were regulated by the markets themselves, and lightly regulated at that. By the closing decades of the nineteenth century the City had elaborated a distinctive regulatory ideology: this was that financial markets were delicate and complex mechanisms which could not be effectively ruled by anything as rigid as the law, and which could only be controlled by the development of cultures of discipline in the markets, and by the independent organization of those markets (Moran 1981).

This system of independent self-regulation developed before the age of the interventionist state and under an oligarchic system of government. Both features were transformed by World War One. Total war transformed the regulatory ambitions and resources of the state. The war also transformed the party and electoral systems. Labour emerged as the opponent of the main business friendly party, the Conservatives; the franchise was widened to something close to universal adult suffrage.

These developments potentially posed a major threat to business power generally, and to the autonomy of City interests in particular. The City responded with particularly successful adaptations. These endured for much of the twentieth century, and even now exercise an important influence over the regulatory system. The Bank of England, which had hitherto been fairly marginal in the regulation of the City, now emerged as a critical institution. It used its authority to reshape the governance of markets. The war had destroyed the kind of open international economy of which the City had been a centerpiece. After 1918, City markets were organized into a series of cartels policed by trade associations. The cartelization of the markets, coupled with the authority of the Bank of England, was sufficient to sustain what the City called self-regulation: accepting the discipline of self-regulation was the price firms paid for being allowed into the privileged cartels. The stability of the self-regulatory system in the decades after 1918 allowed the City to develop its regulatory ideology further. This pictured the City as a special part of the economy, claiming exemption from one of the main features of twentieth century economic government in Britain, the apparently inexorable rise of the state as a regulator of economic life (Moran 1986).

The system created after 1918 to protect the City from the threats of the new political environment proved very effective. A portrait of the City's regulatory world in, say, 1979, would have looked remarkably like the picture in 1919. But even in 1979 important changes were taking place in the economic and political environment. These changes accelerated in the 1980s. The wider globalization of financial markets, and the rise of rival financial centers, lay behind the "Big Bang" of 1986. The Big Bang deregulated many of the key restrictions which had supported the cartels that in turn had provided the foundations for the system of self-regulation. The market reforms of that year were thus accompanied by a reconstruction of regulatory institutions. The City still clung to the language of self-regulation, and was still determined to minimize the dangers of intervention by the democratic state, but it now needed a replacement for the disciplines of the cartelized world of government by elite trade associations. A Securities and Investments Board (SIB) was created which in turn oversaw a complex range of Self-Regulatory Organizations that covered the main city markets. As their title suggests, their aim was to preserve self-regulation, and indeed the constitution of both the Securities and Investments Board, and of the Self-Regulatory Organizations, was designed to ensure that they were controlled by the elite of the markets (Moran 1991). But this attempt to preserve the old autonomy in a world of competitive markets and global organizations turned out to be profoundly unstable. It could not deliver what it was supposed to provide: effective regulation. It was bedeviled by scandals and failures, of which the most catastrophic was the Barings Bank collapse of 1995. Although strictly speaking outside the SIB system—the Bank of England retained responsibility for banking supervision—the crisis proved the occasion for a wholesale reconstruction of the system of financial regulation. The New Labour government, which was returned to office in 1997, gave the Bank of England the considerable prize of control over short-term interest rate policy, but simultaneously stripped it of responsibility for bank supervision. It created a new Financial Services Authority which inherited both the Bank's supervisory powers and the responsibilities of the system created under the Securities and Investments Board in 1986. It was the Financial Services Authority which was the centerpiece of the regulatory system that collapsed so dramatically after 2007—and it is to this regulatory system that we now turn.

The pre-crisis institutional set up

One of the many puzzles of institution-building in the UK is why the system established in 1997 performed so badly; solving that puzzle has an important bearing on the way things have turned out since. It is a puzzle because the regulatory system created in the wake of the Barings fiasco seemed like a radical break with the past, and indeed a radical departure from the regulatory systems that existed in many other advanced financial centers. The centerpiece was a single institution, the Financial Services Authority, a body that, for the first time, laid out in statute the powers and responsibilities of financial regulators. At a stroke the United Kingdom was equipped with a uniquely powerful financial regulator. The creation of the FSA built on a major institutional innovation in British government in recent decades—the creation of what is sometimes called a regulatory state. Across the governing system there have developed specialist regulatory agencies, in fields as diverse as the regulation of human fertility and the regulation of economic practices in the public utilities (Moran 2007). There was plainly some influence here from the long history of the American regulatory state, but the formal arrangements for the FSA suggested something much more powerful than the United States had achieved, at least in the domain of financial markets. In the United States, as is well known, regulatory jurisdiction for financial institutions has been divided at federal level between many different agencies, and regulatory jurisdiction also has to be shared between institutions at the federal level and numerous agencies within individual states. In the United Kingdom, under the 1997 reforms, all this was concentrated in the hands of a single statutory body. The Bank of England, while gaining control of short-term interest rates via a newly created Monetary Policy Committee, lost its historic responsibility for bank supervision as a consequence of its perceived failings in the Barings collapse (for Barings, see Moran 2001).

Recall that the historical project of the City of London had been to insulate the markets from "political" control—for which read "democratic control." Recall, also, that despite the dismantling of the cartel system that had underpinned regulation, and the creation of the Securities and Investments Board in 1986, the markets had nevertheless managed to secure control over the regulatory system even in the age of the financial services revolution. The creation of a new statutory body by Parliament centralizing all regulatory functions seemed like the realization of the City's worst nightmares. That it did not turn out in this way at all is a key to understanding how the system functioned after 1997—and a key to understanding what has succeeded the crisis. Three influences ensured that the FSA never remotely realized the potential that its formally dominant position would suggest.

First, despite the bare letter of statute, the Authority was always conceived of as the property of the markets. This sense of ownership began with funding, because the Authority was paid for by a levy on the markets. A related important institutional sign of this lay in the practical functioning of the Authority. It was physically located in the City, rather than in the governing quarter in "Whitehall", the cluster of buildings around Westminster where the most important institutions of the core executive are located. It recruited its staff, not from the civil service, but from the City itself, and it tried to pay salaries appropriate to financial markets rather than to the public sector—which is to say, salaries considerably higher than those in the public sector.

These institutional features were in turn linked to the second sign of the Authority's weakness: its operational regulatory philosophy. Some of the inspiration for establishing the Authority lay in the example of the American regulatory state; but none of its regulatory style came from the well documented tradition of adversarialism which has marked American regulation (Kagan 2001, 2007; Vogel 1986). From the beginning, the Authority had an explicitly formulated philosophy of cooperative and consensual regulation: any kind of adversarial confrontation with actors in the markets was only to take place as a last resort. The origins of this regulatory philosophy lay partly in an instinctive cultural subordination to the markets, who after all provided its funding. In addition, while the Authority paid well by the standards of the public sector, in the overheated City labor market of the late 1990s, it certainly did not pay well enough to attract outstanding talent from the City. It suffered from high staff turnover and, as the detailed review of its dealings with the first high profile casualty—Northern Rock—showed, its relatively junior and inexperienced staff were easily overawed and dominated by the powerful personalities who led the most aggressively competitive institutions (Financial Services Authority 2008). Thus, while the creation of the Authority represented an institutional break with the past, it was nothing like so great a cultural break. Despite the fiasco of Barings—which was attributable precisely to the absence of a questioning, adversarial style—the prevailing cultural assumption before and after 1997 was that a consensual regulatory style was what was needed to foster the health of London's financial markets. This assumption not only united regulators in the Authority—it was also a value held across the policymaking system more widely. The advent of New Labour in office from 1997 produced a culture of extraordinary triumphalism. Across the political and economic elite there developed a consensus that the future of the British economy lay in a dynamic financial services sector, and that this dynamism depended above all on creating the most benign conditions possible for financial innovation in London (Froud et al. 2010a). The FSA did not therefore pluck the commitment to a consensual regulatory style out of the air; had it tried to regulate adversarially it would have faced hostility not only from the City, but from right across the governing elite.

Two critical features therefore made the FSA a much less formidable regulator than the bare institutional appearance might have suggested: its closeness to its market clients and its subordination to a widely held regulatory ideology. A third feature played a particularly important role in the actual unfolding of the crisis. The system created in 1997 made the FSA the institutional kingpin of the system, but it could not monopolize regulatory authority. Two other important institutions—the Treasury (Finance Ministry) and the Bank of England—also had big stakes in regulation. The Treasury had a stake because it had a general interest both in financial stability and in the contributions of the financial markets to the wider economy; the Bank of England had a stake because, while it had lost responsibility for narrowly conceived supervision, it plainly retained a deep interest—in all senses of that word—in the health of the financial system, notably of the banking system. In short, there existed perfectly traditional problems of coordination in the new system. The authorities were quite alert to the potential for coordination problems created by this tripartite system, and as late as 2006 had elaborated a Memorandum of Understanding designed to spell out the division of regulatory labor between the three institutions. This tripartite system was coordinated by a Standing Committee which met monthly, was chaired by the Treasury, and on which sat representatives of the three key institutions (HM Treasury 2006). But from the beginning the Standing Committee failed in its coordinating function. This was partly because it never seriously engaged the most important actors. While membership was formally composed of Principals—which meant the heads of the institutions, such as the Governor of the Bank and the Chancellor of the Exchequer—they in practice rarely attended meetings, and the workings of the Committee were relegated to the level of administrative routine (House of Commons Treasury Select Committee 2007). Moreover, when the crisis broke it became clear that the coordinating system simply did not have an effective alignment of responsibilities and resources: the FSA was responsible, but had neither the authority nor the fiscal resources to stem the crisis; the Bank of England had the authority, and in some eyes the duty, but had neither the requisite statutory responsibility nor the fiscal resources; and the Treasury had the fiscal resources, but did not have the expertise or the statutory responsibility. This helps explain why the actual rescue, and the reconstruction in its wake, had relatively little to do with the coordinating arrangements that were supposed to manage the tripartite system. It is to the experience of the crisis that we now turn.

Managing the crisis

Understanding how the crisis was managed is critical to understanding what came afterwards because crisis management both opened up and closed off possible paths to the post-crisis institutional order. We can see this by examining how crisis management unfolded.

The initial effect involved what we can summarily call the repoliticisation of financial regulation. Financial regulation under the system created by New Labour after 1997 belonged to a domain of low politics. With the run on Northern Rock in September 2007, the sight of depositors queuing to withdraw deposits shifted both the terms of regulatory argument and the arenas where it took place. The issue suddenly was of the highest priority for the Prime Minister and the Chancellor (finance minister). Institutionally, the sign of the change was the transformation of the role of the Standing Committee, which from the Northern Rock crisis onwards drew the principals into attendance (House of Commons Treasury Select Committee 2008a). The systemic crisis of October 2008 deepened the transformation, for it widened the range of regulatory issues now commanding the attention of elected politicians at the apex of the core executive, beyond questions about the stability of particular institutions and the arrangements for depositor protection to the macro-stability of the whole banking system. Moreover, the combination of the collapse of particular institutions such as Northern Rock and the systemic crisis pulled in a wide range of other democratic actors: the most significant, because it succeeded in generating wide publicity about its activities, was the House of Commons Treasury Select Committee, which from 2008 published a series of reports on the unfolding crisis (House of Commons Treasury Select Committee 2008a, 2008b, 2009). The Committee was chaired by an astute Labour Party backbencher who showed a striking capacity to turn Committee hearings into soundbites suitable for TV news broadcasts.

The crisis also transformed the state's ownership responsibilities. In November 2008, the authorities were obliged to establish United Kingdom Financial Investments (UKFI) as a vehicle for managing public ownership of a huge tranche of the banking system. As we show below, the government of UKFI is complex: although the holding institution for the state's share of bank ownership, it operates at arms length from the Treasury and, in both its internal organization and culture, is closely integrated with the financial markets. By July 2009, UKFI owned 70 percent of the voting share capital of Royal Bank of Scotland and 43 percent of the Lloyds Banking Group (UKFI 2009: 2). State ownership was symptomatic of another key aspect of repoliticisation: the exposure of the financial elite to popular scrutiny—precisely what the historical regulatory strategy had been designed to prevent. Protecting financial markets from democratic control in the decades before 2007 depended heavily on naturalizing their functions: that is, on depicting the markets as responding to forces born of quasi-scientific laws. But during the crisis, and in the Parliamentary post-mortems, a narrative developed that traced the catastrophe to pathological features of the banking industry: to a system that produced "excessive" rewards, and stimulated excessive risk taking by a banking elite driven by the search for huge bonuses. Opinion polls also showed that these perceptions were widely shared by the public at large (Glover 2008). This was a moment of great danger, for it precisely rejected the assumptions of naturalization, tracing the crisis to a combination of institutional defects in markets and a culture of human greed. That phase probably culminated in two sets of events: the arraignment of several former heads of the stricken banks before the House of Commons Treasury Select Committee, which was accompanied by wide broadcasting of selected clips from their cross examination on mass TV news, and headlines in the tabloid press such as "Scumbag millionaires," in *The Sun* on February 11, 2009; and the extended campaign against Sir Fred Goodwin, head of one of the most spectacular casualties (Royal Bank of Scotland), which focused on the huge pension which he had succeeded in negotiating as a price of departure in the crisis-ridden weekend in October 2008 that saw the rescue of RBS.

But what had seemed like the very peak of a democratic assault—the ferocious criticism of Goodwin—coincided with a reassertion of influence by the financial elite over crisis management. The crisis had thrust the Treasury into the frontline of managing the financial markets, but the Treasury, as a small, elite policy advice institution, has very little operational expertise. The period of reconstruction after the crisis thus saw the Treasury—and the wider core executive—turn wholesale to the City itself as a source of expertise. We can see this most clearly in the case of United Kingdom Financial Investments, the body created by the Treasury to manage the large chunk of the banking system which had come into public hands as a result of the crisis. The Treasury provided UKFI's first chief executive (John Kingman, the most successful career civil servant of his generation) and it was physically located in the Treasury buildings. But otherwise, UKFI was a City institution: its chairs have all been City grandees; its staff at the most senior level have been drawn from City institutions; and its philosophy from the beginning has been expressed in the traditional financial doctrine of maximizing shareholder value—it rejects any radical reconstruction of the banking system in favor of maximizing the profits and share price of the institutions it controls, with a view to resale as soon as possible back to the private sector (Froud et al. 2010a). Nor was UKFI unusual in adopting this cautionary, conservative stance. Although, as we show below, there has been some support for radical regulatory changes, and some radical structural reform of the banking system from within the Bank of England, the crisis was striking for the way in which the pre-crisis elite consensus about the role and importance of the City in the British economy was maintained. Just about the only prominent political figure who argued for radical structural reform—for example, a Glass-Steagall-like separation of investment and retail banking—was the economic spokesman for the Liberal Democrats, Vince Cable. We further examine Cable's role later in the chapter.

This institutional penetration by the financial elite was accompanied by the restatement of the traditional City narrative (see above) about the social value of finance. Two key reports in this respect were Bischoff and Wigley, conventionally named after the chairs of the groups that produced them. But these two City grandees were not just producing private sector statements. The Bischoff Report should more accurately be called the Bischoff/Darling Report (2009), for it was published by the Treasury and was signed off by both Bischoff and Alistair Darling, as Chancellor. Wigley (2008) was commissioned by the Mayor of London, and its report, stressing the importance of a regulatory regime that maintained London's traditional attractiveness as a financial centre, was warmly welcomed by the Mayor. The significance of both these reports is that, in reasserting a traditional City story about the value of financial markets to the economy, they restated, in spite of the crisis, the traditional narrative which had supported policy before the great crash. The closing down of reform possibilities was plain in the changes proposed and enacted by the Labour government before it lost office in May 2010. The most comprehensive statement of the government's philosophy came in the White Paper (the conventional form for legislative proposals in the UK system) which was eventually incorporated into banking reform legislation just before the general election of May 2010 (HM Treasury 2009). The White Paper has a double significance: it represented, after nearly two years of banking crisis, a distillation of official thinking about regulatory reform; and its proposals were faithfully enacted in the government's banking legislation before it lost office. This summary of the White Paper is also a summary of what was enacted as the Banking Act by the Labour government during the last days of the Brown premiership in 2010.

What is most remarkable is its caution in the face of the greatest banking crisis since at least the Great Depression. It rejected any move to reshape the structure of the industry and, specifically, to break up large, complex banking conglomerates. It reasserted, in language that could have been used at any time in the past thirty years, what it called the "pivotal" (p. 18) role of the City and of finance in the economy. It rejected any Glass-Steagall-like measures separating investment and retailing banking (p. 75). Moreover, only the most marginal changes were proposed to the institutional architecture of regulation itself. The FSA's dominant position as regulator was retained. Only marginal changes in the coordinating institutions were proposed. The old Standing Committee was to be replaced by a statute-based Council for Financial Stability. While there would be an annual report to Parliament, the White Paper committed itself only to the vaguest move to more democratic control: it announced merely that the authorities would "discuss mechanisms for increasing the democratic accountability of the [Council]" (p. 50). Had we been writing this chapter as recently as May 2010, therefore, the story we would have told would have been one of a brief reform moment quickly closed off by the reassertion of both City power and a traditional narrative about the key role of financial services in a post-industrial economy. But understanding what has happened subsequently to the regulatory system depends on understanding the forces that helped shape the system after the Labour government's reforms. Two things reopened the closure that had apparently been achieved in May 2010.

First, the reform debate could not be shut out of democratic politics. The reform of the system played only a small part in the 2010 general election campaign, but it was nevertheless critical. In order to distinguish itself from the Government's essentially conservative reforms, the Conservative Opposition was obliged to position itself at a more radical point on the reform spectrum, at least as far as the reform of regulatory institutions was concerned: it committed itself, for instance, to the abolition of the Financial Services Authority. Moreover, the outcome of the election obliged the government to enter into a coalition with the Liberal Democrats who, under the influence of their deputy leader and economic spokesman, Vince Cable, had developed the most radical critique of the financial markets of all three main parties (Johal/Moran/Williams 2011).

Second, the reform of the institutions became entangled—as it had done in the United States—with bureaucratic politics. The Financial Services Authority partly survived in the Labour reforms because, in the form of a report by its new chair, Adair Turner, it had repositioned itself as a more adversarial regulator, something we discuss below. But the Bank of England continued to see the aftermath of the crisis as an opportunity to recapture the regulatory jurisdiction lost in 1997. In June 2009, with the debate about reconstruction at its height inside government, the Governor went public on the Bank's claims, in the presence of the Chancellor, at his annual set piece address to the City at the Lord Mayor's banquet (King 2009a).

Those arguments fell on deaf ears while Labour was in office; but the result of the 2010 general election reopened the terms of regulatory debate and allowed the Bank, and other actors, a new chance to shape the system. It is to this that we now turn.

The present state of regulatory change—and what we will get

This chapter goes to press in September 2011, so it is not possible to describe regulatory developments after that date. That is an obvious consideration, but an important one, since much of the formal institutional reconstruction, and much of the policy reshaping, will not become evident until at least 2012; so the reader has an advantage over the authors.

The present state of regulatory reform can be described under three headings, and they correspond to three key questions which policymakers have had to answer in reshaping regulation in the UK (and in other jurisdictions, for that matter). First, what is to be the institutional shape of regulation? Second, what kind of daily relations are regulators to have with the markets? That is a critical question in the UK because the culture of cooperative regulation described earlier gave market operators great freedom in their everyday dealings and, as we shall see, it was widely concluded that cooperative regulation of this kind was an important contributory cause of the catastrophe? Third, what policy stance is to be adopted on wider issues of systemic regulation? As we saw in the preceding section the outgoing Labour government gave a conservative answer to that question: there was to be no fundamental structural reform along the lines of, for instance, a Glass-Steagall-like separation between investment and retail banking. As we shall now see, the result of the 2010 election reopened that third question.

Of these three, the answers to the first question are the clearest, but also the least illuminating, because while they tell us what the bare institutional structure will look like, we know little about how the new institutions will work in practice. In summary, the system, which will be fully operational by 2012 when the legislation is finally on the statute books, involves the creation of three distinct institutions. (All presently exist in an interim form.) Although legislation is awaited, preparations are now well advanced for the creation of this new structure, including the appointment of heads of the new agencies, as we shall now see.

First, there will be a Financial Policy Committee, "with responsibility for macro-prudential regulation, or regulation of stability and resilience of the financial system as a whole," to be established within the Bank of England (HM Treasury 2011: 4). An interim version of this already exists and held its first meeting in June 2011. The Committee is intended to have 13 members, of whom four will be external (to the Bank) members. Although the Committee has held an initial meeting it has not yet proved possible to fill all four external positions.

Second, there will be a Prudential Regulatory Authority, which will have responsibility for "micro-prudential" (firm-level) regulation. The Authority will be "an operationally independent subsidiary of the Bank of England" (HM Treasury 2011: 4). In effect, this is replacing the Financial Services Authority, but how much of a break with an incompetent past this will be remains to be seen. The need for continuity has ensured that the first head of the Prudential Regulatory Authority is Hector Sants, the outgoing chief executive of the FSA (Treanor 2011).

Third, there will be a standalone Financial Conduct Authority, which will largely take over the responsibilities for consumer protection formerly administered by the FSA. At the time of writing this institution is in the process of construction; from September 2011 it will have a chief executive designate, Martin Wheatley, former chief executive of the Hong Kong Securities and Futures Commission.

Although many questions obviously remain unanswered about this institutional structure, some things are clear. The most important is that in the bureaucratic politics which was prompted by the crisis and its aftermath the central bank, which initially made little headway in the face of the conservative institutional preferences of the Brown government, has now emerged victorious: the Prudential Regulatory Authority is an arm of the Bank of England, and the Financial Policy Committee has a majority of members drawn from officers of the Bank. And this, as we suggested in the preceding section, is the result of something which historically has played little part in financial politics in the UK: the influence of electoral politics, as the Conservatives maneuvered to stake out a distinctive position on institutional change in the 2010 general election. But what is not clear is how big a change this institutional reform denotes. As with the changes in other jurisdictions, such as the Dodd-Frank reforms in the USA, much will depend on implementation. As the appointment of Hector Sants to head the Prudential Regulatory Authority suggests, the sheer practicalities of putting together the new institutional structure at short notice have meant that much has depended on cannibalizing the old FSA. How far the new institutions will break with the old culture only time will tell.

Nevertheless, some important clues are provided by the way the policy system is answering the second question posed above: what kind of daily relations are policymakers to have with the markets? There has indeed been a striking change here, at least in some of the language used. Virtually every regulator and public policy actor has repented of the pre-crisis language of cooperative regulation, and has suggested that there is now a need for a turn to an aggressive and adversarial style. A typical example is provided by Adair Turner, the chair of the Financial Services Authority, in a report designed to lay out the lessons learnt from the crisis. Turner acknowledged that in the case of Northern Rock the Authority "fell short of high professional standards in the execution of its supervisory approach." The new approach would be "underpinned by a different philosophy of regulation" which would be "more intrusive and more systemic" (Financial Services Authority 2009: 88). Turner's use of this language was, admittedly, part and parcel of the bureaucratic maneuvering which accompanied the struggles to reconstruct the regulatory system in the wake of the crisis, a process that involved, as we have seen, the reinvention of the FSA as a less market friendly institution. But it is plainly significant that, in the wake of the catastrophe, the tactically appropriate measure involved abandoning the language of cooperative regulation.

The language used by regulators to describe their philosophy has changed. It is less certain that regulatory practice has altered correspondingly. What is striking about the period since the crisis is the continuity in actual regulatory style, whatever the language used in restatements of regulatory philosophy. A good instance is provided by two issues which have become intertwined: the bonus reward regime operated by the banks, and their lending policies, especially their lending to small and medium-sized enterprises. Substantively, the bonus issue is of secondary importance because it does not go to the heart of the larger structural problems of the system (on which, see below.) But it nevertheless has both substantive and symbolic importance. Substantively, it is linked to an incentive structure which was connected to the kind of risk taking which was implicated in the crisis, and the failure to curb bonuses is an indication of the failure to eradicate that culture of risk taking. Symbolically, large bonuses have been a sensitive political issue in an era of austerity when real incomes for most of the population are falling. The main shareholder in the part of the system taken into public ownership, UKFI, has supported the doctrine of maximizing shareholder value, and has supported the continuation of the bonus system as a means of incentivizing the management of the publicly owned banks. Moreover, faced with widespread hostility to the bonus system the banks have engaged in a classic piece of regulatory circumvention: bonuses have been absorbed into salaries, thus circumventing even the voluntary restraints (Groom 2011). The government's most systematic attempt yet to address the problem is embodied in "Project Merlin," which attempts to link a voluntary settlement of the bonus issue with the vexed issue of bank lending after the crash to small and medium-sized enterprises. In return for hitting agreed lending targets the banks were allowed to operate a voluntary system of bonus restraint. With only a first quarter's returns so far in on the Merlin bargain, it is hard to be certain about its effectiveness; but the key point is that attempts to solve the problem of both bonuses and bank lending are still shaped by the search for cooperative, voluntary arrangements. Above all, Merlin is not a legally enforceable regime: it is a bargain made between the banks and the government. Project Merlin is an attempt to cope with a legacy of the Brown government. In 2009, faced with criticisms of the reappearance of large bonuses in the banks, the Government announced a one off tax on bonuses. The tax was largely ineffective: the banks simply consolidated what would have been bonuses into salaries. But the expiry of the tax left the coalition with a problem: what measure could be created to meet this public disquiet? Project Merlin was the result.

There remains the experience of a bigger picture which is, strictly speaking, not the subject of a chapter which is only about the UK: that is, the wider changes in the supranational regime of prudential regulation focused on the Basel system. But the workings of the Basel system illustrate one of the recurring themes of this chapter: the way the policy process is now heavily conditioned by a world of highly technocratic debate in which those who can command most expertise are best able both to intervene in the decision-making process, and shape—or circumvent—its implementation. What is striking about the 2010 Basel III regulations is how undemanding they are, and how much room their leisurely implementation leaves for regulatory circumvention. The minimum ratio of "tier 1 capital" to "risk weighted assets" was set at 7 percent. There was some tightening of the definition of core capital but the denominator remained "risk weighted assets," not total assets (for more detailed discussion, see Goldbach/Kerwer in this volume). Meanwhile, non-compliant banks did not face full implementation of the new code until January 2019.

The question of bank lending is in turn linked to the third big question identified above: what sort of structural features should mark the reformed banking system—and should reform, indeed, do anything to ownership and competition in the industry? In advance of the general election, the Conservatives had been silent on this structural question, and the Labour government, in its very cautious reforms (see above) had given a clearly negative answer to the question: there would be no structural reform, and the main structural aim would be to restore to the private sector, in financial health, the banks which it had been obliged to acquire in the crisis. The only significant dissenting voice was provided by the Liberal Democrats, the UK's third national party (roughly equivalent to the FDP in the Federal Republic). Its economic spokesman, Vince Cable, argued in advance of the election that the crisis had much to do with the way retail and investment banking were tied together, and advocated the kind of separation between the two created in the US Glass-Steagall Act—an act that, of course, had been first circumvented, and then effectively repealed, at the height of euphoria about the financial services boom (Johal/Moran/Williams 2011).

Had the General Election of May 2010 produced the result usual in the British system—a clear majority for one of the two leading parties, Conservative and Labour—then this third question would undoubtedly have been answered in the negative: had the Conservatives been returned with a workable majority there would have been no question of structural reform of the banking system. But the outcome deprived the Conservatives of a majority, and obliged them to form a coalition with the Liberal Democrats—a coalition in which the main critic of the banks, Vince Cable, now occupied the position of Business Secretary. More directly still, the formation of the coalition involved the creation of an agreed program of policy measures for the new government. The crucial issue was what this program would say about the issue of structural reform. In the event, it temporized. Since the two parties had different views of the desirability of reform, the program committed to the establishment of an Independent Commission on Banking, with a recommendation not to produce a final report until September 2011. Unsurprisingly, the membership of the Commission was a thorny issue, since composition was likely to have an impact on the final report. In the event, it was a predictable compromise. The chair, John Vickers, made his name in public policy circles as an advocate of competition in the age of deregulation in the Thatcher years, as did Clare Spottiswoode, who was a regulator of one of the main sectors—energy—deregulated by the Thatcher government. On the other hand, the Commission also contained the *Financial Times* correspondent Martin Wolf, who has offered sustained criticisms of the banks.

The Independent Commission on Banking is an advisory body. Its reports and recommendations have no statutory force, and the formation of the Commission in May 2011 was a delaying tactic: an effort to push into the future a decision on an issue where there were serious differences of view between the two coalition partners. But it has now produced two reports, and the appearance of the second (final) report in September 2011 was a moment when an elite consensus about banking reform in the UK crystallized. It is plain with the benefit of hindsight that the publication of the first (interim) report in April 2011 allowed the formation of an elite consensus around a set of limited reform proposals. The consultations invited in the wake of that report provided an opportunity for the banks to lobby hard against the most radical option, full separation between their investment and retail arms. On the critical question of the structural reform of ownership the interim report used cautious language, but that language was skeptical about radical reform. It said: "Some form of retail ring-fencing appears therefore preferable to full separation to the extent that: a) the rules around the subsidiary are firm enough to secure most or all of the benefits of the reform; and b) the costs of ring-fencing are substantially lower than those of a full split." But it added: "Unless both of these conditions hold, however, the balance of arguments might favour strict separation" (Independent Commission on Banking 2011a: 89). In his speech to the Lord Mayor's banquet in June 2011 (an annual opportunity to address the City elite) the Chancellor appeared to support this "ring fencing" option (HM Treasury 2011a). And indeed the final report, when it was published in September 2011, opted for this less radical solution (Independent Commission on Banking 2011b.) As the Commission's chair Sir John Vickers put it, introducing the final report: "The first thing to say about our final recommendations to promote financial stability is that they are squarely in line with the provisional position set out in our *Interim Report*" (Vickers 2011). The recommendations for ring fencing were immediately welcomed by the government, in the figure of the Chancellor (Finance Minister).

In summary, these recommendations are, in the Commission's own words, the following:

that a high ring-fence be placed around vital retail banking activities in the UK. In summary, such ring-fenced banks should:
– contain all deposits from individuals and SMEs, along with any overdrafts supplied to them;
– not be allowed to engage in trading or other investment banking activities, provide services to financial companies, or services to customers outside the EEA;

– within these constraints, be allowed to take deposits from larger companies and provide non-financial larger companies with other intermediation services such as simple loans; and
– where they form part of a wider corporate group, have independent governance, be legally separate and operationally separable, and have economic links to the rest of the group no more substantial than those with third parties—but be allowed to pay dividends as long as they maintain adequate capital levels, which will preserve diversification benefits.
(Independent Commission on Banking 2011b: 29–30)

In addition, the Commission has recommended an equity capital to risk weighted assets ratio which is more stringent than the latest Basel requirements. The outcome of the Commission's inquiry thus fulfils three critical political functions. First, for the coalition it has allowed the formation of a unified position between parties that had entered the election in 2010 with very different views: the Conservatives resisting any significant structural reform, the Liberal Democrats advocating a complete separation between investment and retail banking. It thus defuses one of the most explosively divisive policy problems faced by the government. Second, since the Commission's status is only advisory, the recommendations have to be embodied in legislation. That will be preceded by extensive consultation, and this allows the banks to mobilize their full lobbying capacity to shape the details of the legislation; and in banking regulation the devil always lies in the detail. Finally, the time-scale envisaged by the Commission for the full implementation of its proposals is, even if legislation is relatively speedy, quite leisurely: the banks will have until 2018 to adapt to a new regime. And in banking systems, especially in banking systems as volatile as those presently in Europe, the world of 2018 is quite unknowable.

In summary: the single most striking feature of the system of bank regulation which has been reconstructed since the great crisis of 2007–2008 is the limited character of change. Institutionally, there have been losers—notably the Financial Services Authority—but the system now being brought into existence marks a variation on an old set of themes. It is in principle possible that the new institutions will behave in a way very different from their predecessor, but the other evidence from the regulatory system casts doubt on this. Nothing radical is to be attempted with the chunk of public ownership acquired after 2008—on the contrary, it is, via UKFI, being guided by the pre-crisis notion of the maximization of shareholder value. The outcome of the debates about bonuses and the nature of bank lending in the post-crisis system likewise suggest that the traditional culture of cooperative regulation persists. And the Independent Commission on Banking has helped to establish an elite consensus which removes radical structural reform from the policy agenda and gives the banks plenty of opportunity to lobby on legislation and shape implementation.

To understand why the post-crisis system is marked by this striking degree of continuity, despite having experienced a regulatory fiasco which produced the greatest banking and economic crisis for at least a generation, we have to understand the character of regulatory politics in the financial sector since 2007. That is the purpose of the next section.

The new economics and the new politics of the City of London

Understanding the way the policy outcomes sketched above were produced demands an understanding of two sets of forces, economic and political. There are powerful structural interests in the markets, but these structural interests do not mechanically produce policy; they are mediated by political structures through which interests are mobilized and decisions made. That is why understanding what is going on demands that we understand both the economics and the politics of the financial sector.

The structural character of the financial system created in the United Kingdom in the decades since the financial services revolution of the 1980s has a key bearing on outcomes after 2007. As we have seen, the financial elite and its political allies from the 1980s told, and retold, a story about the central role of finance in creating jobs and employment in a post-industrial economy—in replacing the jobs and prosperity lost by the liquidation of the UK's industrial base. But as we have demonstrated elsewhere that account was largely ideology—a narrative, in other words, created to legitimize the position of key elites (Froud et al. 2010a). The evidence shows that, in the period of the economic boom that in the UK stretched from 1992 to the start of the crisis, when the narrative was that the country was creating a new economy based on post-industrial sectors such as financial services, employment in financial services was actually flat. This was because jobs in the sector are predominantly in retail finance. Much of retail finance was indeed dispersed across the whole country and large parts of retail banking were labor intensive because they required a branch-based sales force and back office support. But the expense of these labor intensive operations precisely meant that firms constantly sought efficiencies, and thus constantly sought to cut back employment. London had the dominant cluster of financial services employment. By the time of the great crisis, London as an international financial centre was the centre of UK financial employment despite the dispersion of retail finance employment. The 324,000 working in finance in London accounted for 31 percent of the national financial services workforce and more than 7.5 percent of the London workforce. The backward linkages from finance to supporting London professional services such as law and accountancy were significant but much weaker than in the case of a manufacturing sector assembling a complex product. On our estimates each worker inside the finance sector supports no more than half a worker outside the sector. (This passage draws on the detailed calculations in Ertürk et al. 2011.)

The most important reason for this London dominance is well known: London as an international financial centre concentrates on wholesale finance, where small numbers of highly paid workers lift huge values. Within London, wholesale finance in turn concentrates affluence in a tiny number of areas of the capital. A small number of working rich, senior bankers and financiers in and around the City of London earn ever increasing incomes. Their lucrative employment is highly concentrated in the local government area covered by the Corporation of the City of London—a correspondence that we examine in more detail below. The new working rich of senior bankers, hedge fund partners and such like are a small group commuting from a few suburbs of choice to places of work in the old City in the square mile behind St Paul's or to the main new City location in Canary Wharf, with alternative investment colonizing a Mayfair village. When it comes to finance, "London" is thus actually shorthand for a highly concentrated geographical space which has very little connection with the rest of the metropolis except insofar as nondescript middle class suburbs supply PAs and secretaries for the working rich, and poorer boroughs supply office cleaners. The structural interests created by the financial services revolution thus had, by the moment of crisis, created a very particular constellation of interests: one highly concentrated geographically and, as we shall see, corresponding to a particularly important system of government in the capital.

This structural uniqueness was reinforced by an allied feature of the sector after the financial services revolution. It is sometimes summarized as the Wimbledon effect—the observation that the UK can host what is probably the world's premier tennis tournament, but consistently fails to produce players who excel in it. Foreign firms dominate the new City, which is located in London but cannot find a British champion to cheer on. Most of the British financial services firms which joined the new competition after Big Bang in 1986 lost out and were quickly sold on. Barclays Capital is the only successful surviving large investment bank which can claim to be British owned. Private equity is the only subsector of finance in which several British firms—such as Permira and Apax—have met the US challenge by successfully upscaling. More generally, the entrepôt trade in money has created something rather like an offshore financial centre which just happens to be located on the muddy Thames rather than on a sandy Caribbean island. The City is dominated by foreign institutions performing functions for international, especially EU, markets. The UK banking sector originates more cross-border bank lending than any other country—18 percent of the world total in June 2010—and around half of European investment banking activity is conducted in London. There were 241 branches and subsidiaries of foreign banks in London in March 2010, more than in any other centre worldwide and a third of these banks were from the euro area. Foreign banks manage over one-half of UK banking sector assets, totaling over £7.6 trillion at the end of 2009, mainly on behalf of foreign customers. Even the stock exchange is increasingly dominated by non-UK companies (The City UK 2011).

The structural interests embodied in financial markets at the time of the crisis therefore do not represent a widely dispersed financial sector powering the UK economy; they are a socially and geographically narrowly confined elite. The location of that elite in London, its integration with key parts of the metropolitan political elite, and the workings of its own system of government are all critical to explaining outcomes since the crisis. Above all, explaining the post-crisis world demands recognizing the importance of the new politics of the City. The observation that the financial markets, and the interests embodied in them, are powerful in shaping economic policy in the UK is hardly novel. But the striking development of recent decades has been the reconfiguration of the institutional mechanisms that convert this economic muscle into influence over policy, and this reconfiguration holds the key to making sense of what is going on. Three forces are at work: the reorganization and professionalization of lobbying capacities within the City; the changing institutional configuration within the core executive, notably the way this has affected the capacity of financial interests to make their voices heard at the heart of government; and the changing relationship between democratic actors, especially the major political parties, and City interests. We shall examine each in turn.

For much of the twentieth century the City was barely recognizable as a "lobby": its considerable influence over policy depended on social and cultural integration with governing elites, and on the Bank of England as an informal mediator between City interests and the core executive. The development of more open and transparent systems of interest representation, and the growing relative autonomy of the Bank from City interests, made this informal regime of representation increasingly anachronistic (Moran 1981, 1986). The financial elite has responded with professionalization and more formal organization of its lobbying operations.

Davis (2000, 2002) has documented the growth of professional financial PR and lobbying services in the City in recent years. The Corporation of the City of London—until near the end of the twentieth century largely a body with narrow local government and social functions—has likewise reorganized into a systematic lobby for City interests. A key change occurred in 2002, when the constitution of the Corporation was reformed: it had hitherto escaped every reforming measure in local government since the original Municipal Corporation Act of 1835. The City of London Ward Elections Act (2002) did something unique in British local government. The business vote in all other local government systems of the UK had finally been abolished in 1969. (The business vote—sometimes in other jurisdictions called the corporate vote—was an extra vote, additional to the normal franchise, exercised by business owners in elections.) The Act of 2002 not only retained the business vote in the City, but greatly expanded the business franchise, so that business votes now actually outnumber the residential vote in the City. In other words, the financial elite is unique not only in British society but within the British business community: it controls its own system of local government. The Corporation has applied its considerable historical endowments to building up its advocacy and economic intelligence capacities: it was the Corporation, for example, which provided much of the research work for the Bischoff Report, and it was closely involved in the Wigley Report referred to above (Bischoff/Darling 2009: 54; Shaxson 2011; House of Lords 2002). Not all sections of the City, true, have absorbed the lessons of lobbying professionalism. The newer, more buccaneering markets, like many new business sectors, have found it harder to operate as an institutional lobby, something that emerges from Woll's chapter on hedge funds in this volume. But in general the financial elite entered the crisis of 2007–2008 with a lobbying operation which in its professionalism and command of resources was vastly superior to that commanded in similar earlier crises.

A parallel change had also taken place within the core executive—the second major force that shaped how the financial crisis was converted into public policy. A significant legacy of the Brown Chancellorship has been a great augmentation of the range and depth of Treasury power across the core executive (Thain 2004). A striking index of the change is provided by a comparison of the Treasury's role in successive banking crises: in the great systemic crisis that preceded that of 2007–2008, what is usually called the secondary banking crisis of the 1970s, it played only a marginal role, the key manager in those events being the Bank of England (Moran 1986). But in 2007–2008 the Treasury was the dominant manager in the crisis (Froud et al. 2010b). The crisis saw the use by the Treasury of public funds on a huge scale to support the stricken banks. This second important force shaping post-crisis politics, therefore, involved the domination of the process by a Treasury which had greatly enhanced its position in the core executive during the Brown Chancellorship, and which in turn had developed close relations with the elite of the financial markets.

The strengthening of the nexus between the core executive and the elite of the City has in turn been reinforced by the third force identified earlier: the rise of a financial nexus between the leading parties and City interests. The link is symbolized by the family backgrounds of the present Prime Minister and Deputy Prime Minister, both offspring of the City working rich. In the case of the Conservatives the symbolism is particularly apt, for it points to key long-term changes in the financial relationship between the Party and City interests. Pinto-Duschinsky's landmark study of party finance in the UK showed that in the golden age of the mass party the Conservatives, contrary to many myths, raised most of their income through membership dues and fund-raising activities at local level: for instance, in the decade from 1967 only about 30 percent of Conservative party income came from companies (Pinto-Duschinsky 1981: 234). The bulk of income came from the constituency parties—large in the age of the mass party, and highly effective fund-raising operations. This mass party has now disappeared: there are presently only about 200,000 individual members, most of them elderly. The decay of mass membership has an important financial consequence: the Party in the country is no longer a significant source of income. Moreover, increasing transparency about donations to parties—beginning with the 1967 Companies Act and culminating in the regulatory regime now run by the Electoral Commission—has made large corporations hesitant to contribute. The Party has to rely heavily on rich individual backers. The result can be seen in its financial history under David Cameron: in 2005, when Cameron became Leader, the financial services industries were the source of just under a quarter of total cash donations to the Party; by 2010 the figure had risen to just over 50 per cent (Bureau of Investigative Journalism 2011; Watt/Treanor 2011). A large proportion of this money comes from the working rich created by the financial services revolution—high net worth individuals who have the means to make significant donations, and who as individuals do not feel constrained by the delicacies that hem in major corporations. A key threshold is a £50,000 annual donation, because this makes the donor a member of the "Leader's Group," with an entitlement to meet "David Cameron and other senior figures from the Conservative Party at dinners, post-PMQ lunches, drinks receptions, election result events and important campaign launches" (Conservative Party 2011). In 2010, 57 individuals from the financial services sector made donations sufficient to join the Leader's Group. The withering of the Party's non-metropolitan roots is thus closely connected to its increasing reliance on the working rich created by the financial services revolution.

The future: Closure or a democratic opening?

This picture represents the post-crisis world of financial regulation in the UK as one of closure: one where the financial elite has been able to use its lobbying and financial muscle to shape institutional arrangements, and to elaborate a dominant regulatory ideology. Yet there are countervailing forces, and they mean that the future may be more open than this account might suggest. Three forces are particularly significant.

The first impacts on regulatory ideologies and on the kind of narrative which the financial elite uses to legitimize its dominant position. The most economical way to think about the destabilizing possibilities here is to consider the role of the Bank of England. As we have seen, the Bank historically has been a key institution in maintaining the autonomy of the financial elite: institutionally, it stood between the state and markets; and ideologically, from the era of Montagu Norman, it privileged the tacit regulatory knowledge of market practitioners over any kind of explicit knowledge that might reside, for instance, with professionals like economists or lawyers—a stance that legitimized self-regulation by market actors. But in the last generation, and at an accelerating pace in recent years, the Bank's character changed. Institutionally, it acquired relative autonomy from the interests in the markets, guided instead by a self-image as an institution pursuing the public interest goals of a publicly accountable central bank. Intellectually, it underwent something similar to the experience of other leading central banks: in Marcussen's word, it became "scientised," which is to say that it became increasingly dominated by figures whose legitimacy depended on their professional accreditation as economists, and who moved in an epistemic community of other professionally qualified central bankers (Marcussen 2006, 2009). And while that epistemic community has its own technocratic ideologies, it nevertheless exposed the Bank, as it did other leading central banks, to a range of heterodox economic argument much wider than the range available in the markets. A good example of this is the position of Andrew Haldane. Haldane's importance lies partly in the fact that he is a senior advisor to another professional economist—the governor, Mervyn King—and is also the executive director responsible for financial stability. In the debates that succeeded the crash, both the Governor and Haldane have been publicly skeptical of much of the narrative offered by the financial elite: skeptical of particular claims (for instance the worth of large bonuses in the reward system of banking, and of the threat of banks to relocate operations elsewhere if they find regulation too onerous); and skeptical also of the grand narrative about the contribution of the financial sector to the wider health of the economy. That in turn has led to the public argument that the financial sector in the UK may be too large, and in the direction of heresies like the notion that there should indeed be some structural Glass-Steagall-like separation between investment and retail banking (Haldane 2009a, 2009b, 2010; King 2009a, 2009b). The institutional reforms summarized in the previous section amount to a resounding victory for the Bank of England in the bureaucratic political struggles that accompanied the reconstruction of regulatory institutions. Thus if the effect of Brown's long reign as Chancellor was considerably to increase the power of the Treasury over the range of economic policy, the impact of the regulatory changes since the 2010 General Election has been to increase the Bank's control over the narrower domain of financial regulation. We of course know little beyond general statements of intent about what the actual practice of regulation will be like when the institutions are up and running, but we can fairly confidently predict that the culture of the Bank as a regulator will be very different from the culture of the old Financial Services Authority.

The second countervailing influence lies in the role of transnational institutions and networks in shaping the rules of financial supervision. That is primarily the subject of other contributions to this volume, but it must at least be mentioned as a potential influence on the future of the UK case. Since at least the formulation of the prudential rules by the first Basel Committees following the banking crises of the 1970s, the game of financial supervision has been an international, not just a national, game. The London elite has to formulate strategies that can work in the complex, multi-level and multi-actor system of the European Union and the institutional world of Basel. These are worlds in which the usual complications of coalition creation—divisions between sectors, markets and institutions—are magnified. They are worlds in which, to some degree, London-based institutions have to be "takers" of regulatory standards hammered out in other arenas—in the institutional worlds of Basel and Brussels. They are worlds in which the epistemic communities of "scientised" regulators described by Marcussen (2006, 2009) are particularly important. And they are worlds—especially in the case of Brussels—where new lobbying and advocacy skills have to be acquired beyond those that work in the national setting in London. There is plenty of evidence that the London financial elite is able to master these skills, and plenty of evidence that, notably in the "comitology" of the European Union, it can create effective cross-national coalitions supporting financial elites (Macartney 2011). Moreover, the Brussels elites are often strikingly insulated from wider societal pressure. A vivid example is provided by the most important attempt yet made by the European Union to respond to the regulatory implications of the crisis: the de Larosière Report published in 2009. The diagnosis in the report bears a striking resemblance to that offered for the UK by the Turner Report—that there has been insufficient understanding and close scrutiny of the workings of the markets. That is unsurprising, perhaps, because de Larosière's high level group was composed of national financial regulators, including Turner's predecessor as chair of the Financial Services Authority. But what is most striking about the report is the extraordinarily narrow range of interests and actors to whom it listened. Beginning in November 2008, at the moment of greatest fragility in the financial system, it held eleven day-long meetings. Those who gave evidence included neither a single elected politician nor any of the numerous groups in civil society with views about the organization of finance. The witnesses consist of two sets: the members of the regulatory elite, such as Trichet, Governor of the European Central Bank, EU Commissioners and Baron Lamfalussy; and representatives of the trade associations (mostly EU wide but including some national voices) for the main corporate interests from insurance, banking and securities (de Larosière 2009: 70).

In short, the institutional worlds of the EU and Basel set new tactical challenges for financial elites in London, but there is not much evidence that they are unable to meet these challenges, nor is there evidence that the mindworld of the EU, in particular, threatens to open up the world of financial regulation to more heterodox influences—something we could not say with as much certainty about the epistemic world of central bank regulation.

This leaves the third possible influence that might destabilize the elite settlement arrived at in the aftermath of the crisis: democratic politics. What the UK and all the other members of the European Union share is the fact they are democratic political systems—if only, in many instances, of a rough and ready kind. Events of recent years have illustrated strikingly the possibilities and limits of democratic intervention. There is, in the case of the United Kingdom and United States, a striking pattern in democratic responses to the crisis: initial outrage, the construction of a scandal, and the arraignment of the "guilty men" (they are all men) in highly televisual hearings of committees of the legislature. But this is characteristically circumscribed by the inability of democratic political debate to cope with the complexities of regulatory argument, the reclaiming of the debate so that it largely takes place within elite networks, and the opportunities this has opened for financial interests to use their considerable lobbying and financial muscle—especially in meeting the often desperate need of democratic politicians for campaign funds.

A more intriguing possibility lies in the potential for movements in civil society in democratic political systems. One of the themes of this chapter has been the increasing sophistication of the lobbying machines operated by financial interests, a sophistication that of course is not confined to the UK. But the mirror image of this world of professional lobbying and PR is the multiplication of civil society groups that are critical, not just of the workings of the financial markets revealed by the crash, but also of the workings of corporate power as a whole. As the case of de Larosière shows, it is perfectly possible for the financial elite to conduct its regulatory debates without reference to these groups, and there exist huge disparities in the resources available to corporate interests and those mobilizing in civil society. But modes of mobilization beyond the political parties, exploiting the declining attachment to the parties, the lessons of single issue success and failure, and new technologies of communication and mobilization probably offer the best chance of destabilizing the elite accommodation which has so far marked the regulatory reconstruction that has taken place in the wake of the great crisis.

Conclusions

This account of the regulatory aftermath of the great financial crisis in the UK has a particularly conditional quality. That is in part for reasons which will have recurred in accounts of other systems given in this volume: even now, four years after the crisis began, we are still at the beginning of the process of reconstruction. In the UK the reconfigured institutions will not be fully operational until well into 2012. We know that in regulation the devil lies in the detail: we probably will not be able to offer with certainty any judgment about the regulatory regime until perhaps 2015—when the institutions will have been observed over a prolonged cycle. And we also know that structural reform of the banking system itself will take until 2018 to unwind.

But apart from this commonsense caution, there is a more analytically revealing reason for contingency in the UK case: the impact of the crisis has been to leave partly open the future of the UK regulatory system. The reason for this is that the crisis has destabilized the system of politics that has long governed financial regulation in the United Kingdom. As we have seen, that system has deep historical roots. The City was already a great economic and political power before the rise of democratic politics in Britain. For much of the twentieth century both the institutions and ideology functioned to protect financial markets from the attentions of the democratic state. Even the statutory system of regulation created in 1997 reflected the preference for light touch public control. The catastrophes of 2007–2008 dealt a tremendous blow to all this: they undermined the claims that the system was competent at the job of securing financial stability; they resulted in the forced transfer of a big part of the banking system to public ownership; and they opened up debate about the control of the City in wider democratic arenas like Parliament.

As the outcome summarized in these pages shows, financial elites have met these challenges robustly. They have had several powerful advantages: they are embedded in key parts of the core executive, notably in the Treasury; they control key institutions of crisis management, such as United Kingdom Financial Investments; and in recent years the organized lobbying capacity of the City has been transformed, allowing it to operate in a sophisticated way in interest-group struggles. The best guess about the future is that financial elites will control regulation as effectively as in the past. But as we have also noted, there are uncertainties. The elite is nowhere as socially, politically or economically integrated as in the past. As the leading financial centre in Europe, London also imports the diversity of interests of many different national elites. Key institutions, notably the central bank, that once were reliable allies of market elites, are now swayed by alternative forces—notably the influence of "scientised" epistemic communities. The impact of crisis has accelerated a process which was already under way: it has demystified the traditional regulatory ideology and emboldened those in the democratic political arena, and in the wider civil society, who are critical of the banks and of the City elite more generally. That elite will probably still succeed in future struggles; but that there will indeed be struggles over the future of the regulatory system in democratic political arenas in the UK is now pretty certain.

References

Bischoff, Win/Alistair Darling, 2009: *UK International Financial Services—The Future: A Report from UK Based Financial Services Leaders to the Government.* London: HM Treasury.

Bureau of Investigative Journalism, 2011: *City Financing of the Conservative Party under Cameron.* <http://thebureauinvestigates.com/2011/02/08/city-financing-of-the-conservative-party-doubles-under-cameron/>

Cannadine, David, 1990: *The Decline and Fall of the British Aristocracy.* London: Picador.

Conservative Party, 2011: *Donor Clubs.* <www.conservatives.com/Donate/Donor_Clubs.aspx> (accessed April 28, 2011)

Davis, Aeron, 2000: Public Relations, Business News and the Reproduction of Corporate Elite Power. In: *Journalism* 1, 436–455.

———, 2002: *Public Relations Democracy: Politics, Public Relations and the Mass Media.* Manchester: Manchester University Press.

de Larosière, Jacques, 2009: *The High Level Group on Financial Supervision in the EU: Report.* Brussels: Commission of the European Union.

Ertürk, Ismail, et al., 2011: *City State Against National Settlement UK Economic Policy and Politics After the Financial Crisis.* CRESC Working Paper No. 101. Manchester: Centre for Research on Socio-Cultural Change. <www.cresc.ac.uk>

Financial Services Authority, 2008: *The Supervision of Northern Rock: A Lessons Learned Review.* London: Financial Services Authority, Financial Services Authority Internal Audit Division.

——, 2009: *The Turner Review: A Regulatory Response to the Global Banking Crisis.* London: Financial Services Authority.

Froud, Julie, et al., 2010a: Opportunity Lost: Mystification, Elite Politics and Financial Reform in the UK. In: Leo Panitch/Greg Albo/Vivek Chibber (eds.), *The Crisis This Time.* London: Merlin Press, 98–119.

——, 2010b: Wasting a Crisis? Democracy and Markets in Britain after 2007. In: *Political Quarterly* 8, 25–38.

Glover, Julian, 2008: Voters Blame Bankers—and Everyone Else. In: *The Guardian,* October 21.

Groom, Brian, 2011: Fall in Bonuses Negated by Rise in Regular Pay. In: *Financial Times,* April 26.

Haldane, Andrew, 2009a: *Rethinking the Financial Network.* Speech delivered at the Financial Student Association, Amsterdam, April 2009, 3.   <www.bankofengland.co.uk/publications/speeches/2009/>

——, 2009b: *Small Lessons from a Big Crisis.* Remarks at the Federal Reserve Bank of Chicago 45th Annual Conference, May 8.   <www.bankofengland.co.uk/publications/speeches/2009/>

——, 2010: *The Debt Hangover.* Speech at a Professional Liverpool dinner, January 27.   <www.bankofengland.co.uk/publications/speeches/2010/speech422.pdf>

——, 2011: Our Brief Is Simple, But Critical: Keep the System Strong and Stable. In: *The Observer,* June 12.

HM Treasury, 2006: *Memorandum of Understanding between HM Treasury, the Bank of England and the Financial Services Authority.* London: HM Treasury.   <www.hm-treasury.gov.uk/fin_money_index.htm>

——, 2009: *Reforming Financial Markets.* London: HM Treasury, CM 7667.

——, 2011: *A New Approach to Financial Regulation: Building a Stronger System.* London: HM Treasury, CM 8012.

——, 2011a: *Speech at the Lord Mayor's Dinner for Bankers and Merchants of the City of London by the Chancellor of the Exchequer.* Mansion House, London, June 15.   <www.hm-treasury.gov.uk/press_58_11.htm>

House of Commons Treasury Select Committee, 2007: *Minutes of Evidence, Inquiry into Financial Stability,* 11, 1 February.   <www.publications.parliament.uk/pa/cm200607/cmselect/cmtreasy/292/7020101.htm>

——, 2008: *Banking Reform.* Seventeenth Report. Session 2007-8, HC 1008.

——, 2008a: *The Run on the Rock.* Fifth Report. Session 2007-8, HC 56–I.

——, 2009: *Banking Crisis: Dealing with the Failure of the UK Banks.* Seventh Report. Session 2008-9, HC 416.

House of Lords, 2002: *Select Committee on City of London (Ward elections) Bill: Examination of Witnesses, Dr Maurice Glassman,* October 8.   <www.publications.parliament.uk/pa/ld200102/ldselect/ldcolweb/21008/2100812.htm>

Independent Commission on Banking, 2011a: *Interim Report: Consultation on Reform Options.* London: Independent Commission on Banking.

——, 2011b: *Independent Commission on Banking Final Report: Recommendation.* London: Independent Commission on Banking.   <http://bankingcommission.independent.gov.uk/>

Johal, Sukhdev/Michael Moran/Karel Williams, 2011: The Financial Crisis and Its Consequences. In: Nicholas Allen/John Bartle (eds.), *Britain at the Polls 2010.* London: Sage, 89–119.

Kagan, Robert, 2001: *Adversarial Legalism: The American Way of Law.* Cambridge, MA: Harvard University Press.

——, 2007: Globalization and Legal Change: The "Americanization" of European Law? In: *Regulation and Governance* 1, 99–120.

King, Mervyn, 2009: *Speech to Scottish Business Organisations,* Edinburgh, October 20, 2009. <www.bankofengland.co.uk/publications/speeches/index.htm>

——, 2009a: *Speech at the Lord Mayor's Banquet for Bankers and Merchants of the City of London at the Mansion House,* June 17. <www.bankofengland.co.uk/publications/speeches/index.htm>

Kynaston, David, 1994: *The City of London,* Volume I: *A World of Its Own 1815–90.* London: Chatto & Windus.

——, 1995: *The City of London,* Volume II: *Golden Years 1890–1914.* London: Chatto & Windus.

——, 1999: *The City of London,* Volume III: *Illusions of Gold 1914–1945.* London: Chatto & Windus.

Macartney, Huw, 2011: *Variegated Neoliberalism: EU Varieties of Capitalism and International Political Economy.* London: Routledge.

Marcussen, Martin, 2006: Institutional Transformation? The Scientization of Central Banking as Case. In: Tom Christensen/Per Lægred (eds.), *Autonomy and Regulation: Coping with Agencies in the Modern State.* Cheltenham: Edward Elgar, 81–109.

——, 2009: Scientization of Central Banking: The Politics of A-politicization. In: Kenneth Dyson/Martin Marcussen (eds.), *Central Banks in the Age of the Euro: Europeanization, Convergence and Power.* Oxford: Oxford University Press, 373–390.

Moran, Michael, 1981: Finance Capital and Pressure-Group Politics in Britain. In: *British Journal of Political Science* 11, 381–404.

——, 1986: *The Politics of Banking.* London: Macmillan.

——, 1991: *The Politics of the Financial Services Revolution.* London: Macmillan.

——, 2001: Not Steering But Drowning: Policy Catastrophes and the Regulatory State. In: *Political Quarterly* 72, 414–427.

——, 2007: *The British Regulatory State: High Modernism and Hyper-innovation.* Oxford: Oxford University Press.

Pinto-Duschinsky, Michael, 1981: *British Political Finance 1830–1980.* Washington, DC: American Enterprise Institute.

Shaxson, Nicholas, 2011: The Tax Haven in the Heart of London. In: *New Statesman,* February 24.

Thain, Colin, 2004: Treasury Rules OK? The Further Evolution of a British Institution. In: *British Journal of Politics and International Relations* 6, 123–130.

The City UK, 2011: *Key Facts about UK Financial and Professional Services,* March. London: The City UK. <www.thecityuk.com/assets/Reports/Economic-Trends-Series/Key-facts-about-UK-FS.pdf>

Treanor, Jill, 2011: Spotlight Falls on City Watchdog Sants. In: *The Guardian,* May 19.

UKFI (United Kingdom Financial Investments Limited), 2009: *Annual Report and Accounts 2008–2009.* London: UKFI.

Vickers, John, 2011: *Final Report: Opening Remarks.* <http://bankingcommission.independent.gov.uk/>

Vogel, David, 1986: *National Styles of Regulation: Environmental Policy in Great Britain and the United States.* Ithaca: Cornell University Press.

Watt, Nicholas/Jill Treanor, 2011: Revealed: 50% of Tory Funds Come from the City. In: *The Guardian,* February 8.

Wigley, Bob, 2008: *London: Winning in a Changing World.* London: Merrill Lynch Europe.

4

International Radicalism, Domestic Conformism: France's Ambiguous Stance on Financial Reforms

Nicolas Jabko

Listening to senior French government officials, one may get the impression that the financial crisis that started in 2007 has revolutionized France's approach to international financial governance. President Nicolas Sarkozy has repeatedly castigated "speculators" for triggering the crisis, and has called for a "moralization" of financial capitalism. He has also been very active on the international stage, using the French presidencies of the EU in 2008 and of the G8 and G20 in 2011 as pulpits to demand a radical reform agenda and repeatedly calling for "a new Bretton Woods."[1] On October 23, 2010, Finance Minister Christine Lagarde hailed the newly adopted *Loi de régulation financière et bancaire* (LRFB) with the following statement: "With this law, France is turning its back on deregulated finance," implying a major change in France's domestic financial policy framework. This law was the main result of a year of legislative work, as the finance ministry had drafted its bill after the G20 summit of September 2009 and the government had introduced it to the French parliament in early 2010. But a closer look at the law, and more generally at France's financial reforms since 2007, suggests a large gap between the ambitious rhetoric of official statements on taming unfettered global finance and the modest scope of actual regulatory initiatives.

In this chapter, I trace the French reactions to the financial crisis at the international, European, and domestic levels. The puzzle that I attempt to explain is the distance between the modest reality of these reforms and France's ambitious rhetoric in the global debate on financial regulation. The inertia of the French financial policy framework could be due to the limits of France's power in the European Union (EU) and on the world stage; to cognitive and sociological biases in the French decision-making process; or to pressures from domestic interest groups. Against conventional wisdom, I argue that the first explanation

Nicolas Véron's input to this paper is gratefully acknowledged.

1 The first presidential statement in this vein was on September 25, 2008: "We have to redesign the entire financial and monetary system, as was done in Bretton Woods after the Second World War." See Nicolas Sarkozy, Discours de M. le Président de la République à Toulon, September 25, 2008 (www.elysee.fr/president/les-actualites/discours/2008/discours-de-m-le-president-de-la-republique-a.2096.html?search=Toulon&xtmc=toulon_25_septembre_2008&xcr=2).

is the least convincing. The modesty of French reforms is primarily due to a biased technocratic and political process that gives disproportionate weight to the status quo. France's relatively weak impact on the European and the global stage is more often a pretext than a genuine rationale for limited domestic reform. France's internal continuity, in turn, casts doubt on its capacity to significantly shift the global debate on financial regulation.

International initiatives

In the documentary film *Inside Job*, French political leaders appear full of resolve and good will in their approach to the global financial crisis, in contrast with hapless and captured US authorities. That is certainly the image that French leaders projected early on in 2008–2009. President Sarkozy used the French presidency of the EU in the second half of 2008 as an advocacy pulpit for a strong multilateral response. Speaking on behalf of the EU, he claimed credit for convincing President George W. Bush to convene a series of high-level international summits and to extend the invitation to a more open circle than the G8. As Sarkozy explained at the end of a meeting with Bush at Camp David on October 18, 2008: "The crisis is global, we must find a global solution [...] In order for the summit to succeed, we must collect ideas from everybody."[2] The direct sequel of this meeting was the first and unprecedented summit of G20 political leaders that took place in Washington on November 15, 2008. Since 1999, the G20 had operated only as a forum of finance ministers and central bankers. The raising of its profile echoed recurrent French critiques of US tendencies to go it alone, but was also in line with longstanding French demands for sturdier global governance. It was also reminiscent of President Valéry Giscard d'Estaing's initiative in the 1970s to establish a forum, which later became known as the G7, for "fireplace chats" between the leaders of the leading industrialized nations. In both cases, the underlying rationale for the creation of a new forum was that high political momentum and hands-on multilateral leadership were necessary in order to address global economic challenges.

   As for the substance of France's positions, the rhetoric of France's political leaders was also quite radical. French leaders repeatedly called for deep reforms of the international financial system. Although the first G20 summit in November 2008 in Washington produced a generic declaration calling for "needed reforms in the world's financial systems," Sarkozy reportedly wanted a blunter

---

2 "Crise: L'idée d'une série de sommets retenue," *Le Monde,* October 19, 2008.

indictment of US-style financial deregulation as the main source of the crisis.[3] Shortly afterwards, he took advantage of the advent of a new administration in the United States to push for tougher regulation. Before the following G20 summit in London in April 2009, he published an open letter calling for more "urgency" in "the regulation of financial markets," focusing especially on credit rating agencies, hedge funds, and tax havens.[4] In September 2009, the G20 summit in Pittsburg appeared to move further in the French government's favored direction with its pledge "to turn the page on an era of irresponsibility and to adopt a set of policies, regulations and reforms to meet the needs of the 21st century global economy."[5] G20 political leaders also "designated the G20 to be the premier forum for our international economic cooperation" and pledged to increase by \$500bn the capital of the International Monetary Fund—which, at the time, was led by Dominique Strauss-Kahn, another Frenchman. At the EU level, Sarkozy successfully pushed for his agriculture minister Michel Barnier to be appointed as internal market commissioner (a portfolio that includes financial regulation) within the incoming European Commission to replace his deregulation-friendly predecessor Charlie McCreevy. In a speech on November 28, 2009, Sarkozy hailed the "triumph of French ideas about regulation" when Barnier was appointed. He proclaimed Barnier would "represent France in Brussels"—a controversial point, as European commissioners are bound by EU law to exercise their mandate in complete independence from the member states. Perhaps the culmination of President Sarkozy's international activism was the stern lecture that he delivered to the world's economic elite at Davos in January 2010. On this occasion, he argued against "unregulated globalization" and called for "restoring the moral dimension of capitalism" (Sarkozy 2010). In that speech, the French President also praised the G20 for "regulating bonuses, closing down tax havens and changing the rules of accounting and prudential standards," advocated "taxing the exorbitant profits of finance," and reiterated his call for a "new Bretton Woods." In January 2011, the French President returned to Davos. As France was holding the presidency of the G20, his speech struck a more cautious tone. But he again called for moralization: "There is no market economy without a minimum of morals, in the same way as there are no markets without rules" (Sarkozy 2011).

When one looks beyond summit pronouncements, however, the picture that begins to emerge is more ambiguous than the bold international initiatives and the radical rhetoric of French political leaders would suggest. Although

---

3 "Le G20, théâtre de la discorde franco-américaine," *Le Monde,* November 16, 2008.
4 Nicolas Sarkozy, "The Practical Steps the G20 Must Take," *Washington Post,* April 1, 2009.
5 Preamble of the Leaders' Statement, Pittsburgh summit, September 24–25, 2009.

French leaders were certainly active in advocating change at the beginning, I will show that their initiatives often petered out due to design weaknesses, inadequate implementation, or outright resistance by domestic interest groups. In some cases, of course, French initiatives also ran into opposition from France's partners. However, this external opposition was a less important factor than the lack of political determination to implement reform in the face of domestic opposition. To illustrate this point more concretely, I consider three issue areas of international initiatives, at both the global and the EU level. At the global level, I highlight France's approach to global negotiations and in relation to specific financial reforms. Second, I look at France's role in EU crisis management, and third, at its impact in advancing a concrete agenda of EU legislative reforms.

Global negotiations

The crisis triggered an unprecedented wave of discussions about financial reform. These were comprehensively outlined in the conclusions of the first G20 summit in November 2008. France appears to have repeatedly pushed for ambitious measures as regards the regulation and/or supervision of rating agencies, hedge funds, traders' bonuses, tax havens, CDS markets and short-selling rules, high-frequency trading, commodities markets, and shadow banking, as well as the possible introduction of a financial transactions tax. In 2008–2009, Nicolas Sarkozy personally led the charge at the G20 against tax havens and in favor of regulating of bankers' bonuses. Independently of their high symbolic value in the domestic context of French politics, these two topics also provided a platform for Sarkozy to build a common position with German Chancellor Angela Merkel. This was an increasingly important goal for the French President after the acute tensions that had surfaced between him and the German Chancellor on the issue of economic stimulus during France's six-month presidency of the EU in 2008.[6]

By contrast, France has been widely reported as being among the less ambitious states in the negotiations within the Basel Committee on Banking Supervision that resulted in the adoption in 2010 of the Basel III accord on capital, leverage, liquidity, and risk management. France has appeared similarly lukewarm in the ensuing discussion on how to tackle so-called systemically important financial institutions (SIFIs), steered by the Financial Stability Board (FSB) under instructions from the G20. In the important area of accounting standards, France has effectively worked against efforts to reach global convergence as it successfully advocated direct political intervention of the European Commis-

---

6 Interview with a government advisor, Paris, July 13, 2009.

sion on International Financial Reporting Standards (IFRS) standard-setting, most visibly in October 2008 with the hurried revision of a much-debated standard on financial instruments. French officials criticized the fair value accounting approach promoted both by the International Accounting Standards Board (IASB) and its US counterpart. They also called for greater involvement of national prudential regulators in setting accounting standards, a proposal that is the subject of considerable resistance in the United States and at the IASB itself.

The overall picture that emerges from this brief overview is that France's more radical positions are in areas that would only have a limited impact, if any, within its own territorial remit. France does not host large-scale activities on the part of rating agencies or hedge funds. Few traders work in France compared to the United Kingdom or other major international financial centers. And France is generally a high-tax jurisdiction, rather than a tax haven, for most financial market segments. On issues that directly affect large French financial intermediaries, as was the case with capital standards (Basel III), the SIFIs discussion or IFRS, France has however tended to rank among the least ambitious, or most defensive, players at international level.

EU crisis management

France took a leading role in EU crisis management at the height of the financial crisis in the fall of 2008, as it was holding the EU six-month rotating presidency at that time. Early efforts failed to coordinate the stances of the bloc's largest members in an entirely intergovernmental manner. The leaders of France, Germany, Italy, and the United Kingdom in Paris met on October 4, 2008, but did not achieve any concrete results and added to the markets' sense of helplessness. On October 12, however, President Nicolas Sarkozy was more successful when he convened another summit, this time of all eurozone leaders plus the British Prime Minister. The heads of state and government presented a joint approach inspired by the British crisis-management plan introduced a few days earlier. They agreed on targeted recapitalizations, liquidity support, and extensive public guarantees. This framework was subsequently adopted by all EU member states on October 15, putting an end to the most panicky phase of the crisis. Sarkozy's decisiveness was widely—and in my opinion, rightly—credited with this significant achievement.

In the later phases, crisis-management discussions at the EU level were held in three successive and partly overlapping contexts. First, there was a targeted intervention to avoid a shortage of liquidity in Central and Eastern Europe, a region that had become heavily dependent on West European banking groups, including French banks such as Société Générale. This effort, known as the

Vienna Initiative after a series of meetings that took place in the Austrian capital (and later formally called the European Bank Coordination Initiative), was primarily spearheaded by private-sector participants through the Institute of International Finance, and then by the European Bank for Reconstruction and Development (EBRD), as well as the International Monetary Fund (IMF) and the European Investment Bank (EIB), with the involvement of the European Commission. The most prominently involved member state was Austria, and France never appeared to take a leading role. Second, after the peak of volatility in late 2008 it gradually became evident that investor confidence would not return to the European banking sector before a system-wide process of triage (in other words, the assessment of all systemically important banks' capital strength on a truly comparable basis) and, if necessary, recapitalization and restructuring. Three successive half-hearted attempts at conducting such a process through so-called "stress tests" were implemented in September 2009, July 2010, and July 2011. Even though Germany was widely reported by media and professional sources as the least constructive member state in this process, France's voice was subdued at best in the discussion on how to make the European financial system more transparent, the leading advocates for which were the IMF, the ECB, and (in 2011) the newly formed European Banking Authority. Among member states, Spain (at least from mid-2010 onwards), the United Kingdom, and the Nordic countries took a more visible leadership role in this process. Third, since early 2010 the fiscal difficulties of peripheral Eurozone countries including Greece, Ireland and Portugal have become a major risk factor for the entire EU and beyond. Germany has been the pivotal player among "core" Eurozone countries. France has played a significant role in mediating the dialogue between Germany and other Eurozone member states, but can hardly be described as the agenda-setter.

EU legislation and regulation

In the United States, crisis management and crisis-related legislation succeeded each other in a relatively straightforward sequence. First, there were two major crisis-management initiatives, namely the Troubled Asset Relief Program (TARP) introduced by the Bush administration, and then the Supervisory Capital Assessment Program ("stress tests") initiated in early spring 2009 by the newly formed Obama administration. Together with major interventions by the Federal Reserve, these initiatives led to significant stabilization around mid-2009. By then, the major US financial institutions were generally considered safely capitalized, even though smaller banks continued to default in large numbers in the following two years. Second, in June 2009 the administration presented an initial blueprint for structural regulatory reform. This marked the start of the legislative process that eventually led the US Congress to adopt the Dodd-Frank Act in July 2010. The subsequent rule making by specialized agencies on the basis of the Dodd-Frank Act is still ongoing at the time of writing (see Woolley/Ziegler in this volume).

In Europe, developments have been less neatly sequential. Crisis management continued on and off and has not yet come to a conclusive end. Since early 2010, it has evolved largely in reaction to market developments on the front of sovereign debt crises in peripheral Euro-area member states. Meanwhile, financial legislation has been an ongoing process, with many different texts being successively discussed, rather than one single all-encompassing piece of legislation as in the United States with the Dodd-Frank Act.

To simplify, in the EU two main areas of legislative reform can be identified (see Quaglia in this volume). First, the EU has embarked on a major transformation of its financial supervisory architecture, which resulted in the legal and operational start of four new EU-level bodies on January 1, 2011. Second, it has introduced or is considering various changes to its financial legislation in areas that broadly parallel those covered by the Dodd-Frank Act. In both areas, I find ambiguous evidence of France's specific impact.

As regards the EU's financial supervisory architecture, reform started with the initiative by European Commission President José Manuel Barroso in November 2008 to request a report from an ad hoc "high-level group" headed by former French central banker (and IMF and EBRD head) Jacques de Larosière. The de Larosière Report, delivered in February 2009, suggested the creation of three European Supervisory Authorities (ESAs) replacing existing consultative committees: the European Banking Authority (EBA) based in London, the European Securities and Markets Authority (ESMA) based in Paris, and the European Insurance and Occupational Pensions Authority (EIOPA) based in Frankfurt; and of an additional "macro-prudential" body hosted by the ECB in Frankfurt and now called the European Systemic Risk Board (ESRB).

The French government broadly supported this reform agenda, while other EU member states, including the United Kingdom and Germany, repeatedly dragged their feet. More than a specific input from a particular government or individual leaders, France's relative openness to the implementation of the de Larosière Report reflects long-standing French positions in EU negotiations, even though they have not always been put forward consistently. The idea of creating EU financial supervisors was described in the United Kingdom as early as 2000 as a "French plot." Jacques de Larosière embodied this position throughout the 2000s as he personally lobbied for more consistent EU financial supervision. However, it is important to remember that Commission President

Barroso chose Jacques de Larosière because of his widely recognized international financial expertise and credibility rather than as a representative of France or of "French" ideas. In fact, de Larosière often seemed to be a voice in the wilderness. When his report was initially published, the Banque de France was far from enthusiastic as it felt the creation of the EBA would encroach on its supervisory prerogatives. Now that the ESAs and the ESRB have been set up, it remains to be seen how constructively France will engage with these authorities, both in general and on specific issues. The fact that key figures of the French financial establishment, such as de Larosière or head of the French securities regulator Jean-Pierre Jouyet, initially favored the principle of centralization does not necessarily mean that French officials will be constructive in practice further down the road. On the contrary, early indications suggest that French authorities may take a more lukewarm view of the power of the ESAs now than in the discussion that led to their creation, especially since comparatively few French nationals have been appointed as their chairs or as members of their management committees.[7]

As for the rest of the EU's post-crisis regulatory program, a comprehensive assessment is made more difficult by the fact that most of the legislative work remains incomplete. Specifically, three crucially important pieces of legislation—on the structure of securities and derivatives markets (known as the MiFID review[8]), the transposition into EU law of the Basel III capital accord (known as CRD4[9]), and bank crisis management and resolution—are yet to be negotiated or finalized. Legislation adopted since the start of the crisis—most notably on deposit insurance (2009), securitization (CRD2, 2009), credit rating agencies (2009 and 2011), private equity and hedge funds (AIFM Directive,[10] 2011), and remuneration policies (CRD3, 2010)—have been more limited in their ambitions, even though some of them were far from finding consensus. As regards France's position, the same remarks apply to these texts as my previous comment on negotiations at the international level: France, like Germany, has specifically pushed for harsh measures in those areas in which it did not have significant domestic interests at stake, rather than for across-the-board regulatory tightening that would also have constrained the large universal banking groups that dominate its domestic financial system.

---

7 Interview with senior French financial regulatory official, March 15, 2011.
8 MiFID stands for Markets in Financial Instruments Directive, the first version of which was adopted in 2004.
9 CRD stands for Capital Requirements Directive, of which there have been three iterations so far, adopted in 2006, 2009 and 2010.
10 AIFM stands for Alternative Investment Fund Managers.

The domestic response to the crisis

In this section I assess the French domestic response. As we will see, the forms of institutional change in the regulation of French financial markets were quite varied. The government used many institutional levers in order to formulate its response to the financial crisis. From this perspective, formal changes in laws and regulations were only the tip of the iceberg. They are inseparable from other dimensions of the regulatory reform process—crisis management, financial supervision, tax policy, and other measures that the government adopted in response to the crisis. In all cases, I find continuity with previous practice, and no change of direction for the French state's approach to financial regulation and oversight.

Crisis management

The French government's first measures were an immediate reaction to the fast-moving developments of the financial crisis. To be sure, BNP Paribas's decision on August 9, 2007 to freeze three investment funds due to a sudden shortage of liquidity marked the start of the financial crisis. However, there were fewer dramatic developments in France than in Germany (with the failures of IKB and Sachsen LB) or the United Kingdom (with the bank run on Northern Rock) in the initial phases of the crisis in the second half of 2007. In January 2008, the revelation of a major trading loss at Société Générale eventually led to a change of that bank's management. Contrary to initial fears, however, this did not result in the bank's loss of independence, let alone a systemic collapse.

Things became more volatile, in France as in the rest of Europe, following the bankruptcy of Lehman Brothers in mid-September 2008 and rapid contagion that followed. Two prominent French financial institutions were among the most massively hit by the fear of contingent liabilities: Natixis, a publicly-listed corporate and investment banking firm jointly controlled by Caisses d'Epargne (the French Savings Banks group) and Banques Populaires, and Dexia, a French-Belgian bank specializing in the financing of municipalities. In both cases the problems were related to their investments in bond insurers in the United States: CDC IXIS Financial Guaranty (CIFG) in the case of Natixis, and Financial Security Assurance (FSA) in the case of Dexia. Dexia was rescued jointly by the French and Belgian governments with a massive capital increase on September 27–28, 2008. Its senior management was dismissed and a senior executive from BNP Paribas, Pierre Mariani, was appointed as the bank's new CEO. The state-coordinated restructuring of Natixis precipitated the merger of its two parent groups to form the newly branded BPCE group in February 2009. François

Pérol, until then President Sarkozy's senior economic adviser, was appointed chairman of the merged group.

To help manage the crisis, the French government in September 2008 created two new corporate bodies: the Société de Prise de Participation de l'Etat (SPPE), a financial investment vehicle specifically designed to shore up the capital of the banks; and the Société de Financement de l'Economie Française (SFEF), to refinance the economy. SPPE was created as a 100-percent state-owned corporate entity that could inject public capital into French financial institutions. It had 40 billion euros at its disposal for re-capitalization. SFEF represented a less direct approach to state intervention. It was set up as a commercial company in which private-sector banks own 66 percent of the stock and the French state holds 34 percent. SFEF could raise up to 320 billion euros in order to help the banks refinance themselves; the banks' stock of SFEF benefited from a state guarantee and could therefore be used as collateral to borrow yet more funds from the European Central Bank. In practice, SFEF later raised the equivalent of 77 billion euros on the market, while re-capitalization was broken down into two hybrid equity tranches of 10.5 billion euros each, plus 3 billion euros to bail out Dexia and 2.5 billion euros for the BPCE group.

Thus, the French government's crisis management was swift and effective. The creation of SPPE and SFEF avoided singling out the weaker financial players and enabled the entire French banking sector to remain afloat. At least up to the time of writing, France has thus steered away from any major banking collapse—unlike some of its big neighbors across the Atlantic Ocean, the English Channel, or even the Rhine. But this crisis management framework can hardly be described as a radical break from the past, and it is not without its downsides. As in previous financial crises, the French government played a major role and liberally committed taxpayers' money to rescue ailing banks. The government also utilized all the usual channels of influence, although without asserting bold new objectives beyond the immediate goal of putting out the fire. The Inspection des Finances, an elite corps within the Finance Ministry, remained at the center of all crisis management operations. This is significant because the Inspection also happens to be the perennial breeding ground for France's banking establishment. The same corps had played a critical role in the French state's initiative to liberalize the financial sector in the 1980s and the 1990s.[11] Now the Inspection was called to the rescue of the banking sector. None of this was particularly new.

---

11 On the beginnings of this process, see especially Philip Cerny (1989).

Supervisory architecture

Beyond the immediate task of crisis management, the most visible domestic initiative was the creation—by way of a governmental decree adopted in January 2010—of a new Prudential Supervisory Authority (Autorité de Contrôle Prudentiel, ACP). This was achieved by merging two previously separate bodies: the Commission Bancaire, hosted by the Banque de France, which supervised banks and other financial intermediaries; and the Autorité de Contrôle des Assurances et des Mutuelles, the insurance supervisor. This resulted in a "two-pillar" regulatory structure, with an unchanged Autorité des Marchés Financiers (AMF) as the securities regulator, and the ACP assuming prudential oversight of most French financial services firms. Both the AMF and the ACP are independent public authorities, separate from both the Ministry of Finance and the Banque de France. However, the AMF board includes a non-voting representative of the Ministry of Finance and the 19-member executive college of the ACP is chaired by the governor of the Banque de France.

Although this reorganization was occasionally presented as a bold response to the financial crisis, it was once again anything but revolutionary. Similar mergers between banking and insurance supervisors had been conducted in other EU countries in previous years, for example, in the United Kingdom in 2000 and in Germany in 2002 (in these cases the mergers also, and more controversially, included securities regulation). The corresponding move in France was arguably long overdue and cannot be labeled groundbreaking. Irrespective of the merits assigned to different models of supervisory architecture, post-crisis change in this respect was less significant in France than in some other countries. In the United Kingdom, the Cameron government in 2010 announced the return of most prudential supervisory competencies to the Bank of England, which had lost them to the Financial Services Authority (FSA) in the late 1990s. In the United States, Congress conducted an extensive series of hearings up to the Dodd-Frank Act, mandating the creation of a consumer protection watchdog within the Federal Reserve and an across-the-board overhaul of regulatory rules and bodies. By contrast, France approached the topic of regulatory reform through the same channels as before. In a spirit of continuity characteristic of France's regulatory reforms, the reform was assigned to the Inspection des Finances. The Inspection's report was itself drafted by Bruno Deletré, who ironically had previously been one of the senior executives of Dexia and had been associated with that bank's questionable investments in the United States.

Another new item—introduced by the LRBF—is the creation of a Financial Regulation and Systemic Risk Council (Conseil de Régulation Financière et du Risque Systémique, CRFRS). This paralleled the creation of macro-prudential policy bodies elsewhere, such as the Financial Stability Oversight Council (FSOC) in the United States, the Financial Stability Council in Belgium, or the European Systemic Risk Board, an autonomous EU body hosted by the ECB. The CRFRS is chaired by the Finance Minister and is in charge of coordinating the action of France's main regulatory bodies, namely the Banque de France, ACP, AMF, as well as the accounting standard-setter, Autorité des Normes Comptables (ANC). On the occasion of its first meeting on February 7, 2011, Christine Lagarde declared that "France is one of the very first European countries to create a genuine traffic controller to monitor financial risk." However, there is no indication that this new body will actually be making any impactful decisions. Its competencies are much more restricted than those of the US FSOC or even of the Belgian Financial Stability Council, which is tasked with determining which financial firms are systemically important in the Belgian financial system. Instead, the CRFRS will probably serve as an incubator of official French positions that the minister will use in order to assist her in European negotiations.

Other regulatory reforms

A myriad of other measures were included in the LRBF. In addition to ratifying the merger of preexisting regulatory bodies into the ACP and creating the CRFRS, the law for example extended the powers of the Autorité des Marchés Financiers; it mandated tighter corporate governance and greater transparency of compensation for banks and financial establishments; and it introduced a series of measures aimed at protecting small and medium-sized enterprises and households from a contraction of bank credit. But none of these measures went markedly beyond the scope of the ordinary regulatory maintenance that is included in French legislation on a more-or-less yearly basis, such as the transposition of EU financial directives. Although French Members of Parliament did harden some of the government's provisions in the original bill, most of the amendments were marginal. As finance minister Christine Lagarde declared, "the legislative base is international by essence, and European by default." The government's constitutional prerogative to set the parliamentary agenda sharply circumscribed the Parliament's initiatives—all the more so that financial reforms were a highly technical subject, in which parliamentary expertise is typically scarce. The Parliament's discussion of the bill did not attract much publicity, and the parliamentary debates never involved more than 15–20 Members of Parliament; only 15 members were present when the National Assembly adopted the law on June 10, 2010. On the part of the government, there was no attempt to add idiosyncratic French rules to the ones coming from the European level. On the contrary, there was a deliberate attempt to avoid any overly strict regulation, for fear that financial skills or institutions would leave the country.

The law did increase the possibility of financial sanctions for wrongdoing and reckless risk taking; but these sanctions are capped at a relatively low amount (100 million euros) and the imposition of sanctions remains subject to several political and administrative vetoes. The law also establishes a regulatory framework for derivative markets for the first time in France. However, most of the legal provisions are about the imposition of greater transparency, rather than actual limits on derivative trading—and in any case, not much derivatives trading activity is located in France at the present juncture. The regulation of credit rating agencies, which was presented to the press as a major change, mainly mirrors EU developments and consists of registration requirements. The French law additionally includes a possibility of financial sanctions (also limited to 100 million euros) in case of egregious mistakes in rating corporate or sovereign debts. Since such mistakes are hard to prove, however, the legal impact of this provision remains unclear for the moment.

Tax policy[12]

The taxation regime applied to the financial industry is another area of financial reform. Although there were obvious limits to how far France could go on its own, the government could have changed its tax policies at the margin in order to try to influence the corporate governance of financial firms. In contrast to other European Union countries such as Germany and the United Kingdom, however, France did not require that banks benefitting from public support suspend the distribution of dividends to shareholders. When France's bank support plan was announced, BNP Paribas congratulated itself on these measures, which would have "consequences for neither the shareholders nor the governance of the group."[13] The government merely asked employers in October 2008 to draft a "code of conduct" for business managers. France's two biggest employers' associations therefore issued a document that advocated a restriction of bonuses, supplementary retirement schemes, golden parachutes, as well as the awarding of shares and options to executive officers.[14] But the adoption of these recommendations was purely voluntary, since the code was not made legally binding. And while the executive directors of big banks voluntarily renounced their 2008 bonuses in the aftermath of a scandal that erupted in March 2009 around the

---

12 This section builds on Jabko and Massoc (2011).
13 Press Release, BNP Paribas, October 21, 2008.
14 *Code de Gouvernement d'entreprise des Sociétés cotées,* AFEP-Medef, October 2008, pp. 20–31.

Société Générale decision to award generous stock options, retirement packages and bonuses were not at all abandoned.

This state of affairs evolved slowly as the conditions of the state's support to the banks began to stir controversy. As the issue became more politicized, many elected officials began to criticize the conditions imposed by the government's bank support plan as insufficiently restrictive. From opposition and majority parties alike, voices began to condemn the government's refusal to legislate on the remuneration of bank managers and on banks' use of tax havens. They denounced "the disdain for national representation" and the tactic of "decreeing a state of emergency on almost every text."[15] As the rescue plan unfolded and the situation of emergency receded, MPs and the government came into confrontation. The Parliament demanded to be involved in overseeing the rescue plan. Didier Migaud, a Socialist Party member, and Gilles Carrez, from the governing UMP party, managed to achieve a certain level of agreement within the Finance Committee of the National Assembly. The impact of the Parliament on the rescue plan nevertheless remained limited, with the exception of two amendments relating to transparency. Only in March 2009, when a scandal broke out over the payment of bonuses to executives of state-assisted banks, was the Parliament able to impose legal restrictions on executive pay (Culpepper 2011: 173–174). Meanwhile, President Sarkozy's speeches increasingly struck a moralizing and interventionist pose vis-à-vis the excesses of the financial sector: "The law of the market alone, it's over; self-regulation, it's over; excessive remuneration, it's over" (Sarkozy 2008). The managers of big banks were summoned to the Elysée Palace on several occasions, after the President declared himself outraged by their remuneration packages. But these highly publicized interviews did not lead to any formal restrictions until the end of 2009.

When government policy finally began to change in earnest, it happened under the pressure of events rather than as the result of an independently defined government strategy. On December 6, 2009, British Prime Minister Gordon Brown—already in a poor electoral position—made a surprise announcement of an exceptional tax on banks, primarily targeting bonuses paid to traders. The French government announced several hours later that it planned to align itself with the British mechanism. Without delay, Sarkozy and Brown co-signed an article in the *Wall Street Journal* in support of a "one-off tax" on bonuses and calling for action "at the global level" on this issue (Brown/Sarkozy 2009). The French Ministry of Finance was then tasked with drafting a corrective finance bill to be presented to parliament on January 20. The French initiative was an exact copy of the British mechanism, establishing a tax rate on banks of 50 per-

---

15 Interviews, Paris, June 10 and June 22, 2009.

cent of the total volume of bonuses and starting from a threshold of 27,500 euros per employee (equivalent to 25,000 pounds in Britain). It seemed as though the French government had finally decided to punish French banks. By contrast, German Chancellor Angela Merkel feared that the Constitutional Court would rule against targeted taxation and she therefore did not follow the example set by her British and French counterparts.

The French government's belated enthusiasm for taxing the banks remained limited, however. As Christine Lagarde stated after the Council of Ministers' meeting on December 16, 2009, the tax on bonuses was an "exceptional tax for exceptional circumstances." Moreover, the impact of this tax remained relatively modest, much more so than in Britain given the large difference in the number of traders between the two countries. The banks in the City of London responded to the British government's announcement by denouncing Gordon Brown's populism, even convincing the Mayor of London to take up their cause. In France, the reaction of the bankers was more muted.[16] This difference is more easily understood when the total amounts involved are considered. Expected revenues in France from this exceptional tax were less than 320 million euros[17]—far less than what was reaped by the British Treasury.[18] Finally, the French government kept a narrow focus on the issue of "excessive" bonuses for traders. Even if justified by the traders' colossal losses, this focus diverts attention from the significant compensation of senior bank executives, who also bore responsibility for the crisis. After the meager diet of 2008, executive compensation packages climbed in 2009 and they were again awarded sizeable bonuses.[19] In the absence of a public outcry, the French government seemed little inclined to intervene heavily in the banks' governance and remuneration schemes.

The government's caution in the area of tax policy and its narrow framing of tax reform also had some partisan-political roots. Before the financial crisis even started, Nicolas Sarkozy himself had committed significant political capital to the creation of a "tax shield" (bouclier fiscal). This new policy enabled French taxpayers to limit their total taxes up to a ceiling of 50 percent of their income. It was ostensibly designed to make France more attractive for entrepreneurs, but it also disproportionately benefitted financiers. After the beginning of the crisis, the President's agenda ran into a dilemma. On the one hand, the government had to show that it was doing what it could to discourage reckless behavior and to crack down on "speculation," including by means of taxation. The pressure

16 "Taxe sur les bonus: les Banquiers français grognons mais discrets," Les Echos, January 12, 2010.
17 "En France, la recette attendue ne devrait pas rapporter plus de 300 millions d'euros," Les Echos, January 7, 2010.
18 "Londres: la taxe sur les bonus pourrait rapporter plusieurs milliards," Les Echos, January 7, 2010.
19 "Retour des bonus pour quelques dirigeants de banques françaises," Les Echos, June 3, 2010.

mounted even within the governing UMP after its massive setback at the regional election of March 2010. Members of the government's majority in Parliament worried about the impression of "social unfairness" that the tax shield created during a period of budget cuts and across-the-board tax increases.[20] On the other hand, the President did not want to acknowledge defeat and antagonize core constituencies. In the end, the government decided in May 2011 to abolish the tax shield, but at the same time to reform (and presumably alleviate) France's wealth tax, the *Impôt de Solidarité sur la Fortune* (ISF). Nicolas Sarkozy's government did not abolish the symbolically loaded ISF altogether, for fear of a political backlash against the "president of the rich." However, the threshold of exemptions was raised from 800,000 euros to 1.3 million euros and the taxation rate above that level was considerably decreased, which may result in an overall tax cut for a majority of ISF taxpayers.

In sum, the government did not use its taxation powers to significantly modify the framework of financial firms' corporate governance. The government had to face the pressure of public opinion and growing hostility in Parliament, including within its own majority. It attempted to neutralize critics on both the right and the left with the slogan of "moralizing capitalism." This posture should not be taken at face value, however. Above all else, the rhetoric of "rupture" apparently served to deflect attention from a mostly hands-off approach to corporate governance and to the taxation of financial firms' activities. It is possible to justify this restraint by pointing out that French bankers, as they were groomed within the state's financial establishment, were not awarded bonuses as high as those of some of their British and American counterparts.[21] There is no question that executive compensation among senior French bank executives remained much lower than in the United Kingdom or the United States, especially after the bailout-related restrictions and the special UK tax on bonuses were relaxed in 2010.[22] But this relative self-restraint pre-existed the financial crisis and partly reflects the fact that France's marketplace is not nearly as developed, competitive and lucrative as the City of London or Wall Street. The relatively moderate level of executive compensation in France thus cannot be considered a consequence of the government's professed desire to radically reform the financial system.

---

20 "Bouclier fiscal: Nicolas Sarkozy face à la fronde de la majorité," *Le Monde,* April 1, 2010.
21 Interview, Paris, March 15, 2011.
22 "Ahead in the Clouds," *Financial Times,* March 15, 2011.

A choice of no change

In the view of the overwhelming majority of French financial executives and policymakers, at the time of writing, the French financial model has been vindicated rather than undermined in the crisis. A few powerful universal banks, under the attentive but ultimately benevolent gaze of the prudential supervisor, are at the apex of this system. Unlike some of their unfortunate counterparts in the United States, the United Kingdom, or even Germany, no major financial institution in France has collapsed, even though Dexia and Natixis came close, Caisses d'Epargne had to be merged into BPCE, and further consolidation may lie ahead. France did not experience a highly visible near-bankruptcy of a systemically important financial establishment like Northern Rock, Hypo Real Estate, or Lehman Brothers. As the Banque de France's Governor Christian Noyer declared in a speech on January 17, 2011, the French model of universal banking "has proved itself valuable." This judgment is in sharp contrast with the US drive to prevent financial establishments from remaining or becoming "too big to fail." A meaningful French debate on this topic has not even started—and it is not clear that it ever will (Goldstein/Véron 2011).

This sense of success (or limited failure) in the face of crisis is arguably one of the most important dimensions of France's relative post-crisis institutional inertia. Rather than going in the direction favored by US lawmakers—in other words, the corporate separation of risky proprietary trading activities from banking and financial intermediation (the so-called Volcker Rule), or the different but similarly radical UK attempts to "ring-fence" retail banking from wholesale operations (Independent Commission on Banking Interim Report, April 2011)—the French financial establishment professes the belief that the combination of universal banking and effective regulation provides a reliable response to financial risks. Bankers point out the unique capacity of large universal banks to successfully adopt a balanced portfolio approach, in which the risky nature of trading activities is offset by the conservative nature of the traditional banking business. French regulators are often critical of their American and British counterparts, arguing that lax regulation and sketchy or contested regulatory enforcement bear more responsibility for the financial crisis than the sheer size or structure of financial groups.

France's crisis management measures were undeniably effective in preventing disorderly developments. However, the massive support provided has arguably increased moral hazard, as the government made it crystal-clear that no French bank would be allowed to fail, thereby exacerbating the too-big-to-fail problem in France. In fact, the French government has consistently appeared reluctant to acknowledge the very existence of that problem. A revealing episode was when Prime Minister François Fillon, just after the disclosure of the multi-billion loss at Société Générale following Jérôme Kerviel's trading fraud, declared that the bank would "remain a major French bank."[23] In the context of the moment, this unambiguously meant that if another group was to acquire Société Générale because of its Kerviel-induced weakness, the acquirer would have to be a French group, ruling out potential foreign bids by HSBC, Santander, or UniCredit. Indeed, the market consensus quickly crystallized on an acquisition by BNP Paribas as the most likely outcome if Société Générale could not remain independent. The government thus expressed a clear preference for a combination of two major French banking groups, rather than the loss of a "national champion" to a European peer, regardless of the fact that such a combination would not only diminish competition in the French banking sector and potentially lead to numerous layoffs, but also and above all increase the already very high concentration of the French banking sector and therefore the too-big-to-fail problem.

In sum, the government's crisis management is marked by strong continuity with past practice. As in previous crises, most notably Credit Lyonnais and Comptoir des Entrepreneurs in the early 1990s, the government gave priority to the avoidance of bank failures, at the price of increasing moral hazard and committing massive public financial resources. When restructuring could not be avoided, as happened in the case of Natixis and nearly happened to Société Générale, it gave unambiguous preference to domestic acquisitions over cross-border ones. This combination will probably not change in the near future. Judging from recent history, France is more likely to try to address systemic risk by further consolidating its universal banks than by cutting into the flesh of a highly concentrated banking sector. Although this makes local bank failures unlikely, it also increases the risk of catastrophic and system-wide crisis if one of France's large financial conglomerates ever runs into serious trouble.

Conclusion: The ambiguity of France's reformism

French reformism in the face of the financial crisis is ambiguous. There is an obvious gap between the ambitious rhetoric of official French statements on taming unfettered finance at the global level and the modest scope of French

---

23 "La Société Générale, c'est une grande banque française [et] le gouvernement entend que la Société Générale reste une grande banque française acteur de la mondialisation," quoted in *L'Express,* January 29, 2008.

regulatory reforms at the domestic level. I see three possible explanations of the inertia of French financial policy: it could be due to the limits of France's power in the EU and on the world stage; to cognitive and sociological biases in the decision-making process; or to pressures from domestic interest groups. All three explanations are plausible, as they echo international relations theory, cognitive theories of decision making, and political economy theories of interest aggregation and capture by powerful domestic actors. In the foregoing narrative, we highlighted various explanatory elements that could be classified under one or, in some cases, several of these headings. I recognize that the matter is complex and that these explanations are not always mutually exclusive. In other words, institutional inertia could be overdetermined. However, I believe it is useful to consider different explanations as distinct hypotheses, and to assess their relative weight in the outcome. The advantage of proceeding in this way is that it produces a pointed depiction of France's actions since the outbreak of the global financial crises. These actions are a far cry from the radical vision that French political leaders have projected to domestic and foreign audiences.

Limited sovereignty

A first explanation for the limits of institutional change in France is that it is mostly driven by EU and international developments. Realizing their limited domestic leeway, French policymakers may have consciously decided to focus their energies on trying to enact change at the European and the global level.

This explanation is not completely devoid of relevance. As we have seen, Finance Minister Christine Lagarde made it very clear that France would prioritize reforms at the global and the EU level. France's inclination towards cooperative solutions was not just an abstract goal. France did play an active role in several broad global and EU initiatives on regulatory reform. Far from dragging his feet, the French President acted closely in concert with Germany to obtain results from the G20 summit in Pittsburgh in spring 2009. He encouraged independent French figures such as de Larosière, Barnier, and Strauss-Kahn to carry the flag of regulatory reform beyond French borders. He praised and emulated the British government in October 2008 for its leadership on rescuing banks, and again in December 2009 for taxing bank bonuses.

Although France had a role in launching some global and EU processes of regulatory reform, I have argued that its support for reform was fraught with ambiguity. At the outset, French reform initiatives were often cast in such broad terms and flamboyant rhetoric that it was difficult for policymakers to follow up on French promises and translate them into actual reforms. When it came down to specific issues, French state officials who specialized in financial issues sometimes acted differently from the stated intentions of French political leaders. President Sarkozy painted a very big picture indeed—but in financial regulation, the devil is generally in the details. When bureaucrats had to negotiate on policy details, they received little guidance from their political masters. Thus, they often reverted to the path of least resistance, namely the defense of French financial services firms' interests and institutional status quo. Even political leaders were remarkably cautious once they got into specific details. The fact that this conservative attitude contrasted with the government's ambitious rhetoric became apparent only late in the game. The loss of momentum of many French initiatives, such as the taxation of "speculative profits," highlights ambiguous attitudes toward reform.

Ostrich attitude

The second possible explanation for the timidity of French reforms resides in the cognitive and sociological biases of France's decision-making process. I believe that this explanation works much better than the first one, partly for reasons that are peculiar to the social composition of France's financial and policy-making establishment.

Among that group, there appears to be broad consensus that extreme ("tail") risk scenarios should not be envisaged, reinforced by politicians who are confident that most problems in the recent crisis did not originate or manifest themselves dramatically in France. Only the insider circle at the Autorité de Contrôle Prudentiel, the Banque de France that hosts it, and the major banks, know how close they were to disaster, what exactly has been done to avert it, and what is the true current condition of the banking system. Anecdotal reports suggest considerable anxiety, among both supervisors and bankers, from the summer of 2007 and throughout 2008. But the general public and much of the political class and media were not directly made aware of any apparent risk of national banking collapse. Problems could not be withheld from public view at Société Générale (the Kerviel story), Dexia, Calyon (Credit Agricole's corporate and investment bank unit, which suffered heavy trading losses) and Natixis. But they remained much less dramatic than Northern Rock, Lehman, Fortis, or Hypo Real Estate. There was also public outrage at the level of bonuses, but with no specific lightning rod, given that the most prominent financiers and bank executives renounced some of their compensation to avoid public ire, this petered out. Politicians and bankers have held to the belief that in France there are effective informal ways of dealing with the problems of France's biggest banks. With such a small number of big banks, executives representing virtually the entire system can easily sit around a table. The extraordinary degree of sector concentration—which has even increased since the crisis with the giant merger that gave birth to the BPCE group—also means that bank failures are less frequent. From a sociological perspective, the financial establishment is largely staffed by the Inspection des Finances, an elite group within the public service from which private banks massively recruit their top management.[24] After graduating at the top of their ENA class, they had all started their careers on the same protected executive track at the Ministry of Finance. These bankers have the same educational background; they know how the state operates, having often served at the Finance Ministry or in the staff of government ministers or both. The *inspecteurs* are groomed to think of large banks as "national champions" whose role enhances France's prosperity. Cognitive and sociological factors thus reinforce each other to produce institutional inertia.

Domestic interests

A third way to explain the paucity of reforms is the resistance from domestic interest groups. Unlike the limited sovereignty and ostrich hypotheses, this third explanation foregrounds sectional interests rather than international-structural or sociological-cognitive impediments to change. As I have made clear throughout this chapter, I find that this explanation works rather well. It is perhaps best understood as complementary to the above sociological-cognitive (ostrich-like attitude) explanation.

To be sure, the French government was under political pressure to react to the excesses of the financial sector. There were cases of rogue traders putting large banks at risk (Kerviel at Société Générale, smaller cases at Natixis and Calyon) and the awkward coexistence of generous bonus awards with bank rescues using taxpayers' money. The government thus had to act, as it did for example in December 2009 by emulating the United Kingdom when it decided to create a special tax on traders' bonuses. The rhetoric against reckless risk taking by "thirty-year old traders" and "speculators" then flourished. But fundamentally the French government remained protective of the interests of large banks and their most senior executives.

Obviously, this interest group would not happily welcome financial reforms that could have the effect of reducing profitability, strategic margins of maneuver, and compensation packages. The links between the financial and policy

---

24 As Massoc and Jabko (2011) point out, ten out of the 19 executive directors of the four biggest French bank networks in October 2008 were ENA alumni (including eight *inspecteurs des finances*); six were alumni of the Ecole Polytechnique; and two were alumni of both schools. Only five bankers were neither *énarques*, nor *polytechniciens*, and four of these five relative outsiders were at Crédit Agricole, a bank that remains influenced by its origins as a grassroots-level credit union.

elites, both at the level of elected officials (for example, through the UMP's fundraising) and unelected senior bureaucrats (through the sociological compact of the *Inspection des Finances* and other networks), thus could create powerful obstacles to change. When push comes to shove, French leaders' radicalism remained superficial and rhetorical. As it ran into powerful sociological, cognitive, and material countervailing forces, it quickly ran out of breath.

References

AFEP-MEDEF (Association française des entreprises privées/Mouvement des entreprises de France), 2008: *Code de Gouvernement d'entreprise des Sociétés cotées,* October.

Brown, Gordon/Nicolas Sarkozy, 2009: For Global Finance, Global Regulation. In: *Wall Street Journal,* December 9.

Cerny, Philip, 1989: The "Little Big Bang" in Paris: Financial Market Deregulation in a Dirigiste System. In: *European Journal of Policy Research* 17(2), 169–192.

Culpepper, Pepper D., 2011: *Quiet Politics and Business Power: Corporate Control in Europe and Japan.* Cambridge: Cambridge University Press.

Jabko, Nicolas/Elsa Massoc, 2011: *French Capitalism under Stress: How Nicolas Sarkozy Rescued the Banks.* Conference paper. 18th International Conference of Europeanists, Barcelona, June 20–22.

Sarkozy, Nicolas, 2008: *Discours de M. le Président de la République à Toulon,* September 25. <www.elysee.fr/president/les-actualites/discours/2008/discours-de-m-le-president-de-la-republique-a.2096.html?search=Toulon&xtmc=toulon_25_septembre_2008&xcr=2)>

———, 2010: *Discours de M. le Président de la République.* 40th World Economic Forum, Davos, January 27. <www.elysee.fr/president/les-dossiers/economie/preparer-l-avenir/world-economic-forum-2010/le-president-au-forum-de-davos.6771.html>

———, 2011: *Intervention de M. le Président de la République. 41st World Economic Forum,* Davos, January 27. <www.elysee.fr/president/les-actualites/discours/2011/41e-forum-economique-mondial.10535.html?search=Davos&xtmc=davos_27_janvier_2011&xcr=5>

5

Institutional Change in German Financial Regulation

Stefan Handke and Hubert Zimmermann

Introduction

Without any doubt, the financial crisis of 2008/2009 posed the most serious challenge to the German regulatory and supervisory system since the turmoil of the 1920s and 1930s. Prior to the crisis, Germany was among the most internationally active proponents of a comprehensive regulatory framework for global finance (Zimmermann 2008). National regulation, on the other hand, was seen as prudent and the financial system as less crisis-prone than others. Germany had been very hesitant in adopting the full range of financial innovations created in the past two decades. In many respects for example, permission for hedge funds and private equity to operate in the country or liberalization of the housing market—it lagged behind the Anglo-Saxon countries and even many other European countries. During the negotiations about the Basel I and Basel II frameworks, Germany had fought a rearguard campaign to preserve elements of its peculiar banking landscape. The German banking sector is characterized by a unique three-pillar structure, with public sector banks (such as the *Landesbanken*, state-owned regional banks, and savings banks), cooperative, and private commercial banks. This traditional structure has endured, despite the severe problems of some Landesbanken and the widely lamented small size of most German financial institutions. The often predicted transformation from a quintessentially bank-based to a market-based financial system has not yet happened in Germany, despite the progressive disintegration of the cozy network of banks and firms which characterized the postwar "Deutschland AG" (Lütz 2004; Streeck/Höpner 2003). For all these reasons, it came as an unpleasant surprise when, in autumn 2008, despite the supposedly low exposure to the financial excesses in Anglo-Saxon countries, the German government had to resort to unprecedented measures to avert a meltdown of its financial system, including the nationalization of banks and comprehensive government guarantees on savings. After this shock, many observers expected and asked for a complete makeover of the regulatory and supervisory system. However, this has not yet happened and this chapter deals with the reasons.

The analysis traces the evolution of German financial regulation after the crisis, emphasizing the historical dimension of institutional change (Streeck 2009). The objective is to detail the extent and direction of institutional change, both of rules and agencies, in German financial market regulation. We observe that there is no radical, but only incremental change in the aftermath of the latest crisis, despite the severity and comprehensive scope of the distortions. What explains this relative stasis? We argue that functional requirements and complementarities emphasized by the Varieties of Capitalism school played only a limited role: institutional change in German financial regulation is fairly decoupled from developments in the markets. Those changes which actually happened were rather conditioned by a political game structured by the German polity. The German financial system is closely linked to political structures at the federal, regional and local level. This creates numerous veto opportunities for actors with a stake in existing institutional structures. Partisan veto-players, *Länder* governments and influential lobbying associations hinder every attempt at a radical overhaul of the system. As a result, incremental change dominates, despite the violence of the external shock. Our explanation therefore confirms a simple veto-player constellation (Tsebelis 2002). To account for the limited changes we have recourse to recent concepts of institutional change, such as "institutional layering" and "institutional drift." *Institutional layering* involves a step-by-step establishment of new institutions without abruptly replacing old ones (Streeck/ Thelen 2005; Van der Heijden 2011). We use the concept in the sense originally established by Kathleen Thelen: "layering [...] involves the partial renegotiation of some elements of a given set of institutions while leaving others in place" (Thelen 2003: 225). Over time, a web of institutions emerges which has a propensity for overlap and inefficiency. *Drift* emphasizes how stagnant institutions slowly fail to adapt to their fast-moving erstwhile target through non-decisions and inertia. Contrary to Streeck/Thelen (2005), who summarized and deepened these concepts we do not see slow transformative change at work in observing these modes of change in German financial regulation.

We first discuss regulatory change as a consequence of specific failures identified by political actors during the crisis. The bailout of Hypo Real Estate (HRE), the establishment of the Financial Market Stabilisation Fund, and the controversial ban on naked short selling were quickly implemented emergency measures. We then examine more long-term regulatory programs and decisions, such as the Financial Market Stabilisation Act *(Finanzmarktstabilisierungsgesetz)*, proposals for better market regulation via capital requirements or financial transaction taxes (BMF 2010b), and the adoption of the so-called *Restrukturierungsgesetz* (Restructuring Law). We also deal with the debate on reform of the German system of deposit insurance. National supervision as the only exclusive administrative competence of the Federal Government is covered by the second part of the analysis where we discuss the German governance structure of financial markets, with its two pillars, the Bundesbank and the integrated supervisory agency BaFin *(Bundesanstalt für Finanzdienstleistungsaufsicht)*. Of course, financial regulation in Germany is strongly conditioned by the international or European level (BMF 2010c). Reform initiatives at these levels are discussed in other chapters of this volume and we mention German reactions to these initiatives only briefly and selectively. Finally, our conclusion offers an explanation of incremental policy change based on the specific pattern of political veto-players in financial regulation.

Regulatory change as a result of crisis management

Restructuring banks

Among all the industrialized nations, Germany was the country which, prior to the crisis, was most active in arguing at the global and European level for new institutions to govern global finance (Zimmermann 2009). It regularly lectured its partners on the dangers for financial stability and social cohesion posed by new actors in global finance, such as private equity, hedge funds or sovereign wealth funds. Given the supposedly low exposure of the German financial system, the government reacted to the first reverberations of the crisis with complacency. Early warning signs, such as the August 2007 bailout of the rather small IKB Bank, traditionally a lender to small and medium-sized enterprises, were treated as isolated incidences. In late 2008, however, the crisis hit Germany with full force. By far the most serious event was doubtless the barely averted crash of Hypo Real Estate (HRE). Its de facto nationalization, as well as the aid packages for other banks (particularly Commerzbank) dominated headlines and talk-shows in Germany for months, along with stories of the losses incurred by individual savers who had made the mistake of investing in Lehman certificates or Icelandic banks. The crisis also brutally exposed the longstanding problems of the Landesbanken which got into trouble due to risky international investments and speculative transactions. The result was a several billion euro bill for German tax payers. Traditionally, the Landesbanken as state-owned regional banks had a threefold task: first, to function as a kind of central bank for the savings banks *(Sparkassen)*; second, to finance regional projects of the Länder; and third, to support small and medium-sized companies (SME) in cooperation with the Sparkassen (Schrooten 2009). However, EU competition policy had long fought against the competitive advantages of the Landesbanken because of the implicit state guarantees which gave them easier access to credit than other banks. Faced with the impending loss of their privileges, the Landesbanken joined the global securitization game as late-comers and incurred heavy losses. Two smaller Landesbanken were merged with the more successful Landesbank Baden-Württemberg and in June 2011 it became known that West-LB—as it was now known—would be split up into several parts, but the debate on the future of this German peculiarity is still ongoing (Spiegel-Online 2010). The decade-long struggle about the future of the Landesbanken shows the resilience of the German financial system against any change which touches on the fundamental interests of the Länder.

A strong influence of the regional level was also evident in the fields of bank restructuring and deposit protection which reflected the core interests of the political system: avoiding further burdens on state governments due to bank failures and ensuring the stability of German savings. The most prominently proclaimed objective immediately prior to the crisis and during its first phase, the regulation of new financial actors, became a secondary issue and was delegated to the international level (see Quaglia and Woll in this volume). An exception was the controversial unilateral ban on short-selling. Up to the financial crisis, investors in Germany, with the exception of investment funds, were allowed to engage in this practice. In May 2010, under the impression of the escalating Greek sovereign debt crisis, the government introduced a unilateral ban on the short-selling of the stocks of ten of the country's largest financial institutions. A following draft law planned to extend the ban to Eurozone government bonds and Credit Default Swaps (CDS), among other instruments. The unilateral step was criticized heavily by many other countries (NYT 2010). However, soon afterwards the EU started to work on its own proposal. In May 2011, European Union governments agreed to curb so-called naked short-selling of government bonds and stocks. The German government welcomed the step, adding that the ban should have gone further and included CDS tied to the debt. Apart from this episode, the German authorities took care to embed their regulatory reform steps in the concurrent European and international efforts.

The crisis of Hypo Real Estate was the most profound shock to the German financial system at least since the crash of the private Herstatt bank in 1974. This event had led to the establishment of a deposit insurance system for private banks and the strengthening of banking supervision by the state. HRE was among the biggest players in the German bond and housing markets and it was highly exposed to global capital markets, in particular because of the recent acquisition of offshore conduits, such as the Irish affiliate Depfa. The German government was convinced that the insolvency of HRE would result in "Armageddon", dwarfing the Lehman disaster (Steinbrück 2010: 207). Earlier episodes of struggling banks could be ascribed to mismanagement at smaller banks under the radar of supervisory authorities: HRE threw a glaring spotlight on the inadequacy of financial regulation and supervision. Successive and massive bailout packages led to the de facto nationalization of the bank in October 2009. This met the dogged resistance of some shareholders. To the government the whole affair constituted a severe threat to its autonomy in dealing with financial emergencies. Its responsibility in the disaster came under intense scrutiny and a parliamentary committee investigating the affair garnered enormous media attention (Bundestag 2009). Clearly, the restructuring of banks had to be based on new legal procedures which minimized the risks for taxpayers and the threat to the stability of the financial system posed by systemically important financial institutions (SIFIs). Existing insolvency laws were not adequate for this task, since they protected shareholders from a so-called "bail-in." The need to socialize the costs of cases such as IKB or HRE (while the profits had been privatized in previous years) was considered explosive in terms of the legitimacy of the overall political system (Steinbrück 2010: 164). Thus, the most important objective of institutional reform in Germany after the crisis was to avoid bank rescue operations by the state that were financially and politically extremely costly, while at the same time the investors in these banks and their managers escaped political and financial liability. However, rather than attempting an overhaul of the existing system of banking regulation, the reform efforts focused on the more limited objective of avoiding another HRE and satisfying public calls for a legally binding mechanism which would ensure that managers and other stakeholders had to bear the cost of ill-judged investment decisions. Given these limited objectives of the reform and the fact that even the banking industry was calling for a stricter resolution regime, the reform was uncontroversial—as long as it did not impinge on the competences of the Länder. The following paragraphs trace the development of the so-called Restructuring Law from its beginnings as an emergency measure to save troubled banks during the height of the crisis, to a new institutional feature in the German regulatory landscape.

On October 5, 2008, the same day that Chancellor Merkel gave a guarantee with regard to all individual savings deposits, a distinguished group of people met at the Federal Chancellery: the state secretary in the Federal Chancellery Jens Weidmann, Finance Minister Peer Steinbrück and his state secretary Jörg Asmussen, Bundesbank president Axel Weber, the bosses of Deutsche Bank, Commerzbank and Allianz, and the president of the Federation of German Banks (*Bundesverband deutscher Banken,* BdB). Together they represented the major decision-makers in German financial regulation. According to Steinbrück (2010: 211) the goal of this meeting was to devise a quick solution for the stabilization of the German financial system. The immediate result was the German Financial Market Stabilisation Act of October 17, 2008. Its purpose was to restore confidence in the financial system and to jumpstart bank lending to businesses. Another immediate goal was to save systemically important banks—a task which many governments had to embark on in the hot days of autumn 2008.

For this purpose, the law set up a fund administered by a new Federal Agency for Financial Market Stabilization (FMSA). FMSA was established as a dependent agency under public law at the Bundesbank but it was kept organizationally separate from the central bank and supervised by the Ministry of Finance (BMF) because of its political nature. It was supposed to finance stabilization measures through the *Sonderfonds Finanzmarktstabilisierung* (SoFFin) which provided funding to banks in difficulties. This made the state co-owner of the banks which had recourse to these funds.[1] To an even larger extent (102 billion euros), SoFFin extended guarantees for loans of struggling banks, permitting them affordable refinancing on capital markets.[2] Originally, SoFFin was to be a short-term remedy, to be abolished at the end of 2009. However, the continuing stress in the German banking system required an extension until the end of 2010. This dateline also passed and instead of demise, SoFFin acquired new responsibilities, as shown below, resulting in another layering of institutions dealing with financial regulation. The perpetuation of this institution resulted from the government's attempt to reform its financial regulation in such a way as to avoid another HRE-type drama. The government felt misled by the HRE management and was confronted with recalcitrant stockholders resisting the takeover of the bank by the government.

On February 18, 2009, the Financial Market Stabilisation Act was supplemented by a provision which allowed the nationalization of failing SIFIs. Obviously, such a step evoked historical memories of expropriation. The government, amid a chorus of concerned voices, tried to avoid this extreme measure (NYT 2009). While this difficult debate was under way, the government asked the Federal Ministry of Justice, led by SPD minister Brigitte Zypries, and the Federal Ministry of Economics and Technology (BMWi) under CSU minister Theodor zu Guttenberg to draft a plan for the orderly restructuring of banks. With the electoral campaign in full swing, neither ministry was able to agree on a common plan. The BMWi plan was presented in early August 2009 and foresaw rapid nationalization of systemically important institutions in case they were threatened by insolvency (BMWi 2009). The plan was heavily criticized in

---

1 To date, the following banks have requested and received capital from SoFFin: Aareal Bank €0.38 billion; Commerzbank €18.2 billion; Hypo Real Estate Holding €7.7 billion; WestLB €3.0 billion. Overall, SoFFin has provided €29.28 billion (FMSA 2011).

2 HRE, IKB and HSH Nordbank are the biggest beneficiaries to date. In 2009 and 2010, SoFFin amassed annual losses of more than €4 billion.

the press because it was seen as too interventionist and because the draft was written by the private law firm Linklaters. Soon afterwards, Zypries and Finance Minister Steinbrück (SPD) presented their own plan which argued that in case of trouble the concerned bank and the supervisory agency BaFin would first try to negotiate a solution without proceeding towards government control of the bank. In case these talks achieved no result, the plan foresaw the separation of systemically important parts of the bank. These parts were then to be administered by SoFFin. The goal was to supplement the existing insolvency law in such a way as to preserve the autonomy of the state, without, however, resorting to expropriation as in the Guttenberg plan (Welt-Online, August 26, 2009). The plan was well received, but it was obvious that a proper law could be agreed on only after the federal elections of October 2009.

Despite the CDU/CSU and FDP majority resulting from this election, the Steinbrück/Zypries plan turned out to be the basis from which the new government proceeded. In March 2010, the cabinet approved a key-issues paper (BMF 2010a) which contained the outlines of the Federal Government's response to regulatory failures: the creation of an orderly procedure for the restructuring and wind-down of troubled banks, a bank levy to build up reserves for future emergencies, and new rules on the pay and conduct of employees of financial institutions. These plans were far from the radical overhaul demanded by the opposition parties, in particular *Bündnis 90/Die Grünen* und *Die Linke*.[3]

The cabinet meeting of March 2010 was attended by French Finance Minister Christine Lagarde. This was a signal that Germany would not step out of line with regard to parallel financial reform talks in the EU. In fact, the final restructuring act was very much along the lines proposed by the European Commission in May 2010 (Euractiv 2010). Contrary to the position of some EU countries, such as France, the United Kingdom and the Netherlands, which wanted to use a bank levy to bolster state budgets, Germany sided with the Commission in its demand that these funds should be used only for the purpose of bank restructuring. In July 2010, the government published a first draft for a bank restructuring law which fleshed out in detail the measures proposed in the key-issues paper (Bundestag 2010). The draft law (Act on the Reorganization of Credit Institutes or *Kreditinstitute-Reorganisationsgesetz*) stipulated specific procedures for the reorganization of such institutions. Among the core provisions were limits on the rights of minority shareholders of troubled banks to block a necessary restructuring procedure with reference to laws protecting the rights of stockowners. Shareholders could be forced to turn some of their investment into eq-

---

3 Both focussed particularly on a Europe-wide financial transaction tax. See: Bündnis90/Die Grünen (2008); Höll (2010).

uity, thus incurring high losses. The burden on the state and the taxpayer would be reduced while private shareholders would participate in the cost of failed investment strategies. Such an infringement of property rights (violating Article 14 of the German Constitution) was justified by the public interest of preventing a collapse of the financial system. In line with the Steinbrück/Zypries plan, troubled banks would first attempt their own restructuring process, under the supervision of a BaFin administrator. If this process failed, BaFin would be allowed to transfer assets to a "good bank" which could be sold. Investors would be left with the rest, a "bad bank" (*Financial Times* 2010). In addition to this procedure, a bank levy was introduced. Banks were expected to pay part of their profits into a restructuring fund with a target size of 70 billion euros. The levy on individual banks would vary in accordance with their liabilities and exposure to capital markets. The German bank levy was among the first in the OECD world, in accordance with IMF proposals from April 2010 (IMF 2010) and a Communication from the European Commission from May 2010 (European Commission 2010). Finally, the draft law provided for restrictions on the remuneration of employees in financial institutions in which the state had a stake.

The bank levy was originally a bone of contention between the CDU/CSU and the FDP. However, after similar ideas were discussed in other countries, in particular the United States, the FDP gave up its resistance (SZ 2010). Nonetheless, the levy attracted a lot of criticism. Most experts are highly skeptical about whether the target size of 70 billion euros would be reached anytime soon. However, the coalition argued that higher levies would cut too deeply into the earnings of many German banks which were characterized by fairly low productivity. The banking industry, notably Deutsche Bank and the BdB, strongly attacked the bank tax as well as new rules on the pay of top executives, alleging that German regulation went far beyond internationally envisioned rules (Wilson 2010). The BdB also lamented that actors such as the insurance industry and hedge funds were to be exempted (BdB 2010). However, their lobbying effort was futile (Öchsner/Bohsem 2010).

The Restructuring Law was pushed through parliamentary deliberations in the *Bundestag* and the *Bundesrat* with great haste. The opposition parties, which had tried to induce the government to establish a proper financial transaction tax (Tobin tax), sharply criticized the swift process. Overall, they agreed with the general purpose of the law. The hasty parliamentary procedure limited their chances, and those of other societal actors, to shape the content of the law. In October 2010, notwithstanding the protestations, the law speedily passed the Bundestag, with the SPD abstaining, and the Greens and Die Linke voting against the law because of its too lenient treatment of the banking industry.

However, the law also had to clear the hurdle of the Bundesrat which turned out to be much more difficult. The finance and economic committees of the upper chamber recommended suspending a vote on the law and instead to move it to a conciliation committee of the two chambers. The major contentious issue was the bank tax since it applied also to savings and mutual banks in which the Länder have a major voice through co-ownership and co-decision. These institutions argued vociferously that they should be exempted from the tax, because they had proven their resilience during the crisis and were now unfairly punished (Deutscher Sparkassen- und Giroverband 2010). Nonetheless, only public sector banks with specific mandates for public investment (such as the *Kreditanstalt für Wiederaufbau* and many Länder institutions) were exempted from the law.

In November 2010, the Bundesrat passed the law but only after having reserved for itself the right to have a say in the implementing legislation. Predictably, the formulation of implementing legislation caused new conflicts. In spring 2011, the Bundesrat tightened the rules on estimating the bank tax. It had turned out that Deutsche Bank, despite high profitability, would only pay a very small sum after using International Financial Reporting Standards (IFRS) to drastically reduce its reported income in Germany (Handelsblatt 2011a). Some Länder governments also once more demanded the exemption of smaller institutions, while the Federal Government argued that this would violate the constitutional principle of equal treatment. In July 2011, a compromise was reached between the Federal Government and those Länder with Grand Coalition governments: bigger banks would have to pay a higher percentage of their annual profits whereas small banks were exempted (Handelsblatt 2011b).

Since January 2011, the *Restrukturierungsgesetz* has been in force and broadens the competences of FMSA. In addition to SoFFin (which will give no new loans to banks), FMSA now also manages the restructuring fund, which will be filled with contributions from the new bank levy. The restructuring law also expands BaFin's competences with regard to preventive action. It can now declare failing banks "systemically important" which would then bring them under the remit of FMSA. This is an advance on the initial set-up of SoFFin which did not distinguish between systemically important and other banks (Sachverständigenrat 2010). However, such a decision will remain a political one. The restructuring law brought about institutional layering, with the new institution FMSA inserting itself uneasily between the previous two pillars of supervision, BaFin and the Bundesbank. FMSA is a new actor which might incrementally gain additional competences but it does not constitute a bold departure (and was never intended to become a new regulatory agency). It increases the number of actors in German financial regulation. Numerous grey areas in the competences of Ba-

Fin, Bundesbank, FMSA and BMF indicate the likelihood of a perpetuation of the institutional turf-wars characterizing financial regulation in the past decade.

Deposit insurance

On October 5, 2008, the German government extended a guarantee to all deposits of German savers. The potential amount encompassed by this guarantee was a staggering 600 billion euros, roughly double the size of the German state's annual tax revenue. Doubtless, this step was among the politically most relevant responses of the government to the crisis. A bank run similar to the one on Northern Rock in the United Kingdom would have potentially catastrophic consequences for the German financial system. The protection of savings is a core task of the state, particularly in a country with a savings rate as high as Germany's. The government guarantee on savings glaringly exposed the limitations of the existing national system of deposit insurance.

Deposit insurance mirrors the three-pillar structure of the German banking system. When the crisis erupted, no less than eight different deposit protection schemes existed, most of them private. The cooperative banks had already introduced a scheme in the 1930s; commercial and savings banks followed in the mid-1960s. In the mid-1970s, reacting to the bankruptcy of Herstatt bank, commercial banks introduced full-fledged deposit insurance guaranteeing individual deposits up to an amount of 30 percent of the core capital of each bank. Obviously, this entails potential sums which cannot be met during a systemic financial crisis. The fund is financed by the contributions of the over 180 member banks. Savings banks, including regional central banks, provide indirect insurance via a broad array of schemes which safeguard the viability of single banks. In case one bank fails, the other banks in the sector have to jump in. The scheme of the cooperative banks foresees 100 percent coverage, guaranteed by all member banks (BVR 2010a). These funds are used to bail out member banks in difficulties.[4] In addition to these private schemes, there is a guarantee by the state which used to cover up to 20,000 euros. In July 2009, the government legalized an augmentation of the state guarantee on private deposits to 50,000 euros, to be followed by another rise to 100,000 euros from January 2011 onward, in compliance with EU prescriptions.

After the collapse of IKB in 2007, which cost the fund of the private banks a hefty 925 million euros, Finance Minister Steinbrück commissioned a study on reform of the German deposit insurance system. According to this study, pub-

---

4 In 1998, in compliance with EU directives, deposit insurance was made compulsory for all private and public deposit institutions.

lished in early 2008, the conflicts about the recapitalization of IKB had shown that the fragmented system was inefficient and undercapitalized (Bigus/Leyens 2008). Consequently, it recommended centralization, forcing the three pillars to extend guarantees to each other (Drost 2010a). Predictably, the heads of the associations representing the three pillars strongly denounced the necessity of such a reform and pointed to the stability of their respective systems. Since nobody at that time felt enough urgency to take up this potentially controversial issue, the study was shelved.

Unsurprisingly, the Lehman collapse depleted the deposit insurance system of the BdB immediately, given its very high guarantee sums, unprecedented in Europe (Böhmcke 2009). When it had to reimburse the German victims of the Lehman collapse, the commercial banks had to have recourse to a 6.7 billion euro guarantee from SoFFin. Adding to this disaster, the press reported that the guarantee scheme was already in a critical condition well before the crisis toppled it, possibly since 2001 (Frühauf 2009). In August 2009, the BdB decided to double the contribution of its members, but it was obvious that the fundamental problem persisted. The protection scheme of the savings banks and Landesbanken was overwhelmed by the losses incurred by banks such as WestLB. The Länder and the Federal Government, again via SoFFin, had to extend huge guarantees. The only deposit insurance system which withstood the crisis was that of the cooperative sector which was able to stabilize two struggling members *(Deutsche Zentral-Genossenschaftsbank* and *Apotheker- und Ärztebank)* without aid from the state.

These obvious deficiencies of the German deposit insurance schemes gave proponents of reform powerful arguments. The BdB president, Andreas Schmitz, publicly called in late 2009 for a reform of the system along the lines of the 2008 Steinbrück idea, suggesting that not only the private banking sector but also the savings and cooperative banks should join a centralized scheme (Frühauf 2009). The FDP, usually an advocate of consolidation at the Federal level, supported such a position which would have resulted in a concentration of deposit insurance (Drost 2010). It was also in accordance with an EU-wide plan published by the internal market commissioner, Michel Barnier, in July 2010, which recommended harmonized and centralized deposit protection schemes across Europe (FT 2010). However, the cooperative and local savings banks strongly came out against such an EU-wide scheme because it would have been introduced in addition to their scheme and therefore would have caused high additional costs (BVR 2010b). In September, both government parties had come round to the position of the savings and cooperative banks. The Bundesrat took the same stance but even more strongly, accusing the Commission of violating the subsidiarity principle (Drost/Menzel 2010). As it did during the Basel III negotiations, Germany staunchly protected its decentralized banking system. Supported by Austria and MEPs, the Germans were able to block those parts of EU legislation which endangered the deposit protection schemes of the savings and cooperative banks (FAZ 2011). In late 2010, the Commission caved in to the demand for the preservation of these schemes; however, it demanded that the Landesbanken should not be included. In all likelihood, this would have been the end of the Landesbanken (Stock/Drost 2010). Influential economists demanded that this chance should be used to finally push the Landesbanken towards a more sustainable business model (Hilgert et al. 2011). To date, however, the Landesbanken are still covered by the overall deposit protection scheme of the savings banks. The regulation of deposit insurance exemplifies once more the resilience of German institutions, even in the case of obvious inefficiencies and strong EU objections. Political actors were able to stop any meaningful reform.

Failed supervisory reform

The crisis also turned out to challenge the German supervisory system, which had been tampered with on an on-and-off basis since the 1990s (Frach 2010). From 2002, the system rested on a two-pillar structure constituted by the German Bundesbank and the single supervisory authority the *Bundesanstalt für Finanzdienstleistungsaufsicht* (BaFin). The establishment of BaFin, which is responsible for the supervision of the whole financial sector, was a reaction to the rising importance of new financial products and the inefficiencies of the existing supervising structure (Frach 2008: 74–83). In 2002, the coalition government of the Social Democrats and the Green Party merged three formerly separated supervisory institutions and created BaFin following the model of the British Financial Services Authority.

The liberal-conservative government of Christian Democrats (CDU) and Free Democrats (FDP), which took office at the end of 2009, announced in its coalition agreement the intention to reshuffle the existing supervisory structure. Administrative failures were seen as a major element in the belated response of supervisory authorities to the serious over-leverage of many financial institutions (Mülbert 2010). One central element of this reform was supposed to be the concentration of banking supervision under the roof of the Deutsche Bundesbank (Coalition Agreement 2009). According to the *Kreditwesengesetz* (§7 KWG), the Bundesbank and BaFin shared competences in banking supervision. BaFin represented the single supervisory authority, answerable to political oversight (see §2 FinDAG [*Gesetz über die Bundesanstalt für Finanzdienstleistungsaufsicht*];

FTD 2010b), whereas the central bank was responsible for on-site inspections. Although organized as a single supervisor, BaFin has three different directorates for the supervision of banks, insurances and securities firms and a fourth directorate which deals with cross-sectoral tasks. Removing banking supervision from its remit would have seriously downgraded the importance of BaFin. The plan of the new coalition was an attempt to cut the agency's competences and its alleged growth in power during the previous years (Handke 2010). This increasing influence of the agency was due not only to BaFin's strong domestic position as a single supervisor, but also to its increasing involvement in transnational networks which gave it more autonomy in management and implementation matters than politically intended (Döhler 2006). Another demand of BaFin critics—that it be brought physically closer to the government by relocating it from Bonn to Berlin—was not tackled. Bonn was the constituency of the FDP party leader Guido Westerwelle who feared the anger of almost 2,000 employees and their families. Nonetheless, the mere suggestion of removing banking supervision from BaFin's remit caused a major debate in the following months.

After the coalition plans became public, the Bundesbank moved quickly, sensing a major opportunity to expand its range of tasks after its loss of importance due to the introduction of a common European currency. Bundesbank president Axel Weber presented the so-called "integration model" *(Integrationsmodell)*, in which the Bundesbank was to become the only authority to supervise banks, insurance companies, and other financial service firms (Frankfurter Rundschau 2009). The integration of BaFin into the structure of the Bundesbank would have demoted the agency to an appendix of the central bank, with minor competences in consumer protection and market supervision. Of course, BaFin resisted these plans. It was supported by the insurance industry which rejected the idea of being supervised by the Bundesbank, an alleged ally of the banking business (GDV 2009). It also quickly became clear that the integration of BaFin, which was under legal and technical oversight of the Federal Ministry of Finance, would pose thorny questions with regard to the hallowed independence of the central bank.

In March 2010, Leo Dautzenberg, the Finance Spokesman *(Finanzpolitischer Sprecher)* of the CDU/CSU faction in the Bundestag, proposed a so-called "holding model" *(Holding-Modell)* as an alternative option, which would have maintained BaFin as one pillar of a newly created Bundesbank holding (Wallstreet-Online 2010a). The model sought to unite BaFin, the central bank, and the newly created SoFFin under the roof of this holding, which would have been headed by an executive board of the representatives of all three pillars. Within the holding, not only the structure of BaFin as the single supervisory authority—including the authority to supervise banks—would have been maintained, but also the ministerial oversight over the whole supervisory pillar. This part of the model conflicted with the self-conception of the central bank as the independent guardian of the stability of the financial system (Bundesbank 2007). Therefore, the central bank strongly opposed this model. It was supported by the FDP, which disapproved of ministerial oversight over the central bank (Handelsblatt 2010b).

During the debate, which lasted for one year, each model pretended to enhance the efficiency of supervision by abolishing the dual system with split competences between BaFin and the Bundesbank. However, the goal of "efficiency" was not operationalized and therefore remained an empty term. Specific ways of promoting better performance or the problem-solving capacity of supervision were not defined. The advantages of pooling competences under the roof of the Bundesbank could not be derived from objective evaluations or the observation of administrative deficits (Hartmann-Wendels 2011). Much of the debate became couched in legal terms. The question was raised concerning whether a merger of banking supervision under the roof of the Bundesbank was in line with the German Constitution. Some financial law experts doubted that the plan of the governing coalition could have been realized without changing the German Basic Law (*Grundgesetz* or GG), since according to §88 GG the Bundesbank is not authorized to perform sovereign acts such as shutting down a bank (Häde 2009; FTD 2010a). However, this legal argumentation against reform does not explain actors' strategic behavior. Basically, questions of political influence dominated and issues of efficiency or legal appropriateness were only of secondary importance (Hartmann-Wendels 2009; Interview CDU 2010; Interview FDP 2010).[5] This is best expressed by the dissent between the FDP and the CDU on the question of ministerial oversight over BaFin and the Bundesbank. Whilst the CDU—including the CDU finance minister—was willing to submit parts of the central bank to such oversight, the FDP was the guardian of the Bundesbank's independence. Parts of the CDU were keen to implement ideas they had held for a long time and to kill two birds with one stone: on the one hand, the reduction of BaFin's power and on the other hand, getting a foot in the door of the central bank, at least in supervisory matters (FAZnet 2009).

At the end of 2010, the government gave up its far-reaching goals and presented a vague ten-point plan which intended modifications of the existing supervisory structure with divided responsibilities between BaFin, SoFFin, and the Bundesbank. Apart from the announced further development of macroprudential supervision, the plan promises that the relationship between the

---

5 In 2010 and 2011, one of the authors (S. Handke) conducted structured interviews with representatives of political parties and the BMF. The interviewees requested anonymity.

three administrative bodies and the exclusive tasks of BaFin were to be defined more clearly (Dautzenberg et al. 2010). However, as of 2011 there is still no organizational change in comparison to the supervisory structure of 2008 and the announced reforms are nothing more than abstract political declarations of intent, which may be picked up in the future (Bundestag 2011). Thus, the opportunity to reorganize the German supervisory system was missed, although the financial market crisis had opened a wide policy window for significant change. Irreconcilable differences between the central actors—especially BaFin, the Bundesbank, the BMF, and political parties—obliterated the chance of establishing a common position on which supervisory reform could have been based.

The major reasons for the failure of the reform lay in politics and the fact that BaFin, the Bundesbank, and each of the three supervisory models were backed by different partisan veto-players. During the debate those veto-players were the governing parties, the CDU, the CSU, and the FDP, which had to agree on a unanimous policy position for any change in the supervisory status quo. Remarkably, the line of conflict was drawn not between government and opposition parties but among the coalition partners themselves. After it was voted out of office, the SPD, which had been instrumental in creating BaFin, was not really interested in the fairly arcane debate on supervisory reform.

The differences among the governing parties were widened by splits among interest groups. The financial industry was not able to agree on a unanimous position with regard to the three solutions on the table: the coalition agreement, the integration model, and the holding model. The banking sector with its Association of German Banks (BdB) was in favor of a model which would have given the sole responsibility for banking supervision to the Bundesbank (Schmitz 2010). Initially, the CDU/CSU and FDP government predominantly focused on the banking business as the most affected branch of the financial sector. Consequently, the coalition agreement of 2009 took into consideration the specific interests of the banking industry, which conceded the improvement of regulation and supervision, but insisted on the single banking supervision under the roof of the Bundesbank (Bundestag 2009). The insurance industry, however, opposed the government's plan of concentrating banking supervision at the expense of BaFin, as well as the integration model and the holding model since the branch expected to be worse off when supervised by the Bundesbank (GDV 2009). They feared that insurance interests—for example, specific internal risk models and softer capital requirements—could be violated by the dominant bank-centered perspective of banking supervisors. Consequently, not only the GDV but also the giants of the insurance industry, Munich Re and Allianz, lobbied against the government's reform plans (Afhüppe 2010).

Apart from the industry, the affected administrative bodies pursued their own interests. In accordance with a political economy perspective on organizational behavior (see, for example, Downs 1967; Blais/Dion 1990) it can be assumed that the BMF, BaFin, and the Bundesbank as bureaucratic organizations share distinctive preferences. All three try to keep their institutions alive and foster their growth in terms of staff and budget (Niskanen 1979). Despite similar strategic orientations they nonetheless had to expect quite different support in the political sphere. Although BaFin had no strong institutional support, it survived. Dissent among the coalition parties and in the industry was enough to kill any proposal.

Neither the CDU nor the FDP were able to force a decision in favor of one of the three models since opinions also differed widely between and within the political parties. In sum, the reform failed because political parties as veto-players did not dare to jeopardize their good relations with either the financial industry or influential and important executive bodies, since the consequences of reform were incalculable and did not guarantee success (Drost 2010a; Wallstreet-Online 2010b). No single reform model was supported by either the whole financial industry or BaFin and the Bundesbank together and therefore none of them gained a majority among the governing parties in parliament (Interview BMF 2011). This is why in the end the old institutions persisted.

Despite the failure of the reform of the overall supervisory structure, the crisis constituted an opportunity for functional changes, for example adding new tasks to the remit of BaFin or modified procedures. However, the internal organization of BaFin has not yet been revised. There have been attempts to alleviate one of BaFin's main problems, the lack of qualified staff, granting it more than 240 additional employees in 2011 (BaFin 2010a). But it is still a severe problem to find trained staff for the supervisory authority, which is bound by collective wage agreements and salary laws and which therefore has problems competing with well-paying banks and insurers. The challenge of recruitment concerns every hierarchical level, from the basic units up to the top positions (FTD 2011). The debate on BaFin's future has probably exacerbated the difficulties of recruitment, as top candidates might have been deterred from entering an agency with an uncertain future.

Apart from personnel matters the implementation of supervision is important. While it is not clear whether BaFin now performs its supervisory tasks more strictly than before the crisis, the agency was at least given more preventive enforcement powers, such as the competence to evaluate the qualifications of members of the supervisory boards and boards of directors of financial institutions (§36 para. 3 KWG). Additionally, BaFin has the right to impose tighter capital requirements (§10 para. 1b KWG) and surcharges on the liquidity (§11

Figure 1   Number of annual supervisory activities and IFG obligations, BaFin

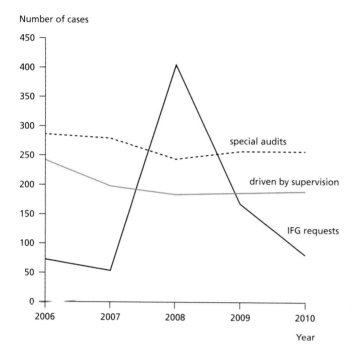

Number of cases

Source: Author's own illustration based on BaFin's annual report 2007–2010.

para. 2 KWG) of individual institutions. In the wake of the latest crisis BaFin has obtained the legal authority to take such measures against a bank or an insurer even when there is merely an assumed violation of solvency requirements (§45 para. 1 KWG). Despite this expansion of competences, which constitutes institutional layering in terms of "adding instruments" (Van der Heijden 2011: 14), the focus is mainly on the micro-prudential level. This is fairly demanding in terms of professional skills and manpower, since BaFin has to perform duties such as on-site inspections and the review of (internal) risk models. Against this background, it is not surprising that supervisory activities have not expanded quantitatively. In the banking sector, for instance, BaFin conducts so-called *Sonderprüfungen* (special audits), which are demanded by law on a regular basis, requested by an institution to approve internal risk models, or driven by BaFin's investigatory needs (BaFin 2010b). Between 2006 and 2010, the total number of annual audits did not increase, as can be seen in Figure 1. The stable number of BaFin-driven audits is particularly noteworthy, since an increasing number of bank failures and default risks should have led to an increasing number of special audits, but this is not confirmed by the data. The absence of extended auditing may be a consequence of BaFin's limited personnel capacities, which did not allow for more inspections even in the case of a severe crisis and the intended tightening of regulation and supervision. Even so, the workload increased due to BaFin's further obligations, which are not an integral part of its supervisory tasks. For one thing, the number of requests for information on the basis of the Freedom of Information Act *(Informationsfreiheitsgesetz, IFG)* rose dramatically. While there were 72 requests in 2006, BaFin had to answer 407 in 2008 (BaFin 2007, 2009). The legal obligation to supply every applicant with the requested information is a time- and resource-consuming duty for BaFin, which can be met only at the expense of others.

The empirical data indicate that supervision in terms of auditing and sanctioning was not tightened during the crisis, since the agency was not able to expand its capabilities at short notice. With some new supervisory competences just a thin institutional layer was added. Hence neither an organizational reform of the supervisory structure nor a radical functional improvement of BaFin's capacities took place. Officially, the supervisory reform was postponed due to other urgent tasks in financial market regulation (Handelsblatt 2010a), but in the end it was simply cancelled without any explanatory statement and the political debate ended abruptly, adjourning the topic *sine die* (Henrich 2010). Fundamental change will, in all likelihood, result only from external pressure: the establishment of a European Banking Authority with far-reaching competences will have a deep impact on national supervisory structures.

Conclusion

This description of institutional change in German financial regulation and supervision has shown that German institutions turned out to be quite resilient despite the upheavals in the markets during the crisis and the breakneck speed of financial innovation in recent decades. Instead of completely reforming and transforming existing institutions, the German system has adapted slowly and rather out of sync with financial market developments, whether this concerned the years prior to the crisis when regulation seemed to work reasonably well and the main target was the so-called "excesses of Anglo-American capitalism" or the crisis shock of 2008. The most frequent patterns of change took the form of institutional layering and drift: while the need for a restructuring regime for banks and closer controls on financial elites led to the establishment of new

institutions, existing structures remained in place despite a partial loss of significance. Even obvious failures, such as in the cases of market supervision and
deposit insurance, did not lead to the abolition of existing institutions. Instead,
new agencies such as FSMA and new committees, such as a reconciliation committee for supervisory authorities, were added to the existing set-up. Institutional drift in which some institutions lost importance but survived while others
assumed new functions was another important mode of institutional change.
This is, for example, the case with the Landesbanken, the Bundesbank's supervisory department, or pre-crisis insolvency laws.

The political space for reforms remained rather small, although technocrats
in the concerned ministries and the regulatory agencies promoted their own
reform agenda and developments in the European Union again and again constituted an incentive for pre-emptive and post-facto adaptation. The main reason for this slow adaptation seems to be the nexus of the political economy
of finance in Germany, with the existence of a multilevel polity, represented
in particular by the Länder governments. Financial regulation and supervision
was up against the realities of Germany's federal structure which also enhances
the resilience of the traditional bank-based system. Both financial actors and
their regulators are battling to preserve their organizational identities. They are
backed by regional and local constituents who then bring their influence to bear
on the parties. The endless debate about the reform of the Landesbanken is a
prime example. Germany's big financial firms have close links to and are coveted
by their regional sponsors, as are predominantly regionally based savings and
cooperative banks. Financial regulation and supervision inevitably touches these
entrenched interests, leading to conflicts among and within parties, and frequently, if proposals are not killed beforehand and in anticipation of Bundesrat
opposition, to ultimate demise in the upper chamber. Slow incremental change,
as the major adaptive strategy, reflects not only the interlocked nature of German decision making in financial regulation, but also the continuing parallel
persistence of traditional and new forms of financial market structures.

References

Afhüppe, Sven, 2010: Regierung verschleppt Reform der Finanzaufsicht. In: *Handelsblatt*, January 11.
BaFin (Bundesanstalt für Finanzdienstleistungsaufsicht), 2007: *Jahresbericht der Bundesanstalt für
Finanzdienstleistungsaufsicht '06.* Bonn: BaFin.
——, 2008: *Jahresbericht der Bundesanstalt für Finanzdienstleistungsaufsicht '07.* Bonn: BaFin.
——, 2009: *Jahresbericht der Bundesanstalt für Finanzdienstleistungsaufsicht '08.* Bonn: BaFin.

BaFin, 2010a: *BaFin: Verwaltungsrat verabschiedet Haushaltsplan 2011.* <www.bafin.de/cln_179/ nn_722802/SharedDocs/Mitteilungen/DE/Service/PM__2010/pm__101125__ver- wrat__stellen.html>

———, 2010b: *Jahresbericht der Bundesanstalt für Finanzdienstleistungsaufsicht '09.* Bonn: BaFin.

———, 2011: *Jahresbericht der Bundesanstalt für Finanzdienstleistungsaufsicht '10.* Bonn: BaFin.

BdB (Bundesverband deutscher Banken), 2010: *Bankenverband Pressemitteilung zur Bankenabgabe und Restrukturierungsgesetz,* August 25. <www.bankenverband.de/presse/presse-infos/ bankenverband-zur-bankenabgabe-und-zum-restrukturierungsgesetz/?searchterm=bank enabgabe>

Bigus, Jochen/Patrick Leyens, 2008: *Einlagensicherung und Anlegerentschädigung: Reformüberlegungen aus ökonomischer und rechtsvergleichender Sicht.* Tübingen: Mohr Siebeck.

Blais, André/Stéphane Dion, 1990: Are Bureaucrats Budget Maximizers? The Niskanen Model and Its Critics. In: *Polity* 22, 655–674.

BMF (Bundesministerium für Finanzen), 2010a: *Key-issues Paper: Preventing Crises with Banks Paying Their Due,* March 31. <www.bundesfinanzministerium.de/nn_103342/EN/Topics/ Financial-markets/Articles/20100816-Key-issues-paper-Preventing-crises-with-banks. html?__nnn=true>

———, 2010b: *Finanzmarktsteuer: Modelle im Vergleich.* <www.bundesfinanzministerium.de/ DE/Wirtschaft__und__Verwaltung/Steuern/20100526__Finanzmarktsteuer.html>

———, 2010c: *Finanzmarktregulierung: Wie geht's voran?* <www.bundesfinanzministerium. de/DE/Buergerinnen__und__Buerger/Gesellschaft__und__Zukunft/finanzkrise/ 20100730-Finanzmarktregulierung.html>

BMWi (Bundesministerium für Wirtschaft und Technologie), 2009: *Gesetzentwurf zur Ergänzung des Kreditwesengesetzes.* <www.bmwi.de/BMWi/Redaktion/PDF/Gesetz/entwurf- gesetz-ergaenzung-des-kreditwesengesetzes,property=pdf,bereich=bmwi,sprache=de,rw b=true.pdf>

Böhmcke, Nikolaus, 2009: *Experteninterview: Reform des Einlagensicherungsfonds dringend nötig,* December 1. <www.wiwo.de/finanzen/reform-des-einlagensicherungsfonds-dringend- noetig-415675/>

Bundestag, 2009: *Beschlussempfehlung und Bericht des 2. Untersuchungsausschusses nach Artikel 44 des Grundgesetzes* (HRE-Untersuchungsausschuss). Bundestagsdrucksache 16/14000, September 18.

———, 2010: *Entwurf eines Gesetzes zur Restrukturierung und geordneten Abwicklung von Kreditinstituten, zur Errichtung eines Restrukturierungsfonds für Kreditinstitute und zur Verlängerung der Verjährungsfrist der aktienrechtlichen Organhaftung (Restrukturierungsgesetz).* Bundestagsdrucksache 17/3024, September 27.

———, 2011: *Effektive Regulierung der Finanzmärkte nach der Finanzkrise.* Bundestagsdrucksache 17/6313, June 29.

Bundesbank, 2007: *The Tasks of the Bundesbank.* <www.bundesbank.de/aufgaben/aufgaben_ aufgaben.en.php>

Bündnis 90/Die Grünen, 2008: *Finanzmärkte besser Regulieren – Krisen künftig vermeiden.* Antrag der Abgeordneten Schick et. al, Bundestag, 16. Wahlperiode. Bundestagsdrucksache 16441, December 16.

BVR (Bundesverband der Deutschen Volks- und Raiffeisenbanken), 2010a: *Statut der Sicherungseinrichtung.* <www.bvr.de>

BVR, 2010b: *BVR zum Entwurf einer Einlagensicherungsrichtlinie,* 12 July. <www.bvr.de/p.nsf/index.html?ReadForm&main=0&sub=10&ParentUNID=1B030A401018621DC125775E003CC7FA>

Coalition Agreement, 2009: *Wachstum, Bildung, Zusammenhalt, Koalitionsvertrag zwischen der CDU, CSU und FDP,* October 26. <www.cdu.de/doc/pdfc/091026-koalitionsvertrag-cducsufdp.pdf>

Dautzenberg, Leo/Bartholomäus Kalb/Michael Meister, 2010: *Koalition einig über Reform der nationalen Finanzaufsicht.* Press Release of the CDU/CSU, December 16. <www.cducsu.de/Titel__pressemitteilung_koalition_einig_ueber_reform_der_nationalen_finanzaufsicht/TabID__6/SubTabID__7/InhaltTypID__1/InhaltID__17465/Inhalte.aspx>

Deutscher Sparkassen- und Giroverband, 2010: *Stellungnahme zum Referentenentwurf eines Gesetzes zur Restrukturierung und geordneten Abwicklung von Kreditinstituten,* July 19.

Döhler, Marian, 2006: Regulative Politik und die Transformation der klassischen Verwaltung. In: Jörg Bogumil/Werner Jann/Frank Nullmeier (eds.), *Politik und Verwaltung: Auf dem Weg zu einer postmanagerialen Verwaltungsforschung.* Politische Vierteljahresschrift, Special Issue 37. Wiesbaden: VS Verlag, 208–227.

Downs, Anthony, 1967: *Inside Bureaucracy.* Boston: Little, Brown and Company.

Drost, Frank M., 2010a: Streit über Reform der Einlagensicherung. In: *Handelsblatt,* January 17.

——, 2010b: Reform auf Abwegen. In: *Handelsblatt,* May 17.

Drost, Frank M./Stefan Menzel, 2010: Streit über den Schutz der Sparer. In: *Handelsblatt,* September 30.

Euractiv, 2010: *EU Proposes 'Preventive' Bank Levy,* May 26. <www.euractiv.com>

European Commission, 2010: *Communication to the EP, the Council, the European Social and Economic Committee, and the ECB,* COM (2010) 254 final, May 26.

FAZ (Frankfurter Allgemeine Zeitung), 2011: EU reformiert Sparerschutz, June 20.

FAZnet, 2009: Union will angeblich Bafin in Bundesbank integrieren, June 22. <www.faz.net/artikel/C30770/bankenaufsicht-aus-einer-hand-union-will-angeblich-bafin-in-bundesbank-integrieren-30135460.html>

FT (Financial Times), 2010: Berlin to Make Debtholders Carry Greater Burden, November 24.

FMSA (Bundesanstalt für Finanzmarktstabilisierung), 2011: *Stabilisierungsmaßnahmen des SoFFin.* <www.fmsa.de/de/fmsa/soffin/instrumente/massnahmen-aktuell/>

Frach, Lotte, 2008: *Finanzaufsicht in Deutschland und Großbritannien.* Wiesbaden: VS Verlag.

——, 2010: *Finanzmarktregulierung in Deutschland.* Baden-Baden: Nomos.

Frankfurter Rundschau, 2009: Bundesbank will BaFin entmachten. In: *Frankfurter Rundschau,* October 5.

Frühauf, Markus, 2009: *Banken wollen Einlagensicherung reformieren.* In: *FAZnet,* November 24. <www.faz.net/artikel/C30770/geldanlage-banken-wollen-einlagensicherung-reformieren-30073474.html>

FTD (Financial Times Deutschland), 2010a: Regierung vor Einigung zur Finanzaufsicht, March 18.

——, 2010b: Streit um Finanzaufsicht: Bundesbank will das letzte Wort haben, April 10.

——, 2011: Personal verzweifelt gesucht, May 9.

Gesamtverband der Deutschen Versicherungswirtschaft, 2009: *Positionen zur nationalen Finanzaufsichtsarchitektur: Versicherungsaufsicht in der Verantwortung der Deutschen Bundesbank und Trennung von Solvenz- von Marktaufsicht?* <www.gdv.de/Downloads/Themen/Position_Aufsicht_141009.pdf>

Haar, Brigitte, 2010: Das deutsche Ausführungsgesetz zur EU-Rating-Verordnung: Zwischenetappe auf dem Weg zu einer europäischen Finanzmarktarchitektur. In: *Zeitschrift für Bankrecht und Bankwirtschaft* 22(33), 185–193.

Häde, Ulrich, 2009: Bankenaufsicht aus einer Hand? – Rechtsfragen einer Neuordnung. In: *Zeitschrift für das gesamte Kreditwesen* 2/2009, 10–11.

Handelsblatt, 2010a: Regierung verschleppt Reform der Finanzaufsicht, January 11.

——, 2010b: Rolle rückwärts bei Finanzaufsicht, November 29.

——, 2011a: Ackermann wettert gegen Bankenabgabe, June 1.

——, 2011b: Roundup: Bund-Länder Kompromiss zur Bankenabgabe, July 8. <www.handelsblatt.com/roundup-bund-laender-kompromiss-zur-bankenabgabe/4380940.html>

Handke, Stefan, 2010: Yes, We Can (Control Them)! – Regulatory Agencies: Trustees or Agents? In: *Goettingen Journal of International Law* 2(1), 111–134.

Hartmann-Wendels, Thomas, 2009: Bankenaufsicht: Konzentration bei der Bundesbank. In: *Wirtschaftsdienst* 89(11), 713–714.

——, 2011: Reform der Bankenaufsicht: Vertane Chance. In: *Wirtschaftsdienst* 91(1), 4.

Henrich, Anke, 2010: Die Reform der Bankenaufsicht ist ein Reinfall. In: *Wirtschaftswoche,* December 21.

Hilgert, Heinz, et al., 2011: *Streitschrift für eine grundlegende Neuordnung des Sparkassen- und Landesbankensektors in Deutschland.* Institute for Monetary and Financial Stability, Working Paper 42/2011. Frankfurt a.M: Institute for Monetary and Financial Stability.

Höll, Barbara, 2010: *Eine vollkommene Finanzmarktregulierung sieht anders aus! Rede vor dem Bundestag,* October 2. <www.barbara-hoell.de/nc/standpunkte/detail/browse/1/zurueck/media/artikel/eine-vollkommene-finanzmarktregulierung-sieht-anders-aus/>

IMF (International Monetary Fund), 2010: *A Fair and Substantial Contribution by the Financial Sector.* Interim Report for the G20, April 16.

Lütz, Susanne, 2004: Von der Infrastruktur zum Markt? Der deutsche Finanzsektor zwischen Deregulierung und Reregulierung. In: Paul Windolf (ed.), *Finanzmarkt-Kapitalismus.* Kölner Zeitschrift für Soziologie und Sozialpsychologie, Special Issue 45. Wiesbaden: VS Verlag, 294–315.

Mülbert, Peter, 2010: Finanzmarktregulierung – Welche Regelung empfehlen sich für den deutschen und europäischen Finanzsektor? In: *Juristenzeitung* 65(17), 834–843.

New York Times, 2009: In Germany, Nationalization Issue Carries Weight of History, November 7. <www.nytimes.com/2009/02/17/business/worldbusiness/17iht-hypo.4.20257846.html>

——, 2010: Germany Drafts Wider Ban on Speculative Trades, May 26. <www.nytimes.com/2010/05/26/business/global/26naked.html>

Niskanen, William, 1979: Ein ökonomisches Modell der Bürokratie. In: Werner W. Pommerehne/Bruno S. Frey (eds.), *Ökonomische Theorie der Politik.* Berlin: Springer, 349–369.

Öchsner, Thomas/Guido Bohsem, 2010: Wirtschaft läuft gegen Bankenabgabe Sturm. In: *Süddeutsche Zeitung,* March 28.

RP-Online (Rheinische Post), 2008: Interview mit Guido Westerwelle: Die Bankenaufsicht hat versagt, October 20. <www.rp-online.de/politik/deutschland/Die-Bankenaufsicht-hat-versagt_aid_628019.html>

Sachverständigenrat, 2010: *Jahresgutachten 2010/11: Chancen für einen stabilen Aufschwung.* Wiesbaden: Statistisches Bundesamt.

Schmitz, Andreas, 2010: *Welche Lehren aus der Krise sind gezogen?* Berlin: Bundesverband deutsche Banken. <www.bankenverband.de/bundesverband-deutscher-banken/presse/vortraege-statements/pressekonferenz-anlaesslich-der-vorstandssitzung-des-bundesverbandes-deutscher-banken-3>

Schrooten, Mechthild, 2009: Landesbanken: Zukunft ungewiss. In: *Wirtschaftsdienst* 10, 666–671.

Spiegel-Online, 2010: WestLB und BayernLB lassen Fusion platzen, November 4. <www.spiegel.de/wirtschaft/unternehmen/0,1518,727218,00.html>

Steinbrück, Peer, 2010: *Unterm Strich.* Hamburg: Hoffmann & Campe.

Stock, Oliver/Frank M. Drost, 2010: Todesstoß für die Landesbanken? In: *Handelsblatt,* November 17.

Streeck, Wolfgang, 2009: *Re-Forming Capitalism: Institutional Change in the German Political Economy.* New York: Oxford University Press.

Streeck, Wolfgang/Martin Höpner (eds.), 2003: *Alle Macht dem Markt? Fallstudien zur Abwicklung der Deutschland AG.* Frankfurt a.M.: Campus.

Streeck, Wolfgang/Kathleen Thelen (eds.), 2005: *Beyond Continuity: Institutional Change in Advanced Political Economies.* Oxford: Oxford University Press.

SZ (Süddeutsche Zeitung), 2010: Banken sollen sich selbst retten, March 23, 23.

Thelen, Kathleen, 2003: How Institutions Evolve: Insights from Comparative-historical Analysis. In: James Mahoney/Dietrich Rueschemeyer (eds.), *Comparative Historical Analysis in the Social Sciences.* New York: Cambridge University Press, 208–240.

Tsebelis, George, 2002: *Veto Players: How Political Institutions Work.* Princeton: Princeton University Press.

Van der Heijden, Jeroen, 2011: Institutional Layering: A Review of the Use of the Concept. In: *Politics* 31(1), 9–18.

Wallstreet-Online, 2010a: Finanzaufsicht – Holding-Modell: Regierung kurz vor Einigung, March 19. <www.wallstreet-online.de/nachrichten/nachricht/2914030-finanzaufsicht-holding-modell-regierung-kurz-vor-einigung.html>

——, 2010b: Reform der Bankenaufsicht: Union steuert auf Grundsatzkonflikt mit Bundesbank zu, October 18. <www.wallstreet-online.de/nachricht/3034146-reform-der-bankenaufsicht-union-steuert-auf-grundsatzkonflikt-mit-bundesbank-zu>

Welt-Online, 2009: Zypries attackiert Guttenbergs Bankenrettungsplan, August 26. <www.welt.de/wirtschaft/article4401400/Zypries-attackiert-Guttenbergs-Banken rettungsplan.html>

Wilson, James, 2010: German Bankers in Attack on Regulations. In: *Financial Times,* October 26.

Zimmermann, Hubert, 2008: *Controlling the Locusts: Germany and the Global Governance of New Financial Markets.* Mario Einaudi Center for International Studies Working Paper 1-08. Ithaca: Cornell University, Mario Einaudi Center for International Studies.

——, 2009: Varieties of Global Financial Governance? British and German Approaches to Financial Market Regulation. In: Eric Helleiner/Stefano Pagliari/Hubert Zimmermann (eds.), *Global Finance in Crisis.* London: Routledge, 121–136.

Interviews

Interview CDU, 2010: Member of the German Bundestag, CDU; Member of the Parliamentary Finance Committee, June 22.

Interview FDP, 2010: Member of the German Bundestag, FDP; Member of the Parliamentary Finance Committee, July 15.

Interview BMF, 2011: Middle Management Level Representatives of the Department for Financial Market Policy, August 8.

6
Increasing Vulnerability: Financial Market Regulation in Switzerland

Simon Steinlin and Christine Trampusch

Introduction

In this chapter, we reconstruct institutional change in the governance of the Swiss financial market before and since 2007. Due to critical press accounts, it is well known that, in the past few years, Switzerland has felt increasing pressure from outside. The tax struggles with the OECD, the EU and Germany, the banking secrecy crisis and the UBS affair in the United States have been ongoing themes on the international political agenda, dominating Switzerland's external relations. After decades of continuity, since 2007/2008 Swiss financial market regulation has been on a new trajectory, which we call "increasing vulnerability." Exogenous pressure and the internationalization of financial markets have long been serious challenges for Swiss financial market regulation. But since the financial crisis, the near breakdown of UBS, and the international pressure on Swiss banks and banking secrecy, the Swiss government has increasingly acknowledged that Switzerland has to adapt its financial system to changing external environments in order to maintain international competitiveness. Thus, even though Switzerland is to a large degree still willing to protect its regulatory peculiarities, the crisis has affected the policy preferences and strategies of the Swiss government, which is increasingly adapting its regulatory agenda to international demands.

As we shall argue, change in Swiss financial market institutions (capital market and banking sector) is traditionally and mainly prompted by international influences (for a similar argument, see Mach et al. 2007; Strahm 2009: 15); that is, by the internationalization and liberalization of financial markets, on the one hand, and by international political pressure, on the other. But while in other countries the financial market architecture has shifted towards stronger regulation, Switzerland until 2007 largely maintained its corporatist self-regulatory model, with little rule-making power on the part of the government, parliament, and political parties with regard to financial policy. The main reason for this resilience is a coalition between the government and the financial industry that defends the traditional governance structure. However, during the financial crisis the Swiss financial market has been confronted with new challenges. The Swiss government seems to have become more aware of Switzerland's dependence on developments in international markets and of the political risks of being a special case *(Sonderfall)*. As a result, the principles of self-regulation and banking secrecy have lost some of their political legitimacy. The government has therefore shown increasing willingness to reform financial market regulation and to adapt the Swiss system to international standards.

This chapter is structured as follows. The next section presents the analytical framework of our study. Here, we argue that studies of change in financial markets should apply a multi-level perspective: in this study defined as a perspective that leaves enough room for the investigation of international and domestic politics. This perspective has the merit of emphasizing the role of actors and how actors and their behavior are constructed within the framework of international influences. It also reveals that domestic actors handle international challenges creatively; the way they do it, however, depends on domestic power constellations. The section that then follows describes the governance structure of the Swiss financial market. It outlines the importance of banking secrecy and the traditional dominance of the self-regulation principle which has often excluded government and parliament from playing a powerful role in the regulation of the financial market. It is in this section that we also discuss institutional change and reforms in the Swiss financial market between 1970 and 2007. The penultimate section explores recent changes in the regulation of the Swiss financial market in reaction to the financial crisis. The final section presents our main findings.

Analysis of changes in financial market regulation in a multi-level perspective

Despite the economic significance of the Swiss financial system, only a few studies analyze Swiss banking and capital market regulation and its change from an institutionalist or a political economic perspective. The most important are Busch (2009), Mach et al. (2007), Maggetti et al. (2011), Nobel (1998), and Zufferey (1998). Furthermore, there are some analyses by economists and lawyers, such as Bischof (1995) and Rime/Stiroh (2003).

The major findings of these studies can be summarized as follows. First, the literature tells us that since the mid-1990s the main reason for reforms and change in Swiss financial market regulation is to be located in changes in the international political economy, namely the liberalization of financial markets and European economic integration, both of which have exerted regulatory pressure. Mach et al. (2007: 8) contend that "profound changes in the international environment […] rendered some self-regulation mechanisms increasingly inefficient." Second, the literature argues that, despite major reforms in the past few years, incremental instead of transformative change prevails as the main pattern of reform (Mach et al. 2007; Maggetti et al. 2011). Third, studies show that the principle of self-regulation is relatively resistant and far from being replaced by the regulatory state model (the same applies to banking secrecy). In accordance with Lütz (2002: 23), we define the regulatory state model as a type of regulation that is dominated by a hierarchical regulatory state which has legislative and sanctioning competencies and establishes independent supervisory agencies.

In recent years, institutional change and reforms in the financial market system have also gained increasing attention in the comparative politics literature. According to Lütz (2004), two events prompted this increasing research interest. First, the internationalization of financial market activities and returning banking crises have led to increasing interstate collaboration in financial market and banking regulation, agreed upon not only in the EU but also by the Basel Committee on Banking Supervision (BCBS) or G10/G20. Second, national governments have increasingly responded to international regulation attempts, as well as national banking crises, with national regulatory reforms. In a number of countries, regulatory systems experienced radical change (Lütz 2002; Vogel 1996). Supervisory agencies have been strengthened and measures for more transparency in banking activities, as well as for protecting the interests of clients and consumers, have been introduced. Often, the trend towards the regulatory state model has been accompanied by a trend away from self-regulation by non-public and private actors. With reference to banking and capital market regulation, in her comparative study Lütz (2002: 309) even concludes that in both domains "the state takes over new tasks […] and [therewith] functionally replaces forms of collective self-regulation." According to Lütz (2002: 309) this development, on the one hand, is caused by the marketization of capital markets which delegitimizes self-regulation from the perspective of both investors and international organizations and, on the other hand, by the increasingly heterogeneous interests of banks.

As to the main causes and patterns of change in financial systems, the two main findings within the literature on financial systems can be summarized as follows. First, following the studies of Coleman (1996: 138), Lütz (2002: 305–330, 2004: 187), and Mach et al. (2007: 22), it seems reasonable to argue that national governments have launched initiatives to reform their systems when public authorities, but also national financial market actors, view international developments as a threat to their economic and political power. Reforms are initiated and implemented when there is a common feeling of vulnerability and loss of international competitiveness. However, Lütz (2004: 191) also reminds us that reforms are not only market-driven but also politically and institutionally mediated. She mentions Germany as an example, where stock exchange reforms are market-driven, while banking reforms are more politically mediated. The second finding concerns the patterns of change, which can be summarized as follows. On the one hand, incremental instead of transformative change seems to be the main pattern (Lütz 2004; Mach et al. 2007). On the other hand, due to strong effects of national regulatory traditions entrenched in national institutions, all-embracing convergence to one regulatory model seems fairly unlikely (Busch 2009; Lütz 2002, 2004; Mach et al. 2007).[1]

Because cross-national diversity in banking and capital market regulation is still observable and countries are not converging on one model, Lütz (2004: 325–330) suggests that an adequate analytical framework for analyzing institutional change and reforms needs to be a multi-level perspective which combines insights from international political economy with comparative historical institutionalism in order to trace the interplay between international influences and domestic factors responsible for specific trajectories of regulatory change in banking and capital market regulation. In this chapter we follow the suggestion of Lütz (2004) and apply a multi-level perspective. We argue that impetus for change may stem from the international level, as well as from domestic factors such as domestic veto players and power relationships. Which level has more impact on change and how these two levels interact in conditioning reforms is an empirical question.

The banks and their Switzerland

In this section, we briefly describe the Swiss financial industry and its economic importance, the governance structure of the Swiss financial market, Swiss banking secrecy, and, finally, the main challenges and reforms the Swiss financial market was confronted with until 2007.

The Swiss financial industry

The financial industry—in particular, the banking and insurance sector—is an important pillar of the Swiss economy and its importance has steadily been

---

1 In contrast to Lütz (2002, 2004), however, Coleman (1996: 227) speaks of convergence in the economic and political structures of financial services.

growing. The GDP share of the financial services sector rose from 7 percent in 1990 to over 12 percent in 2007 (Federal Council 2009: 10). Growth in the financial sector has been faster than in the economy overall: between 1991 and 2005 the annual growth of the financial sector was on average 3 percent (at constant prices), while the rest of the Swiss economy had an annual growth rate of approximately 1 percent. A consequence of this position enjoyed by financial services is that the Swiss economy is highly dependent on trends within the financial market (FDF 2009: 10; Federal Council 2009: 10). Thus, there are good reasons to declare that if important parts of the financial sector slide into crisis the impact on the overall economy will be severe.

The structure of the financial market in Switzerland is highly heterogeneous, especially in the banking sector. At the end of 2009 there were 325 banks in Switzerland. In terms of balance sheet totals or market share, the sector is dominated by the two big banks UBS and Credit Suisse. But there are many other significant types of bank, such as cantonal banks, regional banks and savings banks, *Raiffeisen* banks, commercial banks and stock exchange banks, foreign banks, and a special group of private bankers. Many of these banks are active as universal banks and offer various types of financial services within the same organization (SNB 2010). Furthermore, many financial intermediaries in Switzerland are not characterized as banks by law but are nevertheless active in the banking market. Examples of such actors are independent asset managers or the *PostFinance* which belongs to the Swiss postal services and plays a very important role in the payment transaction system.

According to Rime/Stiroh (2003: 2125), during the 1990s there were two main patterns of change in the Swiss banking industry. First, banking activities in the traditional domain have decreased (lending and deposit-taking), whereas with the internationalization of capital and financial markets their financial market activities gained importance (brokerage, underwriting, and portfolio management). For example, David et al. (2009: 10) show that more and more of the income of Swiss banks stems from capital market transactions instead of interest income: whereas in 1955, 72.6 percent of Swiss banks' income was interest income, in 1980 it was 50.3 percent and in 2000 only 35.7 percent. Second, the Swiss banking industry has consolidated: the number of banks has decreased and mergers led to the emergence of two big banks, namely Credit Suisse and UBS.

Governance structure of the Swiss financial market

Following the comparative political economy literature on banking and capital market regulation, as well as several studies on Switzerland, the Swiss financial market system may be classified as a corporatist regime, with big banks and other financial market actors as well as their associations (such as the Swiss Bankers Association or SBA) acting as "private interest governments" (Streeck/ Schmitter 1985). Self-regulation means that rules are set through agreements among banks and their associations. Rules are internal directives and standards (often called "codes of conduct" or "gentlemen's agreements"), and they are developed and implemented by the banking sector itself (Maggetti et al. 2011: 213) or between banks and larger industrial companies. Swiss banks have also established joint institutions (so-called *Gemeinschaftswerke der Schweizer Banken*) which play an important role in the regulation of the financial market. The SIX Group, for example, is responsible for the operation, regulation and monitoring of the stock exchange trading. Busch (2009: 175) contends that at least until 1970 the Swiss state "never tried to acquire the means to impose government control" and that "neither the finance department nor the central bank wanted to take responsibility for banking regulation."

The significance of the self-regulation principle mirrors the specificities of the Swiss political economy. According to Mach/Trampusch (2011), the strong tradition of self-regulation by economic associations is one of three conditions that play a crucial role in shaping the organization of the Swiss political economy. The other two conditions are the constrained policy capacity of the central state and the dominance of center-right parties (*Bürgerblock* or "bourgeois bloc") and business associations—at the expense of the power of trade unions and social democratic forces. Consequently, in the Swiss institutional and political context, the principle of self-regulation has also ensured the dominance of business interests and center-right parties at the expense of union and social democratic power and has led to a depoliticization of financial market issues (see also Mach et al. 2007: 5, 8). The strong tradition of the self-regulation principle means that the parliament and political parties have only minor steering competencies with regard to financial issues. We must also note that the larger banks UBS and Credit Suisse (as well as other private banks) are important economic actors, influencing the political elites. Several banks donate money to center-right parties (Strahm 2009: 14).

Regulation by federal law did not exist before the 1930s. A first attempt to develop a federal law on banks failed after World War I (Busch 2009: 169–175). However, in the 1930s Swiss banks were badly hit by the international economic crisis. The state had to intervene on several occasions (Vogler 2005: 11–12). In the context of this crisis, agreement on a first banking act increased significantly. Therefore, in 1934 the Swiss Federal Act on Banks and Saving Banks was passed (Busch 2009: 169–175). However, it took a long time until regulation by the state really became a comprehensive pillar of the governance structure of the Swiss financial market. As Mach et al. (2007: 21-26) and Maggetti et al. (2011) note, the regulatory state model—defined as legislative and sanctioning competencies of the state and supervision by independent regulatory agencies (Lütz 2002: 23)—has become important in the Swiss financial sector only in recent decades. According to the study by Barth et al. (2000: 33–34) on regulatory restrictions on commercial bank activities, Switzerland still belongs to the top group of countries—with New Zealand, Suriname and Israel—in which the activities of banks in the domains of securities, insurance, and real estate are relatively unrestricted compared to other countries such as the United States, the United Kingdom, France, or Germany.

Nevertheless, there are several state agencies with regulatory competencies. The tasks of these agencies are based on federal law.[2] Regulatory projects are in most cases prepared by the Federal Department of Finance (FDF) and the Federal Council, often in cooperation with the Swiss Financial Market Supervisory Authority (FINMA) and the Swiss National Bank (SNB). Furthermore, the relevant business associations and other interested groups are usually involved in the preparation of new regulatory projects, too. As a consequence, the influence of financial market associations on state regulation is very high (Busch 2009; Strahm 2009). In the case of federal laws, the finished drafts are discussed and passed in parliament and final approval can be obtained in a facultative referendum. The influence of the parliament, however, has remained fairly low in the area of financial market regulation (Busch 2009: 188-190).

Concerning supervision, the Swiss Financial Market Supervisory Authority (FINMA) is nowadays by far the most important state agency. FINMA is responsible for the supervision of banks, insurance companies, stock exchanges and securities dealers, and other financial intermediaries in Switzerland. FINMA is a new authority, founded in 2009 in a merger of the Anti-Money Laundering Control Authority, the Federal Office of Private Insurance (FOPI), and the Swiss Federal Banking Commission (SFBC) (Arter 2008: 60–70). The foundation of FINMA was not triggered by the financial crisis. According to Federal Council Hans-Rudolf Merz, this integrated financial market authority should "add more weight to the Swiss regulatory and supervisory system in negotiations with foreign organizations and institutions" (quoted in Strebel 2005). FINMA is formally independent from other state agencies and from the financial market. However, as Maggetti et al. (2011) state, the hiring policy of FINMA has often been oriented towards the recruitment of former employees of the

---

2 The most important acts are the following: Financial Market Supervision Act, Swiss Federal Act on Banks and Saving Banks, Collective Investment Schemes Act, Stock Exchange Act, Anti-Money Laundering Act, Insurance Supervision Act, Mortgage Bond Act, and the Insurance Contract Act (SIF 2010a).

financial market. This fact has been criticized in particular during the crisis because it contradicts the model of an independent regulatory and supervisory state (Strahm 2009). Concerning their actual supervisory competencies, FINMA and its predecessors have always been limited. For example, many aspects of monitoring banks' compliance with prudential rules are contracted out to private audit firms. Furthermore, the law has given little authority to the former Banking Commission and to FINMA in the authorization procedure for banks (Maggetti et al. 2011).

Swiss banking secrecy

With banking secrecy the financial privacy of citizens is protected from unauthorized access by third parties or by the state (FDF 2010a). This protection is legally codified. Bankers are obliged to keep the personal information of their clients confidential; they are punished if they violate confidentiality. This rule is derived from Article 47 of the Banking Act, which is the regulatory basis of banking secrecy. Furthermore, banking secrecy is also based on other legal provisions on protection of personality and of data (FDF 2010a). The limits of banking secrecy are also legally defined. In fact, several laws provide for exceptions to banking secrecy. Banks must provide information in cases of civil proceedings, debt recovery and bankruptcy proceedings, and criminal proceedings. The main rule is that in such cases banking secrecy can be lifted against the client's will on the order of a Swiss supervisory or judicial authority (FDF 2010a). Due to international pressure, the Swiss government has also limited the scope of banking secrecy in cases of international administrative and judicial assistance proceedings (SBA 2010).

Swiss banking secrecy has been a contested issue for many years. In fact, the meaning and importance of Swiss banking secrecy have been framed in many different ways. Some point out that it has been a decisive factor of the financial success of Swiss banking sector in the twentieth century and that it is still of crucial importance in protecting the privacy of bank customers with regard to the state. Others, however, claim that banking secrecy has been misused as an instrument to facilitate tax evasion and tax fraud, as well as to disguise money laundering or dormant accounts (Vogler 2005).

Change and continuity before 2007

In the decades before 2007 the Swiss financial market was confronted by several challenges. Many resulted in reforms and most were linked to international developments or international pressure: on the one hand, due to scandals and political pressure, and on the other hand, due to the internalization and liberalization of financial markets. Finally, there is also evidence of Europeanization, in other words, the adaptation of Swiss regulations to EU financial market policies.

Already before the recent UBS affair in the United States (see below), Switzerland was confronted by several scandals that were all more or less connected to banking secrecy. Important examples are the so-called Chiasso scandal of 1977,[3] money laundering activities, the secret bank accounts of dictators, and the debate on dormant accounts *(nachrichtenloses Vermögen)*. The common denominator of all these episodes was that they challenged Swiss banking secrecy. In the cases of the Chiasso scandal, money laundering and dictators' secret bank accounts they challenged banking secrecy because Swiss banks accepted money from tax evaders, from criminal business or from other dubious sources. In the case of dormant accounts, the problem was that Swiss banks did not cooperate enough in clarifying the origins of the assets. All these events received a lot of international attention and endangered the international reputation of the Swiss banking market (Federal Council 1989: 1076; Busch 2009: 190–200). In order to re-establish a stable business environment for the financial market, the government reacted to these scandals by restricting banking secrecy. New legal exceptions were introduced and disclosure of banking secrets with regard to foreign authorities was simplified. The banks, which normally defend banking secrecy, agreed to these institutional changes because they depend heavily on the international reputation of the Swiss financial market (for more details, see Steinlin/Trampusch 2012).

Several other reforms after 1970, however, were not a result of scandals or direct international pressure on Switzerland. Instead, they were motivated by the rapid developments in international financial markets and by financial market actors who stressed that the international competitiveness of the Swiss financial market needed to be improved. One prominent example in this regard is the abolition of certain self-regulating conventions of the Swiss Bankers' Association (see also Maggetti et al. 2011: 214). These conventions regulated prices and charges in the financial market and therefore clearly limited competition. In 1989, the Cartel Commission recommended that many aspects of these conventions should be brought to an end (APS 1989). These de facto cartels were considered inappropriate because of the liberalization trend in the member states of the European Community: the Swiss government wanted accession to the

---

3 A manager of the Ticino branch of the *Schweizerische Kreditanstalt* (SKA, today known as Credit Suisse) had accumulated hot money from tax evaders and criminal sources in Italy and used it for dubious financial dealings in Liechtenstein. However, when the company in Liechtenstein got into a financial crisis the losses of more than 2 billion Swiss francs became public. Details of the scandal are described in Mabillard/de Weck (1977).

European Economic Area and was therefore willing to adapt its economic policies (Busch 2009: 200–201). The Swiss Bankers' Association, however, first tried to defend its de facto cartels. But in 1990 the Federal Council decided in favor of the Cartel Commission and the cartels were thus removed (APS 1989, 1990).

Another important reform which, according to Bischof (1995: 493), was influenced by the internationalization of financial markets, was the reform of the Swiss Stock Exchange by the Swiss Federal Act on Stock Exchanges and Securities Trading of March 24, 1995 (Stock Exchange Act, SESTA). This reform was aimed at enabling "Swiss market participants to compete with other important capital markets in Europe and elsewhere" (Bischof 1995: 493). Before this reform, the regulation of stock exchanges had been a competence of Swiss cantons. However, there were also many aspects of self-regulation, such as stock exchanges' listing requirements (Geiger 2007: 3; Mach et al. 2007: 16). As stock exchanges became more and more internationally intertwined, federal regulation seemed necessary. Furthermore, the new law also had to take account of EU regulation (Geiger 2007: 3–5) and was intended to stabilize the competitiveness of Swiss stock exchanges (Federal Council 1993: 1371; Mach et al. 2007: 17). Concretely, in order to achieve these goals, an increased level of transparency on the part of Swiss companies and the introduction of stricter listing requirements were necessary (Mach et al. 2007: 17). Nevertheless, similar to other reforms of Swiss financial market regulation, the SESTA left many aspects to self-regulation, also in the important areas of organization and stock exchange supervision. In fact, the center-right majority in the parliament built in even more self-regulatory elements than the Federal Council originally intended (APS 1993, 1994, 1995; Mach et al. 2007: 17–18). Thus, according to Bischof (1995: 460), self-regulation was a "major theme" in the reform process and, in the end, it was the parliament that "considerably strengthened the principle of self-regulation and limited the Government's rule-making power."

An important way to constructively meet the challenge of the internationalization of the financial markets, as well as of foreign reservations concerning banking secrecy has been bilateral negotiation. For example, in 1996, after 16 years of negotiations, Switzerland and the United States finally concluded a new double taxation agreement (DTA), within which, however, Switzerland more or less successfully defended its reserved practice concerning information exchange in accordance with Swiss banking secrecy (Neuhaus/Hess 1996). Concerning relations with the European Union, banking secrecy became an important item in the second round of bilateral negotiations between 2000 and 2004. Similar to the DTA with the United States, untaxed money in Swiss bank accounts and exchange of information were controversial issues. With the Agreement on the Taxation of Savings Income (entering into force in 2005) a retention tax of—

originally—15 percent with gradual increases to 35 percent (from 1 July 2011) was introduced. This agreement ensures that the EU Savings Directive cannot be circumvented in Switzerland. However, this solution preserves Switzerland's legal order and the protection of bank customers' privacy. Thus, the tax is not linked to information on the owners of bank accounts (Federal Council 2010: 7274; FDF 2010c). Furthermore, banking secrecy was also an important issue in the negotiations on the Schengen Agreement. At the beginning, the Schengen Agreement did not win much approval among the main economic actors in Switzerland: it was possible that the agreement could include connections with administrative and judicial cooperation against tax fraud and fiscal offences (Lavenex 2006: 235). The largest Swiss business association, *economiesuisse,* and the Swiss Bankers' Association were therefore afraid that, due to the Schengen Agreement, Switzerland could be forced to provide administrative assistance in cases of tax evasion.[4] They thus announced that they would not accept Switzerland's accession to Schengen if the agreement included such provisions. The Federal Council respected these claims and brought this aspect into the negotiations with the European Union. Finally, the European Union conceded Switzerland the possibility to opt out if the Schengen Agreement was changed with regard to direct taxes (Jametti Greiner 2006: 202; Zürcher 2010: 55–59).

To sum up: in the decades after 1970 the Swiss financial market regime was challenged not only by international pressure and scandals but also by the internationalization and liberalization of financial markets. In many cases, self-regulation and banking secrecy were two of the main causes of pressure on the Swiss financial market regime. The examples and cases we have presented concerning this trajectory reveal that the basic elements of self-regulation and banking secrecy have suffered, but have nevertheless been retained. The veto position of Swiss banks hindered transformative change. Therefore, at the outset of the financial crisis, both self-regulation and banking secrecy were still alive (but self-regulation was probably healthier than banking secrecy[5]).

---

4 Until 2009, due to banking secrecy, administrative and judicial assistance from Switzerland was only possible in cases of tax fraud. Switzerland refused assistance in cases of tax evasion, which is considered less severe by Swiss law.

5 For details on changes in banking secrecy, see Steinlin/Trampusch (2012).

Increasing vulnerability since 2007: Regulation as a reaction to the financial crisis

The financial crisis has affected the Swiss financial market in several ways. In our view, the most important consequences were the following. First, the major bank UBS experienced a serious liquidity crisis. Second, due to UBS's illegal activities in the United States and in the wake of the heavy increase of government debt in several countries, international pressure with regard to untaxed money in Swiss bank accounts forced Switzerland to constrain banking secrecy. Third, the salaries of managers also became a major topic in Switzerland. The fourth consequence is that due to the UBS crisis and the accumulation of international pressure, for the first time in history the Swiss government formulated a general strategy for future financial market policies, thereby also initiating institutional reform in the Federal Department of Finance. Although compared to many other countries the effects of the crisis have been less severe in Switzerland (see the other country studies in this volume), the crisis has revealed that Switzerland is increasingly vulnerable to international market developments.

Direct consequences of the crisis: Losses and reactions of the state

The first consequences of the financial market crisis for Switzerland became obvious in October 2007 when the big Swiss bank UBS had to announce its first writedowns in the investment banking branch (FINMA 2009: 14). Therefore, in subsequent months UBS slid into a serious liquidity crisis. The bank's public reputation reached a low point. The bank tried to react to the ongoing losses by increasing its capital on several occasions, always with the help of private actors. However, on October 16, 2008, the Federal Council, the Swiss National Bank and the Swiss Federal Banking Commission announced a rescue package of the federal state in order to save UBS from further damage. As the big bank UBS is one of the most important banks in the Swiss market, this measure was considered absolutely necessary in order to stabilize the financial system (FINMA 2009: 33). The total sum of UBS's writedowns and credit losses amounted to USD 53 billion between 2007 and mid-2009. In the same period, the other big Swiss bank Credit Suisse "only" lost USD 19 billion (FINMA 2009: 15).

Besides the two big banks, other actors in the Swiss financial market were also more or less hit by the crisis. Several insurance companies as well as all types of funds recorded heavy losses. Therefore, many investors started to avoid investment funds and actively managed funds (FINMA 2009: 15–16). It is remarkable, however, that the situation of small and medium-sized banks did not significantly worsen during the crisis. Rather, several banks (such as the

Raiffeisen Group and cantonal banks) even benefitted from the crisis because they registered major inflows of new money as a consequence of the general mistrust in big banks and especially because of the very bad reputation of UBS (FINMA 2009: 15–16).

As described above, in October 2008 the federal state, the Banking Commission, and the Swiss National Bank saw the need to intervene in the financial market. Their main justifications for this step were the systemic importance of the financial sector for the Swiss economy and the threat of a crippling recession. Crisis management was of course focused mainly on rescuing UBS. But at the same time the state took several additional measures, mainly regulatory: depositor protection was strengthened, the big banks' capital adequacy requirements were tightened, and a limit was introduced on the level of indebtedness, otherwise known as the leverage ratio (Federal Council 2009: 13).

However, in an international comparative perspective, the financial commitment and state intervention within the framework of crisis management has been rather low in Switzerland. In fact, the financial extent of state intervention made available until June 2009 was approximately 10 percent of the country's GDP. In this respect, the Swiss state intervention is significantly lower than in many OECD countries, such as France, Germany, Japan, Spain, Sweden, the United Kingdom, the United States, and Ireland (Federal Council 2009: 13–14). Furthermore, the Swiss financial market and the Swiss economy have quickly been able to put the crisis behind them. Compared to many other countries, the Swiss economy and the federal state seem to be in a rather good and stable financial situation today (November 2011).

Nevertheless, even though state intervention in Switzerland was fairly modest by international comparison, it is not the case that UBS's liquidity crisis was a minor problem for the state agencies involved. Considering the systemic importance of the big bank for the Swiss financial market, as well as for the Swiss economy overall, the situation was highly inconvenient: the Federal Department of Finance, the Banking Commission, and the Swiss National Bank were confronted by a serious too-big-to-fail situation and did not see any alternative to direct intervention and stabilization of the bank with public resources (Commission of Experts 2010: 7; FINMA 2009).

Furthermore, the UBS liquidity crisis has triggered a public discussion on financial market regulation in Switzerland. First, a serious public and political discussion on the regulation of big banks has evolved. Due to the UBS crisis, Switzerland will implement stricter capital requirements for big banks than agreed at the international level under Basel III. Second, due to the UBS crisis, the discussion on managers' salaries has become highly controversial in Switzerland. Bank managers' huge salaries and bonuses are considered problematic for the sustainable management of financial institutions. There is even a public initiative that might have significant influence on domestic regulation in this regard. Both these events will be mentioned again below.

Indirect consequences of the crisis: Attacks on banking secrecy

UBS's liquidity problems were not the only major challenge for the regulatory agencies and supervisory authorities during the financial crisis. In winter 2008/ 2009 Switzerland was also confronted by the culmination of political pressure on Swiss banking secrecy. It seems plausible to argue that the financial crisis was an important factor in this political pressure: several governments had to rescue banks and, as a consequence, have suffered huge fiscal deficits since the crisis. Consequently, it became an attractive option for these countries to tap new funds by looking for untaxed money on bank accounts in countries such as Switzerland (Fiechter 2010: 57).

Hence, the focus of foreign governments was on untaxed foreign assets on Swiss bank accounts. These bank accounts were often unknown to foreign tax authorities as banking secrecy made it very difficult or even impossible for them to collect concrete information about account holders in Switzerland. This situation was considered highly problematic by many governments, especially also in the United States and Germany. As a consequence, international pressure on Swiss banks and banking secrecy received so much international support that Switzerland was forced to change its practices concerning exchange of information and, therefore, had to change the implementation of Swiss banking secrecy in international relations. In this context, we can identify two main episodes which we describe in the following.

United States against UBS

The first episode was caused by illegal activities on the part of UBS that came to light in the United States. This episode started in May 2007 when a former UBS banker and whistleblower was arrested. After this, US state agencies started to pressurize UBS: the US agencies accused UBS of knowingly holding the untaxed money of US citizens in its bank accounts. On February 18, 2009, in order to avoid a potentially catastrophic lawsuit, the bank admitted to the US Department of Justice that it had illegally supported US citizens in avoiding paying income taxes. UBS also handed over the names and account information of 285 account holders (Fiechter 2010; Winzeler 2010). The delivery of information on account holders was a remarkable act because it was not in accordance with earlier practice as regards Swiss banking secrecy. However, UBS was under such pressure that no other option seemed possible. The supervision authority FINMA, concerned about the stability of the already troubled bank, shared this view and therefore allowed UBS to hand over this information (Swiss Federal Administrative Court 2010a). Nevertheless, the US state agencies were not satisfied with these steps. Therefore, just one day later, on February 19, 2009, the Department of Justice requested further information on 52,000 bank accounts from UBS. Again, UBS faced severe problems with regard to its reputation in the United States. But with the help of the Swiss government, the bank was able to reduce the number of accounts on which information had to be provided to 4,450 by August 2009. Furthermore, the United States and Switzerland signed a parallel agreement to enable administrative assistance: Switzerland agreed to supply assistance to authorized US agencies not only in cases of tax fraud but also in cases of continued and serious tax evasion (Fiechter 2010: 64; Swiss Federal Administrative Court 2010b). Thus, in order to save the big bank UBS, Switzerland accepted a significant "shrinkage" (Steinlin/Trampusch 2012) of banking secrecy in the bilateral relationship with the United States. In fact, the agreement was later declared unlawful by the Swiss Federal Administrative Court (2010b) but was then legalized again by parliament by turning the agreement into a formal treaty (Fiechter 2010: 64).

To sum up, in 2008 and 2009 UBS not only suffered a liquidity crisis but also faced serious legal pressure from the United States. A lawsuit against UBS would have had very unfortunate consequences for it. The failure of UBS was considered too dangerous for the Swiss economy (Winzeler 2010: 162). However, the pressure was not directed only at UBS as an individual bank but also against Swiss banking secrecy in general. Therefore, this accumulation of catastrophic events involving UBS led the Federal Council to a tipping point: the government saw itself forced to react at the political level by accepting the demands of the US agencies.

OECD, G20, France and Germany against Switzerland

European countries and the OECD were well informed on how Switzerland dealt with the United States (Fiechter 2010: 57). As a consequence, in February 2009 several European governments expressed their wish that the G20 should proceed against countries that refuse to cooperate in the international fight against tax evasion (NZZ 2009). The OECD even announced that it would publish a "gray list" of countries failing to comply with so-called internationally agreed tax standards. Furthermore, Peer Steinbrück, the German Finance Minister, said that he would like to see Switzerland on that list (SRDRS 2008). Thus, Switzerland was confronted by rising political pressure. Finally, on March 13, 2009, the Federal Council decided, along with Austria, Belgium, and Luxembourg, that Switzerland would now accept Article 26 of the OECD Model Convention. With this step, Switzerland agreed to significantly constrain banking secrecy towards foreign countries: concerning international tax matters, Switzerland will in future offer administrative assistance not only in cases of tax fraud but also in individual cases of well-founded suspicion of tax evasion (Bauen/ Rouiller 2010: 120; Fiechter 2010: 57; Strahm 2010: 301; Winzeler 2010: 164).[6]

Public debate on managers' salaries

The salaries of managers in the private sector (including the financial market) have become a major topic in the public debate, both during and after the crisis. In fact, the discussion had already started before the outbreak of the crisis when a popular initiative against so-called "rip-off payments" *(Gegen die Abzockerei)* was successfully launched in 2006. The main objective of the initiative is to delegate the setting of managers' salaries, bonuses and other benefits from the companies' supervisory boards to the shareholders. This change in the setting of salaries should limit excessive bonuses in private companies, especially in the financial sector. In 2007, when the financial crisis broke out, the initiative was not yet ready for a popular vote (Federal Assembly 2011c).

During the crisis, the issue of high salaries and bonuses became a popular topic in the media as well as in parliament. As a consequence, the popular initiative against *Abzockerei* has become an even more popular option for reforming the regulation of salaries and bonuses. According to the official statements of the political parties, the initiative seems to be supported by parties on both the left and the right. However, as of November 2011, the two chambers in the federal parliament had not yet decided whether to recommend approval or rejection of the popular initiative. In fact, the parties were struggling with several counter-proposals that should also be put to a popular vote. Therefore, it was still unclear when the popular vote on the initiative would take place and whether there would be any alternatives (Federal Assembly 2011c).

Furthermore, during the crisis, the youth organization of the Social Democrats successfully launched another popular initiative which aims to limit managers' salaries to a maximum of 12 times the salary of the employees with the lowest income in the company. This popular initiative was handed in to the federal authorities in March 2011. The date of the popular vote has not yet been set (NZZ Online 2011b).

---

6 In fact, Article 26 is not automatically applicable but has to be implemented in new bilateral DTAs. This was why Switzerland was nevertheless temporarily placed on the OECD's "gray list" (Fiechter 2010: 57). As a consequence, the Swiss government showed its willingness to negotiate these DTAs in a very short time (Bauen/Rouiller 2010: 120).

Reforms and government reform strategy

The fact that the crisis has clearly hit Switzerland and that the reputation of the Swiss financial market has suffered was also recognized by the government and the supervisory agencies. They reacted to public opinion by investigating the causes of the crisis and by critically defending their reactions and measures in several reports (see especially FDF 2009; FINMA 2009). As will be shown in the following sections, due to the increasing vulnerability of the Swiss economy to international developments, the government has shown some willingness to reform financial market regulation.

Institutional reform in the Federal Department of Finance

One major reform initiated by the government was an organizational change in the Federal Department of Finance. In December 2009, the Federal Council decided to establish a new State Secretariat for International Financial Matters (SIF) within the Federal Department of Finance. In March 2010 this institutional reform was implemented and the SIF thus commenced work. The new SIF is concerned mainly with matters of international cooperation at the Federal Department of Finance. This means that the SIF "serves the purpose of reinforcing Switzerland's international position in financial and tax matters" (SIF 2010b). Furthermore, the new State Secretariat is also concerned with all questions of financial market policy in Switzerland and will therefore "develop legislation on the financial sector" (SIF 2010b). In sum, the SIF's competencies are in the field of regulation; it is not a new supervisory agency alongside the new FINMA. The SIF therefore takes over a lot of responsibilities previously distributed among several state agencies in the Federal Department of Finance. Nevertheless, it is not yet possible to describe the real influence of the SIF on regulation.

On the one hand, the foundation of the SIF may be considered a major organizational reform within the Swiss federal agency structure: due to the crisis, the government has decided to build up a competence center for financial market policies and for international financial market affairs. On the other hand, when we compare this reform to the level of crisis-induced institutional reforms in other countries, we must note that reforms of the agency structure seem to have remained fairly limited in Switzerland (see other chapters in this volume).

New strategies for reform

More or less in parallel with the decision to build up the SIF, in December 2009, the Federal Council published for the first time a report on "strategic directions for Switzerland's financial market policy" (Federal Council 2009). The report was based on the work of the "Working Group on Strategy." This group consisted of members of state agencies and delegates of the main financial market associations, as well as two external consultants (Federal Council 2009: 60). In the report the Federal Council formulated four strategic directions for Swiss financial market policies: improving the international competitiveness of the financial sector, securing and enhancing market access, strengthening the financial sector's resistance to crisis and dealing with systemically important financial institutions, and preserving the integrity of the financial center. For each of these directions several measures were proposed.[7] In the following, the four strategic directions are presented briefly. Some of the measures implemented by November 2011, after the release of the report, will also be presented.

1. Improving the international competitiveness of the financial sector. The Federal Council names the following as conditions for a competitive financial market: a regulatory framework in line with internationally recognized standards, a robust and stability-oriented monetary and budgetary policy, education, open and flexible labor markets, a functional financial-market infrastructure, the protection of privacy, and an attractive tax regime for the financial sector and the economy as a whole (Federal Council 2009: 31). Thus, concerning the financial market, the goal does not seem to be stricter regulation.

However, looking at the concrete measures that are planned, some new aspects of regulation can be identified. For example, in the field of taxation the government confirms that "Switzerland is about to adapt [the] domestic and international legal framework to Article 26 OECD within the parameters set by the Federal Council" (Federal Council 2009: 51). Concerning supervision, improved transparency for clients is planned (Federal Council 2009: 41). In fact, it has not yet been determined what this measure will look like, but FINMA announced in November 2010 that it plans to enforce the current laws more strictly and will perhaps also propose to adapt the law in the fields of marketing and client information (FINMA 2010). Concerning cooperation, the government intends to "intensify Switzerland's involvement in the main international standards bodies" (Federal Council 2009: 41). In this context, the main goal is recognition of the equivalence of the Swiss supervisory system by foreign countries and international organizations.

---

7 However, these measures will not necessarily be implemented: they are only ideas or proposals on how to achieve the strategic goals formulated in the report. Hence, this government report should be seen as a general strategy only; it should not be compared with concrete regulatory projects implemented in other countries (such as the Dodd-Frank Act in the United States—see J. Nicholas Ziegler in this volume).

2. Securing and enhancing market access. The goal is to improve foreign market access for Swiss financial intermediaries (Federal Council 2009: 42). This strategic direction is not new, but will obviously be of increasing importance. In general, the government intends mainly to enhance international cooperation at the political level in the interests of the national financial market in order to improve acceptance of Swiss financial market regulation and supervision in international organizations and in foreign countries. In this context, the Federal Council stated in 2010 that Switzerland is not effectively represented in international institutions which set the standards for financial markets. Switzerland is a member of the OECD and of the International Monetary Fund (IMF) and it is also very active in the Financial Stability Board. But the fact that Switzerland is not a member of the G20 is clearly seen as a disadvantage when trying to push national interests on the international agenda (Federal Council 2010a: 7282).

The adaptation of national law to EU law is also a major issue (Federal Council 2009: 42–46). According to the Federal Council, recent developments in the EU will become a serious challenge for Swiss market regulation: the government observes a general trend in the EU towards reregulation of the economy (Federal Council 2010a: 7281–7282) and fears that this will have discriminatory effects on Swiss financial market companies. One example is the new EU directive on hedge funds: the new EU passport for hedge funds and for hedge funds managers will probably be available for foreign hedge funds only if these countries accept new standards of cooperation in areas such as anti-money laundering taxation (Federal Council 2010a: 7293; NZZ 2010b). In the view of the Federal Council, Switzerland must therefore increase its efforts to secure and enhance market access for Swiss financial intermediaries in European markets. One way to achieve this is to "[i]ntensify FINMA's dialogue in international bodies and bilaterally with the major supervisory authorities and individual EU bodies […] to obtain international recognition of the equivalence of Switzerland's supervision and regulation" (Federal Council 2009: 45). Second, the Federal Council is also willing to "[e]xamine the arguments for and against a (financial) services agreement with the EU" (Federal Council 2009: 45). However, concrete steps towards such an agreement have not yet been taken.

3. Strengthening the financial sector's resistance to crisis and dealing with systemically important financial institutions. This third strategy is clearly a consequence of the financial crisis. So far, two reforms have been of major importance: primarily, new regulatory solutions for the too-big-to-fail problem and, to a lesser degree, improved depositor protection.

Solutions for the too-big-to-fail problem are dependent on international developments, especially on Basel III. Nevertheless, in June 2010 FINMA and the

SNB put into force a new liquidity regime for Swiss banks. A core element of the new supervisory regime is a new stress test; the banks are required to cover the outflows estimated in such a scenario over a period of at least 30 days (SNB/FINMA 2010). Furthermore, in November 2010, just a few weeks after the conclusion of Basel III in the Basel Committee on Banking Supervision, an expert commission presented its proposals for a national regulatory solution to the too-big-to-fail problem. The solutions proposed by this committee are remarkable. Not only are they compatible with the requirements of Basel III, but they are—to some extent—even stricter (the so-called Swiss Finish). The capital requirements go further than what has been negotiated at the international level in Basel III. Concerning the capital requirements of systemically important banks, the experts propose a progressive component (Commission of Experts 2010). The proposals made by this commission have been worked out not only by the government but in collaboration with private actors, thus for example with the Swiss Bankers' Association and *economiesuisse* (Commission of Experts 2010: 63–64). So far, the proposals have enjoyed broad political support. As of November 2011 the measures had not yet obtained legal status but they had been passed by the two chambers of the federal parliament in September 2011 (NZZ Online 2011a).[8]

Concerning depositor protection, concrete steps towards reform have already been taken. The temporary measures agreed by the Federal Council in autumn 2008 will now become part of the Banking Act, as decided by parliament in March 2011 (Federal Assembly 2011b). One important element of this reform is to increase protected deposits from CHF 30,000 to CHF 100,000. As a consequence, the protection level will be substantially higher than the recent increase in the EU minimum limit (Federal Council 2010b).

4. Preserving the integrity of the financial center. As the problem of tax offences has become a major issue during and after the crisis, with clearly negative consequences for the reputation of the Swiss financial market, the government has decided to take up this challenge. The Federal Council (2009: 49) considers integrity an "important factor in the choice of location."

Concerning international relations, several developments can be observed. First, the government plans to "intensify active involvement in international bodies, such as the FSB, the GF [Global Forum] and the FATF [Financial Action Task Force], in order to combat financial crime, implement an appropriate monitoring system and create a global level playing field" (Federal Council

---

8 The Swiss federal parliament consists of two chambers with equal rights in legislation: while the proposals were approved by the Council of States in June 2011 (with minor adjustments), they have not yet been discussed in the National Council (Federal Assembly 2011a).

2009: 54). Second, additional DTAs shall be negotiated in order to show the country's will to implement Article 26 of the OECD Model Tax Agreement. Third, Switzerland is also willing to enter into bilateral agreements that go beyond the OECD standard in order to promote taxpayer honesty among bank clients (Federal Council 2009: 54). In fact, in October 2010 Switzerland officially agreed with the United Kingdom and Germany to start bilateral negotiations in order to implement a final withholding tax. The two agreements were signed in summer and autumn 2011 but had not yet entered into force as of November 2011 (FDF 2011; NZZ 2010a, 2011). Fourth, despite the willingness of the government to be more active at the international level, it is not yet clear how Switzerland plans to react to a potential problem with the European Union: the European Commission has announced, concerning company taxation, that it wants Switzerland to abandon banking secrecy and to introduce automatic exchange of information (NZZ Online 2010).

Conclusions

The Swiss financial system is a typical corporatist financial services regime with big banks, other financial intermediaries and their associations acting as "private interest governments" setting standards by self-regulation. Traditionally, self-regulatory arrangements were predominant with regard to the regulatory state model, and together with banking secrecy they ensured the dominance of business interests in financial market regulation. For decades, both self-regulation and banking secrecy were highly resistant to change and pressures.

Nevertheless, the Swiss financial system is now on a track which we call "increasing vulnerability." Our historical and process-oriented reconstruction of change in the Swiss financial market regime between 1970 and today has revealed that the leverage of international influences has become stronger. Interestingly, one of the main reasons for international pressure is often banking secrecy in connection with the self-regulation principle. Change in the governance structure of the Swiss financial market is, on the one hand, conditioned by international political pressure (for example, induced by scandals) and, on the other hand, by the internationalization and liberalization of financial markets. Furthermore, from our multi-level perspective it is clear that change is also strongly influenced by domestic politics and institutions: the principles of self-regulation and banking secrecy enjoy broad support in Switzerland, leading to only incremental change of these two principles, sometimes even to greater self-regulation as a reaction to international pressure. For example, in case of the Schengen Agreement bankers and economic actors used the guarantee of banking secrecy as a deposit for their agreement to Schengen. But our historical record also shows that the legitimacy of banking secrecy as well as of self-regulation by banks has significantly decreased at the international level. International organizations as well as foreign governments more and more view both of these sacred cows as obstacles in the international fight against money laundering, tax evasion, tax fraud, and public debt.

As a consequence of the financial market crisis, the Swiss government has currently become more aware of the dependence of Swiss economic and financial market success on developments in the international political economy. Switzerland was not spared in the financial crisis, which generated two serious challenges for the financial market: a serious liquidity crisis for UBS and harsh attacks on banking secrecy due to tax evasion. The government, the financial market supervision, and the Swiss National Bank faced the first challenge by implementing urgent measures to save UBS and to protect the stability of the financial market. Another consequence of the UBS liquidity problems will be stronger capital requirements for big banks (even above the level of Basel III). In the end, the UBS crisis did not have catastrophic economic consequences. However, the attacks on banking secrecy, mainly caused by the illegal activities of UBS and by the appetite of foreign governments for tax revenues, have fundamentally weakened this institution; the pressure of international organizations and foreign governments has been overwhelming.

In the wake of the crisis, the government founded a new state secretariat that is concerned with international matters and with the development of financial market legislation in Switzerland. Thus, there has been at least one larger agency reform. Furthermore, for the first time in Switzerland, the government presented a strategic plan of what it intends to do concerning financial market regulation. However, a closer look at the strategic plan makes clear that the priority of regulation is still to ensure the competitiveness of the Swiss market, as well as to secure the market access of Swiss financial intermediaries abroad. Indeed, in 2009 Federal Councilor Hans-Rudolf Merz stated in an interview with the magazine of the Swiss Association of Asset Managers (SAAM) that the recipe for success is not more regulation but the quality of regulation. Merz insisted that quality rather than strictness is a decisive location factor for the Swiss financial market (SAAM 2010: 16). This way of framing the state's role is probably a consequence of the fact that self-regulation has always played a major role in the Swiss financial market and that new regulatory legislation is usually developed by a coalition between the state and the financial industry, mainly banking. We have already mentioned that even the preparatory work on strategic direction was done by such a coalition.

Thus, despite the vulnerability of the Swiss financial market, the actual number of domestically motivated attempts to reorganize the financial market or the banking system has remained fairly low. In our view, this peculiarity of the Swiss trajectory can be explained by several conditions. Among them, the economic success of Switzerland shortly after the crisis is clearly important, as is the weakness of left-wing parties and the traditional predominance of the center-right and right-wing forces with close connections to the financial industry. The fact that banking secrecy is viewed as part of the Swiss identity is also important. Finally, the insignificance of partisan competition due to the *Konkordanzdemokratie* (Sager/Zollinger 2011) plays a major role. Thus, as major political projects within the framework of *Konkordanzdemokratie* need to be coordinated among all politically relevant actors, the associations of the financial market are often able to control and block serious reform attempts.

However, not everything has remained as it was before 2007. Strategic directions numbers three and four (see "New strategies for reform" above) in the report of the Federal Council (2009) as well as other reforms and reform intentions show that Switzerland is nevertheless willing to partly adapt its regulatory agenda to the challenges that have become obvious during the crisis. First, the foundation of the SIF shows that the government is aware of the interconnectedness between national and international financial markets and is willing to adapt the regulatory agency structure. Similar to the integration of all supervisory matters within the new FINMA, the SIF seems to have become an integrated center of competence for national regulation and international relations. Second, the serious too-big-to-fail problem with UBS was a real shock for the supervisory and regulatory agencies as well as for the economy in general. Considering the importance of such a bank for the Swiss economy, the regulatory agencies have started to insist on stricter regulation of big banks. Basel III and the further Swiss-specific rules have not yet been implemented, but the trend towards more public regulation in this area is obvious. Third, the government has realized that the pressure on Swiss banking secrecy has had serious consequences for the reputation of the financial market. Therefore, the Federal Council seems to have become more willing to cooperate in international bodies and to accept international standards, especially concerning international taxation agreements. In fact, by accepting Article 26 of the OECD model convention, Switzerland has made a major concession with serious consequences for the institution of banking secrecy. Fourth, beyond the government's intentions there is also the intense public and political discussion on the regulation of managers' salaries.

In sum, however, we think that Switzerland is still going to be confronted by further challenges from abroad that may reveal further need for institutional change. First, in comparison to other countries, there may still be considerable regulatory misfit. Self-regulation and banking secrecy are still important pillars of Swiss financial market regulation. This means that there is some potential for pressure to be maintained on Swiss financial market regulation. The policy options for the fight against tax evasion that are being considered in the EU (for example, automatic exchange of information) are just one example. And as history has shown, tax evasion is ever present and so is the desire of governments to overcome it. Therefore, Switzerland will probably experience bad international press in the next few years, too. Furthermore, the financial markets have been developing and changing very flexibly; thus, Switzerland, embedded in international markets, will be challenged to find new ways to react to these developments with its mix of self-regulation and a regulatory state.

Can a broader theoretical lesson be drawn from the pattern of change we have identified in this case study on Switzerland? First, governance in the Swiss financial services regime mirrors the three specificities of the Swiss political economy identified by Mach/Trampusch (2011): business and right-wing party predominance, weak state capacity, and self-regulation by highly organized non-public actors. Second, due to Switzerland's small-country status, we would have expected that Switzerland is an unlikely case for resistance to change (Papadopoulos 2011). However, in the domain of financial services (as in sectors such as agriculture and the labor market for a long time) the Swiss have been highly resistant to change for decades. Nevertheless, this resistance has diminished strongly in recent years. Likewise, as in other political-economic domains (Mach/Trampusch 2011), in financial services the acceleration of economic integration has put increased pressure on Switzerland. This phenomenon may be explained by changes in actors' preferences and strategies: on the one hand, banks have shifted their activities from the traditional domain of lending and deposit-taking to financial market activities (brokerage, underwriting, and portfolio management). On the other hand, the Swiss government increasingly acknowledges that Switzerland must adapt its regulatory system to changing external environments in order to maintain the international competitiveness of the Swiss financial market. Both self-regulation and banking secrecy have turned out to be strongly resistant to institutional change but they are nevertheless shrinking pillars of Switzerland's political economy.

References

APS (Année Politique Suisse), several years: *Année Politique Suisse/Jahrbuch Schweizerische Politik*. Berne: University of Berne, Institute of Political Science.

Arter, Oliver, 2008: *Bankenaufsichtsrecht in der Schweiz: Standortbestimmung und Zukunftsperspektiven am Vorabend der FINMA*. Berne: Stämpfli.

Barth, James/Gerard Caprio/Ross Levine, 2000: *Banking Systems Around the Globe: Do Regulation and Ownership Affect Performance and Stability?* World Bank Policy Research Working Paper 2325. Washington, DC: The World Bank, Development Research Group.

Bauen, Marc/Nicolas Rouiller, 2010: *Schweizer Bank[kunden]geschäft*. Zurich: Schulthess.

BIS (Bank for International Settlements), 2010: *The Basel Committee's Response to the Financial Crisis: Report to the G20*. Basel: BIS.

Bischof, Thomas, 1995: The Swiss Securities Exchange Act and Investment Fund Act: A New Regulatory Framework for the Swiss Capital Markets. In: *North Carolina Journal of International Law and Commercial Regulation* 20, 457–493.

Busch, Andreas, 2009: *Banking Regulation and Globalization*. New York: Oxford University Press.

Coleman, William D., 1996: *Financial Services, Globalization and Domestic Policy Change*. New York: St. Martin's Press.

Commission of Experts, 2010: *Final Report of the Commission of Experts for Limiting the Economic Risks Posed by Large Companies*. <www.sif.admin.ch/dokumentation/00514/00519/00592/index.html?lang=en>

David, Thomas, et al., 2009: The Swiss Business Elite Between 1980–2000: Declining Cohesion, Changing Educational Profile and Growing Internationalization. In: Friederike Boyer/Christoph Sattler (eds.), *European Economic Elites Between a New Spirit of Capitalism and the Erosion of State Socialism*. Berlin: Duncker & Humblot, 197–220.

FDF (Federal Department of Finance), 2009: *Situation und Perspektiven des Finanzplatzes Schweiz: Bericht an die WAK-N*. <www.efd.admin.ch/dokumentation/zahlen/00578/01532/index.html?lang=de>

——, 2010a: *Protection of Privacy in Financial Matters*. <www.efd.admin.ch/dokumentation/zahlen/00579/00607/00621/index.html?lang=e>

——, 2010b: *Stock Market Offences and Market Abuse: Federal Council in Favour of General Market Supervision*. Press release of December 17, 2010. <www.efd.admin.ch/dokumentation/medieninformationen/00467/index.html? lang=en&msg-id=36858>

——, 2010c: *Taxation of Savings Income*. <www.efd.admin.ch/dokumentation/zahlen/00579/00608/00634/index.html?lang=e>

——, 2011: *Federal Council Launches Consultation on the Implementation of the Tax Agreements with Germany and the UK*. Press release of September 30, 2011. <www.efd.admin.ch/dokumentation/medieninformationen/00467/index.html?lang= en&msg-id=41466>

Federal Assembly, 2011a: *Bankengesetz. Änderung (too big to fail)*. <www.parlament.ch/d/suche/seiten/geschaefte.aspx?gesch_id=20110028>

——, 2011b: *Bundesgesetz über Banken und Sparkassen (Sicherung der Einlagen). Änderung*. <www.parlament.ch/d/suche/seiten/geschaefte.aspx?gesch_id=20100049>

——, 2011c: *Dossier Abzockerei*. <www.parlament.ch/d/dokumentation/dossiers/abzockerei/Seiten/default.aspx>

Federal Council, 1989: Botschaft über die Änderung des Schweizerischen Strafgesetzbuches (Gesetzgebung über Geldwäscherei und mangelnde Sorgfalt bei Geldgeschäften) vom 12. Juni 1989. In: *BBl* (Bundesblatt) 1989, 1061–1100.

——, 1993: Botschaft zu einem Bundesgesetz über die Börsen und den Effektenhandel (Börsengesetz, BEHG) vom 24. Februar 1993. In: *BBl* (Bundesblatt) 1993(I), 1369–1462.

——, 2009: *Strategic Directions for Switzerland's Financial Market Policy: Report in Response to the Graber Postulate (09.3209)*. <www.efd.admin.ch/dokumentation/zahlen/00578/01622/index.html?lang=en>

——, 2010a: Bericht des Bundesrates über die Evaluation der schweizerischen Europapolitik (in Beantwortung des Postulats Markwalder [09.3560] "Europapolitik. Evaluation, Prioritäten, Sofortmassnahmen und nächste Integrationsschritte") vom 17. September 2010. In: *BBl* (Bundesblatt) 2010, 7239–7344. <www.admin.ch/ch/d/ff/2010/7239.pdf>

——, 2010b: Botschaft zur Änderung des Bankengesetzes (Sicherung der Einlagen). In: *BBl* (Bundesblatt) 2010: 3993–4036. <www.admin.ch/ch/d/ff/2010/3993.pdf>

Fiechter, Jean-Rodolphe W., 2010: Exchange of Tax Information: The End of Banking Secrecy in Switzerland and Singapore? In: *International Tax Journal* (November–December 2010), 55–67.

FINMA, 2009: *Financial Market Crisis and Financial Market Supervision*. Berne: FINMA. <www.finma.ch/e/aktuell/Documents/Finanzmarktkrise-und-Finanzmarktaufsicht_e.pdf>

——, 2010: *Distribution Rules—FINMA Launches Discussion on Ways to Improve Client Protection*. Press release. <www.finma.ch/e/aktuell/pages/mm-diskussionspapier-vertriebsbericht-20101110.aspx>

Geiger, Hansueli, 2007: *10 Jahre Börsengesetz – Ziel erreicht?* Presentation at the general assembly of the Swiss Association of Independent Securities Dealers. <www.svue.ch/press/10_Jahre_Boersengesetz_HU_Geiger_07_06.pdf>

Jametti Greiner, Monique, 2006: Würdigung der Assoziierungsabkommen der Schweiz zu Schengen und Dublin. In: Christine Kaddous/Monique Jametti Greiner (eds.), *Bilaterale Abkommen II Schweiz-EU und andere neue Abkommen*. Basel: Helbing & Lichtenhahn, 195–205.

Lavenex, Sandra, 2006: Switzerland: Between Intergovernmental Co-operation and Schengen Association. In: Marina Caparini/Otwin Marenin (eds.), *Borders and Security Governance: Managing Borders in a Globalised World*. Zurich: Lit Verlag, 233–251.

Lütz, Susanne, 2002: *Der Staat und die Globalisierung von Finanzmärkten: Regulative Politik in Deutschland, Großbritannien und den USA*. Frankfurt a.M.: Campus.

——, 2004: Convergence within National Diversity: The Regulatory State in Finance. In: *Journal of Public Policy* 24(2), 169–197.

Mabillard, Max/Roger de Weck, 1977: *Der Fall Chiasso*. Geneva: Tribune Editions.

Mach, André, et al., 2007: Transformations of Self-Regulation and New Public Regulations in the Field of Swiss Corporate Governance (1985–2002). In: *World Political Science Review* 3(2), Article 4, 1–30.

Mach, André/Christine Trampusch, 2011: The Swiss Political Economy in Comparative Perspective. In: Christine Trampusch/André Mach (eds.), *Switzerland in Europe: Continuity and Change in the Swiss Political Economy*. London: Routledge, 11–26.

Maggetti, Martino/Alexandre Afonso/Marie-Christine Fontana, 2011: The More It Changes, the More It Stays the Same? Swiss Liberalization and Regulatory Policies in Comparative

Perspective. In: Christine Trampusch/André Mach (eds.), *Switzerland in Europe: Continuity and Change in the Swiss Political Economy.* London: Routledge, 205–223.

Neuhaus, Markus R./Jacqueline Heuss, 1996: Gute Note für das Steuerabkommen Schweiz USA. In: NZZ (Neue Zürcher Zeitung), issue of 12 June 1996.

Nobel, Peter, 1998: Selbstregulierung. In: Claude-Alain Margelisch/Christoph Winzeler (eds.), *Freiheit und Ordnung im Kapitalmarktrecht.* Festgabe für Jean-Paul Chapuis. Zurich: Schulthess, 119–134.

NZZ (Neue Zürcher Zeitung), 2009: *Die EU erhöht den Druck gegen "Steueroasen"; Umfassende globale Finanzarchitektur und Aufsicht gefordert.* February 23, 2009.

——, 2010a: *Brüssel wird Bern zum „Steuerdialog" bitten.* June 9, 2010.

——, 2010b: *Kompromiss der EU-Staaten zu Hedge-Funds; Ecofin vertagt Beschluss über Amtshilfe in Steuerfragen.* October 21, 2010.

——, 2011: *Schweizer Kampf an drei Fronten.* July 1, 2011.

NZZ Online, 2010: *EU-Steuerkommissar will nicht locker lassen.* Published on October 14, 2010. <www.nzz.ch/nachrichten/schweiz/automatischer_informationsaustausch_bleibt_bestes_mittel_1.7996000.html>

——, 2011a: *Die neue "Too big to fail"-Regulierung ist unter Dach.* Published on September 29, 2011. <www.nzz.ch/nachrichten/politik/schweiz/die_neue_too_big_to_fail-regulierung_ist_unter_dach_1.12727861.html>

——, 2011b: *Juso reichen Volksinitiative "1:12" ein.* Published on March 21, 2011. <www.nzz.ch/nachrichten/politik/schweiz/juso_reichen_volksinitiative_112_ein_1.9976737.html>

Papadopoulos, Yannis, 2011: How Much, and in What Ways is Switzerland Changing? In: Christine Trampusch/André Mach (eds.), *Switzerland in Europe: Continuity and Change in the Swiss Political Economy.* London: Routledge, 223–237.

Rime, Bertrand/Kevin J. Stiroh, 2003: The Performance of Universal Banks: Evidence from Switzerland. In: *Journal of Banking and Finance* 27(11), 2121–2150.

SAAM (Swiss Association of Asset Managers), 2010: Finanzplatz Schweiz – quo vadis? In: *Denaris* 3/2010, 15–17. <http://vsv.inettools.ch/upload/dokumente/denaris_10_2.pdf>

Sager, Fritz/Christine Zollinger, 2011: The Swiss Political System in Comparative Perspective. In: Christine Trampusch/André Mach (eds.), *Switzerland in Europe: Continuity and Change in the Swiss Political Economy.* London: Routledge, 27–42.

SBA (Swiss Bankers Association), 2010: *Bank Client Confidentiality.* <www.swissbanking.org/en/home/dossier-bankkundengeheimnis/dossier-bankkundengeheimnis-themen-geheimnis.htm>

SIF (State Secretariat for International Financial Matters), 2010a: *Financial Market Regulation and Supervision.* <www.sif.admin.ch/themen/00489/index.html?lang=en>

——, 2010b: *SIF mandate.* <www.sif.admin.ch/org/00532/index.html?lang=en>

SNB (Swiss National Bank), 2010: *Banks in Switzerland 2009.* Zurich: SNB. <www.snb.ch/ext/stats/bankench/pdf/deen/Die_Banken_in_der_CH.book.pdf>

SNB (Swiss National Bank)/FINMA, 2010: *New Liquidity Regime for Swiss Big Banks.* Press release of April 21, 2010. <www.finma.ch/e/aktuell/Documents/mm-liquiditaetsregime-grossbanken-20100421-e.pdf>

SRDRS, 2008: *Steinbrück: 'Schweiz gehört auf die Schwarze Liste'*. Website. Last updated on: October 21, 2008. <www.drs1.ch/www/de/drs1/sendungen/nachrichten-drs-4/5736.sh10054740.html>

Steinlin, Simon/Christine Trampusch, 2012: Institutional Shrinkage: The Deviant Case of Swiss Banking Secrecy. In: *Regulation and Governance* (forthcoming).

Strahm, Rudolf, 2009: Die Bankenmacht im Schweizer Staat. In: *Das Magazin* 2009/13, 12–17.

———, 2010: *Warum wir so reich sind*. Second edition. Berne: hep Verlag.

Strebel, Brigitte, 2005: Integrierte Finanzmarktaufsicht: Verhandlungsposition verstärken. In: *Schweizer Bank*, September 16.

Streeck, Wolfgang/Philippe C. Schmitter, 1985: *Private Interest Government: Beyond Market and State*. Beverly Hills: Sage.

Swiss Federal Administrative Court, 2010a: *Urteil vom 5. Januar 2009, B-1092/2009*.

———, 2010b: *Urteil vom 21. Januar 2009, A-7789/2009*.

Vogel, Steven K., 1996: *Freer Markets, More Rules: Regulatory Reform in Advanced Industrial Countries*. Ithaca: Cornell University Press.

Vogler, Robert U., 2005: *Das Schweizer Bankgeheimnis: Entstehung, Bedeutung, Mythos*. Zurich: Verein für Finanzgeschichte.

Winzeler, Christoph, 2010: Rechtsentwicklungen um das Bankkundengeheimnis: Standortbestimmung 2009. In: *Aktuelle Juristische Praxis* 2010/2, 158–166.

Zufferey, Jean-Baptiste, 1998: Vaut-il mieux être banque ou négociant? In: Claude-Alain Margelisch/Christoph Winzeler (eds.), *Freiheit und Ordnung im Kapitalmarktrecht*. Festgabe für Jean-Paul Chapuis. Zurich: Schulthess, 193–216.

Zürcher, Isaac, 2010: *Moravcsik, Schengen und die Schweiz*. Masters thesis. Berne: University of Berne, Institute of Political Science.

7

The Regulatory Response of the European Union to the Global Financial Crisis

Lucia Quaglia

Introduction

The global financial crisis that erupted full force in late 2008 challenged the existing architecture of financial services regulation and supervision. The European Union (EU) was severely affected by the crisis, prompting an intense regulatory debate on the revision of existing rules and the adoption of new regulatory measures in the EU. This chapter outlines the EU's regulatory response to the global financial crisis, asking whether it represents a major break from the past, as might be expected following the most severe financial crisis since the Great Depression, or whether it is an incremental adjustment.

The EU's response to the global financial crisis is an important research topic for three main reasons. First, the EU has devoted considerable efforts to the completion of the single financial market in Europe following the Financial Services Action Plan (FSAP) in 1999 (Commission 1999). After the Plan was completed in 2004, it was agreed that there would be a "regulatory pause," the focus shifting to implementation and monitoring (Commission 2004). However, in the aftermath of the global financial crisis, the EU has made a series of regulatory changes. Second, EU rules to a large extent provide the framework for national regulatory changes in the member states. Third, the EU is one of the largest jurisdictions in the world; it is increasingly active in shaping global financial rules in international forums, as argued in the section on "Reform of the financial services," and it is one of the main interlocutors of the United States in the policy debate on this subject (Posner 2009).

This chapter begins with an overview of financial market integration and regulation in the EU prior to the global financial crisis. The section that then follows outlines the regulatory changes enacted or set in motion by the EU in the aftermath of the crisis. The focus here is on the medium to long-term response, hence primarily the legislative measures proposed or adopted by the EU, rather

Financial support from the European Research Council (204398 FINGOVEU) is gratefully acknowledged.

than its short-term crisis management measures. The next section provides an overall assessment of the EU regulatory response to the global financial crisis, teasing out the most prominent features and the main drivers of and the opponents to the EU regulatory reforms. It is argued that the reforms enacted by the EU since 2008 constitute a series of incremental changes rather than path-breaking reform. The changes carried out were those that were politically feasible given the compounded polity of the EU and the complex multi-level governance of financial services, rather than "first best" solutions to the problems at hand.

An overview of financial market regulation in the EU prior to the crisis

In the run up to the final stage of Economic and Monetary Union (EMU) and in the first decade after the introduction of the euro, the pace of financial market integration quickened and financial services governance underwent significant changes in the EU. This process was driven by the Commission (Jabko 2006; Posner 2005) and was actively advocated by an increasingly powerful transnational financial industry (Van Apeldoorn 2002; Bieling 2003; Mügge 2010). From the early 2000s onwards, the completion of the single financial market was achieved through a set of legislative measures outlined in the FSAP. These measures aimed mainly at maximum harmonization and focused primarily on securities markets and insurance (Ferran 2004). Subsequently, attention shifted to post-trading,[1] in particular payment services and clearing and settlement of securities (Quaglia 2009). In the same period, new accounting rules were agreed by the EU, basically adopting the international standards issued by the International Accounting Standards Board (IASB) (Leblond 2011; Véron 2007).

The completion of the single financial market was facilitated by the reform of the framework for financial regulation and supervision in the EU in the early 2000s, when the so-called Lamfalussy reforms were enacted in banking, securities markets and insurance (Mügge 2006; Quaglia 2007). Basically, the main innovation introduced by the Lamfalussy reforms was the fact that implementing measures of level 1[2] financial services legislation were to be adopted by the

---

1 After a trade is complete, it goes through post-trade processing, whereby the buyer and the seller verify the details of the transaction, approve it, exchange records of ownership, and transfer securities and cash.

2 The Lamfalussy architecture was articulated across multiple institutional levels. At level 1, the EP and the Council co-decided framework legislation (mainly directives) proposed by the Commission. At level 2, the implementing measures (generally directives, less frequently regulations)

Commission through the "comitology" process, which involved committees of member state representatives (the so-called level 2 committees). Committees of national regulators were established to advise the Commission on the adoption of legislative measures (the so-called level 3 committees). They also had implementation tasks and could adopt non-legally binding standards and guidelines (Coen/Thatcher 2008; Quaglia 2008). These committees were the Committee of European Banking Supervisors (CEBS), the Committee of European Securities Regulators (CESR) and the Committee of Insurance and Occupational Pension Supervisors (CEIOPS).

In the making of EU financial services regulations prior to the crisis, the United Kingdom (Posner/Véron 2010) and the most competitive part of the financial industry (Mügge 2010) were highly influential for a variety of reasons. To begin with, the United Kingdom and the United States hosted the main global financial centers and had a large financial industry, in particular when compared to the rest of the economy (especially in the United Kingdom; Macartney 2010). Their policymakers therefore had widely recognized financial expertise and were regarded as providing state-of-the-art regulation. Moreover, British policymakers invested a considerable amount of technical and human resources in order to shape the regulatory debate in the EU. Interviews conducted by the author prior to the crisis suggest that British policymakers were on average very well briefed about the financial dossiers under discussion in Brussels and eager to lead the negotiations.

In addition, the United Kingdom and the United States hosted large banks that had the resources to lobby policymakers domestically and internationally (Baker 2010; Helleiner 2010). For example, the Basel Committee on Banking Supervision (BCBS), which is the international standard-setting body in the banking sector, consulted extensively on the so-called Basel II accord (BCBS 2004) that set international capital requirements for banks (see Goldbach/Kerwer in this volume). The Committee received more than 200 responses to its consultation documents, two-thirds of which were from industry, mainly from financial institutions located in the United States and the United Kingdom. The European Commission also consulted on the incorporation of the Basel II rules into EU legislation: the Capital Requirements Directive (CRD). In this case, too, there was a large response from financial institutions located in the United Kingdom.

---

of the level 1 framework legislation were adopted by the Commission through the comitology process, which involved the so-called level 2 committees of member state representatives. At level 3, the committees of national regulators (the level 3 committees) advised the Commission on the adoption of level 1 and level 2 measures and adopted level 3 measures, such as non-legally binding standards and guidelines.

The reform of financial services regulation in the EU after the crisis

A host of new regulatory initiatives were undertaken by the EU in the aftermath of the global financial crisis, besides the short-term crisis management measures adopted in the midst of the turmoil (Quaglia et al. 2009). These changes are summarized in Table 1, which outlines the list of new rules introduced or substantially amended and their content. The EU's actions that did not result in "hard" legislative measures, such as recommendations on managers' remuneration (Commission 2009) and the communication regarding a new EU framework for crisis management in the financial sector (Commission 2010), are not examined because they are not legally binding.

Deposit and investor guarantee schemes

As far as banking is concerned, the global financial crisis brought into the spotlight the inadequacy of the existing Deposit Guarantee Scheme (DGS) Directive, dating back to 1994. This directive set the minimum level of deposit protection schemes in the EU to 20,000 euros per depositor. When the crisis broke out, the depositor protection coverage ranged from 20,000 euros in the new member states and the United Kingdom to more than 100,000 euros in Italy and France. Moreover, uncoordinated decisions on deposit guarantees taken by the member states worsened the crisis. The most notable case was that of depositors in the United Kingdom who moved their money from British banks to branches of Irish banks in the United Kingdom when Ireland unilaterally introduced an unlimited deposit guarantee in October 2008. This caused a severe draining of liquidity away from the British banks.

At the peak of the crisis, the Commission proposed legislative changes concerning the DGS Directive. These changes, which were hastily agreed in 2009, represented an emergency measure designed to restore depositors' confidence by raising the minimum level of coverage for deposits from 20,000 euros to 50,000 euros subsequently to 100,000 euros. The need for swift action meant that several open issues were not tackled and hence the Directive contained a clause providing for a broad review of all aspects of DGSs. In July 2010, the Commission put forward a legislative proposal on Deposit Guarantee Schemes for banks with a view to addressing the remaining issues (Commission 2010b). As of August 2011, the negotiations between the Council and the EP had not been concluded.

The proposed directive contains measures for the harmonization of coverage and the simplification of arrangements for payout. The payout period is reduced from three months to seven days. In order to facilitate the payout pro-

Table 1 Overview of the EU's regulatory response to the global financial crisis

Regulatory change in the EU: – new rules introduced – existing rules amended – institutions established or reformed	Content of new or amended rules
Banking	
Deposit Guarantee Scheme (DGS) directive amended (October 2008)	Minimum level of coverage for deposits increased; payment time reduced
Proposal for new DGS directive (July 2010)	Harmonization of coverage and simplification of payout
Capital Requirements Directive (CRD) III amended (2008–10)	Higher capital requirements on trading book and securitization; sound remuneration practices
CRD IV to be proposed in summer 2011, following Basel III (December 2010)	Redefinition of capital, higher capital requirements, increase of risk weight for certain assets, leverage ratio, liquidity rules
Securities and investment funds	
Proposal for Investor Guarantee Scheme directive amendment (July 2010)	Minimum level of coverage for investor increased; payment time reduced
Regulation on Credit Rating Agencies (CRAs) (May 2009)	CRAs compulsory registration and compliance with rules concerning conflict of interest and quality of rating
Directive on Alternative Investment Funds Managers (AIFMs) (October 2010)	Legally binding authorization and supervisory regime for all AIFM, European passport for AIFMs
Proposed regulation on OTC derivatives, central counterparties and trade repositories (September 2010)	Reporting obligation for OTC derivatives to trade repositories, clearing obligation for standardized OTC derivatives through CCPs, common rules for CCPs and trade repositories
Accounting	
Commission Regulation adopting amended International Accounting Standards (October 2008); see also IASB revisions (October 2008) IASB standards revision in progress	Fair value not applied to certain banks' assets
Institutional framework for regulation and supervision	
Directives on ESRB and ESFS (December 2010), following the de Larosière Report (February 2009)	Transformation of level 3 Lamfalussy committees into European Authorities; creation of a European System of Financial Supervisors at micro-prudential level and of the European Systemic Risk Board dealing with macro-prudential oversight

cess in cross-border situations, the directive designates the host country DGS as a single point of contact for depositors at branches in another member state. The host country DGS would also be responsible for paying out on behalf of the home country DGS. In the preparation of the directive, which would have been legally binding for member countries, the Commission considered setting up a single pan-European scheme. However, it soon realized that there were complicated legal issues that needed to be examined and therefore the idea of a pan-European DGS was shelved for the time being. A report examining this issue will be presented by the Commission by 2014 (Commission 2010b).

The directive on DGS for banks (listed in Table 1) was part of a package on guarantee schemes in the financial sector, which also comprised a review of investor compensation schemes (listed in Table 1) and a White Paper on insurance guarantee schemes, all issued in July 2010. The Investor Compensation Scheme Directive, dating back to 1997, established a minimum level of compensation in cases where an investment firm was unable to return assets belonging to an investor. The Commission's proposal for a revision of this Directive raised the minimum level of compensation for investors from 20,000 euros to 50,000 euros per investor. The payout time was reduced to up to nine months (Commission 2010c).

Whereas in banking and securities specific directives on guarantee schemes had been adopted respectively in 1994 and 1997, this had not been the case in insurance. Only a few member states have insurance guarantee schemes. With a view to harmonizing consumer protection in this area, the Commission adopted a White Paper on Insurance Guarantee Schemes that envisaged the introduction of a directive establishing compulsory insurance guarantee schemes in all member states, subject to a minimum set of requirements (Commission 2010d). The White Paper was subject to public consultation (still pending at the time of writing in August 2011) with a view to a legislative proposal to be put forward by the Commission at a later date.

Capital requirements for banks and investment firms

The main reform enacted in the banking sector concerned rules on capital requirements. Prior to the crisis, international capital requirements were set by the Basel II accord agreed by the BCBS in 2004 (BCBS 2004). In the EU, the main elements of the Basel II accord had been incorporated into the CRD III[3] in 2006. Various revisions of the CRD were carried out in parallel with the inter-

---

3 The first CRD was issued in 1993, incorporating the Basel I accord into EU legislation; in 1998, the CRD II incorporated the amendments of the Basel I accord; and in 2006 the CRD III incorporated the Basel II accord into EU legislation. Actually, what is generally referred to as CRD III includes two directives: Directive 2006/48/EC relating to the taking up and pursuit

national debate on this issue taking place in the BCBS. The revisions of the CRD in 2009 and 2010 set higher capital requirements on the trading book and re-securitizations; imposed stronger disclosure requirements for securitization exposures; and required banks to have sound remuneration practices that did not encourage or reward excessive risk taking (Commission 2009e). The scope of these changes, however, remained quite limited because a comprehensive revision of the Basel II accord was pending. The Basel III accord was eventually signed in December 2010 (see Goldbach/Kerwer in this volume).

The EU was represented in the BCBS by the European Commission, albeit with non-voting observer status, like the ECB. The central banks and the supervisory authorities of the G20 members, including nine EU member states, were full members of the Committee. Hence, the national authorities, as opposed to the EU authorities (namely, the Commission), were in the driving seat in the negotiations in Basel. An EU position, as such, was somewhat lacking, despite attempts by the Commission to coordinate the positions of the European members of the Committee (confidential interviews, June–July 2011). The balance of power shifted, however, once it was time to incorporate the Basel III accord into the CRD IV (discussed below), which was officially proposed by the Commission, after several rounds of consultation with the national authorities and industry.

The negotiations of the Basel III accord were characterized by a division between, on the one side, the United States, the United Kingdom, and Switzerland, which were keen to impose a stricter definition of capital as well as higher capital requirements (for more details see Goldbach/Kerwer in this volume). On the other side, continental European countries—first and foremost, Germany, France, and Italy—were reluctant to accept tighter rules. In part as a result of the state-led recapitalization in the wake of the crisis, the main British banks were relatively well capitalized when the Accord was negotiated. Hence they were likely to have few problems in meeting the new capital requirements set by the Basel III accord. By contrast, the banks in many continental European countries were undercapitalized for a variety of reasons: a lower degree of state-led recapitalization in the midst of the crisis, and other institutional features in place prior to the crisis (as in the case of the public banks in Germany, see Hardie/Howarth 2009). Furthermore, the impact of stricter capital requirements on lending to small and medium-sized enterprises was a major concern for continental European countries, which have a bank-based financial system, where banks provide funding to the real economy. This was less of a concern for the Anglo-Saxon countries that rely more on financial markets for corporate finance.

---

of the business of credit institutions and Directive 2006/49/EC on the capital adequacy of investment firms and credit institutions.

After the Basel III accord was agreed internationally, the process of incorporating it into EU legislation began in earnest. The main difference between the Basel III and the proposed EU legislation are that the former is not a law, but an international "gentlemen's agreement" between supervisors and central banks. Hence, it has to be transposed into EU (and national) law in order to become legally binding. The Basel III accord applies to "internationally active banks," whereas EU legislation applies to all banks (more than 8,000), as well as to investment firms in the EU. These differences had to be taken into account when transposing the Basel III accord into EU law.

In July 2011, the Commission adopted a legislative package designed to replace the CRD III with a directive that governs access to deposit-taking activities (Commission 2011b) and a regulation that establishes prudential requirements for credit institutions (Commission 2011c)—this package is often referred to as the CRD IV. After its approval, the proposed directive will have to be transposed in the member states in a way suitable to their own national environment. It contains rules concerning the taking up and pursuit of the business of banks, the conditions of freedom of establishment and freedom to provide services, and the definition of competent authorities. The directive also incorporates two elements of the Basel III accord, namely the introduction of two capital buffers on top of the minimum capital requirements: a capital conservation buffer identical for all banks in the EU and a countercyclical capital buffer to be determined at national level. Capital requirements are instead set by the regulation which, unlike the directive, will not have to be transposed by the member states and will be immediately applicable.

The proposed EU rules contain prudential requirements for credit institutions and investment firms. It covers the definition of capital, whereby the proposal increases the amount of own funds that banks need to hold as well as the quality of those funds. It introduces a Liquidity Coverage Ratio, the exact composition and calibration of which will be determined after an observation and review period in 2015. It also proposes a leverage ratio subject to supervisory review. Furthermore, the proposal set higher capital requirements for OTC derivatives that are not cleared though CCPs. The use of a regulation which, once approved, is directly applicable without the need for national transposition is designed to ensure the creation of a single rule book in the EU. The regulation eliminates one key source of national divergence. For example, in the CRD III, more than 100 national derogations (differences in national legislation transposing the EU directive) remained.

During the EU negotiations, some of the compromises controversially reached in the BCBS unraveled. Hence the EU is an important arena for setting capital requirements, but because of its implementation power rather than because of its unitary action in the BCBS (as argued above, this was not the case). For example, under the Basel III accord, capital instruments for companies that can issue ordinary shares may comprise only "ordinary shares" that meet certain strict criteria. The EU proposal does not restrict the highest quality form of capital only to "ordinary shares." However, it takes the same approach as the Basel III accord by imposing the same strict criteria that any instrument would have to meet to qualify as capital. This EU "adaptation" of Basel III rules was required because non-joint stock companies such as mutuals, cooperative banks, and savings institutions, do not issue ordinary shares (interviews, July 2011).

The European Parliament called for the taking into account of "European specificities" in incorporating the Basel III rules into the CRD IV. Hence, MEPs argued in favor of counting minority stakes towards equity capital, a looser definition of assets that could be included in liquidity buffers, and rules to ensure that mutually owned and cooperative lenders (common in some continental member states) were not disadvantaged. All these issues had caused friction within the BCBS and were reopened during the EU negotiations of the CRD IV. The EP was also keen to ensure an "international level playing field." Of particular concern was the fact that in the United States, the Basel III accord would be applied only to internationally active banks, whereas the new rules will be applied to all banks in the EU; the United States had not yet fully applied Basel II (EP 2010).

Regulating credit rating agencies

In the securities sector, Credit Rating Agencies (CRAs) were singled out among the main culprits of the crisis for failing to rate financial products properly (Brunnermeier et al. 2009). They substantially overrated many complex securities created through the financial activity of securitization and were slow in revising their ratings once market conditions deteriorated. The overgenerous rating of securities was influenced by the strong competition between CRAs to attract clients and by conflicts of interest because CRAs provided a variety of other services to the potential issuers requiring rating. Hence, they had strong incentives to be generous in their assessment of creditworthiness.

Prior to the crisis, CRAs were regulated internationally by a voluntary Code of Conduct Fundamentals issued by IOSCO in 2004 (IOSCO 2004) and revised in the wake of the crisis (IOSCO 2008). The compliance of CRAs with the Code had been monitored in the EU by the CESR which, prior to the crisis, had opposed the idea of specific EU rules for CRAs, opting in favor of the IOSCO "soft" (non-legally binding) rules. After the crisis, the CESR issued a report on CRAs (CESR 2008) which, like its previous report (CESR 2005), continued to support market-driven improvement, considering the revised IOSCO Code as the standard to regulate CRAs. A second report commissioned by the Commission by the European Securities Markets Experts (ESME)[4] also warned against the introduction of legislation in the EU. Echoing the concerns of the CESR, the ESME concluded that,

> Given the global nature of the business of CRAs and the existing US law, we have doubts as to whether the development of a separate EU law would produce any particular benefits. We think it is important that CRAs are subject to a global approach to their business [...] regulatory cooperation in this sphere is essential to avoid duplication of effort.   (ESME 2008)

The French presidency of the EU in the second semester of 2008 implicitly made EU legislation on CRAs one of its priorities. The European Council called for a legislative proposal to strengthen the rules on credit rating agencies and their supervision at EU level in October 2008 (Presidency Conclusion 2008). Influential MEPs supported the regulation of CRAs in the EU. Indeed, the EP produced two reports that discussed this matter (EP 2007, 2008). The (revised) IOSCO Code provided the benchmark for the Commission's draft regulation on CRAs (Commission 2008a, b). However, the Commission argued that the IOSCO rules needed to be made more concrete and be backed by enforcement.

CRAs initially opposed the idea of EU rules on rating. Subsequently, they focused their lobbying activities on the amendment of certain parts of the proposed legislation that were seen as too prescriptive, such as the requirements that regulators should gather information about the model used by CRAs, the quality of people employed and so on. This criticism was also shared by countries that have traditionally been in favor of light touch, principle-based regulation, as evidenced by the response to the Commission's consultation from the British Treasury, the Swedish Finance Ministry, the Finnish Finance Ministry as well as the main CRAs, namely Standard & Poor's, Moody's, Fitch, and AM Best.

The regulation on CRAs was agreed relatively quickly by the EU in less than a year. According to the new rules, all CRAs whose ratings are used in the EU need to apply for registration there and have to comply with rules designed to prevent conflict of interest in the rating process and to ensure the quality of their rating methodology and ratings. CRAs operating in non-EU jurisdictions can issue ratings to be used in the EU provided that their countries of origin have a regulatory framework recognized as equivalent to the one put in place by the EU, or that such ratings are endorsed by an EU-registered CRA (Council of Ministers and European Parliament 2009b).

---

4 This group was set up in 2006 to advise the Commission on European securities markets legislation. Its members come mainly from the financial industry.

The issue of equivalence was particularly controversial. Many policymakers (the EP was vocal on this, see EP 2008, 2009) felt that a mechanism was needed to recognize third-country regulation of CRAs as "equivalent" to the EU, with a view to facilitate the use in the EU of the ratings issued by CRAs located outside the EU. After extensive lobbying, first and foremost by the British authorities, who were worried about the negative effects that this could have for the financial instruments traded in the City of London, the regulation agreed in April 2009 contained provisions for an equivalence mechanism to be operated by the Commission.

In the end, some concerns remained as to whether the EU rules were fully in line with the IOSCO Code and the US legislation on CRAs, which was also revised in the wake of the crisis. This is an important issue because the main CRAs operating in the EU are headquartered in the United States and are therefore subject to US law. At the same time, the EU rules on equivalence could have implications for regulation in the United States. The main difference between the IOSCO Code and the US and EU legislation is that the former is not (nor could it be) legally binding, whereas US and EU laws are legally binding. The US and EU laws prescribe distinctive processes of registration for CRAs in their respective jurisdictions, unlike the IOSCO rules, which do not envisage the registration of CRAs.

In June 2010, the Commission proposed an amendment of the regulation on CRAs adopted in 2009. Since ratings issued by a CRA can be used by financial institutions throughout the EU, the Commission proposed a more centralized system for supervision of CRAs, whereby the newly created European Securities and Markets Authority was entrusted with exclusive supervisory powers over CRAs registered in the EU, including European subsidiaries of US headquartered CRAs, such as Fitch, Moody and Standard & Poor. The ESMA was given powers to request information, to launch investigations, and to perform on-site inspections. The amended Regulation was adopted by the Council and the EP in May 2011 (Council/EP 2011). In the summer 2011, the downgrading by the (mainly US-headquartered) CRAs of the government bonds in the countries directly hit by the sovereign debt crisis gave new momentum to the debate on the creation of the European rating agency, a proposal that was put forward by the EP (2011).

Regulating alternative investment fund managers

Prior to the financial crisis, in policy discussions in international forums, two different approaches could be detected concerning the regulation of hedge funds: one in favor of regulation, sponsored by Germany and France, and one resisting regulation, championed by the United States and the United Kingdom (Fioretos 2010). During preparations for the April 2009 G20 summit, the split over how to regulate hedge funds re-emerged. Several European countries, led by France and Germany—as suggested by the Sarkozy's and Merkel's joint letter (2009) – with the support of Italy, pushed for a tougher regulatory regime for hedge funds and wanted the funds to be overseen similarly to banks. By contrast, the US and UK authorities favored more disclosure over more regulation (*Wall Street Journal,* March 14, 2009). The G20 agreed "to extend regulation and oversight to all systemically important financial institutions, instruments and markets. This will include, for the first time, systemically important hedge funds" (G20 2009). This was seen as a victory for the continental call for hedge fund regulation.

The attempt to regulate hedge funds in the EU was given new momentum by the financial crisis (for a more comprehensive account, see Woll in this volume). In June 2009, the European Commission presented its proposal for the draft directive on AIFMs, which included managers of hedge funds, private equity funds and real estate funds, hence covering quite a broad range of financial entities. After intense lobbying from industry, the United States and the United Kingdom, the draft directive was partly revised during the Swedish presidency[5] of the EU in the second semester of 2009. The main opponents of the directive on AIFMs were the UK and the hedge fund industry, which is based mainly in London. During the consultation phase, they opposed the prospect of EU rules on hedge funds. Once the directive was proposed by the Commission, they focused their criticisms on certain provisions of the draft directive. In the EP, the Socialists called for hedge fund regulation before and after the financial crisis.

An agreement between the Council of Ministers and the EP was eventually reached in late October 2010, and the directive is due to enter into force in 2013. It introduces a legally binding authorization and supervisory regime for all AIFMs in the EU, irrespective of the legal domicile of the alternative investment funds managed. Hence, AIFMs will be subject to authorization from the competent authority of the home member state and to reporting requirements of systemically important data to supervisors. The directive sets up a European passport for AIFMs. Hence, an AIFM authorized in its home member state will be entitled to market its funds to professional investors in other member states, which will not be permitted to impose additional requirements (Council of Ministers and European Parliament 2011).

---

5 Sweden has a significant private equity industry, hence it was seen as having a vested interest in the revision of the text of the Directive.

Regulating over-the-counter derivatives

Prior to the global financial crisis, a large number of derivatives were traded over-the-counter (OTC), not through stock exchanges, and were not cleared through central counterparties (CCPs). Derivatives trading on stock exchanges increases transparency and central counterparties reduce counterparty risk (that is, the risk of default by one party to the contract), so that the default of one market participant would not cause the collapse of other market players, thereby putting the entire financial system at risk. The OTC derivatives comprise a wide variety of products (interest rates, credit, equity, foreign exchange and commodities) with various characteristics. They are used in a variety of ways, including for purposes of hedging, investing, and speculating. OTC derivatives account for almost 90 percent of derivatives markets. The default of Lehman Brothers and the bail out of AIG highlighted the need to obtain more reliable information on what goes on in the OTC derivatives market, which in the past remained outside the perimeter of regulation.

In September 2009, the G20 Pittsburgh Summit agreed that "all standard OTC derivative contracts should be traded on exchanges or electronic trading platforms, where appropriate, and cleared through central counterparties by end-2012 at the latest." Furthermore, they acknowledged that "OTC derivative contracts should be reported to trade repositories and that non-centrally cleared contracts should be subject to higher capital requirements" (G20 2009). In the United States, this issue was dealt with in the Dodd-Frank reform package. The EU moved almost in parallel with the United States. The EP issued a resolution on June 15, 2010 on "Derivatives markets: future policy actions" (EP 2010), which called on the Commission to "use a differentiated approach to the many types of derivative products available, taking account of differing risk profiles, the extent of usage for legitimate hedging purposes, and their role in the financial crisis." It also called for a "ban on CDS transactions […] which are purely speculative." The Commission issued a series of communications on this matter, arguing that there had been "a paradigm shift away from the traditional view that derivatives are financial instruments for professional use and thus require only light-handed regulation" (Commission 2009f). Commissioner Barnier also stressed the importance of EU–US convergence on the regulation of derivatives markets.

In September 2010 the European Commission proposed a regulation on OTC derivatives, CCPs, and trade repositories. This measure, which at the time of writing (August 2011) is under discussion, envisaged reporting obligations for OTC derivatives to trade repositories; clearing obligations for standardized OTC derivatives through CCPs; and common rules for CCPs and trade repositories. To be authorized, a CCP would have to hold a minimum amount of capital. Trade repositories would have to publish aggregate positions by class of derivatives, offering market participants a clearer view of the OTC derivatives market. The European Securities and Markets Authority (ESMA) would be responsible for the surveillance of trade repositories and for granting and withdrawing their registration. In order to be registered, trade repositories must be established in the EU. However, a trade repository established in a third country can be recognized by ESMA if it meets a number of requirements designed to establish that such a trade repository is subject to equivalent rules and appropriate surveillance in that third country. Interestingly, the regulation also foresees the need to conclude an international agreement to that effect and stipulates that if such an agreement is not in place a trade repository established in that third country would not be recognized by ESMA. CCPs in third countries would be able to operate in the EU subject to equivalence clause (Commission 2010e).

Prior to the crisis, the United Kingdom and the United States had opposed any regulation of derivatives markets (Helleiner/Pagliari 2010). After the crisis, when the Commission consulted on the proposed regulation on derivatives, the UK authorities raised objections to forcing "standardized" OTC derivatives contracts into clearing houses, whereas the Nordic countries were critical of measures contained in the regulation designed to prevent short selling (*Financial Times,* December 17, 2009), a feature that was strongly supported by France and Germany.[6]

Accounting standards

As far as accounting is concerned, the crisis reopened the never settled divide between the (mainly Anglo-Saxon) supporters of mark-to-market accounting, and those criticizing it, primarily in continental Europe (Donnelly 2010; Posner 2010). It also reopened the debate on the governance of the IASB. The EU partly succeeded in its long-standing goal of increasing its influence in the governance of the IASB, whereby the Commission was given observer status in the newly created Monitoring Board of the IASB (for a more detailed account see Lagneau-Ymonet/Quack in this volume).

As a response to the crisis, the EP, the Commission, and policymakers in France and Germany urged the IASB to limit the use of mark-to-market accounting (Nölke 2010). The IASB waived its due process procedures and amended its standards, allowing banks to reclassify financial instruments from the trading book (subject to mark-to-market valuation) to the banking book

---

6 Germany unilaterally and controversially banned short selling as the crisis unfolded.

(subject to historical costs). Shortly afterwards, the Commission endorsed the amended standards (Commission 2011a). Other amendments concerning the valuation of collateralized debt obligations and impairment rules were undertaken by the IASB following its due process, but with strong political pressure from the EU authorities.[7] Despite having urged the IASB to amend its standards, once the IASB did so, the Commission did not approve them. Reportedly, this was due to the resistance of French, German, and Italian banks and politicians in these countries to the new rules, which would have led to significant losses in their derivative portfolios (Bengtsson 2011).

Reforming the institutional framework for regulation and supervision

The global financial crisis triggered the reform of the EU framework for financial regulation and supervision. The crisis revealed the weaknesses of existing macro-prudential oversight in the EU and the inadequacy of nationally-based supervisory models in overseeing integrated financial markets with cross-border operators. It exposed shortcomings in the consistent application of Community law (the lack of a European rule book), as well as insufficient cooperation between supervisors in exchanging information and in crisis management (de Larosière Group 2009). In 2009, a group of high level practitioners and financial experts, chaired by the former governor of the Banque de France, produced a report on the issue, which was named after the chair of the group. Building on the de Larosière Report, in September 2009, the Commission put forward a series of legislative proposals for the reform of the micro- and macro-prudential framework for financial supervision in the EU. The Commission proposals were eventually agreed by the Council and European Parliament in autumn 2010 and were implemented in early 2011.

The main institutional innovations were the establishment of the European Systemic Risk Board, its chair to be elected by and from among the members of the General Council of the ECB and in charge of monitoring macro-prudential risk; the transformation of the so-called level 3 Lamfalussy committees (discussed in the second section on the overview of financial markets) into independent authorities with legal personality; an increased budget and enhanced powers. The newly created bodies—namely the European Banking Authority, the European Insurance and Occupational Pension Authority, and the European Securities Markets Authority—were charged with the tasks of coordinat-

---

7 For example, the Commission wrote several letters to the IASB on this issue, to which the IASB responded. The Chair of the IASB also appeared before the Council of Ministers to discuss the matter.

ing the application of supervisory standards and promoting stronger cooperation between national supervisors.[8] Nonetheless, the new agencies have limited
competences and it remains to be seen whether they will be able to regulate the
financial sector effectively.

In the negotiations on these institutional reforms, disagreements arose in
the Council and between the Council and the EP concerning the powers of
the newly created bodies, as well as the role of the EP in the proposed architecture. In the Council, there were (mainly British) concerns about giving the
new authorities powers over national regulators and the possibility of supervising individual financial cross-border institutions (*European Voice*, March 4, 2009;
April 6, 2009). Besides the United Kingdom, Ireland and Luxemburg were also
reluctant to transfer powers away from national supervisors to bodies outside
their borders (*Financial Times*, March 20, 2009; Buckley/Howarth 2010). Moreover, the UK government was reluctant to grant decision-making powers to
EU-level bodies while public funds to tackle banking crises came from national
budgets. To this effect, Gordon Brown, the British Prime Minister, secured a
guarantee that the new supervisory system would not include powers to force
national governments to bail out banks. The United Kingdom also stressed that
the EU's supervisory architecture should fit in with global arrangements and
should support the development of "open, global markets" (Darling 2009).
That said, a number of member states, particularly those with large financial
centers—namely the United Kingdom, France, and Germany—favored the limited reform approach and were hesitant about transferring substantive power
to the EU level (Buckley/Howarth 2010). This led to a significant reduction in
the scope of the Commission proposals during the negotiations in the Council.

By contrast, the EP argued that the Commission's proposals did not go far
enough and was adamant that the powers of the ESAs should be safeguarded
and its own oversight role enhanced. Hence, the EP called for the strengthening
of the financial and human resources available to the ESAs. It also called for
the presidency of the ESRB to be given to the president of the ECB, so as to
augment the authority of this newly created body. MEPs inserted provisions to
enable the ESRB to communicate rapidly and clearly. They defended the powers of ESAs to take decisions that are directly applicable to individual financial
institutions in cases of manifest breach or non-application of law, and where
there is disagreement between national authorities. The EP was keen for the
ESA to be able to temporarily prohibit or restrict harmful financial activities or

---

8 The Commission also proposed a directive amending the existing directives in the banking,
securities and insurance sectors and a Council Decision entrusting the ECB with specific tasks
in the functioning of the ESRB.

products already covered by specific financial legislation or in emergency situations (*Financial Times*, July 2010). On all these issues, the EP was able to get what it wanted.

The question of which authority (the Council, the EP and the Commission) has the power to call an emergency in the EU's banking sector was a major point of contention. However, in the end the Council—hence national governments—retained the sole power to declare a crisis. The EP was also unsuccessful in arguing that the three authorities should be located in the same city, Frankfurt, for efficiency reasons (EurActive 2010). However, they secured the inclusion of a review clause requiring the Commission to report back every three years on whether it is desirable to integrate the separate supervision of banking, securities, pensions, and insurance; on the benefits of having all the ESAs headquartered in one city; and on whether the ESAs should be entrusted with further supervisory powers, notably over financial institutions with pan-European reach. As far as accountability is concerned, the EP was given the power to veto the appointment of ESA chairs. Indeed, in February 2011 the EP postponed its decision on the proposed candidates for the European supervisory authority chairmen on the grounds that it needed more guarantees from the Commission and the member states regarding the independence of all senior executives of the authorities, appropriate budgetary and human resources, and an improved personnel selection procedure. Moreover, the ESRB President is to keep the chair and vice-chairs of the EP's Economic and Financial Affairs Committee updated on ESRB activities through confidential discussions.

An overall assessment

In the aftermath of the worst financial crisis since the 1930s, the EU embarked on a significant revision of its financial services regulation. It is not easy to evaluate regulatory reform in the EU (as elsewhere) in the wake of the crisis. Analytically, it is difficult to identify measurement standards or benchmarks against which to assess such a reform. Practically, many of the new measures adopted have still to enter into force. Hence, necessarily, this assessment is provisional.

Three main features of the regulatory measures adopted or officially proposed by the EU stand out. First, the reforms enacted either regulated activities or financial institutions that were previously unregulated in the EU and its member states (CRAs), or at the EU level (AIFMs), or at the national, EU and international level (OTCDs). In other instances, they imposed heavier, more prescriptive and more burdensome requirements on financial entities that were already regulated prior to the crisis, as in the case of higher capital requirements for banks and new liquidity management rules (Basel III), or they put in place more substantial protection for depositors (the DGSD). That said, several key controversial issues, such as the problem of financial institutions too big to fail[9] and the management of cross-border banking crises, were not addressed, even though the Commission is likely to come forward with proposed legislation on an EU framework for crisis management in the financial sector later in 2011 (Commission 2011a).

Second, although with some notable exceptions, the new or amended rules were generally resisted by the UK, Ireland, Luxemburg, and a variable mix of Nordic countries, depending on the specific legislative measures under discussion, as well as by the actors representing the country (head of state, minister, ambassador). These were the main members of what Quaglia (2010a, b) identified as the "market-making" coalition, which prior to the financial crisis called for a market-friendly approach to financial regulation in the EU. The market players primarily affected by the new or revised rules, such as CRAs and AIFMs, initially resisted the proposed rules. Subsequently, they engaged in intense lobbying with a view to having the proposed rules amended on the grounds that they would be over-prescriptive and costly to implement, creating potential regulatory arbitrage vis-à-vis countries outside the EU. This argument was also used by banks that lobbied on certain aspects of the Basel III Accord and the CRD IV. The concern about international "regulatory arbitrage" has traditionally been at the forefront of British policymakers' minds, given the fact that London is a leading financial center which hosts many non-British owned financial institutions and successfully competes with other financial centers worldwide to attract business (interviews, London, May 2007; July 2008).

A somewhat special case was the revision of the Basel II Accord, which resulted in the Basel III Accord, as well as the parallel revisions of the CRD. Despite the fact that banking regulation and integration is fairly advanced in Europe (the first banking directive dates back to 1977), the EU was deeply divided in the negotiations on the Basel III accord. The United Kingdom favored strict new rules on capital requirements, whereas France, Germany, and Italy called for "softer" rules and a longer transition period. As explained in the third section on the reform of financial services, this had much to do with domestic political economy considerations related to the existing low level of bank capital and the banking–industry link on the Continent.

---

9 Shortly before the Bank of England took over banking supervision, Governor Mervyn King controversially called for the breaking up of the big banks. He also remarked that "if a bank is too big to fail [...] it is simply too big" (The Guardian, June 17, 2009).

By and large, the new or revised rules, as well as the reshaped institutional framework were actively sponsored, or at least strongly supported, by France, Germany, Italy, Spain, and the EP (especially, the Socialist groups). These were the members of what Quaglia (2010a, b) identified as the "market-shaping" coalition which was active in the making of EU financial regulation well before the financial crisis. The proposed EU measures were seen as necessary to safeguard financial stability and protect investors. Some of the proposed rules, such as those concerning AIFMs, CRAs and OTCDs, also embodied the deeply ingrained Continental dislike of "casino capitalism" (Strange 1997), which was seen as serving the fortunes of the City of London (interviews, Berlin, April 2008; Paris, July 2007; Rome, December 2007; Madrid, March 2009; Lisbon, November 2008).

In the main continental countries, unlike in the United Kingdom, there was limited concern over potential international regulatory arbitrage, or rather they were keen for the EU to act as a pace-setter in international financial regulation. In their response to the Commission's consultation on the proposed measures, many respondents—notably France and Germany—argued that "Europe should play an instrumental role in shaping a global regulatory regime" and that "an EU framework could serve as a reference for global regulation" (Commission 2009b: 8). Although, in the end, those resisting the new rules or parts of their content did manage to have the original legislative proposals amended, the very fact that the rules were proposed in the first place suggests that the balance of regulatory power has shifted in favor of a less market-friendly regulatory approach, which has at least temporarily gained ground in the EU (for a similar argument, see Posner/Véron 2010).

Internationally, the EU and the main member states have often played an important role in the debate on the reform of financial regulation. During the French presidency of the EU in the second semester of 2008, Nicolas Sarkozy argued that the G8 should be enlarged to include emerging economic powers such as Brazil, China, India, Mexico, and South Africa (Sarkozy 2008). In October 2008, the French President, accompanied by Commission President José Manuel Barroso held a meeting with US President George W. Bush, paving the way for the first summit of G20 leaders in Washington, DC in November 2008 (Hodson 2010). Since then, G20 Summits have been held in London and Pittsburgh in 2009, and in Toronto and Seoul in 2010. With the backing of the EU, the G20 has de facto replaced the G7 and G8 as the most important forum for international economic and financial cooperation.

Prior to the G20 summits, the EU attempted to coordinate its positions internally. For example, prior to the G20 summits in Washington and Pittsburgh the Council issued an "agreed language" (Council 2008, 2009b). The EU also agreed on a (rather general) set of priorities prior to the G20 summit in London (Council 2009a). These meetings at the EU level were often preceded by bilateral or multilateral meetings of the main member states, in which the Franco-German alliance was prominent. Prior to the G20 summit in London, the French President and the German Chancellor sent a joint letter to the presidency of the EU, outlining their priorities for the G20 in London (Sarkozy/Merkel 2009). At that summit, several EU priorities were achieved. The decision to enhance the oversight of systemically-important hedge funds and credit rating agencies met European demands. The most overt success for France and Germany was the G20 stance on tax havens, even though the issue had not been included in the EU agreed language. There was no commitment to additional fiscal stimulus, which was vetoed by Germany, but supported by the United Kingdom and the United States. The United Kingdom, however, supported and achieved an increase in the IMF's financial resources. At the G20 in Pittsburgh the EU, France, and Germany in particular, called for and partly achieved rules on bankers' bonuses and exit strategies from fiscal stimuli (Hodson 2010).

With the exception of the Basel III Accord negotiated by the BCBS and accounting standards set by the IASB, the EU did not wait for international action and acted as a (limited) reform promoter in its own right. The regulation on CRAs is much more prescriptive than the IOSCO code, and so is the AIFM directive, whereas the report produced by IOSCO on hedge funds was not even able to agree on whether hedge funds or funds managers should be regulated. The issue of DGS was also discussed by the IMF; however, the EU issued legally binding legislation. At the G20 meetings, the EU and its member states often called for regulatory reforms, even if at times there were different priorities among the European members of the G20, as in the case of the tax havens.

Third, the pace of reform was somewhat piecemeal in the EU. This has partly to do with the interlocking mechanisms of policymaking in the EU, where there are several veto players. The main agenda-setter of the reform efforts was the Commission, which is the only body that can officially propose legislation in the EU. Of course, the Commission did so after consulting the member states informally and after holding open public consultations. In certain cases the Commission was spurred to act by initiatives of the EP, as in the case of CRAs, and by the market-shaping member states, as in the case of AIFM. The Council and the EP were the main decision-makers because they had the power to adopt or amend the legislation proposed by the Commission. Often, the member states had different priorities and they were worried about potential regulatory arbitrage with jurisdictions outside the EU. Lobbying from the financial industry, which was keen to limit the extent of regulatory change at the national, EU, and international levels, watered down the proposed reforms in some cases, such as AIFM.

What is perhaps most remarkable in the politics of financial services regulation in the EU after the crisis is the political salience that the previously obscure topic of financial regulation has acquired. Prior to the crisis, financial regulation in the EU was mainly a "technical" policy area: there was very limited involvement of politicians and it was of marginal interest to the wider public. It was, however, an arena where the competing interests of the member states and the financial industry played out. After the crisis, heads of state and government, such as Sarkozy and Merkel, became interested in financial regulation, at times adopting populist stances to appease public opinion.

References

Alternative Investment Industry Association (AIMA), 2008: *Submission to the Treasury Committee, House of Commons, Banking Crisis, Written Evidence (Part 2)*. London: AIMA.

Apeldoorn, Bastiaan van, 2002: *Transnational Capitalism and the Struggle over European Integration*. London: Routledge.

Baker, Andrew, 2010: Restraining Regulatory Capture? Anglo-America, Crisis Politics and Trajectories of Change in Global Financial Governance. In: *International Affairs* 86(3), 647–663.

BCBS (Basel Committee on Banking Supervision), 2010a: *Basel III: A Global Regulatory Framework for More Resilient Banks and Banking Systems*. Basel: BCBS.

——, 2010b: *Basel III: International Framework for Liquidity Risk Measurement, Standards and Monitoring*. Basel: BCBS.

——, 2010c: *Interim Report Assessing the Macroeconomic Impact of the Transition to Stronger Capital and Liquidity Requirements*. Basel: BCBS.

——, 2004: *Basel II: International Convergence of Capital Measurement and Capital Standards: A Revised Framework*. Basel: BCBS.

Bengtsson, Elias, 2011: Repoliticization of Accounting Standard Setting: The IASB, the EU and the Global Financial Crisis. In: *Critical Perspectives on Accounting*, forthcoming.

Bieling, Hans J., 2003: Social Forces in the Making of the New European Economy: The Case of Financial Market Integration. In: *New Political Economy* 8(2), 203–223.

Brunnermeier, Markus, et al., 2009: *The Fundamental Principles of Financial Regulation*. Geneva Reports on the World Economy 11. London: Centre for Economic Policy Research (CEPR).

Buckley, James/David Howarth, 2010: Internal Market: Gesture Politics? Explaining the EU's Response to the Financial Crisis. In: *Journal of Common Market Studies Annual Review* 48, 119–141.

CEC (Commission of the European Communities), 2011a: *Proposal for a Directive on the Access to the Activity of Credit Institutions and the Prudential Supervision of Credit Institutions and Investment Firms*, 2011/453/EC, July 20. Luxembourg: CEC.

CEC (Commission of the European Communities), 2011b: *Proposal for a Regulation on Prudential Requirements for Credit Institutions and Investment Firms*, 2011/452/EC, July 20. Luxembourg: CEC.

——, 2011c: *Technical Details of a Possible EU Framework for Bank Recovery and Resolution*, January 6. Luxembourg: CEC.

——, 2010a: *Commission Services Staff Working Document: Possible Further Changes to the Capital Requirements Directive*, February 26. Luxembourg: CEC.

——, 2010b: *Directive …/…/EU Of the European Parliament and of the Council on Deposit Guarantee Schemes [recast]*, 2010/368/EC, July 7. Luxembourg: CEC.

——, 2010c: *Directive Amending Directive 97/9/EC on Investor Compensation Schemes*, 2010/371/EC, July 12. Luxembourg: CEC.

——, 2010d: *White Paper on Insurance Guarantee Schemes*, 2010/370/EC, July 12. Luxembourg: CEC.

——, 2010e: *Proposal for a Regulation of the European Parliament and of the Council on OTC Derivatives, Central Counterparties and Trade Repositories*, 2010/484/5/EC, September 15. Luxembourg: CEC.

——, 2010f: *Communication from the Commission on an EU Framework for Crisis Management in the Financial Sector*, 2010/579/EC, October 20. Luxembourg: CEC.

——, 2009a: *Communication from the Commission: An EU Framework for Cross-Border Crisis Management in the Banking Sector*, 2009/561/4/EC, October 20. Luxembourg: CEC.

——, 2009b: *Feedback Statement-Summary of Responses to Hedge Fund Consultation Paper*, March 12. Luxembourg: CEC.

——, 2009c: *Recommendation on Remuneration Policies in the Financial Services Sector, 2009/384/EC*, April 30. Luxembourg: CEC.

——, 2009d: *Proposal for a Directive on Alternative Investment Fund Managers and Amending Directives 2004/39/EC and 2004/…/EC 2009/207/EC*, April 30. Luxembourg: CEC.

——, 2009e: *Commission Proposes Further Revision of Banking Regulation to Strengthen Rules on Bank Capital and on Remuneration in the Banking Sector*. Press release, July 13. Luxembourg: CEC. <http://europa.eu/rapid/pressReleasesAction.do?reference=IP/09/1120&format=HTML&aged=0&language=EN&guiLanguage=en>

——, 2009f: *Financial Services: Commission Sets Out Future Actions to Strengthen the Safety of Derivatives Markets*. Press release, October 20. Luxembourg: CEC. <http://europa.eu/rapid/pressReleasesAction.do?reference=IP/09/1546&format=HTML&aged=0&language=EN&guiLanguage=en>

——, 2008: *Regulation (EC) 1004/2008 Amending Regulation (EC) 1725/2003 Adopting Certain IASs in Accordance with Regulation (EC) 1606/2002 as Regards IAS 39 and IFRS*, October 17. Luxembourg: CEC.

——, 2004: *Financial Services: Turning the Corner, Preparing the Challenge of the Next Phase of European Capital Market Integration, 10th Progress Report*. Brussels: EC.

——, 1999: *Financial Services: Implementing the Framework for Financial Markets: Action Plan*, 99/239/EC, May 11. Luxembourg: CEC.

CESR (Committee of European Securities Regulators), 2008: *CESR's Response to the Consultation Document of the Commission Services on a Draft Proposal for a Directive/Regulation on Credit Rating Agencies*, 2008/671/CESR, September 8, 2008. <ww.esma.europa.eu>

CESR (Committee of European Securities Regulators), 2005: *CESR's Technical Advice to the European Commission on Possible Measures Concerning Credit Rating Agencies 2005/139b/CESR*, March.

Coen, David/Mark Thatcher, 2008: Network Governance and Multi-Level Delegation: European Networks of Regulatory Agencies. In: *Journal of Public Policy* 28(1), 49–71.

Council of Ministers, 2011: *3100th Council Meeting Economic and Financial Affairs*. Press release, Brussels, June 20, 2011.

Council of Ministers and European Parliament, 2011: *Regulation (EU) No 513/2011 of 11 May 2011 amending Regulation (EC) No 1060/2009 on Credit Rating Agencies*, May 11.

——, 2009a: *Directive 2099/14/EC of 11 March 2009 Amending Directive 94/19/EC on Deposit-Guarantee Schemes as Regards the Coverage Level and the Payout Delay*, March 13, 2009.

——, 2009b: *Regulation (EC) No 1060/2009 of 16 September 2009 on Credit Rating Agencies*, November 17.

Council of the European Union, 2009a: *Brussels European Council 19/20 March 2009 Presidency Conclusion*. Brussels, April 29.

——, 2009b: *Agreed Language for the Pittsburgh G20 Summit*. Informal Meeting of EU Heads of State or Government. Brussels, September 17.

——, 2009c: *Brussels European Council 15/16 October 2008 Presidency Conclusion*. Brussels, October 16.

——, 2008a: *Informal Meeting of EU Heads of State or Government on 7 November 2008 Agreed Language*. Brussels, November 7.

Darling, Alistair, 2009: *Letter to Miroslav Kalousek, Czech Finance Minister*. Personal Communication, March 3.   <www.hmtreasury.gov.uk/d/chxletter_ecofin030309.pdf>

de Larosière Group, 2009: *The High-Level Group on Financial Supervision in the EU*. Chaired by Jacques de Larosière. Report. Brussels, February 25.

Dewing, Ian/Peter Russell, 2008: Financial Integration in the EU: The First Phase of EU Endorsement of International Accounting Standards. In: *Journal of Common Market Studies* 46(2), 243–264.

Donnelly, Shawn, 2010: *The Regimes of European Integration*. Oxford: Oxford University Press.

EurActive, 2010: *EU Cuts Deal to Set Up Banking Watchdogs*.   <www.euractiv.com/en/financial-services/eu-cuts-deal-set-banking-watchdogs-news-497410>

European Parliament (EP), 2011: *Beefing Up Credit Rating Agency Rules*. Press release, June 8.   <www.europarl.europa.eu/en/pressroom/content/20110606IPR20812/html/Beefing-up-credit-rating-agency-rules>

——, 2010a: *Resolution on Basel II and Revision of the Capital Requirements Directives (CRD 4)*. Committee of Economic and Monetary Affairs, Brussels, September 21.

——, 2010b: *Resolution on Derivatives Markets: Future Policy Actions*. Brussels, June 15.

——, 2009: *Draft Report on the Proposal for a Regulation of the European Parliament and of the Council on Credit Rating Agencies*. Committee on Economic and Monetary Affairs, Rapporteur: Gauzes, Brussels, January.

——, 2008a: *Draft Report with Recommendations to the Commission on Lamfalussy Follow-up: Future Structure of Supervision*. Committee on Economic and Monetary Affairs, Rapporteurs: Ieke van den Burg/Daniel Dăianu, Brussels, June 13.

European Parliament (EP), 2008b: *Draft Report with Recommendations to the Commission on Hedge Funds and Private Equity.* Committee on Economic and Monetary Affairs, Rapporteur: Poul Nyrup Rasmussen, Brussels, April 18.

——, 2008c: *Report of the European Parliament with Recommendations to the Commission on Hedge Funds and Private Equity.* Committee on Economic and Monetary Affairs, Rapporteur: Poul Nyrup Rasmussen, Brussels, September 11.

——, 2008d: *Report of the European Parliament with Recommendations to the Commission on Transparency of Institutional Investors.* Committee on Legal Affairs, Rapporteur: Lehne, Brussels, July 9.

ESME (European Securities Market Experts), 2008: *Role of Credit Rating Agencies.* ESME's Report to the European Commission, Brussels, June 4.

Federal Chancellery, 2009: *Chair's Summary of the Berlin G20 Preparatory Summit.* Press release, April 22.   <www.bercy.gouv.fr/directions_services/dgtpe/international/090222_prep G20.pdf>

Ferran, Eilis, 2004: *Building an EU Securities Market.* Cambridge: Cambridge University Press.

Ferrarini, Guido/Eddy Wymeersch (eds.), 2006: *Investor Protection in Europe: Corporate Law Making, the MiFID and Beyond.* Oxford: Oxford University Press.

Financial Stability Board (FSB), 2011: *OTC Derivatives Market Reforms Progress Report on Implementation.* Basel: FSB.

Fioretos, Orfeo, 2010: Capitalist Diversity and the International Regulation of Hedge Funds. In: *Review of International Political Economy* 17(4), 696–723.

Geithner, Timothy, 2010: *Letter to European Commissioner Michel Barnier.* Personal communication, March 1.

Group of Thirty/Working Group on Financial Stability, 2009: *Financial Reform: A Framework for Financial Stability.* Special Report, Washington, DC.

Group of Twenty (G20), 2009: *The Leaders Statement.* Pittsburgh Summit, Pittsburgh, September 25.

——, 2009: *The Global Plan for Recovery and Reform.* London Summit, London, April 2.

Hardie, Ian/David Howarth, 2009: Die Krise but Not La Crise? The Financial Crisis and the Transformation of German and French Banking Systems. In: *Journal of Common Market Studies* 47(5), 1017–1039.

Helleiner, Eric, 2010: A Bretton Woods Moment? The 2007–2008 Crisis and the Future of Global Finance. In: *International Affairs* 86(3), 619–636.

Helleiner, Eric/Stefano Pagliari, 2010: The End of Self-Regulation? Hedge Funds and Derivatives in Global Financial Governance. In: Eric Helleiner/Stefano Pagliari/Hubert Zimmerman (eds.), *Global Finance in Crisis: The Politics of International Regulatory Change.* London: Routledge, 74–90.

Hodson, Dermot, 2011: *The Paradox of EMU's External Representation: The Case of the G20 and the IMF.* Conference paper. EUSA Conference, Boston, March 3–5.

IIF (Institute for International Finance), 2010: *The Net Cumulative Economic Impact of Banking Sector Regulation: Some New Perspectives.* Washington, DC: IIF.

IOSCO (International Organization of Securities Commissions), 2009: *Hedge Funds Oversight.* Madrid: IOSCO.

——, 2008: *Code of Conduct Fundamentals for Credit Rating Agencies* (Revised, May). Madrid: IOSCO.

IOSCO (International Organization of Securities Commissions), 2004: *Code of Conduct Fundamentals for Credit Rating Agencies* (Revised, December). Madrid: IOSCO.

Jabko, Nicolas, 2006: *Playing the Market: A Political Strategy for Uniting Europe, 1985–2005.* Ithaca: Cornell University Press.

Leblond, Patrick, 2011: EU, US and International Accounting Standards: A Delicate Balancing Act in Governing Global Finance. In: *Journal of European Public Policy* 18(3), 442–460.

Macartney, Huw, 2010: *Variegated Neoliberalism: EU Varieties of Capitalism and International Political Economy.* London: Routledge.

Mügge, Daniel, 2010: *Widen the Market, Narrow the Competition: Banker Interests and the Making of a European Capital Market.* Colchester: ECPR.

——, 2006: Reordering the Marketplace: Competition Politics in European Finance. In: *Journal of Common Market Studies* 44(5), 991–1022.

Nölke, Andreas, 2010: The Politics of Accounting. In: Eric Helleiner et al. (eds.), *Global Finance in Crisis: The Politics of International Regulatory Change.* London: Routledge, 37–55.

Posner, Elliot, 2010: Sequence as Explanation: The International Politics of Accounting Standards. In: *Review of International Political Economy* 14(4), 639–664.

——, 2009: Making Rules for Global Finance: Transatlantic Regulatory Cooperation at the Turn of the Millennium. In: *International Organization* 63, 665–99.

Posner, Elliot/Nicolas Véron, 2010: The EU and Financial Regulation: Power Without Purpose? In: *Journal of European Public Policy* 17(3), 400–415.

Quaglia, Lucia, 2010a: *Governing Financial Services in the European Union: Banking, Securities and Post-Trading.* London: Routledge.

——, 2010b: Completing the Single Market in Financial Services: The Politics of Competing Advocacy Coalitions. In: *Journal of European Public Policy* 17(7), 1007–1022.

——, 2008: Committee Governance in the Financial Sector in the European Union. In: *Journal of European Integration* 30(3), 565–580.

Quaglia, Lucia, et al., 2009: The Financial Turmoil and EU Policy Cooperation 2007–8. In: *Journal of Common Market Studies Annual Review* 47(1), 1–25.

Rasmussen, Poul Nyrup, et al., 2009: *Letter to the President of the European Commission Barroso.* Personal communication, April 20.

——, 2009: *Letter to the President of the European Commission Barroso.* Personal communication, December 16.

Sarkozy, Nicolas, 2008: *Discours de M. Le Président de la République Française. Speech at the 63rd General Assembly of the United Nations,* New York, September 23. Paris: Elysée, Présidence de la République.

Sarkozy, Nicolas/Angela Merkel, 2009: *Letter to Mirek Topolanek, Prime Minister of the Czech Republic and José Manuel Barroso, President of the European Commission in Preparation for the G20 Summit.* Personal communication, March 16.

Strange, Susan, 1997: *Casino Capitalism.* Manchester: Manchester University Press.

Underhill, Geoffrey, et al. (eds.), 2010: *Global Financial Integration: Thirty Years On.* Cambridge: Cambridge University Press.

Véron, Nicolas, 2007: *The Global Accounting Experiment.* Bruegel Blue Print Series. Brussels: Bruegel.

8

The Defense of Economic Interests in the European Union: The Case of Hedge Fund Regulation

Cornelia Woll

Introduction

After an initial shock caused by its inability to provide a collective response to the financial crisis, the European Union (EU) reacted by drawing up an impressive list of regulatory initiatives (see Quaglia in this volume). The roadmap ranges from financial supervision to the regulation of financial services, covering areas such as capital requirements, deposit guarantee schemes, bank remuneration and credit rating agencies. While some seemed to provide rather technical solutions to problems that were unveiled by the crisis, other proposals were accused of being politically motivated and driven by a pro-regulatory agenda. The financial crisis, the argument went, gave momentum to member states in favor of tighter supranational regulation and disfavored countries with a more light touch approach to financial regulation (Quaglia 2011). In addition, it provided European institutions with an opportunity to seize power and expand their activities, even when there was no direct need for supranational intervention.

The regulation of hedge funds through the so-called Alternative Investment Fund Managers (AIFM) directive adopted in November 2010 seems to be emblematic of this development. Highly politicized, the member state negotiations, that lasted for 18 months, pitted most notably France against the United Kingdom. Since even the Commission's original proposal acknowledged that hedge funds were not responsible for the financial crisis (European Commission 2009b: 3), the battle seemed to represent an ideological commitment to supranational regulation on the one hand, and national autonomy and a continued lack of intervention on the other.

Should one conclude that the AIFM directive arose from mere opportunism, from politicians exploiting the momentum of the financial crisis to drive a pro-regulatory agenda? Did ideologically driven governments instrumentalize the turmoil to attack the suspect industry, all the more because only the UK had considerable economic interests at stake? What explains the regulation of hedge funds in 2010 if they are not directly linked to the financial crisis as some argue?

This chapter counters analyses of European politics that center on ideological battles. By unpacking the positions of the French, British and German governments in the particularly heated debate over hedge fund regulation, I will demonstrate that each defended the interests of their industries, even those that appeared not to have very visible economic stakes. We tend to assume that business interests and the influence of the financial stakeholders are more effective in technical debates, where they benefit from "quiet politics" and the reduced accountability of politicians (Culpepper 2011). However, even in areas of high political salience, business interests can influence the course of European negotiations.

Yet the links between industry and government positions are often surprising and do not neatly reflect the distribution of economic stakes in a given country. Most importantly, *which* industries are most successful in influencing the government depends on how their demands fit the government agenda on financial regulation. In the case of hedge fund regulation, I will show that business influence hinged centrally on its importance to an overarching political objective: a Franco-German alliance on regulatory reform that went well beyond the issue of hedge fund regulation.

In theoretical terms, European negotiations are thus neither driven by economic interests only, as liberal intergovernmentalism assumes (see Moravcsik 1998), nor are they determined entirely by paradigmatic changes or the activism of the supranational institutions, which try to expand their activities. The following account emphasizes the strategic interplay of *some* business interests at the domestic level with the geopolitical strategies of governments at the supranational level.

The empirical account draws on qualitative interviews with industry representatives and policymakers in Brussels and the member states between December 2009 and May 2011, as well as primary documents, such as legislative and policy documents and industry briefs.[1] The chapter is divided into four parts. The first part lays out the history and context of hedge fund regulation prior to the EU's recent regulatory initiative. The second part, "Economic interests in European alternative investment," discusses the lobbying efforts and industry stakes in the member states that most actively influenced the discussion. The fourth part, "Geopolitical stakes and the Franco-German alliance," moves to the intergovernmental level to explain the issue linkage and alliances that were

---

1 Interviewees included officials from the European Commission, members of the European Parliament, representatives of member state governments and regulatory authorities, industry associations and lobbyists representing the affected sectors, as well as a public official from the US Securities and Exchange Commission.

at stake. I conclude by discussing how these two levels became linked and why they explain the final outcome of the negotiations, and lay out the lessons of this case study for the general examination of business–government relations.

A short history of hedge fund regulation

Hedge funds are investment vehicles that are notoriously difficult to define, but they generally refer to highly leveraged funds open only to wealthy or institutional investors who pay a performance fee to the fund's manager. Using a variety of investment methods, they tend to hold both long and short positions, where investment in supposedly overvalued securities is counterbalanced by investment in undervalued securities. Such strategies should rather be termed "leveraged speculation," which is the opposite of how the term "hedging" is traditionally used in finance (Edwards 1999: 189).

Hedge funds have developed in particular in countries where securities markets occupy a central role, most importantly the United States and the United Kingdom.[2] In both these countries, the regulation of hedge funds has tended to be through indirect regulation. Rather than imposing registration or disclosure requirements on the hedge funds themselves, regulation applied to the counterparties. In the United States, hedge fund managers were explicitly exempt from the oversight of the Securities and Exchange Commission (SEC) until recently, while British managers had to be accredited by the Financial Service Authority. In continental Europe, hedge funds were most often directly regulated, including registration, disclosure, and reporting requirements. In Germany, hedge funds, or more specifically the investment techniques they employed, were even prohibited until 2004. By comparison to the United States and the United Kingdom, the French and German hedge fund sector remains negligible (see IOSCO 2009; see Fioretos 2010).

Nevertheless, over the course of the late 1990s and 2000s, hedge funds became an issue of public debate and underwent some scrutiny from international bodies, in particular the International Organization of Securities Commissions (IOSCO) and the Financial Stability Forum (FSF, later renamed the Financial Stability Board, FSB), which both issued a series of principles, guidelines, and recommendations (cf. IOSCO 2009: 39). Even though the indirect supervisory ap-

---

2 The fund itself is a legal entity distinct from its manager and can be domiciled in another country. Most often hedge funds are registered in offshore financial centers, which attract funds through tax exemptions or low regulatory requirements.

proach remained in place, public authorities and industry in the United States and the United Kingdom moved to set up a credible self-governance regime in order to avoid further regulation. In the United Kingdom, the industry created a Hedge Fund Working Group (HFWG) in order to develop an industry-based code and the London-based Alternative Investment Management Association (AIMA) also issued a series of recommendations (IOSCO 2009: 40; Fioretos 2010).

Simultaneously, the European Central Bank became involved in the issue of systemic risks posed by hedge funds and the European Union began working on two directives in the early 2000s that touched directly on the operation of hedge funds. First, it continued revising a directive for collective investment schemes, such as mutual funds, the directive for Undertakings for Collective Investment in Transferable Securities (UCITS). UCITS are investment funds available to retail customers—that is, the general public—rather than to large institutional investors. These mutual funds obtained a European passport through the UCITS directive, originally adopted in 1985, which continued to be revised throughout the 2000s in order to remove barriers to cross-border trade and specify the conditions of their operation. Second, the EU drew up a new directive on investor protection in 2004, the Markets for Financial Instruments Directive (MiFID), which also touched upon certain requirements for alternative investment. But hedge funds were still largely left outside the reach of these initiatives and the European Parliament in particular pressed for tighter regulation of hedge funds and private equity, most notably through the Rasmussen report and the Lehne report in 2008 (see Lutton 2008).

The financial crisis moved the salience of the issue up to a new level (Fioretos 2010; Quaglia 2011). After two decades of simple guidelines and codes of conduct, members of the G20 declared at the London summit in April 2009 that they intended to strengthen financial regulation and to extend it to sectors that were previously not covered, including "for the first time, systematically important hedge funds" (G20 2009: 4).

In parallel, the European Commission published a proposal for the regulation of hedge funds and private equity firms with the intention of imposing registration and disclosure on all funds previously left outside the UCITS directive of 1985. Despite the preceding consultation the Commission had launched and despite the staunch opposition of a substantial part of the industry to the regulatory ambitions, the proposal insisted on the need for a harmonized direct regulatory regime to apply across Europe (European Commission 2009a, 2009b). Specifically, the Commission proposed that all alternative investment fund managers operating in the European market should require authorization and oversight according to commonly defined principles. In exchange, managers authorized to operate in one member state would obtain a "European passport" that enables them to operate anywhere in the European market without having to apply for additional authorization in the respective countries. Significantly, this passport would also be available for managers of funds domiciled in countries outside the EU.

The proposal, which was produced in record time, according to most observers, created an outcry on all sides. The investment industry and representatives from liberal market economies such as the United Kingdom and Ireland complained about the costly regulatory requirements and some even entirely rejected the proposal. Observers from pro-regulation countries were concerned about the scope of the directive and feared the consequences it would have for the access of funds from off-shore financial centers to the European market. In the intensive negotiations that followed in the European Council and Parliament, substantial revisions were introduced and several times the discussion risked breaking down entirely. In the Council, member states defended their national traditions, while party groups and other stakeholders tried to propose amendments in the European Parliament. During the following eighteen months, representatives from the Commission, the Council, and the European Parliament met in eighteen trialogues before jointly reaching an agreement on October 26, 2010. Between the initial proposal and the final agreement, the European Parliament most notably had tabled 1,690 amendments, a record number which testifies to the contestation and incompleteness of the initial draft proposal (Serrouya 2010). The following sections analyze the different positions and study the evolution of negotiations.

Economic interests in European alternative investment

Understanding the stakes and the evolution of the regulatory efforts requires a study of the interests and coalitions within the EU that led to the current regulatory framework. It is therefore important to examine in which countries the affected industries were located and how they developed their lobbying strategies.

Stakeholders within and beyond the hedge fund industry

The hedge fund industry is divided into several stakeholders: investors, the fund itself, the managers/advisors of the fund and the prime broker/dealers who provide lending to support leverage and facilitate short selling, but also clearing and settlement of trades, and custodial services. In some cases, prime brokers can outsource services to separate custodians. Similarly, hedge fund managers can outsource administrative functions such as accounting or risk analysis to fund administrators. All in all, this implies that a considerable number of financial service activities are linked to the hedge fund industry (see Hardie/MacKenzie 2007).

The United States is the largest center for hedge fund management, accounting for 68 percent of the total industry in late 2009, followed by Europe with 23 percent, and Asia with 6 percent. Within Europe, 76 percent were managed out of London. Other important locations include Sweden (5 percent), Switzerland (4 percent), France (2 percent), and the Netherlands (2 percent). The funds themselves are predominately domiciled in offshore financial centers: the Cayman Islands are the most popular with 39 percent, followed by Delaware (US) with 27 percent, the British Virgin Islands with 7 percent, and Bermuda with 5 percent of funds. Another 5 percent of global hedge funds are registered in the EU, primarily in Ireland and Luxembourg.

The attraction of the United Kingdom for hedge fund management is linked to the concentration of related services. With approximately half of European investment banking activity conducted through London, it is a central location for prime brokerage, but also administration, custody, and auditing. However, among the largest hedge fund prime brokers, one can also find Deutsche Bank (6 percent share of the brokerage industry), and among hedge fund administrators the French CACEIS Investor Services (6 percent), and the Fortis Prime Fund Solution (6 percent) which is currently owned by the French bank BNP Paribas (all figures from International Financial Services London 2010). Ireland is another important location for hedge fund administration.

Finally, many hedge funds in Europe have recently launched fund vehicles targeting retail investors in order to benefit from the European market for mutual funds established through the UCITS directive. In other words, hedge funds not only offer institutional investors products but have adapted to the regulated retail investor market in order to provide funds which qualify for the European UCITS passport. UCITS services under hedge fund management grew an impressive 50 percent in 2009, in particular in the United Kingdom, but also in France and Luxembourg (International Financial Services London 2010). This development is significant because it implies that hedge funds are beginning to enter into competition with the traditional mutual fund industry, which has been regulated since 1985 under the UCITS directive, prohibiting both leveraging and short-selling. Second only to the United States at the global level, France is a prime location of UCITS funds in terms of both management and domicile: 23 percent of European UCITS funds are managed in France, followed by Germany (20.1 percent), and the United Kingdom (15.8 percent). In terms of domicile, France comes in second with 20.3 percent of funds, after Luxembourg (26.2 percent) (Association française de la gestion financière 2010).

However, the AIFM directive is not just an issue for the hedge fund industry and their competitors. Indeed, one of the most central and most controversial decisions of the initial proposal was to address hedge funds through a directive that covers *all* investment funds that were previously left outside the realm of EU legislation. The definition of the scope of the AIFM directive is therefore a negative definition, seeking to cover "the management and administration of any non-UCITS in the European Union" (European Commission 2009b: 5). While pension funds and non-pooled investment—such as sovereign wealth funds—are excluded, private equity and venture capital funds, real estate funds, commodity funds, infrastructure funds, and other types of institutional funds will have to comply with the AIFM provisions. The private equity industry in particular was very concerned about the directive. Private equity firms, which provide funding for companies that are not publically traded on stock exchanges, are mainly managed in the United Kingdom (12.4 percent), but also in France (4.7 percent), Germany (3.3 percent), and Sweden (1.7 percent) (TheCityUK Research Center 2010). In Germany, real estate funds also play an important role.

It is thus incorrect to state that only the United Kingdom had considerable economic interests at stake because it is home to almost 80 percent of the hedge fund industry. To be sure, the City of London was concerned in almost all aspects of the hedge fund industry and also as a location for all other affected investment funds. But France and Sweden also have important hedge fund activities, all the more so if one includes related services, such as prime brokerage. As preferred locations for the registration of funds within Europe, Ireland and Luxembourg also had an interest in keeping the hedge fund industry flourishing. If one includes private equity and other investment vehicles, the spread of economic stakeholders becomes even broader. The industries and firms that we would expect to lobby in support of light-touch regulation can thus be found in the United Kingdom, France, and Germany. Further support would be likely from Sweden, Luxembourg, and Ireland, if one considers industry stakes only.

However, what is mostly overlooked is that a specific branch of the investment industry was quite concerned about the growth in the unregulated investment sector: collective investment funds falling under UCITS began to enter into the hedge fund market and were in competition with hedge funds offering UCITS-compliant products. This implied that UCITS funds had a strong interest in ensuring that this competition happened within the UCITS regulatory framework, where everybody bore the same costs. UCITS funds were located predominantly in France. In what follows, I will argue that it is the political influence of the UCITS industry that led to the French government's refusal to accept a European passport for third-country funds.

Lobbying strategies

Many members of the investment industry realized how imminent EU regulation was only when they read the first proposal of the European Commission in April 2009. Investment funds had become used to being unregulated and only paid partial attention to the consultation procedure the Commission had launched between December 2008 and January 2009. For the private equity industry in particular, the draft was a cold shower they did not expect because they had done their utmost to insist on being exempted from investment regulation (interview with a business representative, Brussels, March 4, 2011). For a long time, private equity firms felt that they were "legitimately not regulated" because they provided financing to small and medium-sized companies; in the case of venture capital "they were the nice guys" helping firms focusing on technological innovation, even in risky contexts (interviews with a business representative, Paris, February 10, 2011; European Commission, March 10, 2011).

In the period following the publication of the proposal, the CEOs of investment funds relied on their well-established ties with national politicians and sometimes insisted even on their most basic desire: to be exempt from the pending regulation. This initial lobbying period was somewhat awkward and unsuccessful at the European level. According to one representative:

[Within the EU] if you fail to convince at the technical and technocratic level, it does not help you to be friends with the finance minister of your country or be able to stand on your head. [...] Knowledge of the procedure is very important. [The investment managers], taken individually, may be falcons, but taken together, they behaved like a bunch of frightened sparrows trying to stop a steam roller.　(Interview, Brussels, March 4, 2011)

A learning period had to be gone through before investment firms got organized and begin to contribute constructively to the negotiations in order to limit the negative impact on their sector of activity. Eventually, most business associations ended up endorsing the general ambition of the proposal, but suggested substantial modifications in the heart of the text. The private equity industry's lobbying strategy is illustrative of this evolution: their European association EVCA withdrew an initial policy statement where they had spoken out entirely against the proposal and began to support the idea of European harmonization in order to be able to shape the details of the directive (interview, European Commission, Brussels, March 10, 2011).

Simultaneously, the national associations lobbied their ministries, regulators, and national Members of the European Parliament (MEPs) to gain support for the common position. British industry representatives from all concerned domains, furthermore, coordinated their lobbying in both London and Brussels and deployed a tremendous effort to shift the details of the draft, as well as the general attitude in the European Parliament, and also the Commission, in favor of light-touch regulation.

Still, the British industry was initially not used to collective action because they had never been the object of substantial regulatory efforts. Firms could choose to be represented by AIMA, the Association of Investment Companies (AIC), or the Investment Management Association (IMA), but membership was not an obligation, in contrast to France, for example. A 2009 parliamentary report highlighted that the Hedge Fund Standards Board, which collectively defined industry standards, AIMA's voluntary code of conduct, had only 34 members out of 400 to 450 firms (House of Commons 2009: 128). To ward off what felt like a European attack on the British regulatory model, Her Majesty's Treasury, the FSA, and the industry mobilized in several working groups. As one public official explained:

Treasury held town hall meetings with hedge fund managers. You had guys worth hundreds of millions sitting on the floor because there was not enough space. They thought it would all be fine, that there was no way [the regulation] could happen. They would just shout or yell when we told them otherwise.   (Cited in Prabhakar 2011: 119)

In contrast to these big investment funds, which grasped the importance and functioning of the European policymaking process only during the course of the negotiations in 2009 and 2010, the UCITS industry had been playing the game since 1985. Having been active in several revisions of the UCITS directive, they monitored developments in Brussels much more closely and already had well established ties at the national level with public officials working on EU regulation, as well as in Brussels. This difference in EU public affairs experience would turn out to matter immensely, since the UCITS industry was able to make a very forceful case against some of the provisions of the AIFM directive from very early on (interview with a business representative, Frankfurt a.M., February 21, 2011). According to one observer, the relationship between these funds and the French finance ministry is the only plausible reason that can explain the rigid position France defended throughout the negotiations. He argued,

[French finance minister] Lagarde and [other French representatives] took issue with third country passports, even though it was not the position of the banking or private equity industry or the French investors. But a small portion of the UCITS industry ended up being in competition with hedge funds and was afraid that these would be exempted from the regulatory costs weighing on the UCITS industry. They therefore said "If they get a passport, we are dead" and the government went with it all the way.   (Interview with a business representative, Brussels, March 4, 2011)

Indeed, a French public official declared himself to be puzzled by his governments' positions, since it "does not reflect the interests of the French investment industry, which looks much more similar to the British industry than one is led to believe" (interview, Paris, November 25, 2009).

While the French government argued that their position was in line with the battle against tax havens, which often hosted alternative investment funds, several observers doubt the validity of this argument. According to the proponents of the proposal, including French MEPs such as Jean-Paul Gauzès, the acceptance of the passport system was a more efficient way of imposing constraints on tax havens than its rejection (interview, Paris, May 19, 2011).

Why was a small portion of the French industry so efficient in its lobbying that it outweighed all other business interests on these issues and almost brought the AIFM negotiations to a standstill? In what follows, I will argue that we need to consider the member states' strategic alliances on financial regulation more generally to understand which demands translated into the ones the member states defended at the EU level.

Geopolitical stakes and the Franco-German alliance

In particular, a Franco-German alliance on regulatory reform in international finance turned out to be crucial for the evolution of the AIFM negotiations. The joint interest in hedge fund regulation began as early as 2007, at the G8 summit in Heiligendamm, but at the time, proponents of a more regulatory approach had little momentum. As the financial crisis unraveled, both French and German policymakers realized that they should seize the opportunity to move ahead on their respective objectives.

Germany had remained suspicious of hedge funds since they allowed their operation in 2004 and wished to regulate them tightly. The experience of the Deutsche Börse takeover and a general public mistrust of alternative investment funds such as private equity, made hedge funds fertile ground for political activism in Germany (cf. Milne 2008). French President Nicolas Sarkozy, in turn, sought to capitalize on the financial crisis to become known for a new financial architecture he wished to push under the French presidency of the EU in the second half of 2008 and later the French presidency of the G20 from 2010 to 2011, just months before his upcoming election. Facing countries with a more light-touch tradition on financial regulation, the two governments made a pact to support each other in order to defend a pro-regulatory agenda against the Anglo-Saxon laissez-faire tradition. This general agreement fundamentally shaped alternative investment negotiations. According to a French government representative:

Ten years ago, we were like the Germans, but we have liberalized a lot recently [...]. But on [alternative investment] we do not argue against the German position for political reasons, which come from the highest level. President Sarkozy has asked us to support Germany all the way. (Interview, Paris, November 25, 2009)

The first person to succumb to the pressure of the Franco-German alliance was Internal Market Commissioner Charlie McCreevy. Initially, he had declared publically that hedge funds would not be regulated under his leadership, and allegedly signaled his staff that anybody working on such a proposal would be fired (interview cited in Prabhakar 2011: 110). However, as Commission President José Manuel Barroso faced re-election in 2009, the French and German governments indicated that progress on a hedge fund directive was important in order to obtain their support. With similar signals from the European Parliament, Barroso insisted that a proposal be ready as soon as April 2009. As a result of these political imperatives, a proposal was produced in record time and without much exchange with national officials after the official consultation in January 2009. The inspiration for much of the original text came from existing European directives, in particular UCITS and MiFID, simply in order to save time, which explains why even supporters of the regulation were disgruntled when they read the first draft (interview, Paris, December 10, 2009). Arguing that British mistrust was partly unjustified, a French official underlined, "[the British] are convinced that France is behind this directive, but I can assure you that it came from DG Market, maybe with some help from the Germans" (interview, Paris, November 25, 2009).

Most importantly, German government representatives were concerned about the effects of alternative investment on the company structure and corporate governance regime of German firms. They therefore wanted the most comprehensive regulation possible to ensure that no type of investment would threaten co-decision procedures and workers' rights. France might have not been behind hedge fund regulation in general, but they did have strong opinions when it came to the details. A European solution was advantageous because the UCITS blueprint that was copied into the AIFM proposal reflected many of the particularities of the French market. However, they were very concerned about the third-country passport, whose negative effects had been highlighted by their UCITS industry. Throughout the 18 months of negotiations and the 18 trialogues between the Commission, the Council, and the European Parliament, this issue became the most important bone of contention. The French showed no intention of opening the European market to offshore funds, which effectively made the proposal inacceptable to the British industry.

After repeated stalemates in July, September, and October 2010, it became clear that France had become isolated in its opposition to the third-country passport in the Council. Nevertheless, in preparation for an Ecofin Council meeting, the representative from the treasury who was supposed to represent Germany got a call from the finance minister, Wolfgang Schäuble, who insisted "I promised Christine Lagarde that you will not isolate her" (interview, Brussels, March 4, 2011). In spite of their doubts about the substance, the Germans thus dug out time for France to propose a last compromise, suggesting that the new European Securities Market Authority (ESMA) should be charged with the licensing of third-country fund access to the EU market (EurActiv 2010a). The British refused to grant such powers to a European authority and even US Treasury Secretary Timothy Geithner intervened by writing to French Finance Minister Christine Lagarde to warn about the consequences of French protectionism.

With strong opposition from the United Kingdom and German backing waning, the French finally decided to accept a compromise, which allowed third-country access and left it up to national regulators to grant third-country funds access. In exchange, the United Kingdom agreed to delay access for third-country funds until 2015. Moreover, ESMA was charged with drawing up the requirements these funds will have to fulfill and is expected to settle disputes between national regulators if they disagree on whether a fund should have been eligible (EurActiv 2010c).

This final agreement was reached on October 26, 2010, leading to the adoption by the European Parliament on November 11, just in time to present the new EU regulatory framework at the G20 meeting in Seoul on November 12, before it was approved by the Council of Ministers on November 17. While member states concentrated on national fault-lines, the European Parliament advanced on substantial changes. The unusually high number of 1,690 amendments was necessary, according to MEP Jean-Paul Gauzès, rapporteur of the directive, to build support from both camps: those who insisted on the need for more control and those that pointed to the ensuing costs for the affected industries (interview, Paris, May 19, 2011). Bringing the hastily written draft in line with the realities of different alternative investment funds required him to hold 198 meetings with industry representatives (Serrouya 2010). The European Commission official following the directive admits having stopped counting by the time he reached 150 meetings (interview, Brussels, March 2011).

The directive came into force in January 2011. From this date on, each Member State has two years to transpose the directive into national law, accompanied by ESMA, which will provide advice on the most appropriate implementation measures for the 210 pages of the directive. This means that the directive becomes practically effective only in January 2013. The passport for third-country funds and managers will become available after an additional two-year transition period in January 2015.

Conclusion

The AIFM directive was one of the EU's most disputed post-crisis regulations, which most importantly pitted France against the United Kingdom. As with most political compromises, none of the negotiators obtained what they initially aimed for. While the United Kingdom had to accept that alternative investment would be regulated at the supranational level, France was not able to exclude off-shore funds in principle from the European market. Although the British press continued bashing French protectionism and the unjustified regulatory push of the EU, even *The Economist* defended the proposal as a useful attempt to simplify and harmonize the existing regulatory frameworks (Anonymous 2010). Indeed, the fund industry in London now has the advantage of a one-stop regulatory interaction for all operations in the European market. Rather than applying for a license from each regulatory authority of the countries they wished to operate in, they could now use a license granted in one country to operate anywhere else in Europe.

France in turn obtained a regulatory framework for institutional investment that looks quite similar to the one they initially helped to shape for the retail mutual funds market. However, despite the insistence of the French government, the origin of funds is not an issue, as long as they comply with the regulatory requirements imposed on hedge fund managers.

For the German government, any encompassing regulation is satisfactory, as the economic interests of their industry are least directly exposed. Concerned with the preservation of the German company structure, German MEPs were most interested in issues such as asset stripping, which was a central issue for private equity firms. The final agreement now limits the selling off of capital—or asset stripping—in the years after the company is bought by a private equity investor. Regulating asset stripping reduces the attractiveness for private equity firms to buy a company in order to sell off its assets and make a quick profit (EurActiv 2010b).

In sum, despite the heated political debates, the hedge fund regulation resembles other initiatives to harmonize operations in the European market. Nevertheless, the most important issue will be the implementation of the ambitious project. One will have to judge in several years whether the framework merely opened up a pan-European market or actually provided additional control mechanisms over alternative investment that can be used effectively.

What this case study has tried to demonstrate is the strategic nature of business–government interactions and intergovernmental negotiations in the EU. It is insufficient to study the distribution of business interests or to state that paradigmatic change can trigger important reorientations in the regulatory agenda. To be sure, each government is very concerned with its industry interests and tries to make sure that policy proposals do not damage vital parts of their economies. Likewise, new economic ideas and the reorientation of public intervention after the crisis are also important to understand the momentum of political activism. However, one needs to ask *which* economic interests a government will ultimately defend and *when* paradigmatic change leads to political action.

The answer given in this study is that it depends on the strategic constellation of actors at both levels: domestically and internationally. Domestically, a specific portion of the French industry skillfully lobbied the French government from very early on to protect the competitive conditions in their sector. This lobbying turned out to be very consequential for most of the negotiations because it allowed the French government to build and maintain an alliance with Germany, which was very eager to advance on hedge fund regulation.

The feedback loops between the initial interests and the strategic advantages these provided are thus context-specific and can evolve over the course of negotiations (Farell/Newman 2011). We should therefore expect the politics of financial regulation in the EU to vary depending on the alliances countries chose to engage in but also in response of the lobbying strategies of the financial industry and other stakeholders. Importantly, those interest groups that are able to fit their demands into the overarching geopolitical objectives of their governments are most likely to influence the evolution of these international negotiations.

References

Anonymous, 2010: Britain's Phoney War Over Hedge Funds. In: *The Economist,* May 18.

Association française de la gestion financière, 2010: *L'industrie française de la gestion d'actifs.* Paris. <www.afg.asso.fr/index.php?option=com_docman&task=doc_download&gid=1686&Itemid=82&lang=fr>

Culpepper, Pepper D., 2011: *Quiet Politics and Business Power: Corporate Control in Europe and Japan.* New York: Cambridge University Press.

Edwards, Franklin R., 1999: Hedge Funds and the Collapse of Long-Term Capital Management. In: *Journal of Economic Perspectives* 13(2), 189–210.

EurActiv, 2010a: *English Papers Lead Campaign to "Ditch the Directive."* <www.euractiv.com/en/financial-services/english-papers-lead-campaign-ditch-directive>

——, 2010b: *EU Agrees "Imperfect" Deal to Regulate Hedge Funds,* October 27. <www.euractiv.com/en/euro-finance/eu-agrees-imperfect-deal-regulate-hedge-funds-news-499194>

——, 2010c: *Paris Attempts Last-ditch Power Grab on Hedge Funds,* September 29. <www.euractiv.com/en/financial-services/paris-attempts-last-ditch-power-grab-hedge-funds-news-498232>

European Commission, 2009a: *Feedback Statement: Summary of Responses to Hedge Fund Consultation Paper,* March 12. DG Market Services Working Document. Brussels: European Commission.

European Commission, 2009b: *Proposal for a Directive of the European Parliament and of the Council on Alternative Investment Fund Managers*, 2009/0064 (COD), April 30. <http://eur-lex.europa.eu/LexUriServ/LexUriServ.do?uri=COM:2009:0207:FIN:EN:PDF>

Farell, Henry/Abraham Newman, 2011: Making Global Markets: Historical Institutionalism in International Political Economy. In: *Review of International Political Economy* 17(4), 609–638.

Fioretos, Orfeo, 2010: Capitalist Diversity and the International Regulation of Hedge Funds. In: *Review of International Political Economy* 17(4), 696–723.

G20, 2009: *The Global Plan for Recovery and Reform,* April 2. <www.g20.org/Documents/final-communique.pdf>

Hardie, Iain/Donald MacKenzie, 2007: Assembling an Economic Actor: The *agencement* of a Hedge Fund. In: *The Sociological Review* 55(1), 57–80.

House of Commons, 2009: *Banking Crisis,* Volume I: *Oral Evidence.* Sessional Papers, 2008–2009. Treasury Committee. <www.publications.parliament.uk/pa/cm200809/cmselect/cmtreasy/144/144i.pdf>

International Financial Services London, 2010: *Hedge Funds 2010,* April. <www.thecityuk.com/media/2358/Hedge_Funds_2010.pdf>

IOSCO (International Organization of Securities Commissions), 2009: *Hedge Funds Oversight: Consultation Report,* March. <www.iosco.org/library/pubdocs/pdf/IOSCOPD288.pdf>

Lutton, David, 2008: *The Regulation of Hedge Funds at an EU level: The US Sub-prime Crisis in Context.* Unpublished manuscript. Strathclyde: University of Strathclyde.

Milne, Richard, 2008: "Locusts" of Private Equity Help Grohe. In: *Financial Times,* June 5.

Moravcsik, Andrew, 1998: *The Choice for Europe: Social Purpose and State Power from Messina to Maastricht.* Ithaca: Cornell University Press.

Prabhakar, Rahul, 2011: *Varieties of Regulation: Domestic Preferences and Global Outcomes in Finance.* MPhil thesis. Oxford: University of Oxford.

Quaglia, Lucia, 2011: The "Old" and "New" Political Economy of Hedge Funds Regulation in the European Union. In: *West European Politics* 34(4), 665–682.

Serrouya, Thierry, 2010: Le Parlement européen adopte la directive gestion alternative. In: *La Tribune,* November 12.

TheCityUK Research Center, 2010: *Private Equity 2010.* <www.thecityuk.com/assets/Uploads/Private-equity-2010.pdf>

9

What's the Problem? Competing Diagnoses and Shifting Coalitions in the Reform of International Accounting Standards

Paul Lagneau-Ymonet and Sigrid Quack

Introduction

It does not happen very often that a technical matter such as accounting makes it into the final declaration of a G20 summit, agreed by the heads of government of the world's leading nations. Nevertheless, this happened on November 15, 2008, two months after the bankruptcy of Lehman Brothers terrified capital markets, and roughly eighteen months after the first signs of the financial crisis had become tangible and started to impact the balance sheets of most banks worldwide. After holding their initial meeting as a Group of Twenty in Washington to deliberate about the means to cure the most severe financial crisis since the interwar period, the leaders of the G20 called on their finance ministers to formulate recommendations in areas such as "Mitigating against pro-cyclicality in regulatory policy" and "Reviewing and aligning global accounting standards, particularly for complex securities in times of stress" (G20 2008). Ever since, measures to reform international accounting standards—namely, those produced by the International Accounting Standards Board (IASB)—have been on the working agenda of G20 meetings, even if they have moved from front to backstage and are increasingly repeated using similar phrases (see the Declarations of the London, Pittsburgh, Toronto, Seoul, and Paris summits: www.g20.utoronto.ca).

Accounting standards are rules for valuing different types of assets and liabilities that are entered into a firm's balance sheet for the purposes of financial reporting and supervision. At the international level, so-called International Financial Reporting Standards (IFRS) have been developed since 1973 by a private standard-setting body, the International Accounting Standards Board (IASB) and its predecessor, the International Accounting Standards Committee (IASC), predominantly staffed by accountants from large international accounting firms (Botzem/Quack 2006; Nölke/Perry 2008). The rising number of countries adopting IFRS and, in particular, the decision of the European Union to make

Acknowledgement: Solomon Zori kindly prepared the tables presented in this paper.

IFRS binding for all publicly listed companies in its member states from January 2005 onwards, gave rise to debates on the political accountability of the standard-setter and the rule-setting process itself (Botzem 2010; Nölke 2009).

Prior to the EU's decision to adopt IFRS, the US Securities and Exchange Commission (SEC) had been rather reluctant to consider IFRS for use by American companies abroad or to let foreign issuers in the United States file financial statements according to IFRS without reconciliation with US Generally Accepted Accounting Principles (US GAAP) as developed by the US Financial Accounting Standards Board (FASB). It had, however, initiated and supported a project by the International Organization of Securities Commissions (IOSCO) to produce core standards by 1998. After the EU adopted IFRS, concerns about additional costs that American companies might encounter if they had to prepare a second set of financial statements according to IFRS in Europe, fostered more openness on the side of the SEC. In 2007, the SEC voted to allow foreign issuers in the United States to file financial statements according to IFRS without reconciliation to US GAAP. Therefore, the stage seemed set for convergence of the two leading accounting standards systems worldwide prior to the financial crisis (Posner 2010).

Accounting rules themselves, however—with one exception relating to financial instruments—had not received extensive political attention but rather had been treated as a technical matter before the crisis unfolded. Therefore, the appearance of such an arcane issue on the G20 agenda provides an interesting case on the basis of which to explore why and how this issue came to be considered a problem worth being included on the global political agenda for restoring the stability and improving the robustness of the financial system. According to Kingdon (1995), the financial crisis can be seen as a window of opportunity to be exploited by different actors in their struggle to connect problems, politics, and policy streams in order to identify which issues are relevant for "the active and serious consideration of authoritative decision-makers" (Cobb/Elder 1983: 86). Interest-based as well as epistemic community explanations would typically focus on agenda-setting as a programmatic phase in the policy process, followed by less politicized decision making and implementation. Other authors, however, have argued that bringing up an issue for political consideration does not tell us much about what is going to happen next, and that instead, it might be more promising to study how problem definitions shape the subsequent policy process. They argue that problem definition consists of more than the identification and description of difficulties.

As Stone (1989: 282) points out, problem definitions always imply causal stories and potential solutions, and they provide images that attribute cause and responsibility. Weiss (1989: 118) agrees that problem definition is "concerned with the organization of a set of facts, beliefs and perceptions—how people think about circumstances." According to this author, problem definition can be the "overture" to jointly building an "intellectual framework" for further action (Weiss 1989: 98–99). However, problem definition can also become a "weapon of advocacy" that actors use strategically to form coalitions with other actors that have the potential to shape decision making. Furthermore, problem definition can also be an "outcome" of policymaking, in so far as the solutions pursued and the policy instruments used to achieve them may change problem definitions over time by raising awareness of new issues, changing preferences of actors, or weakening the stance of formerly dominant groups (Weiss 1989: 116–117).

While policy analysis has widely recognized that the initial definition of a problem has implications for the subsequent policy process, less consideration has been given to the ways in which problem definitions may remain contested and continue to shift throughout a reform process, and what the implications might be for reform outcomes. In the case of the global financial crisis, exploring how competing problem diagnoses and related reform proposals shaped the policy process is particularly promising for two reasons.

First, given the urgent need to act and the complexity of global financial markets, proposals to fix the problems underlying the financial turmoil were developed under conditions of high epistemic uncertainty. It is therefore likely that different sets of actors brought partial views of root causes and reform proposals to the table. One would expect them to strategize by building on their respective expertise to foster their goals in the policy response. Hence, there was a strong likelihood that competing diagnoses and proposals would emerge.

Second, theories of regime complexity (Alter/Meunier 2009) would lead us to expect that the polyarchic, fragmented, and multi-layered structure of the global financial regulatory system provided opportunity and incentives for competing diagnosis and proposals to co-exist throughout the reform process without necessarily converging towards a shared view of problems and solutions. Debates on the causes of and remedies for the unfolding financial crisis took place in many different policy forums. Although one of the goals of reform was to coordinate these bodies within the framework of a more coherent and comprehensive global financial architecture, we suggest that most of the process took place in a fairly decentralized and networked manner, providing a breeding ground for continued struggles between competing diagnoses and solutions, as well as shifting coalitions.

In this chapter we present a case study of debates and reform activities concerning the role of international accounting standards in the global financial crisis. This case study is based on process-tracing using publicly available documents and interviews with key actors, complemented by insights from recently published studies by other authors (André et al. 2009; Posner 2010; Stellinga 2011; Thiemann 2011). While the reform of accounting and prudential capital rules is closely interlinked this chapter focuses on accounting (for the reform of Basel standards, see Goldbach/Kerwer in this volume).

We argue that the reform process concerning international accounting standards unfolded as continued struggles over two competing diagnoses—arising from a transparency and a prudential approach—and gave rise to shifting and sometimes fairly counterintuitive coalitions across typical industry–regulator or private–public divides. Continued competing problem diagnoses did not prevent reform altogether—in fact international accounting standards and the governance of the standard-setter were modified significantly between November 2007 and November 2011. However, the reform process unfolded in such way that it generated new differences between the international and US standard-setters. Paradoxically, the reform process has produced as one outcome something that it aimed to resolve at its beginning.

International accounting standards for financial instruments: The choice of valuation principles

The financial crisis has provoked a controversy about how and what banks and other financial institutions should publicly report about their economic performance. In order to analyze this controversy and its outcomes, it is helpful to look at two broad changes in the economic and regulatory environment of financial institutions which have occurred since the 1980s and have impacted on the disclosure and reporting requirements of (financial and non-financial) companies dealing with financial instruments. The first trend, often referred to as financialization, consists of the rise of capital markets, increasing securitization, and the proliferation of complex structured financial instruments, such as derivatives. Partly fostered by the business strategies of financial institutions themselves, this trend has resulted in the disproportionate growth of the trading book, containing financial instruments held for sale, as compared to the banking book, containing traditional loans and savings. It has also blurred the lines of demarcation between the two books since financial products on the banking book are now often secured with financial instruments on the trading book (Matherat 2008). Another development was that more assets of banks were held by conduits in the growing shadow banking sector, which remains outside the financial reporting of the sponsoring company (Thiemann 2011). Financialization has also fostered investor demands for transparent and time-sensitive reporting on the value of the assets held by the company at a given point in time over the demands of other stakeholders, such as creditors, prudential regulators and, to a lesser extent, managers who might have taken a long-term view on the company's economic performance.

The second important change refers to a shift in the policy approaches of national and international financial and monetary regulators, characterized by Wade (2008) as the emergence of a standards/surveillance/compliance regime for global financial regulation. Regulators increasingly relied for their macro- and micro-prudential policies on instruments that assumed that market discipline and disclosure of investor-relevant information would limit harmful and excessive risk taking (Allen/Carletti 2008). Regulators also increasingly relied on financial companies' internal risk management and auditing data for prudential supervisory purposes (Laux/Leuz 2009, 2010), as is particularly evident in the Basel regime for calculating risk exposure and capital requirements (Helleiner et al. 2009). This regulatory approach—built on the theory of rational and efficient markets—assumed that market prices provided a good approximation of the worth of assets and that securitization and financial innovation would even promote financial stability because more liquid markets would enhance allocative efficiency (FSA 2009: 39; Orléan 2011). In many respects, it signified a departure from previous prudential approaches, particularly prevalent in continental European countries (Richard 2005), which had relied more strongly on the principle of prudence and on counter-cyclical buffers to shield financial institutions from market fluctuations.

From the 1980s onwards, the development of financial reporting standards by the two leading standard-setters worldwide, the International Accounting Standards Board (IASB) and the US Financial Accounting Standards Board (FASB), mirrored and promoted a market-based approach to disclosure and supervision. By initiating a standard-setting project for Fair Value Accounting (FVA) in 1991, the IASC followed the FASB. In the United States, the shift towards FVA had been a response to accounting scandals during the savings and loan crisis in the 1980s and early 1990s, as well as to the rise of securities markets and increasing securitization through derivatives (Hellwig 2009), accompanied by the empowerment of financial professionals (Useem 1999).

Historically speaking, there are at least three ways to provide information about financial assets and liabilities in a company's balance sheet: Historical Cost Accounting (HCA), Fair Value Accounting (FVA) and accounting at amortized cost. In HCA, an asset or liability is reported at the original monetary value at the time it was acquired or incurred and amortized over its lifetime. In principle, this method relies on past transaction prices resulting in accounting values. HCA is considered "prudent" and "conservative"; it tends to buffer the balance sheet of an entity against market price fluctuations. It also potentially sets counter-cyclical incentives for economic entities' behavior in so far as market prices above acquisition costs might trigger sales, while market prices below acquisition costs should lead companies to hold on to assets. One of the downsides of HCA, as shown in the US savings and loan crisis, is that it is insensitive to current price signals and can lead financial companies to ignore the depreciation of their assets under current market conditions. Underlying HCA is an understanding of the firm as an ongoing concern, as well as a certain skepticism about market prices providing the most accurate estimate of "true value." HCA was the prevalent approach to accounting for financial instruments well into the 1970s in most industrialized countries.

In contrast, FVA reports the value of an asset or liability based on the price that it would receive if transacted in markets at the time of measurement. FVA is thus a method that shows the assets and liabilities of an entity at a value that would be achieved in arm's length transactions on markets at the date of the balance sheet. The advantage of FVA is that, under conditions of functioning and efficient markets, it provides an accurate representation of the price at which assets could be realized in transactions. FVA is also seen as providing management with up to date information relevant for decision making. Proponents consider FVA as an early warning system against mistakes in handling risk since declining prices will be immediately reflected in the balance sheet and profit and loss statement. While elegant in theory, however, in practice FVA raises a number of questions concerning how fair value can be empirically established (Whittington 2010). This is an issue especially in inactive or illiquid markets. One problematic feature of FVA, according to a critical report by the European Central Bank (2005), is that by relying on market prices for the valuation of company assets it can have undesirable pro-cyclical effects. Rising asset values during "boom" periods can lead companies to take on high risks while declines in market prices in "bust" periods might lead to panic sales and thereby exacerbate a downward spiral. Accordingly, in good times, banks tend to lend more (which implies to some extent taking on riskier clients) whereas in times of distress they tend to limit lending, and thereby reinforce recession. Underlying FVA is a view of the firm as a bundle of assets and liabilities of which the investors should be able to establish the realizable or exit/liquidation value, i.e. the value of the firm at the time of sale. Compared to HCA, it is optimistic about the efficiency of markets in generating prices that approximate the "true value" of the firm's assets.

A third method, accounting at amortized cost, is usually used for the subsequent measurement of financial instruments initially acquired at fair value. The value of such a loan or receivable is reported using the effective interest rate method taking into account changes in the macroeconomic environment[1].

In the 1990s, FASB and IASB were both in favor of expanding FVA beyond financial assets held on companies' trading books. They considered that this approach provides a more comprehensive and accurate picture of the different classes of financial assets held by an entity. In their view, FVA provided more appropriate and high-quality information for investors interested in transparent and timely disclosure of economic performance data. In both cases, however, their proposals met fierce opposition from the banking industry (Laux/Leuz 2009). When the FASB proposed FVA in the United States, American banks argued that this accounting method did not suit their business model and was not relevant for their investors either. Only investment banks were more receptive to FVA because most of their business consisted of trading financial instruments on a daily basis. After negotiations with the industry and some revisions, FASB published a fair value standard in 1991. Two years later, it expanded the requirement for FVA to debt and equity securities that were held for trading or for sale. In 1998, derivatives were required to be measured at fair value.

Finally, in 2006, FASB issued FAS No. 157, Fair Value Measurements, which was aimed at providing a single and consistent definition of fair value and established a hierarchy of valuation techniques. When applied as mark-to-market accounting, prices in existing markets were used as fair value. In the absence of active markets, fair value was to be calculated on the basis of prices in reference markets or, in situations where market prices were not available or reliable, by using market valuation models (Laux/Leuz 2009: 827). Companies had to classify their assets and liabilities in one of three categories: while financial instruments Available for Sale (AfS) and Held for Trading (HfT) were to be valued according to fair value, financial instruments Held to Maturity (HtM) continued to be valued according to amortized cost. While generally moving towards FVA, US GAAP retained some categories for loans at amortized cost (see Table 1).

At the international level, IAS Exposure Draft 40 for financial instruments was published by the International Accounting Standards Committee (IASC) in 1991. It was subsequently modified and separated into IAS 32, "Financial Instruments: Presentation" (adopted in June 1995), and IAS 39, "Financial Instruments: Recognition and Measurement," which was revised several times before being adopted as the last core standard required by the International Organization of

---

1 For technical details see the definition provided by PriceWaterhouseCoopers (2006: 23): "The carrying amount of a financial instrument [...] is computed as the amount to be paid/repaid at maturity (usually the principal amount or [...] face value) plus or minus any unamortized original premium or discount, [...] and less principal repayments."

Table 1   Financial Instrument Categories—US GAAP

Categories of financial asset	Characteristics	Balance sheet measurement
Held to maturity assets	Usually debt instruments purchased with the intent and ability to hold until maturity	Amortized cost
Financial assets as held for trading	Possibly debt or equity instruments bought and held principally to sell in the short term	Fair value
Available for sale financial assets	Debt or equity instruments which are held neither to maturity nor for trading	Fair value

Source: Bragg (2010: 254).

Securities Commissions (IOSCO) in 1998. Among the reasons for this lengthy standard-setting process was once again resistance from the banking sector, this time mainly in continental Europe (André et al. 2009; Botzem 2010). French banks, in particular, were opposed to expanding FVA to financial instruments other than those on the trading book, and especially to financial instruments held for hedging purposes. Camfferman and Zeff (2007: 367) report that IAS 39 was approved at the December 1998 meeting of the IASC with a very tight vote of 12 members in favor, Australia voting against and France, United Kingdom, and the United States abstaining for different reasons. As a result of long and controversial negotiations, IAS 39, published in 1998, consisted of a mixed model combining different measurement methods. It established a hierarchy of valuation techniques for fair value similar to that in US GAAP. But as a result of complicated negotiations, IAS 39 distinguished between five categories of financial instruments (instead of three, as in the case of US GAAP) which are displayed in Table 2.

As a result, more financial instruments were subsequently measured at amortized costs under IAS 39 than under the FASB's FAS 157. In addition, the so-called Fair Value Option in IAS 39 allowed companies irrevocably to classify financial instruments, independently of category, to fair value to increase consistency of financial reporting. From the beginning, IAS 39 was criticized for its complexity and there was agreement among the parties involved that it would require revision in the medium term. Controversies surfaced again following the European Union decision to adopt IFRS. IAS 39 was the only IFRS standard that was not endorsed by the EU at the outset, following strong opposition from continental European banks. In 2005, the European Union endorsed the Fair Value Option in a revised version. However, the so-called hedge accounting option was still pending when the financial crisis broke in 2007 (Botzem 2010). Hedge accounting includes rules for financial instruments, often derivatives,

Table 2   IAS 39-Categories of Financial Instruments—IFRS

Categories of financial assets and liabilities	Characteristics	Initial valuation	Subsequent measurement
Held to maturity assets	*Includes* Investments in debt Instruments quoted in an active exchange *Excludes* Equity shares Loans and receivables Held for trading	Fair value	Amortized cost
Available for sale financial assets	*Includes* Ordinary share investments Convertible notes Preference share investments *Excludes* Derivatives held for trading	Fair value	Fair value
Originated loans and receivables	*Includes* Accounts receivables Loans to other entities Credit card receivables *Excludes* Instruments quoted on an active exchange Held for trading derivatives Preference shares	Fair value	Amortized cost
Financial liabilities at fair value through profit or loss	*Includes* Share portfolios held for short-term gains Forward contracts Interest rate swaps Call options	Fair value	Fair value
Other financial liabilities	Any other category not described above	Fair value	Amortized cost

Source: Compilation based on IAS 39 as issued by the IFRS Foundation (www.ifrs.org/IFRSs/IFRS.htm).

which are used as a defense (hedge) against future financial risk arising from a change in the price of the underlying asset.

As indicated by this brief—and unavoidably somewhat technical—overview of accounting for financial instruments, by the mid-2000s IASB and FASB were still some distance from convergence in their rule-setting. The US side was unhappy about the complexity of the categories in IAS 39 as compared to the

FASB standard and the EU Commission's decision not to endorse the rules on hedge accounting. On other items, FASB standards were—as the crisis would show—still more problematic. FASB standards on consolidation—in other words, which financial instruments, and particularly special purpose vehicles, were to be included in the financial report of an entity—left significant leeway to American banks, whereas IFRS standards were more stringent, although by no means perfect in this respect (Thiemann 2011). Nevertheless, the roadmap towards a convergence of standard-setting appeared to be set. In 2002, IASB and FASB had signed the Norwalk agreement in which they indicated their willingness to work towards making their "existing financial reporting standards fully compatible as soon as practicable" and to "coordinate their future work programs to ensure that, once achieved, compatibility is maintained" (IASB-FASB 2002: 1). Four years later, in February 2006, this commitment was further detailed and specified in the form of "A Roadmap for Convergence between IFRSs and US GAAP 2006–2008." According to this roadmap, convergence on the Fair Value Option and impairment (rules for writing off assets that have a higher carrying value than what could be earned in the market) were supposed to be concluded by 2008. Other topics already on the working agenda but not yet to be concluded by 2008 were issues of consolidation and guidance on fair value measurement (IASB-FASB 2006: 3, updated by IASB-FASB 2008).

In sum, it seems fair to conclude that critical voices highlighting possible undesirable effects of the shift in valuation methods from amortized costs towards fair value were in a minority before the crisis. In the case of banks, their concerns seem to have been overridden by the gains for financial institutions and their professionals (Philippon/Reshell 2009; Godechot 2011) that could be derived from booming financial markets under FVA. Moreover, the main focus of international regulators, concerning accounting, was on the reduction of the remaining discrepancies between the sets of standards issued by IASB and FASB, and fair value seemed a promising approach to work towards more convergence, overriding concerns about possible undesirable effects on macro-financial stability (Erturk et al. 2008). Thus, judging from the mid-2000s, there appeared to be increasing agreement on the future development of accounting standards between a significant number of financial institutions, accounting standard-setters, and national and international financial regulators. This changed significantly as the first signs of a major financial crisis became visible, first in the United States and then worldwide. In the following section we will analyze how certain aspects of accounting standard-setting came to be considered problematic by some actors, and how shifting coalitions of actors shaped the way in which accounting standards became part of the reform agenda.

Putting accounting standards on the international policy agenda

Following a long period of sustained financial market growth and credit expansion, defaults on subprime loans in the US mortgage sector increased significantly throughout 2006 and the first two quarters of 2007, followed by a drying up of interbank markets. The customer credit run on Northern Rock, a UK bank, in September 2007 showed that the financial turmoil was not limited to the United States but was spilling over into Europe (FSA 2009: 27). During this period, representatives of the banking industry, first in the United States and then in Europe, increasingly expressed concerns about the implementation of recently introduced accounting rules for financial instruments (FAS 157 in the US and IAS 39 in Europe). Banks reported practical problems with establishing mark-to-market values in markets under stress, and uncertainty about the conditions under which assets could be moved from fair value to amortized cost categories. The concerns voiced by representatives of banks and banking associations thus referred to a lack of guidance on how to implement fair value for financial instruments under changing market conditions, as well as re-articulating their more general skepticism, voiced earlier, about the appropriateness of fair value accounting for banks. On both continents, the banking industry lobbied standard-setters to suspend their accounting rules for financial institutions in order to allow them to accommodate illiquid markets. In the first instance, the FASB and the IASB resisted doing so, arguing that accounting consistency should be protected independently of market conditions and that it was exactly the function of FVA to signal where risk management strategies in banks had been mistaken or had failed. Changing the rules would give rise to management manipulation and harm investor confidence instead of re-establishing it.

In the fall of 2007, US and European banks experienced further losses on their trading books valued on a mark-to-market basis because of the drying up of commercial paper markets, a problem that triggered the return, for reputational reasons, of assets from special investment vehicles from the shadow market onto banks' balance sheets (Thiemann 2011). Governments and regulators, too, started to worry about the causes of the escalating crisis. There was considerable uncertainty about underlying cause–effect relations and cross-sectoral and international interdependencies. In the case of accounting, the recent introduction of new measurement methods and classification categories made the role of FVA in the unfolding of the crisis rather opaque and difficult to assess empirically. As a consequence of this epistemic uncertainty, several international bodies set up working groups to investigate the causes of and propose remedies for the crisis, considering also the role of capital ratios and accounting rules.

Three reports, produced during this period by the Financial Stability Forum (FSF), IOSCO and International Institute of Finance (IIF), deserve attention because they demonstrate that at this stage, apart from the banks themselves, most actors still adhered to a transparency approach which emphasized that accurate and timely disclosure of business information, if implemented correctly and consistently, would not only enhance the efficiency of financial markets, but also send clear signals to banks that their risk management required corrections, thereby helping to resolve the crisis in the medium term.

The FSF report "Enhancing Market and Institutional Resilience" was published in the run-up to the G7 meeting in Washington in April 2008. The FSF, a group of major national financial authorities—such as finance ministries, central banks, and international financial bodies—founded in 1999 to promote international financial stability, had been asked to prepare this report by the group of G7 finance ministers and central bank governors in October 2007. The FSF (2008) identified severe problems with financial industry practices, including poor underwriting standards, weaknesses in valuation, failures in risk management, and a lack of disclosure, particularly in regard to special purpose vehicles and off-balance sheet financial instruments. The report also pointed to the bad performance of credit rating agencies. Weaknesses in regulatory frameworks and other policies were seen as an exacerbatory factor contributing to the financial crisis. FSF recommendations focused on strengthening prudential oversight of capital, liquidity, and risk management in the context of the existing Basel II Accord, improving the quality of disclosure and valuation, changing the role of credit agencies, strengthening authorities' responsiveness to risks, and enhancing arrangements for dealing with stress in the financial system.

Thus, while maintaining a market-based regulation approach, recommendations were directed towards improving prudential oversight, information, and disclosure where it seemed to have failed and had sent the wrong signals. In the area of disclosure and valuation, the FSF report (FSF 2008) urged the Basel Committee on Banking Supervision (BCBS) to strengthen its risk disclosure and asked accounting standard-setters to take urgent action to improve and converge financial reporting standards for off-balance sheet assets, thereby pointing at an early stage to the role of the shadow banking sector in amplifying the crisis. Furthermore, it pressed FASB and IASB to provide more guidance on valuations when markets are no longer active and to suggest ways of reporting uncertainty about valuations. In order to achieve these goals, it urged the IASB to establish an Expert Advisory Panel (EAP) on Fair Value in Declining Markets. Interestingly, the FSF report made no reference to possible pro-cyclical effects of accounting rules at this time.

In parallel, an IOSCO task force constituted in November 2007 had studied how the subprime crisis in the United States led to instabilities in global financial markets. IOSCO's report, published in May 2008, came to similar conclusions to those of the FSF, which was not surprising since the two working groups had liaised during preparations. However, IOSCO (2008a) highlighted the spillover effects from mortgage banking, derivatives markets, and structured finance leading to a liquidity crisis of hedge funds and institutional investors in the fall of 2007 and a near failure of several investment banks in the spring of 2008. In the section on valuation and accounting, the IOSCO report engages more explicitly with the question of whether FVA is adequate for the task of financial reporting on financial instruments or whether there are better alternatives. While acknowledging that difficulties of valuing at market prices in illiquid markets can exacerbate risk aversion and can lead to pro-cyclical worsening of market conditions, the report emphasized the beneficial role of FVA in providing early warning signals. It stated that banks lacked experience and skill in dealing with valuations under conditions of stress. Consequently, the report called for better guidance related to the measurement of FVA and better training of banking staff in preparing disclosure for investors.

In response to FSF and IOSCO, the Institute of International Finance (IIF), a global industry association of 400 large banks, investment banks, insurance companies and investment firms, formed a working group in October 2007. The IIF Committee on Market Best Practices seized the opportunity provided by the upcoming G7 meeting in April 2008 to publish an Interim Report (IIF 2008a), followed by a final report in July 2008 (IIF 2008b). While the Interim Report acknowledged the responsibility of the industry and urged IIF member banks to adopt improvements in risk management and accounting practices, it also made recommendations regarding public regulation. In particular, the report pointed to pro-cyclical effects of the implementation of Basel II. Like the FSF and IOSCO, the IIF called for more guidance on the application of FVA under stress and in illiquid markets. However, the IIF also suggested a need for a broad dialogue on the long-term implications of fair value accounting. More specifically, the report (IIF 2008a: 17) stated:

A critical subset of issues revolves around whether mark-to-market exacerbates the overall degree of risk aversion in the marketplace and thereby contributes in a procyclical manner to the continuation and possible worsening of market stress. [...] broad thinking is needed on how to address such consequences, whether through means to switch to modified valuation techniques in thin markets, or ways to implement some form of "circuit breaker" in the process that could cut short damaging feedback effects while remaining consistent with the basics of fair-value accounting.

As a lobbying association, the IIF emphasized the need to reduce pressure on banks in order to prevent the collapse of individual institutions, although it also referred strategically to macro-prudential arguments about pro-cyclicality to bolster its claims. Less affected competitors, investors' and analysts' associations denounced this as a self-serving call for exceptional measures. Financial regulators and banking supervisors were also wary of moral hazard. The common view at the time was that existing accounting rules, despite their imperfections, could have a strong purgative effect, enabling a faster recovery.

This view was also reflected in the G7's communiqué of April 11, 2008, which incorporated recommendations made by the FSF. Among many other proposals, it suggested that the "International Accounting Standards Board (IASB) and other relevant standard-setters should initiate urgent action to improve the accounting and disclosure standards for off-balance sheet entities and enhance guidance on fair value accounting, particularly on valuing financial instruments in periods of stress" (G7 2008). André et al. (2009: 11) conclude that the IASB's response to the financial market crisis resulted from this period: the IASB established, as requested by the FSF, an Expert Advisory Panel (EAP) on Fair Value with the FASB as an observer. The IASB also amended disclosure rules in IFRS 7 to provide more information about model-based estimations of fair value, the maturity of derivatives, and liquidity risk (André et al. 2009: 12). Finally, the IASB asked its staff to urgently advance the consolidation project which was already on the active working agenda of the convergence program. The purpose of the EAP was not to discuss the general issue of fair value accounting, but instead to consider the specific technical problems of asset valuation in markets under stress. As the draft report of the EAP released by the IASB on September 16, 2008 observed (IASB EAP 2008: 15):

Some think that, in periods of market turmoil, adverse market sentiment can create an apparently illogical view of risk and that fair value measurement should not consider the effect of this on model inputs, such as credit and liquidity premiums charged. However, the objective of measuring fair value is to establish what the transaction price would have been on the measurement date in an arm's length exchange and market sentiment is a factor in determining any transaction price.

As a general orientation, the IASB continued to pursue fair value as a single measurement principle for all financial instruments, as documented by the release of a discussion paper "Reducing Complexity in Reporting Financial Instruments" (IASB 2008) to coincide with the April 2008 G7 meeting (see Stellinga 2011 for a highly critical response to this draft).

By late summer 2008, "Fannie Mae" and "Freddy Mac" had become increasingly reliant on government funding in the United States; the funding of UK mortgage banks became more difficult; and the interbank market was nearly at a standstill (FSA 2009: 27). The opportunistic demands of individual banks, American and European banking associations, and the IIF to reconsider the appropriateness of FVA beyond technical questions of valuation remained largely unheard. International prudential and securities regulators recognized that there had been an inappropriate implementation of FVA under illiquid market conditions which might have had feedback effects, and that valuation methods in banks might not have been sophisticated enough. However, they also maintained that a transparent surveillance regime based on market discipline was still the most appropriate regulatory model to pursue. Accounting standard-setters responded halfheartedly to FSF pressure to provide clearer rules on consolidation and guidance on FVA but they continued to pursue their convergence agenda based on fair value accounting as the underlying paradigm. The prevailing problem definition was that, if anything, the implementation of accounting standards in practice had been weak and needed to be fixed by more explicit guidance.

How can an equal playing field be established for banks under stress?

September 2008 brought the global financial system to the brink of collapse. After Lehman Brothers filed for Chapter 11 bankruptcy protection on September 15, financial institutions operating internationally faced a double squeeze. Their exposure to illiquid assets forced them to make massive new write-downs and fire-sales of other classes of financial products in order to meet their capital requirements. This precipitated a run by investors eager to disinvest from the institutions which seemed to be the most vulnerable according to their deteriorating books (Hellwig 2009). While stock indexes plummeted because of liquidity pricing, and the cost of interbank lending rocketed because of the general mistrust among surviving banks, major banks became strongly reliant on central bank support (FSA 2009: 27). During this period accounting debates were profoundly redefined (Humphrey et al. 2009; Ojo 2009). Heads of government, finance ministers, prudential banking regulators, and central bankers gradually reformulated their views on the role that accounting rules played—in conjunction with the implementation of Basel II—in the unfolding of the financial crisis, and what steps needed to be taken to revise them in ways that would help to re-establish financial stability and bolster the robustness of the financial system. The major push to do so came from Europe. It was framed by governments and legislators as a problem of competitive disadvantage affecting some banks rather than others.

As documented in more detail by André et al. (2009: 13–15), a meeting of the finance ministries of European members of the G7 (France, Germany, Italy, and the United Kingdom), called by President Sarkozy on October 4, 2008, took place in the heat of the financial turmoil following the collapse of Lehmann Brothers. It was followed by an announcement by the EU Council of Finance Ministers (ECOFIN) some days later that urged the IASB to amend the rules of IAS 39. The revision should allow banks to move certain assets and liabilities from FVA to amortized cost categories. The European Commission threatened that if the IASB did not amend IAS39 accordingly by the end of October 2008, the European Accounting Regulatory Committee (ARC), formally in charge of endorsing IFRS, would meet in mid-October to pass a draft removing paragraphs from IAS39 which prevented reclassification from FVA to amortized cost.

According to André et al. (2009: 13–15) this initiative can be traced back to French banks taking advantage of the financial crisis to renew their earlier calls on the government to intervene to support them and to press the international accounting standard-setter to revise its FVA rules. More specifically, the authors report that President Sarkozy, responding to lobbying by large French banks, had asked for an expert report by René Ricol—a French accountant who had served as the president of the International Federation of Accountants—on whether existing US GAAP standards would allow American banks to reclassify mortgages and financial instruments in the Available for Sale (AfS) category under the current unusual circumstances in ways that would leave European banks at a competitive disadvantage. The Ricol Report concluded that this was indeed the case, and the European Commission's Internal Market and Services Directorate General (DG MARKT) took action based on the requirement of EU directives that IFRS must not disadvantage European companies as compared to those in other major markets.

The IASB, fearing major damage to its legitimacy by a further departure by the EU from the application of IFRS standards, responded by suspending their constitutional due process and passing the requested amendments of IAS 39 on October 13, 2008, against the votes of its American members who argued that the European reading of US GAAP was mistaken. However, the European Commission through DG MARKT, and the French government through a meeting of European members of the G20, stepped up its pressure for further-reaching reforms of international accounting standards. On October 27, 2008, DG MARKT sent a letter to the IASB—discussed in more detail by André et al (2009: 15)—raising questions about the reclassification of assets categorized under the Fair Value Option (which by definition excluded moving them to amortized cost), a revision of the specific impairment rules, and issues related to the valuation of embedded derivatives. The response of the IASB, transmitted by letter on November 14, 2008, was that it would set up a series of roundtable discussions on the financial crisis by the end of the year, and that any further steps to amend standards would need to take place within the established standard-setting due process and in conjunction with the FASB to ensure global convergence (cited according to André et al. 2009: 16).

Thus, in the face of the mounting crisis, the European Commission and member state governments supported banks in their demands for greater managerial leeway to reclassify assets that were rapidly losing value and forcing fire-sales or write-offs. They did so based on concerns that individual banks would collapse and exacerbate the crisis. The problem definition, however, was rephrased somewhat instrumentally in order to find a lever to break the resistance of the IASB. In the first instance, DG MARKT justified its demands with arguments that a level playing field needed to be established between US and European banks in dealing with the crisis. In the second instance, justification was again based on the need for a level playing field, but this time between different European banks (those that been allowed to reclassify by the amendment of IAS 39 and those that had not been allowed to do so because they had chosen the fair value option in the first place). The issue of derivatives, in turn, referred once more to equal treatment of US and European banks. There was little reference to a more long-term perspective concerning how to define accounting standards in line with steps undertaken to reform Basel capital requirements. Longer-term macro-prudential considerations were mentioned only in a side note. In other words, the European Commission and member state governments were concerned about transparency of disclosure in a competitive environment. As their realignment with the banking industry became visible and pressure on standard-setters rose, security regulators, unaffected parts of the banking industry, and standard-setters became increasingly concerned about the negative effects of piecemeal reforms on the transparency of disclosure standards.

Convergence on immediate policy steps, yet continued divergence of problem definitions

Various diagnoses and suggestions for remedies to the escalation of the crisis crystallized around the G20 meeting on November 15, 2008, in Washington. An analysis of the reports, letters and communiqués submitted in the run-up to this meeting confirms the realignment of problem definitions by European banks and governments, as well as the re-articulation of a distinctive view of both problem definitions and remedies by securities regulators and standard-setters.

On the one hand, EU heads of state and government moved beyond their earlier level-playing-field strategies, pursuing a more principled prudential approach to encompassing regulation and supervision of all kinds of financial markets and products. This regulation was required to follow principles of accounting and transparency that prevent "creating bubbles in periods of growth and make crises worse in periods of downturn." To achieve this end, they urged accounting standard-setters to reform their governance structure to allow for "a genuine dialogue with all the parties concerned, in particular, with prudential authorities" (French Presidency of the European Union 2008). The Institute of International Finance, as a voice of the banking industry, sent a letter pointing to the need for reform of the Basel II Accord to avoid future pro-cyclical effects, a reconsideration of the reliance on ratings, and a broader dialogue about the application of FVA in financial institutions (IIF 2008c).

On the other hand, IOSCO (2008b), in its open letter to the G20, highlighted the importance of investor confidence in transparent disclosure and accounting as crucial to the success and liquidity of financial markets, and hence the stability of global financial systems. As a "community of authorities responsible for capital markets" it reiterated its commitment to the development and enforcement of global high-quality accounting standards that provided clear, accurate, and useful information to investors. While IOSCO acknowledged that accounting standard-setters needed independence to develop high-quality standards, it underlined that its "members must have a means of ensuring that accounting standard-setters are working in the best interests of investors." The letter referred to previous coordinated work with the IASB to establish a Monitoring Board to enhance the accountability of the IASB to capital market authorities worldwide. A group of national standard-setters, as well as the Basel Committee, supported the IASB as standard-setter and called for its independence, as did investor associations (André et al. 2009; Stellinga 2011). The SEC, having just commissioned a report on the role of FVA in the crisis under pressure from Congress, also maintained a transparency view (as fully explicated in the final report, SEC 2008).

Thus, while the alignment between European governments and commercial banks on a critical view of fair value continued and was increasingly framed not only as support for banks under stress but also as a macro-prudential issue, security regulators, standard-setters, and investors continued to emphasize their transparency view. While these two camps had some common ground for policy measures, they diverged on others. There was by no means a clear line of demarcation between public regulators, as the differences between the pronouncements of governments, prudential regulators, and securities regulators show. Even among prudential regulators, there was no unanimity. For example, Daniele

Nouy, head of the French bank commission, in March 2008 declared that "mark-to-market accounting is changing the dynamics of this crisis—the pain comes very fast [...] But hopefully the recovery will come very fast too" (Hughes/Tett 2008). Also among banks, there was no unified opinion. In the United States, Goldman Sachs dismissed IIF proposals, coining them "Alice-in-Wonderland accounting" and Morgan Stanley publicly distanced itself from the Institute. In July 2008, Goldman even announced it was quitting the IIF (Dauer 2008).

The Trustees of the International Accounting Standards Committee Foundation (IASCF 2008) sent a letter to the G20 acknowledging policymakers' and prudential supervisors' concerns about issues of pro-cyclicality. However, it emphasized that the primary goal of accounting standard-setters was to provide investors with adequate information. Since pro-cyclical effects were arising, if at all, from interactions between accounting standards and Basel capital requirements they should be addressed by a dialogue with prudential supervisors—in the first instance, the Basel Committee. Furthermore, it was announced that the IASB and the FASB were about to establish a high-level advisory group—consisting of senior leaders with broad experience in financial markets and official observers representing key global regulators—to consult on how improvements in financial standards could contribute to re-establishing investor confidence in financial markets.

Faced with the urgent need to develop a regulatory response to the escalating crisis, the G20 summit in Washington on November 15, 2008 saw an alignment of different actors that focused on commonalities in immediate measures to be taken rather than agreement on cause–effect analysis. The G20, in its declaration and among many other recommendations, reiterated some of the calls made by the FSF in April of the same year, such as asking the accounting standard-setters to provide guidance on the application of fair value to financial instruments during times of illiquid markets and to work on disclosure standards for off-balance sheet vehicles. It increased pressure on the IASB to enhance its governance to "ensure transparency, accountability, and an appropriate relationship between this independent body and the relevant authorities" (G20 2008), leaving it thereby open to whom the IASB should be accountable in the end—to securities regulators as demanded by SEC and IOSCO, or to prudential regulators as suggested by the European Union. The G20 statement also reiterated that regulators should work towards financial statements that include "a complete, accurate, and timely picture of the firm's activities (including off-balance sheet activities) and are reported on a consistent and regular basis"—which was closer to the suggestions of IOSCO than the concerns about potential pro-cyclicality articulated by banks and EU governments. Still, concerns that regulation might reinforce pro-cyclicality were not entirely pushed off the agenda. The IMF and

FSF were asked to review how "valuation and leverage, bank capital, executive compensation, and provisioning practices may exacerbate cyclical trends" in preparation of the next summit in April 2009 (G20 2008).

Coping with the systemic crisis

The period between October 2008 and April 2009 saw exceptional government recapitalization of banks across the United States and Europe. From November 2008 onwards, it became clear that the financial crisis was spilling over into the real economy. Banks with large impairments of assets started to ration credit and economies went into recession. Other near failures of banks required governments to infuse even more money to rescue them in order to prevent further escalation of the financial crisis (FSA 2009: 27). As these developments unfolded, politicians and regulators became increasingly wary of possible pro-cyclical effects of existing regulation, at the same time as a number of high-level expert groups and international regulatory bodies published reports with theoretical reflections on and empirical analyses of such pro-cyclical effects. In February and March 2009 alone five expert group reports and policy papers were published which, among other issues, included a review of possible pro-cyclical effects of prudential and accounting rules: the de Larosière Report, the FSA Turner Review, the FSF and IMF reports, and an European Council Key Issues Paper deserve more detailed consideration because they express a major shift in the problem definition of international financial supervisors, combined with a more systematic articulation of revisions to be considered by the two leading standard-setters.

First, a high-level group on financial supervision in the EU, chaired by Jacques de Larosière, former Managing Director of the IMF, released its report on February 25, 2009 (High-Level Group 2009). This group had been convened by EU President Barroso in October 2008, and included a number of senior experts with experience in prudential regulation and central banks. The report concluded that the existing regulatory framework had been insufficient and had partly reinforced downward spirals as the crisis unfolded. In particular, it pointed to the need for a fundamental review of the Basel II regulations and their implementation with the aim of introducing counter-cyclical measures. The report also stated that mark-to-market accounting under conditions of market stress had reinforced the downswing, and that as a consequence fair value accounting of financial instruments needed to be limited. The report argued that FVA accounting as implemented under IFRS had not been neutral but had produced biased incentives for short-term business strategies. It advocated embedding the "public good of financial stability" (High-Level Group 2009: 21) in accounting standard-setting and pushed strongly for more accountability of the IASB by giving the "regulatory community" a permanent seat in its decision making bodies.

Second, the Turner Review published by the UK Financial Service Agency under the leadership of Lord Turner in March 2009 (FSA 2009: 39), commissioned by the Chancellor of the Exchequer in October 2008, also concluded—based on a similar diagnosis—that "major changes in our approach to capital, liquidity, accounting and institutional coverage" were necessary. However, the report went further and also questioned some of the assumptions underlying the previous market-based regulatory system. It asked whether market prices really were good indicators of value; whether securitized credit really fostered economic stability; and whether market discipline could limit excessive risk taking. The Turner Review highlighted a need for higher capitalization of banks, a serious revision of the Basel II regime to avoid pro-cyclicality, the creation of counter-cyclical buffers, and measures to offset pro-cyclicality in published accounts (FSA 2009: 61–62). The report also argued that while the fair value "accounting philosophy is appropriate from an idiosyncratic perspective—an individual bank operating in a reasonably stable financial and economic environment—from the point of view of regulators, and of systemic financial risk, it has serious disadvantages. On both the trading book and banking book sides, it can fuel systemic procyclicality" (FSA 2008: 65). The FSA believed that a dialogue with accounting standard-setters was required on how a counter-cyclical approach to bank capital could become visible in published accounting figures to raise managers' and shareholders' "awareness of the need to assess the performance of banks in the light of the position in the economic cycle" (FSA 2009: 67). Both the Turner Review and the de Larosière Report referred to the existing and successful practice of dynamic provisioning implemented by the Bank of Spain as a best practice model.

Furthermore, in fulfillment of their mandate, the FSF and IMF also published reports and papers on the issue of pro-cyclicality in the run-up to the G20 summit in April 2009. The FSF, based on consultation with various prudential and supervisory agencies as well as stakeholders, came to the conclusion that the current financial crisis had illustrated the "disruptive effects of pro-cyclicality." Pro-cyclicality was defined as "dynamic interaction (positive feedback mechanisms) between the financial and the real sector of the economy" that tends to "amplify business fluctuations and cause or exacerbate financial instability" (FSF 2009: 9). The report suggested that elements of the existing prudential and accounting regimes had been a contributory factor. The FSF highlighted the importance of a macro-prudential assessment of the weaknesses of existing regulation and suggested policy measures in four areas to dampen pro-cyclical effects in financial systems. First, the FSF (2009) recommended revising capital requirements under Basel II in such a way that they would promote prudential capital buffers over the credit cycle. Second, it argued that earlier recognition of losses—which current accounting rules excluded—would have dampened cyclical fluctuations. Hence, it suggested that accounting standard-setters should reconsider their incurred loss model and establish alternatives. Under the incurred loss model a provision for loan losses is recognized only after a credit event has been identified that is likely to result in non-payment of a loan. Third, the FSF pointed to the likelihood of pro-cyclical effects arising from parallel increases in risk taking and fair value valuation in banks. It argued that FVA also needed to be considered from a macro-prudential perspective. As a consequence, prudential regulators and accounting standard-setters were urged "to examine the use of valuation reserves or adjustments for FVA when data or modeling needed to support their valuation are weak" (FSF 2009: 25). Finally, accounting standard-setters should consider "possible changes in their standards to dampen adverse dynamics potentially associated with fair value accounting" (FSF 2009: 26). An IMF Working Paper (Novoa et al. 2009) published the same month took a more moderate line. While it found that weaknesses of FVA may introduce unintended pro-cyclicality, it still considered fair value to be the preferred framework for financial institutions. In line with the other reports, capital buffers, forward-looking provisioning, and more refined disclosure were seen as measures that could mitigate the pro-cyclicality of FVA.

Finally, a Draft Key Issues Paper prepared by the Economic and Financial Affairs Council of the European Union (Council of the European Union 2009), adopted by the European Council in the run-up to the G20 summit in London on April 2, argued pretty much along the same lines, referring to the de Larosière Report, to request financial regulation that would dampen rather than amplify economic cycles and an improvement of accounting standards on provisioning and valuation.

At the London G20 summit (2009a) heads of government took a fairly unified approach to financial regulation (while disagreeing on other issues, such as fiscal stimulus packages). Their "Declaration on Strengthening the Financial System" incorporated the problem analysis of the above mentioned reports and many of their policy recommendations. It explicitly urged the Financial Stability Board and BCBS to work with accounting standard-setters to implement its recommendations. While reaffirming the framework of fair value accounting, the G20 asked accounting standard-setters to take action by the end of 2009 to reduce the complexity of standards and improve accounting standards for loan-loss provisions, off-balance sheet exposure, and valuation uncertainty. Standard-setters were called to work with supervisory regulators to achieve clarity and consistency in the application of valuation standards worldwide. They were to make progress with developing a single global standard and improve the involvement of stakeholders, including prudential regulators and representatives from emerging markets.

At the height of the financial crisis, the IASB saw itself surrounded by a shift of emphasis in diagnoses on the secondary causes of the financial crisis: while excessive risk taking, bad underwriting standards, and ill-directed financial innovation were still considered root causes, views on the role of prudential and accounting standards in the unfolding of the crisis had gradually changed. At the beginning of the crisis, the focus had been either on their coverage (for example, disclosure and accounting of off-balance sheet vehicles), their implementation (insufficient skill and experience of banking staff in dealing with new Basel II and FVA accounting rules), or equal playing-field issues (amendments of reclassification under IAS 39). Now the interface between prudential and accounting standards was considered a potential secondary cause that had reinforced the crisis. Demands and recommendations for reform, while formally confirming the fair value framework, argued increasingly from a prudential perspective that favored a more long-term horizon for the valuation of assets and liabilities than fair value accounting did.

At the end of March 2009, probably in light of the recommendations expected from the G20 summit, the IASB and the FASB had already decided at a joint board meeting to accelerate the process of standard revision. The Chair of the Financial Crisis Advisory Group (FCAG), which had met for the first time in January 2009, sent a letter to then Prime Minister Gordon Brown, as the host of the London G20 summit, highlighting that the group was in the process of considering various studies, including those mentioned above, and soliciting further input from other interested parties to advise the IASB and the FASB on accounting issues related to fair value, loan provisioning and off-balance sheet vehicles (FCAG 2009a). Following the April Summit, the IASB announced that it would undertake the development of a new standard for financial instruments (IFRS 9 to replace IAS 39) instead of pursuing further piecemeal revisions. In press releases, dated April 7 and April 24, 2009, the IASB (2009a, 2009b) explained that it was willing to take up the issues identified by the April summit and committed to working with the FASB towards convergence, but that it also believed that reforms should be undertaken in the context of a comprehensive project rather than in response to pressures from interested governments and business parties for piecemeal changes. The IASB project was subdivided into three parts, dealing with (i) classification and measurement of financial instruments, (ii) impairment of financial instrument, and (iii) hedge accounting.

Pending further research, it appears that the establishment of a Financial Crisis Advisory Group (FCAG) and the Monitoring Board of the IASC Foundation, established in January 2009, together with extensive outreach work undertaken by the IASB, shaped the direction of the new standard-setting project. The resulting IFRS9 standard represented a compromise that included a revisited and simplified mixed model for the classification of financial instruments and consideration of more forward-looking alternatives for loan loss provisioning. The FCAG included senior prudential and supervisory regulators, central bankers, bankers, investors, and accountants from a range of countries, including India and South Africa. The Monitoring Board was a response to long-standing criticisms by IOSCO, the European Commission and others concerning a lack of public accountability. The members included IOSCO, Japan's Financial Services Agency, the SEC, and the European Commission (which, however, withheld signing the Memorandum of Understanding for several months), with the Basel Committee on Banking Supervision present as an observer.

In the press release announcing the publication of its final report, the FCAG (2009b) stated: "Accounting was not a root cause of the financial crisis, but it has an important role to play in its resolution." The report itself (FCAG 2009c: 3) presented a modified transparency approach: it recognized that financial reporting played an important role in the financial system and was of "great importance to investors and other financial market participants, [...] and to regulators and other users." However, the limitations of financial reporting figures also needed to be recognized because "regulators and others cannot rely exclusively on the information" (FCAG 2009c: 9). The report recommended that the IASB and the FASB "explore alternatives to the incurred loss model for loan loss provisioning that use forward-looking information," including expected loss and fair value models (FCAG 2009c: 7). For remaining differences between prudential and accounting standards, the Boards were asked to "develop a method of transparently depicting any additional provisions or reserves that may be required by regulators" (FCAG 2009c: 8). Furthermore, improvements in the standards for consolidation and off-balance sheet assets were requested.

The FCAG and the Monitoring Board underlined and supported the need for independence on the part of the accounting standard-setter. While the range of actors who should have a voice was defined more broadly—including regulators and not just investors—it was argued that independence was required to maintain a coherent and reliable standard-setting process shielded from the strategizing of interested parties. In its Statement of Principles made public on September 22, 2009, the Monitoring Board declared: "We view the primary objective of financial reporting as being to provide information on an entity's financial performance in a way that is useful for decision-making for present and potential investors" (IASCF Monitoring Board 2009: 2). Therefore, the institutionalization of public oversight on the IASB did not fundamentally alter the priority given to investors as addressees of the accounting standards it produced. Nevertheless, it redefined the independence of the standard-setter by giving public authorities a lever in the nomination of trustees and in raising issues concerning the standards themselves.

The re-emergence of convergence as a key problem

When the G20 met six months later for their summit in Pittsburgh on September 24, 2009, the emphasis had changed once more. There was a strong call on "national authorities [to] implement global standards consistently in a way that ensures a level playing field and avoids fragmentation of markets, protectionism, and regulatory arbitrage" (G20 2009b: 7). International accounting bodies were urged to "redouble their efforts to achieve a single set of high-quality, global accounting standards" and complete their convergence by June 2011 (G20 2009b: 9–10). Overall, there were increasing concerns that governments would implement regulatory changes in different ways, leading potentially to divergence and regulatory arbitrage. The background of this shift of emphasis from pro-cyclicality to divergence was manifold: while in April 2009 governments had been meeting under the threat of a severe economic downturn, September 2009 saw a gradual relaxation of the crisis as individual banks started to recover thanks to massive public support, and to the reclassification of financial instruments in their books. Furthermore, the work on problems of pro-cyclicality had been taken up by the Basel Committee, and to a lesser extent had also been considered by the IASB in dialogue with the former. However, some of the reform responses of governments and regulators under the threat of failing financial institutions were endangering a coordinated global response because they had created new sources of disparity between prudential and accounting standards rather than reducing them. Furthermore, the crisis had shown how such discrepancies could lead governments and business to engage in regulatory arbitrage and piecemeal rule changes which endangered overall coordination of responses.

   This had become particularly apparent in the field of international accounting where, in contrast to other issue fields, such as capital requirements, two leading standard-setters were operating in parallel and liaising with each other. As time went by, it became increasingly clear that the way the revision of accounting standards had unfolded between the two standard-setters had generated a number of side-effects which were increasingly complicating the policy goal of convergence.

One underlying problem was that both standard-setters worked with different timelines in their responses to the crisis. While the IASB chose to subdivide its project into three phases, the FASB decided to develop a single proposal. As a result, they presented their drafts at different times for public comment to distinct audiences and received quite different responses. A second, and related, source of disparities consisted of distinctive dynamics in their socio-economic and political contexts. For example, the SEC (2008) report on fair value, published in December 2008, which dismissed any role for accounting standards in amplifying the crisis, shielded the FASB from industry lobbying and pressure from Congress to review its standards, while several reports by European and international bodies increased such pressure on the IASB. Finally, a kind of intellectual vacuum emerged after the IASB-FASB joint Discussion Paper on "Reducing Complexity in Reporting Financial Instruments" received broad and virulent criticism. Stellinga (2011: 54) shows that this included disagreement between the standard-setters and the broader accounting community. With the FVA approach as the basis for convergence questioned, it was unclear what the broader intellectual framework for convergence would be.

Three different standard-setting projects illustrate these new sources of divergence: the project on the measurement of financial instruments, the work on impairment, and the standard on consolidation. We will treat them in sequence.

In July 2009, when the IASB and the FASB published their respective proposals for new standards for the classification and measurement of financial instruments within the course of a day, it became apparent that the two standard-setters were diverging in their broader orientations. The IASB Exposure Draft for IFRS 9, "Financial Instruments: Classification and Measurement," published on July 14, distinguished between assets accounted for at amortized cost and at fair value. Broadly speaking, financial instruments with loan characteristics would be held at amortized cost, provided banks could show they would hold them for the long term. Everything else, including equities, derivatives, and more complicated securities, should be accounted at fair value. Responding to multiple criticisms from banks, regulators, and accounting communities (Stellinga 2011: 58–61) the IASB revised the standard in such a way that the final document published in November 2009 took into account the loan characteristics as well as the business model to allow for classification in an amortized cost category, and allowed for reclassification if the business model changed in a way that could be demonstrated to external parties. In contrast, the FASB proposal for addressing the classification and measurement of financial instruments, impairment and hedge accounting published on July 15 (finalized as an exposure draft in May) proposed much greater use of fair value measurement than IFRS 9, with almost all financial instruments at fair value and only a few financial liabilities under the amortized cost option. While the latter received considerable criticism for FVA of loans, the FASB nevertheless continued a full fair value approach up to 2010.

Similarly, the approach taken by the IASB on impairment issues, published as an exposure draft in November 2009, was receptive to suggestions made by the FCAG that loss impairment and provision should be more forward-looking. The recognition of a credit event was removed. In contrast, the FASB proposal developed a different solution that would write off losses at a given time and maintain the logic of a credit event. As stated by the IASB itself (2011: 5), "In redeliberating their original impairment proposals each board began to develop a model for impairment accounting that was a variant of its original proposal." Given the strong urgency that the FSB and the G20 attributed to convergence on the issue of impairment for reasons of prudential and supervisory oversight, the Boards then decided to address the discrepancies by developing and publishing a supplementary document which suggested a kind of meta-frame consisting of two open portfolios, established by the risk management of the banks. Work on this project, as on the one on hedge accounting, is still ongoing at the time of writing, with no easy solution for convergence in sight.

In the area of consolidation of special purpose vehicles and other financial entities which was brought onto the political agenda at an early stage in April 2008, and subsequently followed by the IASB with an exposure draft in December 2008, the approaches taken by the FASB and the IASB again diverged in the course of the crisis instead of converging. After closely monitoring the comprehensive consolidation approach taken by the IASB, the FASB decided not to join this project at the time, and instead is in the process of developing narrower improvements to existing guidance. The IASB, in turn, finalized its standards for Consolidation and Disclosure in May 2011, according to which control (defined in a broad sense) is the defining criterion for consolidated entities. While the IASB argues that developments are broadly in alignment in this area, this remains to be seen, since the FASB's exposure draft of amendments is still under debate at the time of writing (IFRS 2011a, 2011b).

From this short review it is apparent that both Boards are still struggling with substantial differences in their approaches towards accounting for financial instruments, some of which have become even more pronounced in the course of the financial crisis. It remains to be seen whether the FASB will step back from its plans to expand fair value accounting, and what direction it will take towards incorporating IFRS. An SEC (2011) Staff Paper on the latter issue was published in May 2011 and comments received by July are still under consideration by the SEC. In addition, it needs to be mentioned that the EU has so far refused to endorse any part of the new IFRS 9 standards as long as the whole package has not been finished. The EU's opting out of endorsing the standards raises questions about the degree to which revisions in IFRS have been implemented by European banks and financial companies in their accounting practices to date.

Conclusions

The results of our analysis indicate that at no stage in the process have actors converged, either on a single joint problem definition or on a single global reform project. Instead, problem definitions have evolved and changed over time: some actors have aligned their views and strategies, others have continued to articulate a different view of cause–effect relations, and reforms have developed step by step, at times merely responding to uncoordinated short-term pressures. This all points to the need to study problem definition and political action in interaction over time, rather than as two successive phases of the policy process.

As problem definitions have gone hand in hand with specific recommendations on standard-setting and governance reform, they have given rise to shifting actor coalitions. As the crisis unfolded, national governments, the European Commission, and prudential regulators saw accounting rules no longer merely as a means to achieve transparency, but also as a macro-prudential tool. Under the stress of the crisis, this brought them in line with the goals of large parts of the commercial banking sector. However, investment banks, securities regulators, analysts and investor associations, as well as the standard-setters, with some modifications in the case of the IASB, maintained that the principal goal of accounting standards was to provide a timely and accurate picture of the economic performance of an entity to its investors. Thus, coalitions around problem definitions arising from a transparency and a prudential approach cross the traditional divides between industry and regulators, or private and public actors.

The results furthermore suggest that changes in problem definition, as well as their prioritization or deprioritization in the public debate, can be attributed to two main factors: exogenous changes in the economic context—particularly the worsening of the crisis—and the endogenous dynamics of the reform process itself. Two events mark critical moments in the evolution of struggles over problem definition: the collapse of Lehmann Brothers on September 15, 2008, escalated the systemic risk involved in the financial crisis; and the announcements by the IASB and the FASB of their respective proposals on measurement on July 14 and 15, 2009, made visible the potential for divergence between the responses of the United States and international standard-setters to the G20 agenda. While the first event triggered an alignment of views in response to systemic risk, the second event and its aftermath are outcomes of the accounting reform process.

Continued struggles over competing diagnoses arising from the transparency and prudential approaches did not prevent reform altogether. The IASB has revised its standards on consolidation in such a way that it should include all financial instruments held under the (broadly defined) control of a given entity. IFRS 9 provides clearer guidance on fair value measurement and simplifies the classification categories. Proposals on impairment, at least at the time of writing, seem to follow an expected rather than an incurred loss model. The establishment of a Monitoring Board has made the governance structure of the IASB more publicly accountable, although mainly towards securities regulators and less towards prudential regulators, with the underrepresentation of emerging market economies and developing countries persisting.

Nevertheless, the absence of a global governance architecture that would have provided incentives for both standard-setters to pursue a common revision of standards rather than as separate albeit linked projects, seems to be a crucial difference compared to reforms in other areas such as capital ratios. As a result of this specific governance arrangement, the reform process itself has generated new disparities between IFRS and US GAAP in the area of financial standards, while the declared aim of most of the actors involved is to foster convergence between systems. Paradoxically, the reform process itself has produced new problems. It has re-emphasized the problem of how standards can respond to different business models and processes while providing a comparable, relevant, and comprehensible picture of a company's economic situation. Here, as so often, the devil lies in the details.

References

Allen, Franklin/Elena Carletti, 2008: "Fair-value" Accounting and Liquidity Pricing. In: *Journal of Accounting and Economics* 45, 358–378.

Alter, Karen J./Sophie Meunier, 2009: The Politics of International Regime Complexity. In: *Perspectives on Politics* 7(1), 13–24.

André, Paul, et al., 2009: Fair Value Accounting and the Banking Crisis in 2008: Shooting the Messenger. In: *Accounting in Europe* 6(1), 3–24.

Bragg, Steven M., 2010: *Wiley GAAP 2011: Interpretation and Application of Generally Accepted Accounting Principles.* Hoboken, NJ: John Wiley & Sons.

Botzem, Sebastian, 2010: *Standards der Globalisierung: Die grenzüberschreitende Regulierung der Unternehmensrechnungslegung als Pfadgestaltung.* Dissertation. Berlin: Freie Universität Berlin. <www.diss.fu-berlin.de/diss/servlets/MCRFileNodeServlet/FUDISS_derivate_0000000 07292/Botzem_2010_Standards_der_Globalisierung.pdf?hosts=> (accessed on November 25, 2010)

Botzem, Sebastian/Sigrid Quack, 2006: Contested Rules and Shifting Boundaries: International Standard-Setting in Accounting. In: Marie-Laure Djelic/Kerstin Sahlin-Andersson (eds.), *Transnational Governance: Institutional Dynamics of Regulation.* Cambridge: Cambridge University Press, 266–286.

Camfferman, Kees/Stephan A. Zeff, 2007: *Financial Reporting and Global Capital Markets: A History of the International Accounting Standards Committee, 1973–2000.* Oxford: Oxford University Press.

Cobb, Roger W./Charles D. Elder, 1983: *Participation in American Politics: The Dynamics of Agenda Building.* Baltimore: Johns Hopkins University Press.

Council of the European Union, 2009: *Draft Key Issues Paper,* Document 6784/1/09 Rev 1, Brussels, March 5.

Dauer, Ulrike, 2008: Goldman Sachs Quits IIF Bk Lobby Group. In: *Dow Jones Newswires,* July 9.

European Central Bank, 2004: *Fair Value Accounting and Financial Stability.* Occasional Paper Series, No. 13. Frankfurt a.M.: ECB. <www.ecb.int/pub/pdf/scpops/ecbocp13.pdf> (accessed on November 25, 2010)

Erturk, Ismail, et al., 2008: *Financialization at Work: Key Texts and Commentary.* London: Routledge.

FCAG (Financial Crisis Advisory Group), 2009a: *Letter to Prime Minister Gordon Brown as the Host of the G20 Summit on April 2 in London.* London, March 31. <www.ifrs.org/NR/rdonlyres/1B8B6655-501E-4B08-A13B-CE22F7FB1156/0/FCAGLettertoG202 April09.pdf> (accessed on November 25, 2010)

——, 2009b: *Financial Crisis Advisory Group Publishes Wide-ranging Review of Standard-setting Activities Following the Global Financial Crisis.* Press release, London, July 28. <www.ifrs.org/NR/rdonlyres/F0617367-F810-4B3D-85E8-C76AAE12DB1D/0/6PRFinancial-CrisisAdvisoryGrouppublisheswiderangingreviewofstandardsettingactivitiesfol.pdf> (accessed on November 25, 2010)

——, 2009c: *Report of the Financial Crisis Advisory Group.* London, July 28. <www.iasb.org/NR/rdonlyres/2D2862CC-BEFC-4A1E-8DDC-F159B78C2AA6/0/FCAGReportJuly 2009.pdf> (accessed on November 25, 2010)

French Presidency of the European Union, 2008: *Informal Meeting of the Heads of State and Government of the European Union on November 7.* Press release. <www.eu2008.fr/PFUE/lang/en/accueil/PFUE-11_2008/PFUE-07.11.2008/Reunion_informelle_chefs_etat_et_de_gouvernement_de_Union_europeenne_le_7_novembre.html> (accessed on November 25, 2010)

FSA (Financial Services Authority), 2009: *The Turner Review: A Regulatory Response to the Global Banking Crisis.* London: FSA. <www.fsa.gov.uk/pubs/other/turner_review.pdf> (accessed on November 25, 2010)

FSF (Financial Stability Forum), 2008: *Enhancing Market and Institutional Resilience*. <www.financialstabilityboard.org/publications/r_0804.pdf> (accessed on November 25, 2010)

——, 2009: *Report of the Financial Stability Forum on Addressing Procyclicality in the Financial System*, April 2. <www.financialstabilityboard.org/publications/r_0904a.pdf> (accessed on November 25, 2010)

Godechot, Olivier, 2011: *Finance and the Rise in Inequalities in France*. Working Paper No. 13. Paris: Paris School of Economics. Paris.

G7, 2008: *G7/8 Finance Ministers Meeting: Statement of G7 Finance Ministers and Central Bank Governors*. Washington, DC, April 11. <www.g8.utoronto.ca/finance/fm080411.htm> (accessed on November 25, 2010)

G20, 2008: *Declaration: Summit on Financial Markets and the World Economy*. Washington, DC, November 15. <www.g20.org/Documents/g20_summit_declaration.pdf> (accessed on November 25, 2010)

——, 2009a: *Declaration on Strengthening the Financial System*. London, April 2. <www.g20.org/Documents/Fin_Deps_Fin_Reg_Annex_020409_-_1615_final.pdf> (accessed on November 25, 2010)

——, 2009b: *Leaders' Statement: The Pittsburgh Summit*. September 24–25. <www.g20.org/Documents/pittsburgh_summit_leaders_statement_250909.pdf> (accessed on November 25, 2010)

Helleiner, Eric/Stefano Pagliari/Hubert Zimmermann (eds), 2009: *Global Finance in Crisis: The Politics of International Regulatory Change*. London: Routledge.

Hellwig, Martin F., 2009: *Systemic Risk in the Financial Sector: An Analysis of the Subprime-Mortgage Financial Crisis*. Discussion Paper 2008/43. Bonn: Max Planck Institute for Research on Collective Goods.

High-Level Group (High-Level Group on Financial Supervision in the EU, chaired by Jacques de Larosière), 2009: *Report*. Brussels, 25 February. <http://ec.europa.eu/internal_market/finances/docs/de_larosiere_report_en.pdf> (accessed on November 25, 2010)

Hughes, Jennifer/Gillian Tett, 2008: An Unforgiving Eye: Bankers Cry Foul over Fair Value Accounting Rules. In: *Financial Times*, March 13.

Humphrey, Christopher/Anne Loft/Margaret Woods, 2009: The Global Audit Profession and the International Financial Architecture: Understanding Regulatory Relationships in a Time of Financial Crisis. In: *Accounting, Organization and Society* 34, 810–825.

IASB (International Accounting Standards Boards), 2008: *Reducing Complexity in Reporting Financial Instruments*. London. <www.iasb.org/NR/rdonlyres/A2534626-8D62-4B42-BE12-E3D14C15AD29/0/DPReducingComplexity_ReportingFinancialInstruments.pdf> (accessed on November 25, 2010)

——, 2009a: *IASB Responds to G20 Recommendations, US GAAP Guidance*. Press release. London, April 7. <www.ifrs.org/NR/rdonlyres/7603DFF0-D55C-4279-A580-A466CBEF512D/0/IASBrespondstoG20FASBguidanceFINAL.pdf> (accessed on November 25, 2010)

——, 2009b: *IASB Sets Out Timetable for IAS 39 Replacement and Its Conclusions on FASB FSPs*. Press release. London, April 24. <www.iasb.org/NR/rdonlyres/352CE1ED-07DB-474C-B1E3-928A9BCB70C3/0/PRIASBsetsouttimetableforIAS39replacementanditsconclusionsonFASBFSPs.pdf> (accessed on November 25, 2010)

IASB (International Accounting Standards Board), 2011: *Supplement to ED/2009/12 Financial Instruments: Amortized Cost and Impairment, January 2011*. <www.ifrs.org/NR/rdonlyres/2BD9895F-459F-43B8-8C4D-AFE8ACA0A9AD/0/SupplementarydocFinancialInstrumentsImpairmentJan2011.pdf> (accessed on November 25, 2010)

IASB EAP (Expert Advisory Panel), 2008: *Measuring and Disclosing the Fair Value of Financial Instruments in Markets that Are No Longer Active*. Draft document, London, September 16. <www.iasb.org/NR/rdonlyres/F309C029-84B4-4F1F-BFB6-886EE9922A42/0/Expert_Advisory_Panel_draft_160908.pdf> (accessed on November 25, 2010)

IASB-FASB, 2002: *Memorandum of Understanding*. Norwalk, CN, September 18. <www.fasb.org/cs/BlobServer?blobcol=urldata&blobtable=MungoBlobs&blobkey=id&blobwhere=1175819018817&blobheader=application%2Fpdf> (accessed on November 25, 2010)

——, 2006: *A Roadmap for Convergence between IFRSs and US GAAP—2006-2008: Memorandum of Understanding between the FASB and the IASB*. February 27. <www.iasplus.com/press rel/0602roadmapmou.pdf> (accessed on November 25, 2010)

——, 2008: *Completing the February 2006 Memorandum of Understanding: A Progress Report and Timetable for Completion*. <www.fasb.org/intl/MOU_09-11-08.pdf> (accessed on November 25, 2010)

IASCF (International Accounting Standards Committee Foundation), 2008: *Letter of the Chairman of the Trustees to President Bush as Host of the G20 Meeting on November 15 in Washington*. <www.iasb.org/NR/rdonlyres/BE29F49A-188E-4A46-8995-45FAE19DB09A/0/Trustees_letter_addressed_to_US_President.pdf> (accessed on November 25, 2010)

IASCF Monitoring Board, 2009: *Statement of the Monitoring Board for the International Accounting Standards Committee Foundation on Principles for Accounting Standards and Standard Setting*, London, September 22. <www.iasplus.com/iascf/0909monitoringboardstatement.pdf> (accessed on November 25, 2010)

IFRS Foundation, 2011a: *IASB and FASB Report Substantial Progress towards Completion of Convergence Programme*. Press release, London, April 21. <www.ifrs.org/NR/rdonlyres/CA8E48F9-AB0D-49A6-A5ED-5115206C697F/0/PRApril2011progressreport.pdf> (accessed on November 25, 2010)

——, 2011b: *Progress Report on IASB-FASB Convergence Work*. London, April 21. <www.ifrs.org/NR/rdonlyres/1895FCCF-2DC7-499F-BE0B-E01606CE55AC/0/April2011progressreportfinal.pdf>

IIF (International Institute of Finance), 2008a: *Interim Report of the IIF Committee on Market Best Practices*. April 9. <www.iasplus.com/crunch/0804iifbestpractices.pdf> (accessed on November 25, 2010)

——, 2008b: *Final Report of the IIF Committee on Market Best Practices: Principles of Conduct and Best Practice Recommendations. Financial Services Industry Response to the Market Turmoil of 2007–2008*. <www.iif.com/download.php?id=Osk8Cwl08yw=> (accessed on November 25, 2010)

——, 2008c: *Letter to President Bush as Host of G20 Meeting on November 15 in Washington*. Washington, DC, November 7. <www.iif.com/download.php?id=0DkLOqGnjTw=> (accessed on November 25, 2010)

IOSCO (International Organization of Securities Commissions), 2008a: *Report of the Taskforce on the Subprime Crisis*. Final Report. Technical Committee of IOSCO. <www.iasplus.com/iosco/0805ioscosubprimereport.pdf> (accessed on November 25, 2010)

IOSCO (International Organization of Securities Commissions), 2008b: *Open Letter to Messrs. Draghi (as Chairman of FSF), Mantega (as Minister of Finance, Brazil) and Meirelles (Governor of the Central Bank, Brazil) as Participants of the G20 Meeting on November 15 in Washington.* Madrid, November 12. <www.iasplus.com/iosco/0811ioscog20.pdf > (accessed on November 25, 2010)

Kingdon, John W., 1995: *Agenda, Alternatives, and Public Policies.* New York: Harper Collins College Publishers.

Laux, Christian/Christian Leuz, 2009: The Crisis of Fair-Value Accounting: Making Sense of the Recent Debate. In: *Accounting, Organizations and Society* 34, 826–834.

——, 2010: Did Fair-Value Accounting Contribute to the Financial Crisis? In: *Journal of Economic Perspectives* 24(1), 93–118.

Matherat, Sylvie, 2008: Fair Value Accounting and Financial Stability: Challenges and Dynamics. In: *Banque de France: Financial Stability Review* 12, 53–63.

Nölke, Andreas, 2009: The Politics of Accounting Regulation: Responses to the Subprime Crisis. In: Eric Helleiner/Stefano Pagliari/Hubert Zimmermann (eds.), *Global Finance in Crisis: The Politics of International Regulatory Change.* London: Routledge, 37–55.

Nölke, Andreas/James Perry, 2007: The Power of Transnational Private Governance: Financialization and the IASB. In: *Business and Politics* 9, 3.

Novoa, Alicia/Jodi Scarlata/Juan Solé, 2009: *Procyclicality and Fair Value Accounting.* IMF Working Paper 09/39. Washington, DC: International Monetary Fund (IMF).

Ojo, Marianne, 2010: The Role of the IASB and Auditing Standards in the Aftermath of the 2008/2009 Financial Crisis. In: *European Law Journal* 16(5), 604–623.

Orléan, André, 2011: *L'empire de la valeur: Refonder l'économie.* Paris: Seuil.

Philippon, Thomas/Ariell Resheff, 2009: *Wages and Human Capital in the U.S. Financial Industry: 1909–2006.* NBER Working Paper 14644. Cambridge, MA: National Bureau of Economic Research.

Posner, Elliot, 2010: Sequence as Explanation: The International Politics of Accounting Standards. In: *Review of International Political Economy* 17(4), 639–664.

PriceWaterhouseCoopers, 2006: *Financial Instruments under IFRS.* Second edition. October. <http://download.pwc.com/ie/pubs/financial_instruments_under_ifrs.pdf> (accessed on November 14, 2011)

Richard, Jacques, 2005: The Concept of Fair Value in French and German Accounting Regulations from 1673 to 1914 and Its Consequences for the Interpretation of the Stages of Development of Capitalist Accounting. In: *Critical Perspectives on Accounting* 16, 825–850.

SEC (Securities and Exchange Commission), 2008: *Report and Recommendations Pursuant to Section 133 of the Emergency Economic Stabilization Act of 2008: Study on Mark-To-Market Accounting.* Washington, DC: U.S. Securities and Exchange Commission. <www.sec.gov/news/studies/2008/marktomarket123008.pdf> (accessed on November 25, 2010)

——, 2011: *Work Plan for the Consideration of Incorporating International Financial Reporting Standards into the Financial Reporting System for US issuers: Exploring a Possible Framework Method of Incorporation.* Staff Paper, May 26. Washington, DC: U.S. Securities and Exchange Commission. <www.sec.gov/spotlight/globalaccountingstandards/ifrs-work-plan-paper-052611.pdf> (accessed on November 25, 2010)

Stellinga, Bart, 2011: *Too Big to Fair Value: A Study of International Accounting Regulation Reform.* Master thesis. Amsterdam: University of Amsterdam.

Stone, Deborah A., 1989: Causal Stories and the Formation of Policy Agendas. In: *Political Science Quarterly* 104, 281–300.

Thiemann, Matthias, 2011: *Regulating the Off-balance Sheet Exposure of Banks: A Comparison Pre- and Post-crisis*. Foundation for European Progressive Studies. Discussion Paper. Brussels. <www.feps-europe.eu/fileadmin/downloads/political_economy/1106_OffBalanceSheet Exposure_Thiemann.pdf> (accessed on November 25, 2010)

Useem, Michael, 1999: *Investor Capitalism: How Money Managers Are Changing the Face of Corporate America*. New York: Basic Books.

Wade, Robert H., 2008: Financial Regime Change? In: *New Left Review* 53, 5–21.

Weiss, Janet A., 1989: The Powers of Problem Definition: The Case of Government Paperwork. In: *Policy Sciences* 22(2), 97–121.

Whittington, Geoffrey, 2010: Measurement in Financial Reporting. In: *Abacus* 46(1), 104–110.s

10

New Capital Rules? Reforming Basel Banking Standards after the Financial Crisis

Roman Goldbach and Dieter Kerwer

Introduction

In 2008, the failure of the US investment bank Lehman Brothers led to a collapse of the interbank market, threatening banks throughout the OECD world with bankruptcy. The subprime crisis had mutated into a global banking crisis. To overcome this crisis, the United States and other affected states—mostly in Europe—put huge amounts of their taxpayers' money at risk to bail out their banking sectors and to prevent a collapse of the world economy. These events have called into question the institutions designed to prevent a global banking crisis from happening in the first place. At the global level, this is the task of the Basel Committee for Banking Supervision (Kapstein 1994; Tarullo 2008). Since 1974, it has established a highly elaborate and complex set of standards for the capital reserves that banks require to be safe, whatever market conditions may be. Despite these standards, the global financial crisis has brought many banks to the brink of collapse and beyond. Given that the rules of the Basel Committee did not prevent the global banking crisis, significant efforts to reform global banking rules would have been expected.

In this chapter, we analyze the institutional change in global banking regulation after the financial crisis. Given the severity of the crisis, this is a highly important topic in its own right. At the same time, the institutional changes in this area are likely to be influential in other areas of regulatory reform, since the Basel Committee has served as a model for other financial regulators. In our analysis, we address two dimensions of institutional change, procedural and substantial. We analyze changes in how and where decisions are made, and how global banking standards themselves have changed.

Our main finding confirms our expectation only partially. Instead of radical institutional change involving a switch to new decision-making arenas and regulatory approaches, we find that reforms have given rise to only gradual institutional change (Streeck/Thelen 2005). The Basel Committee remains the crucial locus where global banking standards are set (see "Changing organizations" in this chapter). Furthermore, the basic approach to preventing bank failure remains broadly identical with the pre-crisis approach. Nevertheless, within the confines of this approach, some significant reforms have been introduced that are likely to increase banks' capital reserves (see "Changing rules"). However, while the rule changes adopted so far do amount to substantial reform, the extent to which reform actually materializes will depend on future implementation. In this respect, there is less reason for optimism (see "Conclusion").

Changing organizations

Prior to the financial crisis, the most important global regulator for internationally active banks was the Basel Committee (Davies/Green 2008: 32–59). The Basel Committee was established in 1974 within the framework of the Bank for International Settlements (BIS) in response to the failure of the German "Bankhaus Herstatt"; this failure had revealed that for multinational banks, no clear supervisory authority and responsibility existed. The founding G10 were Belgium, Canada, France, Germany, Italy, Japan, the Netherlands, Sweden, the United Kingdom, and the United States, with Switzerland, Luxembourg, and Spain joining later (Buchmüller 2008: 19–20). The members of the Basel Committee are representatives of central banks and banking supervisors. The role of the Basel Committee is to coordinate the work of its subcommittees and working groups and to adopt standards. These have to be approved by the Group of Central Bank Governors and Heads of Supervision (GHOS).

The first goal of the Basel Committee was to establish global rules of banking supervision. In 1975, the central bank governors of the BIS concluded the "Basel Concordat," which for the first time defined the obligations of the home and host countries of internationally active banks. The initial principles of the Concordat were subsequently elaborated, for example to enable information exchange between supervisors alongside national bank secrecy regulations. More recently, the Basel Committee's most important field of activity has been the banks' capital reserves. With the progress of financial globalization, banks were increasingly forced to compete with other banks, and national regulators were increasingly likely to engage in a race-to-the-bottom. As a consequence, capital reserves of banks have declined while risks have increased. In order to prevent an international banking crisis, the Committee adopted a first set of rules to ensure banks' capital adequacy. The first "Basel Accord" was concluded in 1988. Despite a series of updates in the 1990s, the basic structure of the Accord increasingly failed to capture the risks involved in banks' activities. As a consequence, the Committee started to develop a new framework in 1998. This has turned out to be a complex process and has de facto turned the second Basel Accord into a permanent work in progress. In this section, we show that the Basel Committee has remained the pivotal standard-setter for banks after the financial crisis and we address the question of how this has been possible, given the failure of the previous rules to prevent a banking crisis.

Reorganizing standard-setting

As an initial response to the financial crisis, the Basel Committee expanded its membership. Prior to the crisis the Committee consisted of representatives of regulatory authorities from a group of countries deemed to have an internationally significant banking sector.[1] After the crisis, representatives from G20 member states were invited who hitherto had not participated in the Basel Committee. This group consists of Argentina, Indonesia, Saudi Arabia, South Africa, and Turkey.[2] The Basel Committee's governing body expanded accordingly to include central bank governors and heads of supervision from these new member organizations. With this enlargement, the Basel Committee adapted to the shift from the G7/8 to the G20 as the major forum of intergovernmentally coordinated crisis management. However, post-crisis enlargement remains modest as regulators from the most important emerging market economies, the so-called BRIC states, were already members before the crisis.

The major organizational innovation regarding financial standard-setting was the upgrading of the Financial Stability Forum (FSF) to the Financial Stability Board (FSB) (see Donnelly in this volume). While the role of the former had been limited to synthesizing the work of other sectoral standard-setters, the latter was to become a proactive coordinator of post-crisis reform efforts. Due to its broader membership, especially with regard to finance ministries, it has more legitimacy than the Basel Committee and resembles a transnational political body that also represents national political authorities. This would allow the FSB to reduce the institutional power of the Basel Committee by curtailing its agenda-setting power and by introducing new control mechanisms. However, the FSB did not utilize this political mandate to challenge the Basel Committee, but rather sought to optimize the risk regulation approach to bank supervision.

---

1 Before the crisis, the Basel Committee included representatives from Australia, Belgium, Brazil, Canada, China, France, Germany, India, Italy, Japan, Korea, Luxembourg, Mexico, the Netherlands, Russia, Spain, Sweden, Switzerland, the United Kingdom, and the United States.

2 Additional members are regulators from Hong Kong and Singapore.

Standard-setting process

The reform of the Basel banking rules started in 2009 and was concluded by the end of 2010. The decision-making arenas were the G20 and the Basel Committee for Banking Supervision. The role of the Basel Committee was to put together a new set of capital adequacy standards termed Basel III and to submit a progress report to the various G20 summit meetings. The G20 endorsed the various progress reports and gave only very broad guidance. The G20 formally endorsed the Basel III rules in its meeting in Seoul in November 2010.

The Basel Committee thus remained the crucial decision-making arena. In 2009, the Committee members from national bank supervisors and central banks set the initial reform agenda. In spring of 2010, they solicited comments from affected parties and revised the rules accordingly. During 2010, the Basel Committee conducted several quantitative impact studies on how the rules would impact on banks and the economies of its member states. Here, the Basel Committee has been able to counter the claims of the banking industry that Basel III would lead to a credit crunch and as a consequence would be detrimental to economic recovery after the financial crisis.

In comparison, other organizations played only a minor role in the rule-making process. The activities of the G20 were limited to issuing a vague mandate. The first statement of the group on capital standards dates back to the meeting in Pittsburgh in 2009. In the final communiqué, the G20 simply endorsed the Basel Committee proposal (Group of Twenty 2009). At their Toronto meeting in June 2010, the G20 had a chance to comment on the revised proposal submitted by the Basel Committee. However, in general there was little input (*Financial Times,* June 29, 2010: 6): the G20 accepted extensive transition periods giving national regulators time to help their local banks to adjust to new capital standards, easing some industry fears. However, it failed to clarify other important issues such as the definition of capital or the subject of liquidity standards. At the meeting in Seoul in 2010, the G20 accepted the proposals of the Basel Committee without further amendments (Group of Twenty 2010:7).

Other possible decision-making arenas have influenced the Basel Committee, without, however, actually making decisions on standards themselves. The Financial Stability Board (FSB) merely coordinated the reform efforts in the various sub-fields of global financial regulation (see Donnelly in this volume). Nor has the EU directly shaped Basel III (see Quaglia in this volume). Since representatives of EU member-states disagreed in many respects, they were not influential as a single voice within the Committee during the negotiation phase. However, the EU's plan to amend the details of some Basel III standards before adopting them had repercussions for the standard-setting process within the Basel Committee.

The considerable institutional continuity might seem surprising given the magnitude of the crisis in the banking sector. One might have expected a switch to another decision-making arena. Presumably, the approach to dealing with risk would also change. Instead of merely prescribing capital reserves, regulators could downsize banks or ban certain practices such as short-selling. Why did the Basel Committee remain in charge and why did it stick to its regulatory approach?

Explaining continuity

In the field of international relations, the popular state-centric approach conceptualizes the G20 and the Basel Committee as negotiation arenas in which states decide when and how they want to cooperate (Kapstein 1994; Oatley/ Nabors 1998; Singer 2007). In this perspective, incremental rule change is due to the fact that the major states chose to delegate the task of making banks safer to the Basel Committee once again. This decision would explain why the Basel Committee has been able to remain in charge, even though its expertise and its approach to global banking regulation have been called into question by the financial crisis. The act of delegation amounts to a formal empowerment that helps compensate for its tarnished epistemic authority.

There is considerable empirical evidence to support the state-centric hypothesis. All the major states have had an overwhelming interest in setting global standards along established lines. As has been pointed out above, the G20 quickly agreed to delegate the standard-setting process once more to the Basel Committee and had no interest in closely monitoring the rewriting of the rules. This explanation does not exclude political conflict among the G20 member states. In fact, a conflict did arise once the first draft of the new set of standards was published by the Committee. However, the bone of contention was neither the appropriate regulatory forum nor the basic approach, but rather the impact of the new rules in different states. In game theoretical parlance, the conflict can be framed as a coordination game with distributional conflicts only. In fact, the major conflict that did emerge was the conflict between liberal market economies and coordinated market economies.[3] The United States and the United Kingdom both pressed for higher capital standards and wanted short implementation periods, while Germany, France, and Japan called for revisions that take into consideration state banks and smaller regional banks typical of coordinated market economies (*Financial Times,* July 21, 2010: 1; *Financial Times,* July 28, 2010: 5).The conflict over the costs of the reform also split the members of the EU into two opposing camps, with the United Kingdom in one, and most of Con-

---

3 The same conflict emerged during the negotiations on the Basel II rules (Wood 2005).

tinental Europe in the other (*Financial Times,* June 15, 2010: 5). This explains why there was no agreed EU position on these matters. Another piece of evidence supporting the view that the conflict among states concerned mainly distributional issues is offered by the behavior of the new members of the Basel Committee. Major emerging economies such as India and China have remained largely silent, despite being empowered by the new role of the G20, because they did not perceive significant adaptation costs to the new rules. China's banking sector is mostly state owned and operates at the national level. Indian banks seem to be focused on business in India and are already well capitalized (*Financial Times,* September 14, 2010: 26).

Much more problematic for the state-centric perspective is to understand why the G20 states decided to delegate reform of the global banking rules once again to the Basel Committee. The hypothesis that the states followed the pressure of the financial industry (see, for example, Claessens/Underhill 2010) is not plausible. The Institute for International Finance (IIF), the powerful international association of large global banks, warned that the economic repercussions of too much regulation and supervision would be harsh, resulting in financial market turbulence, reduced lending, reduced GDP growth, and higher unemployment (IIF 2010). One of its major suggestions was to implement the new capital requirements of the Accord—namely a "leverage ratio," "counter-cyclical buffers," and "medium-term liquidity"—in such a way as to give banks wider margins of discretion. Whereas the Committee favored prescribing minimum capital requirements through regulation ("Pillar 1"), the IFF suggested that these be determined by banks' internal risk management models ("Pillar 2"). It also objected to the aim of the Committee to establish new permanent standards and instead suggested evaluating the rules in the near future. However, the regulatory outcomes show that regulators have ignored these suggestions of softening up capital adequacy rules (see below).

Given that the influence of banking interests was fairly modest, what other explanations are feasible for why states have chosen conservative reform? One explanation could be that states were under pressure to react promptly to the global financial crisis and lacked the time to establish a consensus on a new regulatory approach and devise a new organization. Another explanation for the difficulties facing more fundamental reform might point to path dependency. After all, for more than two decades, banks, regulators, and other market participants have been using Basel standards. Finally, the Basel Committee's epistemic authority may well have survived the financial crisis. By virtue of being the forum of national bank regulators, it has unique access to sensitive data and can therefore endow its "Quantitative impact studies" with greater authority than private associations (see *Financial Times,* May 31, 2010: 1).

Changing rules: Global banking standards

The new package of rules introduced by the Basel Committee often referred to as "Basel III" does not substitute but rather complements the previous "Basel II" framework. The new regime continues to rest on three pillars. Since the second Basel Accord, this three-pillar structure has characterized international regulatory coordination: Pillar 1 defines amount and calculation models of minimum capital requirements; Pillar 2 stipulates that banks use internally developed risk management systems and outlines principles for the supervisory process, that is, how regulatory agencies investigate the internal risk management mechanisms of banks; and Pillar 3 defines the information banks have to disclose publicly in order to foster market discipline. Changes have been undertaken within all three pillars, while the focus remains on Pillar 1, namely quantifiable capital requirements, with relatively strengthened qualitative supervision (Pillar 2). Due to the many details, the overall picture is hard to grasp. The new rules make the existing elements of the framework of capital requirement regulation substantially more restrictive. In comparison to the previous regime, capital requirements are more demanding and the proprietary trading of banks is severely limited. Furthermore, additional lines of defense against banking failures have been erected, within the framework of which banks' liquidity management is put under supervision and counter-cyclical measures are introduced. We start by presenting the initial adjustments to the existing Basel II Accord and then outline the new Basel III elements.

Reforming banking standards

The first response of regulators to the financial crisis was to amend Basel II, resulting in rapidly applicable and stricter rules. The final amendments raised the (regulatory) costs for trading activities (in contrast to hold-to-maturity investments), and in particular for securitization, as well as for off-balance-sheet assets. These were targeted via a comprehensive Basel II approach, that is, changes in all three pillars, but mostly within Pillar 1.

As most of the banks' losses occurred in their trading books[4] and/or in the form of securitization, in July 2009 the Committee agreed upon measures giving clear-cut guidance to regulate non-hedging securitized assets and other

---

4 Banks' assets are subdivided into two "books": the banking book contains all assets that are held until maturity, and the trading book encompasses all other activities for trading purposes. The distinction is significant because different risks adhere to the two asset classes and accordingly different amounts of capital are required. Before the crisis, trading book items typically were subject to lower capital requirements.

financial instruments of proprietary trading in the trading book (BCBS 2009a, 2009b). The measures reduce incentives to move assets into the trading book by raising the risk weights and bringing them closer to banking book levels. "As a result of these revisions, market risk capital requirements will increase by an estimated average of three to four times for large internationally active banks" (BCBS 2010d). At the same time, the Committee substantially increased credit risk weights for securitization in the banking book.

Changes to the second pillar, the supervisory review of banking activities—in particular, banks' internal risk management—were threefold: first, more requirements for banks' internal risk management processes related to securitization and off-balance sheet trading activities; second, enhanced internal risk management systems, with a view to enhancing short- as well as long-term horizon risk management; and third, new rules on compensation ("bonuses") based on the FSB's Principles (2009) and Standards of Implementation (2010). Combined with the Basel Committee's assessment methodology these measures provide clear rules – for example, the innovation of a board remuneration committee in every bank—with detailed guidance on implementation and enforcement. However, the measures are designed as a compendium of options to implement the fairly general principles. Therefore, success hinges strongly upon national commitment and the newly introduced FSB peer review which is undertaken periodically.

The Basel Committee also amended Pillar 3 rules to enhance transparency and market discipline, as it raised the disclosure obligations of banks in all the three regards touched upon under Pillar 2 above: the very clear stipulations for disclosing securitization (as well as other trading) activities; internal risk management processes; and remuneration practices. These additional disclosure requirements will help to reduce market uncertainties about the strength of banks' balance sheets, as well as internal management practices.

While the revisions to the first and third pillars had to be complied with by the end of 2010, domestic supervisors were expected to start implementation of Pillar 2 changes immediately in July 2009. The revisions are certainly substantial and will impact heavily upon (re-)securitization and off-balance sheet trading.

Once these urgent revisions had been undertaken, the long-term resilience of the financial system and banks came into focus. Basel III is an extensive, comprehensive, and detailed transnational agreement, which continues the tradition of complex transnational financial regulation since the Committee's Market Risk Amendment to the Basel Accord in 1996. Most of the work concerned Pillar 1 issues, in other words, how much capital banks are required to hold, while less development can be seen regarding Pillar 2 and 3 issues, namely risk management and its supervision, or market discipline respectively. The two main documents (BCBS 2010a, 2010b) introduce four amendments/new elements: increased restrictions concerning capital requirements, new capital buffers, a new leverage ratio, and two new liquidity provisioning requirements.

The *minimum capital requirement* in relation to risk-weighted assets (RWAs) has been increased to 10.5 percent, including the new 2.5 percent capital conservation buffer. In addition, risk-weights of several asset categories have been raised (banking and trading book), particularly concerning securitized assets and derivatives. Moreover, the quality of capital will be improved considerably, as definitions are becoming more restrictive. While capital types of lower quality are either no longer eligible (the previously permitted Tier 3 capital) or internationally harmonized (Tier 2), the crucial adjustment is the stricter definition of Tier 1 capital. Under Basel III, 8.5 percent has to be common equity, so-called Tier 1 capital. Of this, 7 percentage points have to be Common Equity Tier 1 (CET1) capital, which is even more restrictively defined capital.[5] An additional 2 percent can be provided using Tier 2, less strictly defined types of capital. Consequently, the composition of the 10.5 percent required minimum capital has to be: 7 percent CET1, 1.5 percent common equity, and 2 percent Tier 2 capital.

While the above adjustments affect banks' costs heavily, we are skeptical concerning the more innovative elements. One new element comprises two *capital buffers*, one to establish a capital stock that can be drawn from temporarily during bad times, another to be built up during good times.

The *capital conservation buffer* ensures against unexpected losses by building reserves above minimum capital levels. An additional 2.5 percent of capital requirements are introduced—as discussed above, this is part of the 10.5 percent overall requirement—the distinctive feature being that this capital can be drawn down during distressed times (as opposed to minimum capital requirements of 8 percent). When banks' capital reserves fall into the range between 4.5 and 7 percent CET1, they are progressively constrained in terms of capital distributions (such as paying dividends, buying back shares, bonus payments and so on). The logic is that banks want to avoid coming into this range where they are substantially restricted as regards compensating their shareholders and employees, which provides them with the incentive to build higher capital reserves.

The second buffer, the *counter-cyclical capital buffer*, provides an incentive to build up buffers during boom times that can be drawn down during bad times by creating a cyclically stable minimum requirement. In extremis, it could result in an additional 2.5 percent of CET1 capital requirements (resulting in the

---

5 Predominantly common shares and retained earnings (with tailored solutions for non-joint stock companies). The 7 percentage points are calculated through deductions from the 8.5 percent common equity—deducted are amounts above an aggregate 15 percent (of the 4.5 percent) limit for investments in financial institutions, mortgage servicing rights, and deferred tax assets from timing differences.

theoretical maximum capital requirement of 13 percent). However, the highly complex process and room for national supervisory discretion beg the question of its real impact. In a complex three-step process a domestic supervisory authority has to (i) identify a boom-episode with system-wide credit risk dissipation and (ii) calculate the additional capital requirements (between 0 and 2.5 percent CET1), for which banks then have twelve months to adjust. Finally (iii), the supervisor has to enforce the buffer when a bank's capital reserves fall below the defined requirement, by progressively constraining capital distributions (stepwise 0, 40, 60, 80, and 100 percent of dividends, share buybacks, bonus payments and so on).

Furthermore, another innovative element was added to reduce capital arbitrage opportunities. The new *"leverage ratio"* defines a minimum level of capital reserves in relation to a bank's portfolio, independent of the risk incurred. It also means equal treatment of balance sheet and off-balance sheet items. The minimum ratio is to act as a "backstop" to prevent banks from building up excessive leverage that is not prevented via risk-weighted regulatory approaches. It will become a parallel requirement to minimum capital requirements and will stipulate 3 percent CET1 capital relative to exposure.

The most innovative element in the transnational banking regulations in question comprises the new *liquidity provisions* that force banks to ensure that their portfolios are sustainable in distressed illiquid markets. The standard requires that banks have a higher reserve of short-term liquid assets (determined by the "liquidity coverage ratio") and longer-term liquid assets (determined by the "net stable funding ratio"). These are not additional to the capital requirements, but overlap. Furthermore, these quantitative requirements are nested within a supervisory framework of liquidity risk management principles (BCBS Principles for Sound Liquidity Risk Management and Supervision 2008) that give detailed guidance on risk management for banks and supervision through regulatory agencies, as well as the Monitoring Metrics that harmonize the minimum information to be gathered by national supervisors.

The Liquidity Coverage Ratio (LCR) stipulates that banks provide sufficient short-term unencumbered high-quality liquid assets to survive a 30-day stress scenario (calculated on the basis of 2007–2009 circumstances, albeit not the worst case scenario of this period). The aim is for banks to have liquid assets available that can be monetized within a few days to finance 25 percent of unexpected cash-outflows; banks have to calculate these provisions internally, based on stress testing, at least monthly, while ensuring operational capacities for weekly/daily recalculation in stressed situations.

The accompanying Net Stable Funding Ratio (NSFR) is aimed at limiting overreliance on short-term wholesale funding during boom times and the underlying revolving market financing of long-term credits. It ensures that a bank's maturity structure of assets and liabilities is sustainable over a one-year time horizon. Banks have to undertake internal stress testing of available funds for servicing maturity structures and report the results at least quarterly.

Summing up, the existing three-pillar architecture of the Basel Accord(s) is stabilized and reinforced by raising quantitative minimum requirements and by increasing qualitative supervisory scrutiny. Furthermore, additional lines of defense are erected that are supposed to ensure prudential banking and prevent failures at an earlier stage (in other words, liquidity management, conservation, and counter-cyclical buffers). The existing supervisory architecture has been considerably strengthened.

Impact assessment and rule effectiveness

These rule changes translate into considerable new capital requirements. However, the question arises as to whether the impact is significant. According to the Basel Committee's "Quantitative impact study" (QIS)[6]—which evaluated how the new standards will affect the banks' capital reserve requirements in comparison to the capital levels in 2009 (Basel Committee 2010c)—large, internationally active banks (Group 1 banks) would have to raise their capital by 4.8 percent to meet Basel III targets. To achieve the 7 percent CET1 requirement, this amounts to additional capital of 577 billion euros (the sum of all profits in 2009 was 209 billion euros, in other words, the additional capital is 2.7 times one year's profits). These figures demonstrate the substantial efforts banks have to undertake in order to raise the necessary capital—although many banks' endeavors to clean their books after the crisis already will improve their capital requirement positions (Zeitler 2011). Smaller, rather regionally oriented institutions (Group 2 banks) have only to accumulate new capital in the amount of 2.7 percent to meet the Basel III standards. To achieve the 7 percent CET1 ratio, this amounts to an overall additional capital requirement of 25 billion euros (1.25 times one year's profits).

While this forecast suggests heavy burdens for the banking industry, the new elements in Basel III will result in some additional restrictions. However, it is unclear whether these will result in substantial additional capital requirements; complying with the minimum capital requirements might already provide sufficient resources to meet the other standards. Regarding the capital conservation buffer, the QIS results suggest that only banks within the highest quartile

---

6 The study's results are contested by the industry, which claims that its own evaluations come to different conclusions.

of profitability would suffer from it. Also, the leverage ratio seems to require fairly modest additional adjustments, as Group 1 banks in 2009 almost fulfilled the minimum requirements (2.8 percent CET1), and the Group 2 banks already over-achieved (3.8 percent CET1). Finally, concerning the new liquidity provisions the QIS indicates that the funding term structure of banks (that is, what time-horizons do a bank's assets have and how fast can banks turn assets into cash under market stresses) must be adjusted substantially. Concerning the short-term measure (LCR), 54 percent of all participating banks did not meet the required liquidity provisions, mirroring a shortfall of liquid assets of 1.73 trillion euros. Regarding the NSFR, the QIS indicated that 57 percent of all participating banks did not meet the required liquidity provisions, mirroring a shortfall of liquid assets of 2.89 trillion euros. However, the additional burden will be less once the LCR provisions are met. In general, these results do not depict additional capital requirements but rather a change in funding structure and maturity management. The costs cannot simply be added, but must be evaluated in more detail.

Switching to the macroeconomic perspective, the Committee—in collaboration with the FSB—came to the conclusion that, based on a static comparison, the increased capital requirements will result in a cumulative GDP reduction of 0.22 percent after full implementation of the new Basel framework, mirroring a 0.03 percentage point reduction in annual growth over that period (MAG 2010). Hence, while the impact will be felt, it is certainly far from threatening.

In sum, banks will have to hold substantial additional amounts of capital. However, the real impact of the described agreement could be weak, due to domestic implementation, international re-negotiation, and continued reliance on banks' internal capacities. Under the future regime, capital arbitrage made possible by varying domestic implementations of Basel III might gain in relevance. One specific danger is that banks may strategically draw down the capital conservation buffer during normal times to enhance competitiveness, and will not be restrained by their supervisors. The design of the buffer is predisposed towards domestic supervisory discretion—time limits on drawing the buffer down can be taken on a case-by-case basis by national supervisors. Furthermore, arbitrage options are provided by discretion regarding the rules' application to parts of a banking group (as opposed to sole consolidated application). Similar challenges are created by the highly sophisticated three-step design of the counter-cyclical buffer, which seems prone to error for two reasons: first, the mechanism does not seem to be real-world applicable, as (a) it needs time for banks to adjust, when it is likely to be too late (given unlikely early intervention by domestic supervisors), and (b) banks have an adjustment time window of up to 12 months, which will make this provision toothless in urgent situations. Second, since the buffer-related additional capital requirements have to be decided upon individually by each country, concerns about national industry competitiveness make application unlikely. The domestic discretion in deciding whether a boom-episode exists and the additional capital requirements should be activated, reduces incentives to implement unfavorable measures when other countries do not do so. In sum, the two new capital buffers are far-reaching but leave too much discretion to national supervisors, which might result in inter-jurisdictional competition via low capital buffer requirements.

Another concern is the potential weakening of Basel III provisions during the lengthy test and implementation period.[7] For the leverage ratio there are two transitional periods—earliest full implementation is 2018—during which results will be generated that are explicitly intended to adjust the framework to prevent unintended consequences. Moreover, in order to arrive at Pillar 1 treatment (that is, actually agree on a harmonized 3 percent rule in contrast to the Pillar 2 approach of domestic supervision) an explicit—new—decision has to be taken by the BCBS. There will be plenty of opportunities to realize the IIF's (IIF 2010: 2) aim of pushing the leverage ratio into Pillar 2 treatment. A third concern is the continued dependence on banks' internal capacities. The success of the liquidity provisions depends heavily upon internal banking calculations and supervisory capacities to supervise compliance with the highly complex and extensive regulations. Furthermore, lengthy test and implementation periods again apply and might weaken the agreements, as could domestic supervisory discretion.

Conclusion

Soon after the outbreak of the financial crisis, efforts commenced to reform global banking standards. In our analysis of these regulatory reforms we have addressed the question of whether they have brought about significant institutional change. Our main finding is that even the severe global banking crisis did not lead reformers to abandon the pre-crisis institutional set-up. We find that institutional change has been mainly gradual, rather than disruptive. Continuity is most pronounced in the way decision making is organized. The Basel Committee remains the sole standard-setter for global banking. The FSB, while more influential than its predecessor, has not emerged as a competing rule-making forum. Also, although Basel II was lenient with large banks, there is no evidence

---

7 In general, compliance with revised standards is due by 2013, while the new standards will be phased in over an additional period of six years until 2019.

that large banks actually captured the Basel Committee during the recent reform process. The reform of the Basel Committee itself was limited to a modest expansion in membership. We also found important elements of continuity in standards. The Basel Committee continues to adhere to its previous approach to banking risks. Reforms merely amend or add to the three regulatory pillars of Basel II. However, within this framework, standards have changed. The new Basel standards define higher capital requirements, stricter capital definitions, and capital requirements for new types of risk, and apply to a wider range of banks' activities so as to close regulatory loopholes. Internal risk management and public information disclosure have to be enhanced and will be subject to stricter supervision. Moreover, a leverage ratio, capital buffers, and liquidity requirements were introduced. The new capital standards will require banks to shore up their capital reserves. Overall, we thus find significant, if incremental change.

While it is important to acknowledge that the Basel Committee has made some headway, it is equally important not to forget that the significance of the new capital standards depends on how they are implemented. In the past, the implementation record has been uneven. While Basel Standards have become mandatory for most banks in the EU, the United States applies them only to a small segment of large multinational banks (Herring 2007: 416–419). There are some signs that implementation will continue to be difficult. Implementation may be jeopardized by generous transitional periods. These may give supervisors time to renege on their commitment or for banks to lobby for softer implementation (see *Financial Times,* September 5, 2011). Furthermore, leverage ratios, capital buffers, and liquidity provisions will be subject to follow-up negotiations on the transnational as well as the national level and will probably be weakened by domestic supervisory discretion when the national agencies face competitiveness issues regarding institutions within their jurisdiction. Before adopting the Basel III rules with minor changes in July 2011, the EU considered altering the Basel deal during EU implementation (see Quaglia in this volume). The Accord Implementation Group, a committee to promote the implementation of Basel standards founded in 2001 (BIS 2001), is likely to be strengthened by a peer review mechanism. However, it remains to be seen how effective this mechanism will be. The mechanism could be weakened considerably if the competitiveness of the national banking industry becomes the prime concern of the participating states. This might allow banks to increase their influence over the reform process in the medium term.[8] Thus, some of the promises of the present reforms may not materialize.

---

8 We owe this point to a comment by Geoffrey Underhill on a previous version of this chapter.

Finally, even if the new Basel standards are implemented fully, they will be significant only to the extent that the Basel Committee's approach to financial market risk prevention is convincing. The Committee continues to be guided by the conviction that the uncertain future of financial markets can be transformed into calculable risk. The more recent financial turmoil has called into question this conception of risk and suggests instead that the development of financial markets entails unknowns that are likely to be missed by preventive risk regulation (Taleb 2007).

References

BCBS (Basel Committee on Banking Supervision), 2001: *Progress towards Completion of the New Basel Capital Accord.* Press release, December 13. <www.bis.org/press/p011213.htm>

——, 2009a: *Revisions to the Basel II Market Risk Framework.* Basel: Bank for International Settlements (BIS).

——, 2009b: *Guidelines for Computing Capital for Incremental Risk in the Trading Book.* Basel: Bank for International Settlements (BIS). Press release, June 10. <www.bis.org/press/p090610.htm> (last access on February 3, 2011)

——, 2010a: *Basel III: A Global Regulatory Framework for More Resilient Banks and Banking Systems.* Basel: Bank for International Settlements (BIS).

——, 2010b: *Basel III: International Framework for Liquidity Risk Measurement, Standards and Monitoring.* Basel: Bank for International Settlements (BIS).

——, 2010c: *Results of the Comprehensive Quantitative Impact Study of Basel III.* Basel: Bank for International Settlements (BIS).

——, 2010d: *Adjustments to the Basel II Market Risk Framework Announced by the Basel Committee.* Press release, June 18. Basel: Bank for International Settlements (BIS). <www.bis.org/press/p100618.htm>

Buchmüller, Patrick, 2008: *Basel II: Hinwendung zur prinzipienorientierten Bankenaufsicht.* Baden-Baden: Nomos.

Claessens, Stijn/Geoffrey R. D. Underhill, 2010: The Political Economy of Basel II in the International Financial Architecture. In: Geoffrey R. D. Underhill/Jasper Blom/Daniel Mügge (eds.), *Global Financial Integration Thirty Years On.* Cambridge: Cambridge University Press, 113–133.

Davies, Howard/David Green, 2008: *Global Financial Regulation: The Essential Guide.* Cambridge: Polity.

Group of Twenty, 2009: *Leader's Statement: The Pittsburgh Summit.* Pittsburgh, September 24–25.

——, 2010: *The G20 Seoul Summit Leaders' Declaration.* Seoul, November 11–12.

Herring, Richard J., 2007: The Rocky Road to Implementation of Basel II in the United States. In: *Atlantic Economic Journal* 35, 411–429.

IIF (Institute of International Finance), 2010: *IIF Comments on BCBS Consultative Documents Strengthening the Resilience of the Banking Sector and International Framework for Liquidity Risk Measurement, Standards and Monitoring*. Basel: IIF.

Kapstein, Ethan B., 1994: *Governing the Global Economy: International Finance and the State*. Cambridge, MA: Harvard University Press.

MAG (Macroeconomic Assessment Group), 2010: *Final Report: Assessing the Macroeconomic Impact of the Transition to Stronger Capital and Liquidity Requirements*. Basel: Bank for International Settlements (BIS).

Oatley, Thomas/Robert Nabors, 1998: Redistributive Cooperation: Market Failure, Wealth Transfers, and the Basle Accord. In: *International Organization* 52(1), 35–54.

Singer, David Andrew, 2007: *Regulating Capital: Setting Standards for the International Financial System*. Ithaca: Cornell University Press.

Streeck, Wolfgang/Kathleen Thelen, 2005: Introduction: Institutional Change in Advanced Political Economies. In: Wolfgang Streeck/Kathleen Thelen (eds.), *Beyond Continuity: Institutional Change in Advanced Political Economies*. Oxford: Oxford University Press, 1–40.

Taleb, Nassim, 2007: *The Black Swan: The Impact of the Highly Improbable*. New York: Random House.

Tarullo, Daniel K., 2008: *Banking on Basel: The Future of International Financial Regulation*. Washington, DC: Peterson Institute for International Economics.

Wood, Duncan R., 2005: *Governing Global Banking: The Basel Committee and the Politics of Financial Globalisation*. Aldershot: Ashgate.

Zeitler, Franz-Christoph, 2011: *Finanzmärkte und Regulierung – Was folgt auf Basel III?* Speech by Franz-Christoph Zeitler, Vice-President of the German Bundesbank at the Bundesbank Symposium „Bankenaufsicht im Dialog" in Frankfurt, May 17.

Newspaper Articles

Financial Times, July 21, 2010, p. 1: Basel standards committee is "succumbing" to bank lobbying.

——, September 14, 2010, p. 26: Regime will reshape business models.

——, May 31, 2010, p. 1: Bankers' "doomsday scenarios" under fire from Basel study chief.

——, June 15, 2010, p. 5: Business chiefs condemn bank capital plans.

——, June 29, 2010, p. 6: Move to reassure on tough new rules.

——, July 28, 2010, p. 5: Watchdog plays down German concerns over accord plans.

——, September 5, 2011: Regulators poised to soften new bank rules.

11

Institutional Change at the Top: From the Financial Stability Forum to the Financial Stability Board

Shawn Donnelly

Introduction

In April 2009, the G20 called for the establishment of the Financial Stability Board. The FSB would coordinate and direct the future development of financial market regulation at the international level, with a view to ensuring the stability of the financial system. It would be a stronger institution than its predecessor, the Financial Stability Forum (FSF), with the capacity not just to compile international standards but actively to promote higher quality and effectiveness for financial market activity as a whole. While other global standard-setting bodies would change incrementally or not at all in the course of improving specific standards, the G20 announced that changes to the Board were intended to help take the quality of regulation, nationally and internationally and as a totality, to the next level. This chapter examines institutional changes from the FSF to the Financial Stability Board and the extent to which they support the conclusion that the Board is a game-changer in international financial market regulation.

A number of reference points can be used to highlight the differences in how the Forum and the Board are structured and operate and what their potential contribution to global economic governance is or is likely to be. There are differences in membership, both in terms of countries and the type of representatives they send, as well as differences in their internal structures, the means by which they interact with national authorities, and the way they interact with a variety of international bodies, including the G20, international standard-setting bodies (ISSBs), and international financial institutions: the IMF and the World Bank.

The Board is more institutionally developed than its predecessor in three ways: internally (to handle an increased workload on standards, supervision and the open method of coordination), internationally (to handle the increased work of coordinating and proposing improvements to international standards), and with regard to the institutional capacities and regulatory policies of national jurisdictions (through the open method of coordination).

These institutional changes reflect and support a higher degree of political commitment within the G20 to use the FSB more forcefully than the Forum to improve the quality of regulatory policy and instruments. It should be noted, however, that this common political commitment is confined to improving the instruments of financial market supervision, data analysis, early warning and emergency intervention. Other goals that demand deeper restrictions on business practices that lay at the core of the 2008 collapse are not part of either the political consensus or the FSB's agenda.

The Financial Stability Forum

The Financial Stability Forum was called into life in 1999 after the collapse of an American hedge fund, Long-Term Capital Management (LTCM), which threatened to unleash a chain reaction of financial collapses in the United States and then Europe. LTCM had incurred losses during a financial crisis that began in Thailand in 1997 and then spread to South-East Asia, then Latin America and Russia. LTCM's heavy investments in Russia, combined with American banks investing heavily in LTCM, completed the chain of contact along which contagion spread from Thailand to American banks (Jorion 2000). While the Federal Reserve Bank of New York organized a bailout by LTCM's largest investors to fight the immediate fire, the American government, together with the rest of the G7, acquired an interest in global institutions that would focus on proactive crisis prevention rather than post-facto emergency management. The Forum was to help this process, while the G20 was formed to bring important emerging market countries to the table with the G7 in overseeing the Forum's work.

The original members of the FSF were the central banks, finance ministries, and financial service regulators from the G7 countries, plus Australia, Hong Kong, Singapore, Switzerland, and the Netherlands, as well as the ISSBs (Basel Committee, International Association Insurance Supervisors (IAIS), the International Organization of Securities Commissions (IOSCO) and the International Accounting Standards Board (IASB), the IMF, the World Bank and the European Central Bank. As with the Basel Committee, the Bank for International Settlements in Basel provided rooms and administrative support for the Forum. The Chair took on the role of setting the agenda in consultation with the members at periodic membership meetings. Ad hoc working groups were formed to study issues of interest.

Institutionally, the Forum was a meeting place without strong institutional diversification, specialization, authoritative decision making powers, or supervisory capacity. The main way that the FSF promoted better regulation on behalf of the G20 was to draw the attention of national regulatory practitioners and lawmakers to existing standards, encourage ISSBs to develop codes of best practice to which national practice could be oriented, and to promote dialogue between the ISSBs. It is here, as the exploratory report for the Forum had suggested (Tietmeyer 1999), that the efforts of the Forum stopped and the responsibility of national governments, regulators, and ISSBs began. The actual review of national implementation was undertaken outside the Forum, by the IMF and the World Bank, without Forum involvement.

The range of standards that the Forum highlighted and that the IMF and the World Bank scrutinized was also limited in nature. The Compendium of Standards that the Forum highlighted as the benchmarks for good economic governance covered three areas: transparency of macroeconomic management (three standards from the IMF); financial regulation and supervision (one set of core principles of good regulation each from Basel, IOSCO, and the IAIS); and institutional and market infrastructure (six standards covering: money laundering (by the Financial Action Task Force), systemic features of clearing systems (by the Committee on the Global Financial System), financial reporting standards (by the International Accounting Standards Board), corporate governance standards (by the OECD), and insolvency standards and deposit insurance (by the Bank for International Settlements). Most importantly, most of the standards did not address the behavior of financial market participants, but instead ensured that regulators had access to sufficient resources, personnel, decision making autonomy and powers of investigation to properly do their jobs. None of them have much to say about banking, securities or insurance regulation directly.

By request of the G7 (Bayne 2000), the IMF examined the application of these limited standards by national governments in the context of Article IV consultations, which audit the economic policies, practices and conditions relevant to economic growth and stability, and specifically in consultations on the Financial Sector Assessment Programme. The IMF's capacity to wield influence rested in turn on the signaling effect to markets of its pronunciations on regulation (Giannini 2000). This reliance on a combination of international standard-setting bodies and international financial institutions to improve regulation generally was subject to two weaknesses: the unwillingness of the United States to undergo such a review of its own practices (Kirton 2000; Walter 2000; Financial Crisis Inquiry Commission 2011: 423), and the lack of consensus on binding standards within any of the ISSBs. This meant that in terms of mission and actual standard work, the FSF had very little to do or room or inclination to grow further institutionally.

The Forum's most important research and strategy reports also came from outside. The Forum allowed a core group of national regulators known as the Senior Supervisor's Group comprising representatives from the United States (the Federal Reserve Bank of New York, which hosts the SSG, the US Federal Reserve, the Securities and Exchange Commission, the Office of the Comptroller of the Currency), Switzerland, France (the respective central banks), Germany and the United Kingdom (the respective Financial Service Authorities) to investigate what had led to the crisis in 2007 rather than compile its own report (Senior Supervisor's Group 2008). Their report revealed that those investment companies that had weathered the crisis well to that point had corporate governance and financial risk management mechanisms that went far beyond the minimum standards that the Forum had put together in its Compendium of Standards.[1] They furthermore declared that they would "continue to work directly through the appropriate international forums (for example, the Basel Committee, International Organization of Securities Commissions, and the Joint Forum) on both planned and ongoing work in this regard," rather than relying on the Forum (ibid.: 2). Although the SSG had no formal status within the Forum, this underlines the irrelevancy of the Forum in actual decision making. In addition to this hard core of powerful countries taking decisions outside the Forum, Davies suggests that ISSBs, too, were reluctant to accept any hint of FSF authority over them. For its part, while the Basel Committee focused on capital standards, it failed to be moved to consider any other regulation of banks (Davies 2010: 188).

In practice, the SSG's 2008 report assigned G7 countries as rulemakers through their dominance in the ISSBs and the Forum (through their status as the home of best practice) and other countries as ruletakers (Kaiser/Kirton/Daniels 2000: 4), with reinforcement by the IMF and the World Bank. The G7 countries Canada and Italy were added to the SSG in 2009, just before the Forum was replaced by the Board. There is no indication that the Forum exercised any independent influence on ISSBs to develop written codes of best practice. The various ISSBs discussed who would take the lead on regulatory standards for various issues in the Forum (Interview 2008), but this is not the same as the Forum having an independent impact. Even as the crisis unfolded in 2008, the Forum's assessment did not stress regulation as a response, even though it blamed a combination of banks, investors, and CRAs for the collapse. Its emphasis was on re-establishing trust in the market (Financial Stability Forum 2008).

---

1 The most important of these practices included treating financial derivatives as inherently risky rather than as secure assets, acquiring information on risks beyond opaque credit ratings, sharing it with all areas of the firm (including supervision of risk management), and subjecting all subsidiaries and company divisions to internal control and evaluation. Policies on financial transparency and directors' pay were also mentioned. See Senior Supervisor's Group (2008), transmittal letter to the Financial Stability Forum.

The Financial Stability Board

The Financial Stability Board was called into life in April 2009 as the successor to the FSF. In contrast to the events of 1997–1998, the financial crisis that started in 2007 had originated in the United States using standards that the Forum had approved and the ISSBs had developed. These facts undermined confidence in the G7's leadership at the expense of emerging markets (Germain 2001) and in the regulatory approach taken to financial market regulation, both nationally and within the Forum. The crisis posed the question: what could be done to prevent similar collapses and contagion from happening again.

The G20's April 2009 communiqué acknowledged the failure of regulation to properly ensure the systemic stability of international finance up until that date and tasked the FSB with increasing the quality and comprehensive scope of regulatory standards:

> Major failures in the financial sector and in financial regulation and supervision were fundamental causes of the crisis. [...] We will take action to build a globally consistent supervisory and regulatory framework for the future financial sector. (G20 2009)

The G20 put particular emphasis on building up real capacity for and the likelihood of enforcement of any new rules, nationally and internationally (Carvajal/Elliott 2009).

The Board's Charter sets out its mission as an enabler and promoter of better regulation not only internationally, but, unlike the Forum, nationally as well:

> The Financial Stability Board (FSB) is established to coordinate at the international level the work of national financial authorities and international standard setting bodies (SSBs) in order to develop and promote the implementation of effective regulatory, supervisory and other financial sector policies. In collaboration with the international financial institutions, the FSB will address vulnerabilities affecting financial systems in the interest of global financial stability. (FSB Charter, 2009: Article 1)

US Treasury Secretary Geithner expressed American hopes that the institution would become "in effect, a fourth pillar" of the architecture of global economic governance, alongside the International Monetary Fund (IMF), the World Bank, and the World Trade Organization (WTO) (US Treasury 2009). However, the FSB lacks any legal personality or attendant formal power to force regulatory change. Nor was there any concerted effort to make the FSB a formal international organization (Interview 2010). This means that it is not entitled to issue rulings that have the force of international law, so that compliance is a matter of political commitment.

The Board's means of influencing policy and implementation at the national level are therefore, for the most part, informal and indirect. Instead of command-and-control mechanisms, the Board employs a rather robust version of the open method of coordination (OMC) to further its agenda of improving regulatory policy and institutions within national jurisdictions. The benchmarking, transparency, and peer review processes on which the OMC depends are all assisted by institutional innovations within the Board that are much stronger than those during the days of the Forum. The institutional development and policy output of the Board place more detailed and more ongoing pressure on the member states to adapt their own policies and institutions, and to network better among themselves. These institutional changes are outlined below. Having said this, the institutional changes stop short of granting the Board direct regulatory authority to intervene in the market. That responsibility remains with national regulators.

Internal decision making and operations

As with the Forum, the FSB's membership consist of national political and regulatory representatives (finance ministers, central bankers, and financial market regulators), representatives of the three ISSBs, the IMF and the World Bank, the Bank for International Settlements, and the BIS's Committee on the Global Financial System (CGFS). A staff of 16 with backgrounds in law and banking supports it, drawn from within the BIS or the Basel Committee or seconded from national regulatory authorities. Figure 1 presents an organigram of the FSB's membership and internal institutions, as well as the roles of those members and institutions in the policy process.

Whereas national FSF members had equal representation, FSB membership rules ensure that input is dominated by those countries with the greatest combined political and economic clout. Member states have between one and three representatives. All member states are represented by their respective central bank. Members with a second seat send a representative from their respective treasury or finance ministry. Members with three representatives also send a financial services regulator, typically covering banking, insurance and securities together. Generally, countries with three seats comprise the traditional G7 and BRIC countries, which supports the view that political and economic clout is important, beyond functionality. There is no objective indicator of which country gets how many seats (Interview 2010). The number of seats is decided collectively based on the economic importance and internal regulatory diversity of the country involved (Griffith-Jones et al. 2010).

The FSB Charter also provides for the body to consult with the private sector and "non-member authorities" on an ad hoc basis on account of being important stakeholders in the policy process (FSB Charter, Art. 8). This po-

Figure 1 Membership and organization of the Financial Stability Board

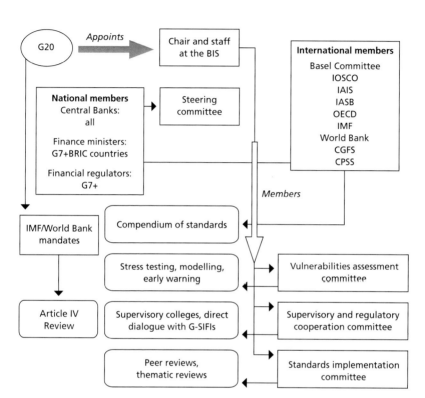

tential for industry but not other stakeholder input, coupled with the restricted membership of the Board, is a key concern in terms of input legitimacy, and as Helleiner (2010) notes, may also be a reason why stronger forms of regulation demanded by strong critics of regulation prior to the crisis remain off the table (New Rules 2011). This cannot be empirically confirmed here, however.

Griffith-Jones et al. note that in terms of structure and procedure, the Board is more formal than its predecessor. There is a formally-recognized Plenary of all the above-mentioned members, which appoints the Chair and Steering Committee by consensus. In practice, the Chair is quite influential indeed. He heads the Steering Committee, which in turn decides the agenda and adjusts the work of the Board in response to feedback from various sources. He also nominates Standing Committee members, who do most of the Board's substantive work, to the Plenary (Griffith-Jones/Helleiner/Woods 2010: 7; Interview 2010).

While the member states sort out their political differences in the Plenum, much of the Board's standard-setting and supervisory work is handled by the ISSBs, individually and inside the FSB's committees. The Basel Committee is the most cohesive, powerful standard-setter represented at the FSB. Its members took on the role of setting standards independently before either the Board or the Forum was established and continue to do so; some of them take part in G10 meetings on global finance and G10 committees studying the global financial system, and attend G20 meetings as well. It is within the FSB that the Basel Committee has more institutionalized contact with the other ISSBs, finance ministers, and other regulators that form its business and political environment. The Committee's overlapping membership in multiple forums, plus the Board's ultimate responsibility for preventing the collapse of banks allows the Committee more points at which to exercise initiative or to make its expertise and interests felt. Conversely, the FSB's interest in regulating non-bank financial actors, such as securities traders and credit rating agencies, appears to be limited to instances in which they might endanger the solvency or liquidity of banks. Wholesale investigations of what market participants like this do, do not appear to be part of the FSB's agenda or of the ISSBs.

A hierarchical relationship between the Board and the Committee, which one might infer from the FSB's responsibility to agree on the appropriateness of ISSB standards, is only theoretical. Instructions for Basel, if they can be called that, come directly from the G20, and the Basel Committee's institutional identity, strength, and cohesion are robust. IOSCO, although it refers directly to the Forum and the Board in reviewing its mandate (Interview 2008), also seems to have a free hand to pursue rule-making and standard development in ways of its choosing.

The prospect of a hierarchical relationship between the Board and ISSBs assumes, of course, that the Board might at some point develop the intention to make demands on the Committee or on the other ISSBs. At the moment, there is no evidence, empirical or anecdotal, to support such a conclusion. Although some of the Board's new members may be critical of pre-crisis business practices, this has not resulted in demands from within the Board for radical changes with regard to regulation (Interview 2010). The Board remains in this sense focused on communication, consensus-building, coordination, and puzzling about the right way to prevent another global crisis, not about handing out instructions to the ISSBs. Although this resembles the open method of coordination, in the case of the FSB, not just the governments are involved in talks as independent actors, but the technocratic standard-setters themselves, among which the Basel Committee is the most ubiquitously involved. The FSB is the arena in which this takes place, rather than a central authority per se.

The FSB's real ability to make a substantial change to global regulation is through its technical committees. There are three Standing Committees: Vulnerabilities Assessment; Supervisory and Regulatory Cooperation; and Standards Implementation. The Vulnerabilities Assessment Committee is headed by the General Manager of the Bank for International Settlements. It reviews potential threats to systemic stability and issues Early Warnings where this is deemed necessary. In one sense, the Vulnerabilities Assessment Committee is the FSB's greatest potential contribution to improving future financial market regulation. It is here that recommendations are raised or dropped, where information is gathered and models developed about how systemic risk works, and how regulations across banking, securities, insurance, and financial reporting standards, both nationally and internationally, affect business behavior and with it, the likelihood of collapse and contagion. It is here that the conceptual toolbox and the informational storehouse are located to put intelligence into the regulatory strategy. The Board is open about the fact that there is a lot they do not know, both in terms of raw data about market transactions, and in terms of how best to go about regulating them. Stress testing and early warnings of possible credit events also happen here.

The Supervisory and Regulatory Cooperation Committee is responsible for ensuring "consistency, cooperation and a level playing field across jurisdictions" (FSB 2009), and for having direct contact with financial market participants considered sufficiently important to accompany closely in the supervision process. It is here that supervisory colleges for financial institutions conduct their work; where the Board considers how cooperation across jurisdictions could be improved; and where the direct dialogue between the Board and the business community takes place.

The Standards Implementation Committee is responsible for organizing and conducting peer reviews of member states' regulatory policies and practices (FSB 2009a). Assuming that the appropriate advances in regulatory understanding have been reached by the Vulnerabilities Assessment Committee, the Standards Implementation Committee is the place where the FSB has the greatest capacity to strengthen regulation globally. Although the IMF conducts its own reviews, the scope of regulations is generally greater in the Board's procedures.

Mechanisms of operation and influence

Overall, the FSB attempts to counter-systemic risk through four main mechanisms, in which all of these institutional features play a role. The first is to promote better standards globally. This means not only reviewing the rules and practices that fall within the remit of the individual standard-setters, but also looking for gaps and contradictions between them (FSB/IMF/BIS 2011). Rather than going back to basics for a total view of systemic risk in theory and in practice, the FSB chooses to focus on particular themes in any given year. The Chair makes suggestions about what these focal points should be to the Plenum, which decides. According to the Board's plans for 2010, for example, the Board wanted to look at regulations requiring companies to disclose information about the financial risks that accompany their businesses (FSB 2010). In 2011, the Board moved on with the IMF to push for new standards on the data provided by governments and regulators themselves in all areas of financial market activity (IMF/FSB 2011). By 2010, the FSB's slate of issues included compensation, bank capital and liquidity, reducing moral hazard, enhancing cross-border resolution, and accounting standards (IASB increasing technical studies of standards) (Financial Stability Board 2010a). At the time of writing, the Board was also working on methodologies for detecting global systemically-important financial institutions (G-SIFIs) that are found to be insolvent, and for managing an eventual bankruptcy (FSB 2011). Of SIFI is any firm whose collapse could cause a cascade effect that undermines the liquidity or solvency of the financial system.

This role will take some time to develop and assess, but the statement of intent is clear, and the list of standards that the FSB collects and reserves the right to comment on is large and growing. In contrast to the Compendium of Standards that the Forum brought together, the standards dealt with by the FSB are quite specific with regard to the regulation of banks, insurance companies, credit rating agencies, and hedge funds, but also of institutional arrangements to govern their transactions.

The FSB's ability in practice to sharpen and expand on international standards appears dependent of the wishes of the members. While the Board has promoted stronger capital adequacy standards for banks and other financial service institutions, for example, a dispute between the United States and the rest of the world continues over the scope, stringency, and timetable of implementing restrictions in the USA (Braithwaite/Spiegel 2011). The US Congress in particular has proven a point of open access for banks and other financial institutions seeking to soften the application of international standards (Davies 2010: 187), and Persaud notes that in national legislation in the United States pertaining to the financial crisis, there is no reference to FSB declarations or the actions of other countries (Persaud 2010: 638).

Given that direct political input by core countries is built into the Board's decision making and deliberative institutions, it seems that the Board provides a suitable mechanism for pushing stronger international standards from standard-setters when political consensus prevails, but not otherwise. The first locus of consensus-building remains the countries belonging to the Senior Supervisor's Group, whereby the interest of the United States in promoting international standards remains very important. Nevertheless, the Board is formally responsible to the G20. The Board, specifically the Chair, refers to G20 communiqués and positions in setting up its agenda and provides regular reports to the G20 on the state of the global economy, and the progress reached in reforming regulation (Draghi 2010).

The second mechanism of Board influence, as with the Forum, is to cultivate a partnership with the IMF and the World Bank. The fact that the IMF in particular is responsible for assessing whether FSB members are establishing and applying regulation properly, and that it is doing so in the context of Article IV consultations, and also that the World Bank does its reviews under the aegis of the Report on Observance of Standards and Codes program (FSB 2010a), allows the IMF and the World Bank to conduct the same certification process for any country if there is demand. Indeed, while all FSB members are expected to undertake peer reviews, the Board sees the IMF in particular as crucial for ensuring standard implementation in non-FSB-member countries. This in turn is viewed as crucial to managing emergent crises in the future (Draghi 2009).

In the case of the United States, this requirement of Article IV consultations and FSAP evaluation as a requirement of membership is a crucial difference to membership in the Board as opposed to the Forum, as the US government had not accepted the need for the IMF to conduct an assessment of financial market regulation in the United States during the Forum's existence. The actual impact will depend on American willingness to accept it, however. Due to voting procedures in the Executive Board of the IMF, which grant the US government a continued blocking minority of 15 percent on crucial issues, it is questionable that the Board and the IMF could exert sufficient political pressure on the United States to converge its regulatory practices with those of the FSB's other members against its will.

The continued role for the World Bank and the IMF in reviewing economic policies and regulatory standards and the added role of the FSB indicate some overlap of the work that the three bodies conduct. This applies particularly to macro-prudential supervision, which asks whether regulatory standards generally are conducive to stability. The FSB appears to go beyond the approach by the World Bank and the IMF in dealing much more thoroughly with macro-prudential supervision by bringing together the micro-prudential supervisory practices for banking, insurance, and securities markets, with the help of the international standard-setting bodies.

The third mechanism by which the Board increases its capacity for influence is to promote regulatory capacity at the national level. This is done by the peer review method characteristic of the open method of coordination, in which country reports are coupled with recommendations for national lawmakers and regulators. The FSB selects a number of countries to review in any given year. To date, the FSB has generated reports for Mexico, Italy, and Spain, in each case recommending more robust tools of regulation and more aggressive approaches to collecting information and enforcing the law.

The fourth mechanism is the supervisory college, which has the primary mission of looking at concrete developments in G-SIFIs. The Board had established 30 colleges at the time of writing, each responsible for supervising a specific financial institution, and each incorporating regulatory supervisors from countries where the financial institution does the most business. This allows the Board to directly impact regulatory supervision alongside the national regulators who are ultimately responsible for them. The colleges, therefore, add value to the home country control model of regulation that remained the official model until the Board's establishment, so that supervisors from home and host countries are working together on an on-going basis to regulate not only the corporate headquarters, but the channels by which contagion can spread across borders (Guardian 2010). To date, however, the college model has not generated any public statements in the way that the Board does for countries.

Summary

The FSB was established to actively transform global financial market regulation. In contrast to its predecessor, the Financial Stability Forum, the Board had a mission to improve on global regulatory standards rather than simply to compile them. The Board discusses standards for financial market participants directly with international standard-setting bodies, with the regulatees themselves, with the national regulators who are on the front line of implementation, and with the national governments who set the legal frameworks in which those regulators do their jobs. Even more, it has the job of trying to model financial complexity and devise regulatory responses to meet the challenge. This means figuring out how different financial market participants—banks, insurance companies, pension funds, hedge funds, credit rating agencies and so on—relate to one another during a possible systemic collapse, and ensuring that standards and interventions support one another before and during a crisis. All of this work is carried out in part in committee, where first principles and generally applicable procedures can be discussed; in the supervisory colleges, where the Board can test and apply its knowledge in a real-life setting; and in the process of peer review, where national application of Board-approved standards can be reviewed and evaluated. This is not just an opportunity for the Board to recommend changes, which it presently does, but to observe how well the application of standards works in practice. Together, these institutional developments and mechanisms do more to develop concrete common goals, enhance transparency and generate peer pressure for institutional strengthening and isomorphism across countries than the Forum once did. They also represent the potential to establish joined-up regulatory standards that close up regulatory gaps. In this sense, the institutional changes at the Board are game-changing for the international financial architecture.

As great as these changes may be, they also preserve some of the self-regulatory practices that preceded the crisis and were identified with its onset. Rather than accommodate a debate about financial market practices in principle, the Board's current approach favors learning more about those practices, both generally and with regard to the world's 30 largest financial institutions. While the FSB's new members may individually critique financial market practices associated with the crisis, such as the widespread use of financial derivatives in banking or the self-regulation of credit rating agencies (for example, the assessment of Lui Mingkang, the President of the China Banking Regulatory Commission) (Wong 2008), the same views are not to be found in the G7 or the SSG, nor in the Board's common positions or in the communiqués of the G20. Instead of rethinking the viability of such practices, the Board prioritizes initiatives that allow "relaunching securitization on a sound basis" (Financial Stability Board 2009b). Indeed, the new members who have no history of using such instruments have remained relatively quiet and uncritical in Board deliberations on how to set systemic standards (Interview 2010). This allows the members of the SSG, expanded again in 2010 to include the jurisdictions of Hong Kong, Spain, and Italy (Senior Supervisors Group 2010), to take the lead on devising disclosure and transparency measures that grant regulators and markets access to information that was previously unavailable to them. Although it is conceivable that the Board's attempt to promote regulation could change in the future, the existing state of research on how consensus is reached in international bodies such as the FSB (Koppel 2010) suggests that a small, cohesive group like the SSG will continue to set the tone for the foreseeable future, even if it has no formal status within the Board. This does not preclude that a more radical change of regulatory direction could happen, but it does mean that the impetus would come from G20 deliberations, rather than from the Board itself.

References

Bayne, Nicholas, 2000: The G7 Summit's Contribution: Past, Present and Prospective. In: Karl Kaiser/John J. Kirton/Joseph P. Daniels (eds.), *Shaping a New International Financial System.* London: Ashgate, 19–35.

Braithwaite, Tom/Benjamin Spiegel, 2011: US Defends its Banking Reforms. In: *Financial Times,* June 2.

Carvajal, Ana/Jennifer Elliott, 2009: *The Challenge of Enforcement in Securities Markets: Mission Impossible?* IMF Working Paper MCM. Washington, DC: International Monetary Fund.

Davies, Howard, 2010: Global Financial Regulation after the Credit Crisis. In: *Global Policy* 1(2), 185–190.

Draghi, Mario, 2009: *Statement to the International Monetary and Financial Committee.* Washington, DC, 25 April.

——, 2010: *Letter to G20 Ministers and Governors: Progress on the Global Regulatory Reform Agenda.* April 19. Basel: FSB.

FSB (Financial Stability Board), 2009: *Charter of the Financial Stability Board.* Basel: FSB.

——, 2009a: *Financial Stability Board Holds Inaugural Meeting in Basel.* Press release, Ref. No. 28/2009, June 27. Basel: FSB.

——, 2009b: *Financial Stability Board Meets in Paris.* Press release, Ref. No. 37/2009, September 15. Basel: FSB.

——, 2010: *FSB Announces Future Peer Reviews.* Press release, Ref. No. 16/2010, March 30. Basel: FSB.

——, 2010a: *Promoting Global Adherence to International Cooperation and Information Exchange Standards.* March 10. Basel: FSB.

——, 2011: *Meeting of the Financial Stability Board.* Press release, Ref. No. 33/2011, July 18. Basel: FSB.

FSB, IMF, BIS, 2011: *Macroprudential Policy Tools and Frameworks: Update to G20 Finance Ministers and Central Bank Governors.* February 14. FSB, IMF, BIS. <www.imf.org/external/np/g20/pdf/021411.pdf>

FSF, 2008: FSF Working Group on Market and Institutional Resilience, *Interim Report to the G7 Finance Ministers and Central Bank Governors.* February 5. Basel: FSB. <www.financialstabilityboard.org/publications/r_0802.pdf>

G20, 2009: *Communiqué.* London, 2 April.

Germain, Randall D., 2001: Global Financial Governance and the Problem of Inclusion. In: *Global Governance* 7(4), 412–414.

Giannini, Curzio, 2000: The Role of the IMF as Lender of Last Resort. In: Karl Kaiser/John J. Kirton/Joseph P. Daniels (eds.), *Shaping a New International Financial System.* London: Ashgate: 143–149.

Griffith-Jones, Stephany/Eric Helleiner/Ngaire Woods, 2010: Introduction and Overview. In: Eric Helleiner/Ngaire Woods/Stephany Griffith-Jones (eds.), *The Financial Stability Board: An Effective Fourth Pillar of Global Economic Governance?* Waterloo: Centre for International Governance Innovation (CIGI).

Guardian, 2010: The Financial Stability Board: How It Will Work. In: *The Guardian,* April 4.

Helleiner, Eric, 2010: *The Financial Stability Board and International Standards?* CIGI G20 Paper 1. Waterloo: Centre for International Governance Innovation (CIGI).

IMF (International Monetary Fund)/FSB (Financial Stability Board), 2011: *The Financial Crisis and Information Gaps: Implementation Progress Report*. June.

Interview, 2008: *Interview with IOSCO Staff Member*. Madrid, August.

Interview, 2010: *Interview with FSB Staff Member*. Basel, June.

Jorion, Philippe, 2000: Risk Management Lessons from Long-Term Capital Management. In: *European Financial Management* 6(3), 277–300.

Kaiser, Karl/John J. Kirton/Joseph P. Daniels (eds.), 2000: Introduction. In: *Shaping a New International Financial System*. London: Ashgate, 3–15.

Kirton, John, 2000: The Dynamics of G7 Leadership in Crisis Response and System Reconstruction. In: Karl Kaiser/John J. Kirton/Joseph P. Daniels (eds.), *Shaping a New International Financial System*. London: Ashgate, 65–93.

Koppel, Jonathan, 2010: *World Rule: Accountability, Legitimacy, and the Design of Global Governance*. Chicago: University of Chicago Press.

Langley, Paul, 2008: Sub-Prime Mortgage Lending: A Cultural Economy. In: *Economy and Society* 37(4), 469–494.

New Rules, 2011: *High-Level Panel on the Governance of the Financial Stability Board: Panelists' Terms of Reference*. Washington, DC. <www.new-rules.org/news/program-updates/358-tor-fsb-hlp> (accessed September 10, 2011)

Persaud, Avinash, 2010: The Locus of Financial Regulation. In: *International Affairs* 86(3), 637–646.

Senior Supervisors Group, 2008: *Observations on Risk Management Practices during the Recent Market Turbulence*. New York, March 6. <www.fsa.gov.uk/pubs/other/SSG_risk_management.pdf>

——, 2010: *Observations on Developments in Risk Appetite Frameworks and IT Infrastructure*. New York, December 23. Basel: FSB, BIS.

Tietmeyer, Hans, 1999: *International Cooperation and Coordination in the Area of Financial Market Supervision and Surveillance*. Report by Hans Tietmeyer, President of the Deutsche Bundesbank, Frankfurt, February 11.

US Treasury, 2009: *Press Briefing by Treasury Secretary Tim Geithner on the G20 Meeting*. Press release, U.S. Department of the Treasury, Pittsburgh, September 24.

Walter, Norbert, 2000: The New Financial Architecture for the Global Economy. In: Karl Kaiser/John J. Kirton/Joseph P. Daniels (eds.), *Shaping a New International Financial System*. London: Ashgate, 134–142.

Wong, Edward, 2008: Booming, China Faults U.S. on the Economy. In: *New York Times*, June 17.

12

The International Financial Architecture:
Plus ça change …?

Geoffrey R. D. Underhill and Jasper Blom

Economic efficiency and financial stability issues are central to the governance of financial systems, and the achievement of either requires effective institutions and policy. The financial crisis that started in 2007 demonstrated that the pre-crisis system of governance was singularly unsuccessful at providing either financial stability or satisfactory market outcomes in terms of efficiency. Even allowing for path-dependency and the role of vested interests, one would expect such a major episode of crisis to generate substantive change through the reform of the system, and reform there has indeed been. This chapter will analyze the changes currently taking place in the international financial "architecture" and its institutions of governance as a response to the crisis. It will also evaluate whether these changes are likely to help in the quest for financial stability. The chapter concludes that it is not yet clear whether the reforms have adequately understood and put to practical use either the knowledge developed and available during the pre-crisis financial architecture debates *or* the lessons of the crisis itself. While the rhetoric of change is considerable, the underlying approach to governance pursued in the reform process has changed little so far.

Introduction

For over thirty years, increasing cross-border market integration has rendered national systems of financial governance and the policies they pursue less and less effective (Underhill/Blom/Mügge 2010). The solution was the slow and ad hoc emergence of market-based forms of financial governance at the national, regional, and global levels. This multi-level "system" was developed by public sector financial elites in concertation with private sector agents and associations

The authors gratefully acknowledge generous financial support from the EU FP7 research programme, theme social and economic sciences, project "Politics, Economics and Global Governance: the European Dimensions" (contract no. SSH7-CT-2008-217559).

and was supposed to respond to the policy dilemmas of both financial sector liberalization and of cross-border financial market integration. Yet liberalization and "governance light" ushered in serial episodes of crisis, to a degree that should challenge the very foundations of this approach to global financial governance itself. As a baseline, two salient features of the pre-crisis international financial architecture should be noted.

First, a shift has taken place from public interventionism to private, market-oriented forms of authority that significantly enhanced the influence of private market agents and their preferences in national and emerging international policy processes. Outcomes ranged from transnational policy cooperation among state agencies to self-regulatory and essentially private regimes. While private sector proposals were central to this outcome, the processes and policy agendas were supported and often generated by state elites responsible for national and international financial governance. State officials and private agents working from a shared agenda together shaped a system of market-based governance built on the wide recognition and prevalence of private interests and authority at the heart of the public domain. The input in terms of preferences and interests from which the substance of the system was drawn was thus singularly limited.

A second salient feature relates to limited inputs into the process at the international level. A small club of creditor states (and therefore their national financial sectors) participated in the policy process that determined substantive outcomes, with the G7 at the top as the "apex policy forum" providing strategic guidance (see Baker 2010 on the notion of apex policy forums). In the domain of banking supervision, the Basel Committee on Banking Supervision (BCBS) was the main technical global-level policymaking forum. The BCBS was a "G10" body with only thirteen members: the G7 plus Belgium, Luxembourg, the Netherlands, Spain, Sweden, and Switzerland. The Joint Forum (comprising banking, securities, and insurance supervisors) and the Financial Stability Forum (FSF[1]) were responsible for international cross-sectoral monitoring of systemic stability issues and were similarly restricted in membership (although the FSF has since 1999 included Hong Kong and Singapore as key emerging market financial centers). In the International Monetary Fund (IMF), responsible for macroeconomic coordination and the promulgation and enforcement of a range of international financial governance standards, the principal creditor states dominated and the G7 countries effectively hold a controlling share of the voting rights (with the United States on its own able to veto changes in the Articles of Agreement). Private sector financial institutions were once again key interlocutors in

---

1 At the London G20 summit (April 2009) the Financial Stability Forum was anointed "Board" (FSB, see Donnelly in this volume).

the process and arguably enjoyed better access to policymaking than most developing or emerging market states (Claessens/Underhill/Zhang 2008).

Many economists reacted essentially positively to enhanced private involvement in global financial governance and the emergence of market-based "governance light." Cross-border integration meant that national systems of public policy should innovate so as to deal with emerging complexity. Private sector involvement could improve policy efficiency; requiring financial institutions to take more responsibility for risk management would promote both market efficiency and financial stability. In essence, it was argued that enhanced private sector involvement in rule-setting in global financial governance was an essential mechanism by which public authorities could pursue their policy goals more effectively in an ever more integrated world economy (see, for example, Cline 2000; Rieffel 2003). On the other hand, a range of studies that sought to explain how and why private market agents acquired their enhanced influence over the policies and institutions of the international financial architecture were more skeptical (Sinclair 2002; Tsingou 2003; Porter 2005; Mügge 2010).

Arguably, the two salient features referred to above have serious implications for political legitimacy before and after the crisis. Scharpf (1999) analytically separates this legitimacy into input-oriented legitimacy (concerning the decision-making process) and output-oriented legitimacy (concerning the outcome of the decision-making process, the effectiveness of governance in achieving socially desirable goals). These two sides of legitimacy are closely linked, however (Underhill/Zhang 2008). As the crisis proved, a process in which the inputs reflected mostly private sector interests resulted in output (market-based "governance light") which failed to mitigate the build-up of risks.

This chapter assesses the post-crisis reform of the international financial architecture through this lens of input- and output-side legitimacy and their relationship. Three arguments will be advanced in relation to the reforms so far to support the conclusions stated at the outset of this article. First, concerning the involvement of public actors (state agencies) on the input side, the replacement of the G7 by the G20 as the apex policy forum in global financial governance has significantly widened the group of states substantively involved in global financial governance and reflects the rising power of, especially, the BRIC countries.[2] The emergence of the G20 as the apex policy forum is also reflected in the expanded membership of the more technical, "executive bodies" of the international financial architecture (for example, BCBS, FSB, and IMF). In this

---

2 The BRICs are Brazil, Russia, India, and China. Smaller poor developing countries must mainly rely on the weaker G24, which prepares input into the G20 and other bodies.

sense, the input side of the policymaking equation has been substantively improved and better outputs may be expected.

The second argument concerns the ideational underpinning of global financial governance. It will be argued that pre-crisis financial governance was based on a limited set of economic ideas, which benefitted certain interests present on the input side at the national and international levels. In the process, much historical evidence and several theoretical contributions warning of the instability of open financial markets under market-based governance were ignored. Despite the wider club of G20 public actors, private interests and the ideational preference set that they supported in the pre-crisis period continue to wield significant influence in the process of reform. The views of state agencies remain ambivalent at best.

Building on these two points, the third argument is that the changes in the international financial architecture in response to the 2007 crisis contain the potential for radical change, but that the jury is still out on whether this potential will be fulfilled. The emerging discourse of macro-prudential oversight and the challenges to proprietary trading by banks, for example, may have significant consequences for the global financial system if fully pursued. However, the reforms have so far been limited to the incremental, only tinkering with the underlying approach to the problem such that the existing market-based approach to regulation remains largely intact.

The linkages between the input and output sides of the equation are thus complex and problematic. In other words, although there is the appearance of improved input legitimacy, the ongoing convergence of public and private actor preference sets means that little of substance in output has changed. Further evidence that reform is only incremental is observable: the phase-in period of the proposed reforms has been extended substantially by private sector pressure and by fears that the banks remain too fragile to survive overly-rapid substantive change (see Goldbach/Kerwer and Woolley/Ziegler in this volume). The more radical elements of the reforms have been pushed into the future. This provides ample opportunity, if relative calm returns to financial markets, for the private sector to water down more radical proposals or eliminate them altogether through a strategy of attritional lobbying during the implementation phase.

The chapter is structured as follows. The next section consists of a general description of the reforms, particularly the advent of the G20. The subsequent section analyses the policy initiatives taken by the executive bodies in response to the crisis (for example, Basel III). The final section concludes by situating the changes in the international financial architecture in the context of input and output legitimacy, assessing the prospects of better outcomes in terms of effective governance and the provision of financial stability.

The input side of the international financial architecture

The international financial architecture has three main fronts on the technical level: (i) the BCBS and related BIS efforts on capital adequacy and the supervision of the financial services industry as increasingly integrated by the banks; (ii) the International Organization of Securities Commissions (IOSCO) process for the regulation and encouragement of cross-border securities markets; and (iii) the macroeconomic imbalances, debt workout, and adjustment/monetary policy front led by the IMF and, to a lesser extent, the OECD. Each process has its own distinct dynamics, but the ubiquity of capital flows implies frequent issue overlap and a need for coordination across domains. The Joint Forum and FSF addressed this problem directly, but coordination was also facilitated by overlapping participation in these forums resulting from their domination by the national agencies of a small number of major creditor countries.

Coordination of the fronts therefore took place through the G7, that served as the input-side apex policy forum bringing together the most senior officials (for example, ministers of finance and central bank governors) to either mandate the technical bodies or endorse their efforts (Baker 2006, 2010). The G7 as creditors developed a common interest in and preference for open financial markets—the better to expand their financial sectors and centers—and market-based forms of governance (see Baker 2006). Private sector partners with their superior understanding of the new market complexities steadily permeated the policy process as new institutions were developed (for example, the Capital Markets Consultative Group of the IMF). Despite their arguably continued relevance, traditional policy instruments such as capital controls were routinely ignored in the discussions (Cohen 2002, 2003). Likewise, the specific interests of emerging market economies afflicted by the frequent episodes of crisis received scant attention. G7 efforts focused on adapting the system to the market-based vision.

The post-crisis reforms have led to change in and a strengthening of the legitimacy of the input side. The rise of China and other BRICs as creditors with huge currency reserves was confirmed when the 2007 crisis erupted in Wall Street, the core of the G7 financial system. If these fast-growing economies were to become part of the solution, then they would have to be consulted. The G20 had been around for some years as a ministerial/central bank governor forum established after the East Asian crisis of 1997–1998 and it soon emerged as the new apex policy forum meeting for the first time at summit level (Washington, November 2008) at the invitation of US President Bush. G20 membership was then extended to the technical bodies such as the FSB (April 2009) and the BCBS (June 2009). While this notionally enhanced the input-side legitimacy of the process, the impact on the output side of these executive bodies will be dealt with in the next section.

The executive bodies: Institutional change and reforms

The first post-crisis reform front concerned the BCBS (see also Goldbach/Kerwer in this volume). During the 1990s it had developed a *modus operandi* of close cooperation between its creditor country members and the large internationalized financial institutions represented by the Institute of International Finance (IIF). The BCBS had introduced the market-based approach to financial supervision and risk management in close consultation with the IIF in 1996, but this was limited to securities market "trading books" of banks. The Basel II Capital Accord of 2004 extended this approach to credit risk as well, and it was being implemented as the 2007 crisis broke out. The logic behind the new approach was that stability could best be provided if the public sector set the parameters while private financial institutions would become directly responsible for risk management on a consolidated, global basis. Based on private sector proposals (with notable input from public agencies), the effects of the accord were skewed and provided competitive benefits to those who had proposed it and discriminated against the developing countries who were not part of the process. The emerging transnational policy process rendered private agents more influential than many sovereign participants in the global financial system (see Claessens/Underhill/Zhang 2008 and Claessens/Underhill 2010). At the time, the accord was also criticized for its lack of attention to systemic or "macro-prudential" oversight, and because it potentially accentuated upside and downside financial market cycles and herd behavior (see, for example, the input by Daníelsson et al. 2001 to the consultative process of the BCBS).

The crisis appeared to confirm the assessment of the doubters, and the Committee was widely regarded as captured by private interests: limited input had produced skewed output. Despite only partial implementation, it was difficult under the circumstances to associate Basel II with financial stability. Reform came in the form of proposed "enhancements" to Basel II in January 2009 (BCBS 2009), including new liquidity risk provisions, better modeling of securitization risks, a stricter definition of bank capital, countercyclical capital buffers to prevent bubbles, and higher capital adequacy requirements for systemically important banks. In addition, a second, simpler measure for capital adequacy was discussed: the leverage ratio (capital to balance sheet total). The next year-and-a-half produced a series of papers developing the proposed Basel III.

The opening of BCBS membership to G20 countries in June 2009 had little apparent impact on the proposals, as the BCBS soon afterwards reached broad agreement on the revised Basel III Accord. The agreement was formalized by the November 2010 G20 summit in Seoul (the final version was published in December 2010, BCBS 2010b). Basel III is presented as the first of the building blocks of a "broad strategy" for a "new approach" to the post-crisis financial system (BCBS 2010a: 1–2) that aims to raise the *quality* and *level* of bank reserve capital and to extend the *coverage* of capital reserves to all market segments and aspects of financial conglomerates (for example, derivatives markets and off-balance sheet activities). (See Goldbach/Kerwer in this volume, for further details.)

Notwithstanding these potentially significant reforms, Basel III builds directly on the approach developed in the Basel II framework for market-based supervision and as such does not constitute a new departure. Market discipline and price signals remain central to the practice of banking supervision despite pre-crisis warnings that such an approach was unwise (Persaud 2000; Daníelsson 2002) and obvious post-crisis doubts. There is no serious institutional innovation beyond the (as yet undefined) proposal to set up "Colleges" to enhance supervisory coordination, and there is no explicit link between macroeconomic policymaking and financial system supervision to accompany the countercyclical measures. Moreover, the improved input legitimacy of G20 representation does not seem to have mitigated possible adverse effects of Basel III on developing countries (La Via 2010) The measures are not yet in effect, in any event, and will be phased in from 2015, with minimum standards finally in force in 2018 (BCBS 2010b: 10). This leaves plenty of time for private sector lobbying to further water down provisions in their actual implementation.

The second reform front concerned securities market governance institutionalized in IOSCO which is devoted to developing regulatory standards that promote efficiency and transparency in international securities markets (see Underhill 1995). IOSCO members are official national securities regulators, usually autonomous government agencies mandated by legislation,[3] supplemented by "associate" members (for example, important official securities regulators at sub-national/provincial level, or other market authorities which work closely with the "national" regulator) and "affiliate" members, which are Self-Regulatory Organizations (SROs), securities exchanges, or trade associations with self-regulatory responsibilities. The latter do not vote but are considered crucial to the IOSCO policymaking process (as regularly stated in Annual Reports, for example, 2006: 5).

Although membership is therefore much broader than the BCBS—seemingly improving the input legitimacy of this institution—until recently the leading role in developing standards was performed by the Technical Committee (TC) with a much more selective membership mainly consisting of the creditor

---

3 This could involve a division of a national finance ministry, an SRO (for instance, a stock market) or even a central bank. See IOSCO website section on membership and other rules.

states.[4] Key decisions were thus deliberated and taken by the developed country membership in consultation with a few prominent emerging market members. Moreover, IOSCO members have been more accountable to SROs and private market participants than to traditional government oversight, yielding a poorly-defined sense of broader public interest in this transnational regulatory regime. Furthermore, technological and product innovations have made regulators heavily dependent on industry expertise for the skills involved in formulating rules. Tellingly, IOSCO considers itself a non-governmental international organization (Underhill 1995: 261).

This skewed nature of the inputs in the policy process led to a regulatory system that failed to prevent the collapse and virtual elimination of the Wall Street investment banking sector in 2008. The alignment of securities market governance to private sector interests produced a system that enhanced risks and ensured that the cost of imprudent behavior would be shared widely, while the profits would be appropriated by the private sector and their bonus-drugged senior management and traders.

Since the crisis, IOSCO has responded to the sense of alarm by increasing the breadth of its policy deliberations and accelerating the publication of reports. From 2008, the areas of intensified work largely mirrored the agenda of pre-crisis years but with a post-crisis urgency and "spin": revision of the supervisory principles; cross-border and also cross-sectoral supervisory cooperation; corporate governance; Credit Rating Agencies (CRAs); market transparency; accounting standards; emerging market issues; and a range of specialized market/product work, such as derivatives, hedge funds, short-selling, real estate products, private equity; special purpose entities and so on. There were also new issues, including the attention to new technologies in the markets and to (naturally enough) systemic risk (IOSCO 2008a: 19).

In advance of the inaugural November 2008 G20 summit, IOSCO offered its assistance in exploring regulatory reforms (IOSCO 2008b: 1). This offer was taken up by the G20 by highlighting the issues concerning CRAs for further IOSCO work. This demonstrates the apex role of the G20, providing guidance and assigning specific tasks to the executive bodies. IOSCO set up a special working group to continue work on a number of crisis-related issues. Also, in February 2009 the membership of the Technical Committee was augmented by Brazil, China, and India, key G20 emerging markets not previously members of the TC (IOSCO 2009a).

---

4 The TC has historically consisted of creditor state members (Australia, Canada, France, Germany, Hong Kong, Italy, Japan, the Netherlands, Singapore, Spain, Switzerland, the United Kingdom, and the United States). From 2007, Mexico became the first emerging market member, joined in 2009 by Brazil, India, and China (www.iosco.org).

The initial set of reports and recommendations to members, emerging over the course of 2009, were remarkable only for their adherence to past practice and some renewed zeal in terms of application and consistency (for example, with respect to CRAs: IOSCO 2009b, 2009c). The consensus was that the codes were being implemented satisfactorily but that new regulatory measures might render the implementation of the codes less consistent across borders and action should be taken to avoid such an outcome. Late in 2009 somewhat more serious questions were being asked in a consultation exercise on the transparency of structured finance products (IOSCO 2009d), yet this only addressed secondary market issues and not the rating of products at issuance nor anything to do with the fundamentals of CRA methodologies.

The year 2010 brought a new flurry of reports and consultations which began to get to the heart of the financial crisis. The core IOSCO concern with establishing standards for supervisory practice was pursued and updated but without any change of approach and little in the way of additions (IOSCO 2010b). Further work on CRAs (IOSCO 2010a) concluded that new national measures largely conformed to existing IOSCO principles, so all was well. Cross-border supervisory issues received a new and final report (IOSCO 2010b) that was a standard defense of previous practice. The one innovation was the notion that "Colleges" or "Networks" of supervisors might supplement the bilateral Memorandum-of-Understanding approach; regulators should avail themselves of as many of these options as were available. No concrete initiatives were proposed, however.

Despite the anticipation of radical reform, it is therefore difficult to characterize IOSCO's post-crisis work as such. The concerns of governments and the public were clearly being addressed, but as in the case of the BCBS, an analysis of the work of IOSCO reveals little in the way of new departures, limited institutional innovation, and no fundamental review of the nature of the financial system or its operation. The controversial and problematic issues were being discussed, but genuine reform was being left to national members. There were no recommendations for institutional enhancements besides the "Colleges" idea.

The third front of reform addresses monetary matters (including sovereign debt workout) and is institutionalized mainly in the IMF. During the 2001–2007 pre-crisis "period of calm," the IMF had been losing prominence and legitimacy as a central player in global financial governance (Helleiner/Pagliari 2010). This was partly because many Asian countries perceived a clear Western-interests bias and excessive intrusiveness in IMF lending conditionality during the 1997/1998 East Asian crisis. The accumulated resentment led them to pursue "self-insurance" against the vagaries of both global financial markets and IMF policies through the accumulation of huge official reserves (and in doing so they inadvertently fuelled the 2007 crisis). The IMF was aware of the dangers to its position and the need to find better solutions to sovereign debt and financial crisis workouts after the 2000/2001 Argentine crisis and default. The response had been the Sovereign Debt Restructuring Mechanism (SDRM) announced with much fanfare by First Deputy Managing Director, Anne Krueger, in November 2001 (IMF 2001). This proposal emerged out of a concern that the IMF was consistently bailing out private creditors, while emerging markets, from South Korea to Argentina, wondered aloud why the burden of adjustment was not shared with the ever-fickle banks that saw fit to lend in the first place and that bolted at the first sign of trouble. The 1996 "Rey report," written by the G10 at the request of the G7, had advocated Collective Action Clauses (CACs) to facilitate debt restructuring talks between bondholders and debtors (G10 1996). This report initially went unheeded (Drage/Hovaguimian 2004). Post-Argentina, the IMF saw the problem in a new light.

The SDRM was supposed to be the crowning achievement in the crisis resolution framework that emerged after the East Asian crisis. It was a form of quasi-legal international bankruptcy procedure that would grant sovereign debtors temporary relief from their creditors. Private creditors would be compelled to negotiate the workout in the calm that would follow, and so rendered more responsible for losses. The formal SDRM project was defeated in 2003 by the private sector and the fears of some emerging markets that publicly embracing it would endanger their access to international capital. The SDRM effort was replaced by a revival of the CACs idea, combined with a set of private sector "Principles for Stable Capital Flows and Fair Debt Restructuring in Emerging Markets" (IIF 2005). The principles were, of course, both voluntary and market-friendly.

Thus the IMF initiative sailed into the doldrums. The period of calm meant less IMF lending and interest income, which led to significant budgetary constraints and internal reorganization. The 2007 crisis gave the IMF a new lease of life in this respect with a rapid and enormous revival of lending. The G20 London summit of April 2009 increased IMF resources by US$ 750 billion (500 billion in lending facilities and other instruments provided by member states, and 250 billion in new Special Drawing Rights). The BRICs contributed 82 billion to this capital increase, signifying their emergence as creditor states (Schilperoort 2010: 191–192).

The crisis also put pressure on the long, fizzling debate on how the IMF quota system might be overhauled better to reflect the growing economic significance of the emerging market membership. Especially the smaller European creditor countries had blocked reforms out of fear for their position in the IMF (for example, loss of their Executive Director seats). The 2007 crisis led to a breakthrough of sorts to the stalemate. The November 2008 G20 summit committed the G20 to addressing this issue (G20 2008: 3), and several emerging markets were promised higher quotas (and hence voting weights). But by 2010 only 5 percent of quotas had in fact been redistributed.

Of the technical forums discussed in this section, it seems the IMF is hence most resilient to changing the input legitimacy. This was also reflected in the appointment of Christine Lagarde as new Managing Director after the untimely and unexpected resignation of Dominique Strauss-Kahn in May 2011. By tradition, a European holds the post. Despite decade-long mutterings by the emerging markets that the process should be more open and transparent, the emerging markets failed to build a coalition around a common alternative to Lagarde (although the Mexican central bank governor Augustín Carstens was an official candidate). To attenuate the negative reaction, Lagarde appointed a Deputy Managing Director from China (Min Zhu), the first time a Chinese national has held such a high position in the IMF.

Somewhat surprisingly, despite the serious sovereign debt crisis in the Eurozone periphery, there have been no new IMF policy initiatives concerning crisis resolution. Eurozone members clearly prefer the problem to remain in European hands and they have the influence to make this happen. The creditor emerging markets will not yet experience a longed-for reversal of roles. In short, IMF input-side legitimacy has changed relatively little, and consequently output remains focused on business-as-usual.

Conclusion: The ongoing quest to secure enduring financial stability

As the previous section has shown, the input side of the international financial architecture has changed since the crisis, enhancing the legitimacy of its decision making by embracing the G20 membership. But the apparently significant enhancement of input-side legitimacy seems in the first instance not to lead to significant shifts in effectiveness of policy output. Reforms coming out of the technical bodies still seem to be directed towards improving the functioning of market-based forms of governance. This highlights the complex nature of the linkages between the input and output aspects of legitimacy referred to at the outset of this chapter.

Two reasons may be advanced as to why input-side improvements have not (yet) yielded new outputs. The first is plainly practical: the shift on the input side came while reform efforts were already well under way, simply too late to have a significant impact on the output of the process. The G20 emerged as the apex policy forum in November 2008, and it began by reinforcing established reform efforts (Helleiner/Pagliari 2009: 276). G20 members joined the BCBS in June 2009, the first trend-setting consultative proposal having been published six months before. A similar situation applied to the IOSCO regulatory reform process, where Brazil, China, and India came into the Technical Committee in February 2009, almost simultaneously with the release of prominent policy proposals. It is possible that given time the impact of the new members on policy outputs will increase.

A second, more fundamental reason why outputs have yet to change significantly is that broadening the range of state actors has yet to be accompanied by a broadening of the set of interests and ideas considered in the policy process. The problem of private financial interests commandeering public policy and taking risks with other people's money in the full knowledge that a bailout by taxpaying citizens will be forthcoming has yet to be properly confronted. This brings us back to the question of how demands for market-based "governance light" initially emerged and were adopted as policy.

Financial firms and their associations have historically close and relatively exclusive relationships with elite state policymakers and with the key international organizations responsible for the design of the reforms. G7 governments generally backed the preferences of their private financial sectors (Baker 2006) in an increasingly transnational policy community. Technical institutions of global financial governance, such as the BCBS and IOSCO, were characterized not only by exclusive policy communities, but also by virtual detachment from political accountability (Underhill 1995, 1997). This problem is further exacerbated by frequent recourse to self-regulation. As a result, the global financial system is increasingly regulated by agencies constituting regimes that are more responsive to private interests than to providers of collective goods (Cerny 1996: 96–99; Porter 1999). There seems to be little reason to think that the situation is different in the emerging market G20 members (see Haggard/Lee/Maxfield 1993, especially the concluding chapter) currently gaining prominence in the policy process.

Moreover, it should be noted that many of the G20 members newly at the apex of financial policymaking have crossed the line from being subject to the financial governance mechanisms (as crisis-ridden countries in need of IMF programs, for example) to being creditor states. Their contribution to the IMF capital increase, which was agreed on by the G20 London summit, bears testimony to this. The lack of radical change in policy outputs (and therefore their eventual legitimacy) despite significant change on the input side may be attributable to forms of groupthink among the central bankers and finance ministers of the G20. These officials and the bodies that they populate appear instinctively to respond better to private sector interests than to those outside their institutional neighborhood.

There has thus been no genuine rethink of the global financial order. Although the reform process is not yet over, financial institutions continue to lobby to counter the strengthening of regulation and supervision (for example, the high-profile IIF study (2010)—clearly based on biased accounting—arguing the high costs of stricter bank capital adequacy standards). Institutional innovation has been minimal. It remains uncertain whether the public authorities responsible for financial governance are any longer capable of absorbing the messages of more skeptical and perhaps more objective economic and political economy analyses which run contrary to the approach that has become institutionalized in the financial architecture. There might be worse advice than to prepare for the next crisis, while the intensifying Eurozone turbulence indicates the present one is not yet over.

References

Baker, Andrew, 2006: *The Group of Seven Finance Ministries, Central Banks, and Global Financial Governance*. London: Routledge.

——, 2010: Deliberative International Financial Governance and Apex Policy Forums. In: Geoffrey R. D. Underhill/Jasper Blom/Daniel Mügge (eds.), *Global Financial Integration Thirty Years On: From Reform to Crisis*. Cambridge: Cambridge University Press, 58–73.

BCBS (Basel Committee on Banking Supervision), 2009: *Proposed Enhancements to the Basel II Framework*. Issued for comment by April 17. Consultative Document. Basel: Bank for International Settlements (BIS).

——, 2010a: *The Basel Committee's Response to the Financial Crisis: Report to the G20*. Basel: BIS.

——, 2010b: *Basel III: A Global Regulatory Framework for More Resilient Banks and Banking Systems*. Basel: Bank for International Settlements (BIS), Communications.

Cerny, Philip, 1996: International Finance and the Erosion of State Policy Capacity. In: Philip Gummet (ed.), *Globalisation and Public Policy*. Cheltenham: Edward Elgar, 83–104.

Claessens, Stijn/Geoffrey R. D. Underhill/Xiaoke Zhang, 2008: The Political Economy of Basel II: The Costs for Poor Countries. In: *The World Economy* 31, 313–344.

Claessens, Stijn/Geoffrey R. D. Underhill, 2010: The Political Economy of Basel II in the International Financial Architecture. In: Geoffrey R. D. Underhill/Jasper Blom/Daniel Mügge (eds.), *Global Financial Integration Thirty Years On: From Reform to Crisis*. Cambridge: Cambridge University Press, 113–133.

Cline, William, 2000: *The Role of the Private Sector in Resolving Financial Crises in Emerging Markets*. Conference paper. NBER Conference on Economic and Financial Crises in Emerging Market Economies, Woodstock, October 19–21.

Cohen, Benjamin J., 2002: Capital Controls: Why Do Governments Hesitate? In: Leslie Elliott Armijo (ed.), *Debating the Global Financial Architecture*. Albany: State University of New York Press, 93–117.

——, 2003: Capital Controls: The Neglected Option. In: Geoffrey R. D. Underhill/Xiaoke Zhang (eds.), *International Financial Governance under Stress: Global Structures and National Imperatives*. Cambridge: Cambridge University Press, 60–76.

Daníelsson, Jón, et al., 2001: *An Academic Response to Basel II*. Financial Markets Group Special Paper Series, No. 130. London: Financial Markets Group Research Centre at LSE.

——, 2002: The Emperor Has No Clothes: Limits to Risk Modelling. In: *Journal of Banking and Finance* 26, 1273–1296.

Drage, John/Catherine Hovaguimian, 2004: *Collective Action Clauses (CACS): An Analysis of Provisions Included in Recent Sovereign Bond Issues*. London: Bank of England, International Finance Division.

G10, 1996: *The Resolution of Sovereign Liquidity Crises*. A Report to the Ministers and Governors Prepared under the Auspices of the Deputies. Basel: BIS.

G20, 2008: *Action Plan to Implement Principles for Reform*. Washington, DC: G20, November 15.

Haggard, Stephan/Chung Lee/Sylvia Maxfield (eds.), 1993: *The Politics of Finance in Developing Countries*. Ithaca: Cornell University Press.

Helleiner, Eric/Stefano Pagliari, 2009: Towards a New Bretton Woods? The First G20 Leaders Summit and the Regulation of Global Finance. In: *New Political Economy* 14, 275–287.

——, 2010: Between the Storms: Patterns in Global Financial Governance, 2001–2007. In: Geoffrey R. D. Underhill/Jasper Blom/Daniel Mügge (eds.), *Global Financial Integration Thirty Years On: From Reform to Crisis*. Cambridge: Cambridge University Press, 42–57.

IIF (Institute of International Finance), 2005: *Principles for Stable Capital Flows and Fair Debt Restructuring in Emerging Markets*. Report on Implementation by the Principles Consultative Group with Comprehensive Update on Investor Relations Programs and Data Transparency, October 2009. Washington, DC: IIF.

——, 2010: *Interim Report on the Cumulative Impact on the Global Economy of Proposed Changes in the Banking Regulatory Framework*. Washington, DC: IIF, June.

IMF (International Monetary Fund), 2001: *Address by Anne Krueger "International Financial Architecture for 2002: A New Approach to Sovereign Debt Restructuring,"* Given at the National Economists' Club Annual Members Dinner, Washington, DC, November 26. Washington, DC: IMF.

IOSCO (International Organization of Securities Commissions), 2006: *Annual Report*. Madrid: IOSCO.

——, 2008a: *An Overview of the Work of the IOSCO Technical Committee*. Madrid: IOSCO, July.

——, 2008b: *IOSCO Open Letter to G-20 Summit*. Media release. Madrid: IOSCO, November 12.

——, 2009a: *IOSCO Technical Committee Invites Brazil, China and India to Join Its Membership*. News release. Madrid: IOSCO, February 19.

——, 2009b: *A Review of the Implementation of the IOSCO Code of Conduct Fundamentals for Credit Rating Agencies*. Madrid: IOSCO Technical Committee, March.

——, 2009c: *International Co-operation on the Oversight of Credit Rating Agencies*. Madrid: IOSCO Technical Committee, March.

——, 2009d: *Transparency of Structured Finance Products*. Consultation Report. Madrid: IOSCO Technical Committee, September.

IOSCO (International Organization of Securities Commissions), 2010a: *Regulatory Implementation of the Statement of Principles Regarding the Activities of Credit Rating Agencies*. Madrid: IOSCO Technical Committee, May.

——, 2010b: *Objectives and Principles of Securities Regulation (revised)*. Madrid: IOSCO Technical Committee, June.

——, 2010c: *Principles Regarding Cross-border Supervisory Cooperation*. Madrid: IOSCO Technical Committee, May.

La Via, Vincenzo, 2010: Financial Rules Must Do More for Developing Countries. In: *Financial Times,* March 6.

Mügge, Daniel, 2010: *Widen the Market, Narrow the Competition: Banker Interests and the Making of a European Capital Market*. Colchester: ECPR Press.

Persaud, Avinash, 2000: *Sending the Herd off the Cliff Edge: The Disturbing Interaction between Herding and Market-sensitive Risk Management Practices*. Jacques de Larosière Prize Essay. Washington, DC: IIF.

Porter, Tony, 1999: The Transnational Agenda for Financial Regulation in Developing Countries. In: Leslie Elliott Armijo (ed.), *Financial Globalisation and Democracy in Emerging Markets*. London: Macmillan, 91–116.

——, 2005: Private Authority, Technical Authority and the Globalisation of Accounting Standards. In: *Business and Politics* 11, 1–30.

Rieffel, Lex, 2003: *Restructuring Sovereign Debt: The Case for Ad Hoc Machinery*. Washington, DC: Brookings Institution Press.

Scharpf, Fritz W., 1999: *Governing in Europe: Effective and Democratic?* Oxford: Oxford University Press.

Schilperoort, Wouter, 2010: Het mondiale anker voor financiële stabiliteit: het IMF. In: Jasper Blom (ed.), *De Kredietcrisis: een politiek-economisch perspectief*. Amsterdam: Amsterdam University Press, 179–204.

Sinclair, Timothy, 2002: Private Makers of Public Policy. In: Adrienne Héritier (ed.), *Common Goods: Reinventing European and International Governance*. New York: Rowan & Littlefield, 279–292.

Tsingou, Eleni, 2003: *Transnational Policy Communities and Financial Governance: The Role of Private Actors in Derivatives Regulation*. CSGR Working Paper 111/03. Warwick: University of Warwick, Centre for the Study of Globalisation and Regionalisation.

Underhill, Geoffrey R. D., 1995: Keeping Governments out of Politics: Transnational Securities Markets, Regulatory Co-operation, and Political Legitimacy. In: *Review of International Studies* 21, 251–278.

——, 1997: Private Markets and Public Responsibility in a Global System. In: Geoffrey R. D. Underhill (ed.), *The New World Order in International Finance*. New York: St. Martin's Press, 17–49.

Underhill, Geoffrey R. D./Xiaoke Zhang, 2008: Setting the Rules: Private Power, Political Underpinnings, and Legitimacy in Global Monetary and Financial Governance. In: *International Affairs* 84, 535–554.

Underhill, Geoffrey R. D./Jasper Blom/Daniel Mügge, 2010: Introduction: The Challenges and Prospects of Global Financial Integration. In: Geoffrey R. D. Underhill/Jasper Blom/Daniel Mügge (eds.), *Global Financial Integration Thirty Years On: From Reform to Crisis*. Cambridge: Cambridge University Press, 1–22.

Contributors

Jasper Blom is a Researcher at the Amsterdam Institute for Social Science Research, University of Amsterdam.

Shawn Donnelly is Assistant Professor at the Department of Public Administration at the University of Twente.

Roman Goldbach is a Researcher at the Institute of Political Science of the University of Göttingen.

Stefan Handke is a Researcher at the Institute of Political Science at the University of Hannover (Leibniz Universität Hannover).

Nicolas Jabko is Associate Professor of Political Science at Johns Hopkins University and at Sciences Po Paris.

Sukhdev Johal is Reader in Management at Royal Holloway College, University of London.

Dieter Kerwer is Professor in International Politics at the Department of Politics at the University of Antwerp.

Paul Lagneau-Ymonet is Assistant Professor of Sociology at the Université Paris Dauphine.

Renate Mayntz is Emeritus Director of the Max Planck Institute for the Study of Societies in Cologne.

Michael Moran is Professor of Government at the University of Manchester Business School.

Sigrid Quack is a Research Group Leader at the Max Planck Institute for the Study of Societies in Cologne.

Lucia Quaglia is Professor of Politics at the University of York.

Simon Steinlin is a Master of Arts in Political Science at the University of Bern.

Christine Trampusch is Professor of International Comparative Political Economy and Economic Sociology at the Faculty of Management, Economics and Social Sciences at the University of Cologne.

Geoffrey R. D. Underhill is Professor in International Governance at the Amsterdam Institute for Social Science Research of the University of Amsterdam.

Karel Williams is Professor of Accounting and Political Economy at the University of Manchester Business School.

Cornelia Woll is a Senior Research Fellow at Sciences Po Paris and leader of an Otto-Hahn junior research group at the Max Planck Institute for the Study of Societies in Cologne.

John T. Woolley is Professor in the Department of Political Science at the University of California, Santa Barbara.

J. Nicholas Ziegler is Associate Professor in the Faculty of Political Science at the University of California, Berkeley.

Hubert Zimmermann is Professor of International Relations at the Institute of Political Science at the University of Marburg.

Abbreviations

ABA	American Bankers Association
ACP	Autorité de Contrôle Prudentiel (French Prudential Supervisory Authority)
AFR	Americans for Financial Reform
AIFM	Alternative Investment Fund Manager
AIMA	Alternative Investment Management Association
AMF	Autorité des Marchés Financiers (French Financial Markets Authority)
BaFin	Bundesanstalt für Finanzdienstleistungsaufsicht (German Federal Financial Supervisory Authority)
BCBS	Basel Committee on Banking Supervision
BIS	Bank for International Settlements
BMF	Bundesministerium der Finanzen (German Federal Ministry of Finance)
BMWi	Bundesministerium für Wirtschaft und Technologie (German Federal Ministry of Economics and Technology)
CDS	Credit Default Swap
CESR	Committee of European Securities Regulators
CFPB	Consumer Financial Protection Bureau
CFTC	Commodities Futures Trading Commission
CGFS	Committee on the Global Financial System
COP	Congressional Oversight Panel
CRA	Credit Rating Agency
CRD	Capital Requirements Directive
CRFRS	Conseil de Régulation Financière et du Risque Systémique (French Council of Financial Regulation and Systemic Risk)
DGS	Deposit Guarantee Scheme
DTA	Double Taxation Agreement
EAP	Expert Advisory Panel
EBA	European Banking Authority

EBRD	European Bank for Reconstruction and Development
ECOFIN	EU Council of Finance Ministers
ENA	Ecole Nationale d'Administration (French civil service academy)
ESMA	European Securities and Markets Authority
ESME	European Securities Markets Expert Group
ESRB	European Systemic Risk Board
FASB	Financial Accounting Standards Board
FDF	Swiss Federal Department of Finance
FDIC	Federal Deposit Insurance Corporation
FFIEC	Federal Financial Institutions Examination Council
FINMA	Swiss Financial Market Supervisory Authority
FMSA	Bundesanstalt für Finanzmarktstabilisierung (German Federal Agency for Financial Market Stabilization)
FRB	Federal Reserve Bank
FSA	Financial Services Authority
FSAP	Financial Services Action Plan
FSB	Financial Stability Board
FSF	Financial Stability Forum
FSOC	Financial Stability Oversight Council
FTC	Federal Trade Commission
FVA	Fair Value Accounting
GAAP	Generally Accepted Accounting Principles
GAO	Government Accountability Office
GLBA	Gramm-Leach-Bliley Act
HCA	Historical Cost Accounting
IAIS	International Association Insurance Supervisors
IASB	International Accounting Standards Board
IASC	International Accounting Standards Committee
IFRS	International Financial Reporting Standards
IIF	International Institute of Finance
IMF	International Monetary Fund
IOSCO	International Organization of Securities Commissions
KWG	Kreditwesengesetz (German Banking Law)
LCR	Liquidity Coverage Ratio
LCTM	Long-Term Capital Management
MAG	Macroeconomic Assessment Group
MiFID	Markets in Financial Instruments Directive
NSFR	Net Stable Funding Ratio

OCC	Office of the Comptroller of the Controller
OTC	Over-The-Counter
OTS	Office of Thrift Regulation
QIS	Quantitative Impact Study
SAAM	Swiss Association of Asset Managers
SBA	Swiss Bankers Association
SEC	Securities and Exchange Commission
SFEF	Société de Financement de l'Economie Française (French Financing Agency)
SIF	Swiss Secretariat for International Financial Matters
SIFI	Systemically Important Financial Institution
SIFMA	Securities Industry and Financial Markets Association
SNB	Swiss National Bank
SoFFin	Sonderfonds Finanzmarktstabilisierung (Special Financial Market Stabilization Funds)
SPPE	Société de Prise de Participation de l'Etat (French state-owned investment company)
SSG	Senior Supervisors Group (Financial Stability Board)
TARP	Troubled Asset Relief Program
UCITS	Undertakings for Collective Investment in Transferable Securities
UKFI	United Kingdom Financial Investments

Social Science

Stefan B. Kirmse (ed.)
One Law for All?
Western models and local practices
in (post-) imperial contexts
2012. Ca. 300 pages, ISBN 978-3-593-39493-0

Kolja Raube, Annika Sattler
Difference and Democracy
Exploring Potentials in Europe and Beyond
2011. 397 pages, ISBN 978-3-593-39502-9

Tina Weber
Drop Dead Gorgeous
Representations of Corpses in American TV Shows
2011. 267 pages, ISBN 978-3-593-39507-4

Tsypylma Darieva, Wolfgang Kaschuba,
Melanie Krebs (eds.)
Urban Spaces after Socialism
Ethnographies of Public Places in Eurasian Cities
2011. 325 pages, ISBN 978-3-593-39384-1

Jörg Feuchter, Friedhelm Hoffmann, Bee Yun (eds.)
Cultural Transfers in Dispute
Representations in Asia, Europe and the Arab World
since the Middle Ages
2011. 335 pages, ISBN 978-3-593-39404-6

www.campus.de/wissenschaft

Frankfurt. New York